The Everyday Lives of Young Children

Culture, Class, and Child Rearing in Diverse Societies

JONATHAN TUDGE
University of North Carolina at Greensboro

CAMBRIDGE
UNIVERSITY PRESS

CAMBRIDGE UNIVERSITY PRESS
Cambridge, New York, Melbourne, Madrid, Cape Town, Singapore, São Paulo, Delhi

Cambridge University Press
32 Avenue of the Americas, New York, NY 10013–2473, USA

www.cambridge.org
Information on this title: www.cambridge.org/9780521803847

First published 2008

Printed in the United States of America

A catalog record for this publication is available from the British Library.

Library of Congress Cataloging in Publication Data

Tudge, Jonathan.
The everyday lives of young children : culture, class, and child rearing in diverse societies /
Jonathan Tudge.
    p.   cm.
Includes bibliographical references and index.
ISBN-13: 978-0-521-80384-7 (hbk.)
1. Children – Cross-cultural studies.   2. Social interaction – Cross-cultural studies.   I. Title.
HQ767.9.T835   2008
305.233089 – dc22   2007026981

ISBN   978-0-521-80384-7 hardback

Dedicated to

Rosanne, about 30 months at the time, without whom the research may
never have begun

and

Lia, without whose love and encouragement the book may never have ended

Contents

Preface

I'm writing this on the last day of the year in 2006 and thinking back to some time in the autumn of 1989 when the idea for the research to be reported in this book was very new. It wasn't supposed to take so long, and I wasn't expecting that what began as an intended comparison of the everyday lives of young children in the United States and the Soviet Union would develop a life of its own. But my initial reasoning hasn't changed much. Then, as now, I felt that there was a real lack of knowledge about how young children spent their time, engaged in what sorts of activities, interacted with whom, and got involved in the myriad aspects of their lives. This was an important lack, because one of the ways in which we can understand how cultures influence children's developments and how, in turn, children influence their own development (and in so doing help change their cultural group) is by focusing on these types of typically occurring activities and interactions. It's not that we don't have any information about this topic, but most of the good observational work that we do have is restricted to the lives of children growing up in rural areas of countries often referred to as "Third World" or "developing," rather than to the lives of children in North America, Europe, or other parts of the industrialized world. For information about children's lives in these parts of the world, we have to rely largely on parents' reports of their children's activities or observations conducted under situations of constraint. Some of those constraints are rather subtle, such as observing periods of play or recording mother–child dialogue in the home (the only constraint being that the mother is at home with the child) or observing children in just one of the many settings in which they find themselves, such as a child-care center. However, others are more obvious, such as recording mealtime activities at home when all family members are required to be present and the television is not to be switched on or asking the mother and child to play with various objects in the confines of the psychology laboratory. My goal, however, was to observe young children wherever they were to be found for long enough to get a sense of the typical activities and interactions in which they were involved, the only constraint being the presence of an observer. This, I think, was accomplished, as the pages of this book will testify. In so doing, I hope to have illustrated the ways in which culture and children's development are intimately connected.

A second goal was to conduct research in which the guiding theory was directly related to the methods of data collection and form of analysis. In this book, I've therefore laid out quite explicitly the metatheoretical assumptions of my work, showing how they are linked both to cultural–ecological theory and to the methods used in the Cultural Ecology of Young Children (CEYC) study, the name I gave to this project. The name was chosen partly to honor Urie Bronfenbrenner's 1979 book, *The Ecology of Human Development*, because his views, as they developed during the 1980s and 1990s, were clearly influential as my thinking evolved. However, I also wanted to stress the fact that human development is above all a cultural phenomenon – whether we treat culture at the level of an entire society or as a distinct group within any society. This, too, I hope, is well illustrated in the pages that follow.

The CEYC project is still continuing, as I write, more than 15 years from when it started. That's partly because the study is longitudinal, with data gathered not only when the children were three years of age (although the book's focus is on the activities and interactions of the three-year-olds) but also through their first years in school. The length of time is also a result of the fact that the data in the various countries were not all gathered at the same time but spread over about a decade. The last children to be included in the project, from southern Brazil, are ending their first year of formal schooling now. As you might imagine, there's a huge amount of data – each child in the study was observed for a total of 20 hours – and, at times, when trying to organize all the coded data and the field notes from the observations, I felt rather like George Eliot's character Mr. Casaubon, in *Middlemarch*, of whom she wrote: "He had assembled his voluminous notes, and had made that sort of reputation which precedes performance, – often the larger part of a man's fame" (1872/1988, p. 77). Fortunately, unlike poor Mr. Casaubon, I not only met and married my "Dorothea" but also wrote this book.

Acknowledgments

First and foremost, I thank all of the families who gave so generously of their time. They allowed us into their homes, let us follow them wherever they went with their children, consented to be interviewed, completed questionnaires, and (although they must, at times, have wished that no one was there to see what was happening) did a remarkable job of appearing to behave quite naturally during the 20 hours or more that we were with each of them. The children, around three years of age during the observations, let themselves be equipped with small wireless microphones and allowed someone to observe them doing all sorts of things in all sorts of places. We are extremely grateful to all of them.

Second, this research could never have been done without a group of highly dedicated observers and collaborators who, because of the nature of this research, had to be from the cultural group they were observing. They first had to learn a complex coding scheme and then spent so many hours following the children around, writing the codes, writing field notes, filming for a while, and becoming, for a short while at least, a part of the families they were observing. Sometimes it was hard for both them and the children when it was time to leave a particular family and move on to the next one. Sarah Putnam and Judy Sidden deserve the greatest thanks of all. Not only did they collect the data from the European American families in Greensboro, but they were also involved from the inception of the project and spent almost two years of their graduate student lives helping to design and refine the coding scheme. We were considerably aided in this endeavor by Barbara Rogoff, Gilda Morelli, and Cathy Angelillo, for it was the six of us who worked together on the early versions of the coding scheme. All of the observers, without exception, are due many, many thanks: Fabienne Doucet and Nicole Talley (the African American families in Greensboro); Natalya Kulakova and Irina Snezhkova (the Russian families in Obninsk);

Marika Meltsas and Peeter Tammeveski (the Estonian families in Tartu); Marikaisa Kontio (the Finnish families in Oulu); Souen Lee (the South Korean families in Suwon); Dolphine Odero (the Luo families in Kisumu, Kenya); and Giana Frizzo, Fernanda Marques, and Rafael Spinneli (the Brazilian families in Porto Alegre).

My graduate students also have contributed greatly to my thinking, even if they did not actually participate in the collection of the data reported in this book, and special thanks must be paid to Diane Hogan, Kathy Etz, Paul Winterhoff, Sherrill Hayes, Sheryl Scrimsher, and Fabienne Doucet (who also collected data). My colleagues in Brazil, in the postgraduate program in psychology at the Federal University of Rio Grande do Sul (UFRGS), have also helped greatly in the course of many stimulating discussions, particularly with Cesar Piccinini, Tania Sperb, and Rita Lopes, my colleagues in the Porto Alegre Longitudinal Study (PALS), which began before the children were born. The Brazilian three-year-olds who appear in this book were all selected from the PALS families. I also thank my colleagues in the Department of Human Development and Family Studies (HDFS) at the University of North Carolina at Greensboro (UNCG), not only for allowing me to travel so much while these data were being gathered (for a time I was jokingly known as a "visiting professor" in my own department) but also for their helpful support.

I also owe debts of thanks to many who read parts of early drafts of this book, in particular my colleagues Marion O'Brien (HDFS) and Dale Goldhaber of the University of Vermont. Natalya Kulakova read the entire book in its close-to-final form and provided invaluable assistance. I also benefited greatly from the insights provided by many of my collaborators in the project into the specific details of life in the various cities from which data were collected. Special thanks should go to Dolphine Odero, Soeun Lee, Marikaisa Kontio, Fabienne Doucet, Marika Meltsas, Natalya Kulakova, Tania Sperb, Cesar Piccinini, and Rita Lopes. I would also like to thank the Brazilian graduate students and postdoctoral Fellows who participated in the seminar I taught in the postgraduate program in psychology at UFRGS, as well as those HDFS graduate students who have taken various classes with me in theories of human development for helping me think more clearly about theoretical issues.

Needless to say, a project as large as the Cultural Ecology of Young Children could not have happened without generous financial support. My grateful thanks go to the Spencer Foundation for multiple funding awards, to IREX (the International Research and Exchanges Board), and to three Brazilian governmental funding agencies, CNPq (Conselho Nacional de Desenvolvimento

Científico e Tecnológico) and FAPERGS (Fundação de Amparo à Pesquisa do Estado do Rio Grande do Sul) for help with part of the Brazilian data collection, and CAPES (Coordenação de Aperfeiçoamento de Pessoal de Nível Superior) for providing me with the position of visiting professor in the postgraduate program in psychology at UFRGS during the period in which I was finishing this book. I also thank the School of Education of the University of Oulu for providing part of the financial support that allowed data collection to occur in Finland and the Department of Psychology at the University of Tartu for providing me the position of visiting professor during the period of data collection in Estonia. UNCG has also helped greatly, partly by providing two sabbatical periods (during one of which part of the data collection occurred and during the other I was able to finish this book) and partly by providing several small grants that supported the research during periods of limited funding from other sources. The Human Environmental Sciences Foundation and the Kohler Fund of the International Program Center, both of UNCG, also provided help with funding. I am extremely grateful to all of them for their financial help.

Special words of thanks are due to Julia Hough, my first editor at Cambridge University Press. She provided the initial encouragement to write this book and, despite having moved away from Cambridge, has continued to support this endeavor over the years. I'd also like to thank Paul Silvia, my colleague from the Psychology Department at UNCG, for letting me read an early draft of his book *How to Write a Lot: A Practical Guide to Productive Academic Writing* (Silvia, 2007). It really helped.

Finally, I express my appreciation to the following copyright holders for permission to quote from the sources indicated:

Basil Blackwell, for material from Vygotsky, L. S. The problem of the environment. In R. Van der Veer & J. Valsiner (Eds.), *The Vygotsky reader*, 1994.

Brookes Publishing, for material from Hart, B., & Risley, T. R. *The social world of children learning to talk*, 1999.

Lawrence Erlbaum Associates, for material from Bornstein, M. H., Tal, J., & Tamis-LeMonda, C. S. Parenting in cross-cultural perspective: The United States, France, and Japan. In M. H. Bornstein (Ed.), *Cultural approaches to parenting*, 1991; Goodnow, J., & Collins, W. A. *Development according to parents: The nature, sources, and consequences of parents' ideas*, 1990.

Grove/Atlantic, Inc., for material from Stoppard, T. *Shipwreck*, 2002.

S. Karger, AG, for material from Van der Vijver, F. J. R., & Poortinga, Y. H. On the study of culture in developmental science. *Human Development, 45*, 2002.

Harvard University Press, for material from Whiting, B. B., & Whiting, J. W. M. *Children of six cultures: A psycho-cultural analysis*, 1975; Vygotsky, L. S. *Mind in society: The development of higher psychological processes* (M. Cole, V. John-Steiner, S. Scribner, & E. Souberman, Eds.), 1978.

Oxford University Press, for material from Eliot, G., *Middlemarch* (D. Carroll, Ed.), 1988; Shakespeare, W., *Coriolanus*. In W. J. Craig (Ed.), *The complete works of William Shakespeare*, 1954.

Penguin Group, UK, for material from Eliot, G., *Adam Bede*, 1980; Eliot, G., *Silas Marner*, 1985.

Springer, for material from Vygotsky, L. S. *The collected works of L. S. Vygotsky: Vol. 2, The fundamentals of defectology* (R. W. Rieber & A. S. Carton, Eds., J. E. Knox & Carol B. Stevens, trans), 1993.

Taylor & Francis, for material from Lubeck, S. *Sandbox society: Early education in black and white America*, 1985; Woodhead, M., & Faulkner, D. Subjects, objects or participants? Dilemmas of psychological research with children. In P. Christensen & A. James (Eds.), *Research with children: Perspectives and practices*, 2000.

John Wiley & Sons, for material from Bronfenbrenner, U., & Morris, P. A. The ecology of developmental processes. In W. Damon (Series Ed.) & R. M. Lerner (Vol. Ed.), *Handbook of child psychology: Vol. 1. Theoretical models of human development* (5th ed.), 1998; Weisner, T. S. Cultural and universal aspects of social support for children: Evidence from the Abaluyia of Kenya. In D. Belle (Ed.), *Children's social networks and social supports*, 1989.

1 Introduction and Stage Setting

Because children grow up, we think a child's purpose is to grow up. But a child's purpose is to be a child. Nature doesn't disdain what lives only for a *day*. It pours the whole of itself into the each moment. We don't value the lily less for not being made of flint and built to last. Life's bounty is in its flow, later is too late.

Tom Stoppard, Shipwreck (2002, p. 100).

BACKGROUND

How do young children spend their time? Who are the people with whom children are engaged in activities and interaction? In which sorts of activities do they get involved, and how do those activities get started? Where do they spend their time? Somewhat surprisingly, we don't have very good answers to these questions. And yet it is when children are young that it is relatively easy to see the ways in which parents and other people attempt to ensure that they become skilled in the practices that are considered important and to learn the values, concepts, and ways of behaving that are valued in the culture in which the children are situated. It is possible to see this by examining the types of activities in which children are encouraged to participate, the types of activities they are discouraged from, the people with whom it is considered appropriate to interact, and the roles played by those social partners. It can also be seen from examining the types of settings into which young children are placed, the lessons they are asked to learn, the behaviors they are asked to practice, and the skills they are expected to master. All of these things are intrinsically linked to the culture in which children are being raised.

Felicia (a pseudonym, as are all children's names in this book) is at the Brownie meeting that her mother runs. Her mother asks her if she'd like to go to the room where her older brother and some other boys are playing, and Felicia does so. She gets a tricycle to ride but is then is "captured" by the boys and put in "jail" behind some tables. She escapes on her bike and is chased by the boys, who then start talking with her about who's going to be the "bad guy." "I want to be the good guy," responds Felicia.

Jonghee is at home with her mother, who gets out a pre-kindergarten activity book and starts to teach her daughter colors, Arabic numerals, and the concepts of "big" and "small" (which she also shows her daughter how to write).

Volodya is watching a cartoon on TV and playing with his toys. His mother mends a broken toy and explains to him that the ostrich in the cartoon is sitting on an egg waiting for a chicken to appear. She asks him to put his toys away: "I won't," says Volodya. "Why not?" "I don't like doing that," he replies.

Olev is at home with his mother and older brother and sister. The children have been jumping on the bed, until their mother tells them to stop. Olev then says, "Let's sit in the car and go on summer holidays." His sister agrees: "Yes, let's go swimming," and the children start playing.

Daniel is at his child-care center, playing outside with other children, first on the slide and then climbing on the bars that separate the center from the street. Andrea is also in child care, although it is set up in someone's home. She's there with her sister and a number of other children. The TV is on, and Andrea watches from time to time but complains when her sister takes her toy away from her. "You have to share," says the watching adult.

Gisela is at home with her father and older sister. Her sister is giving her some mathematical problems. Gisela says that 5 plus 5 is 9, and her sister corrects her. Their father then calls them over and sends the pair of them on an errand to the local shop.

Simo's father and brother pick him up from child care, and after his father puts Simo into his car seat, he cleans the snow from the windows. As they approach a traffic light, his father asks Simo whether they have to stop. "No, we have to wait for the green arrows," replies Simo. "Are we able to go now?" his father asks a little later, "Look at the lights." "No," replies Simo.

These vignettes are all tiny slices of the everyday activities in which some of the young children in our study were involved; they are all taken from the field notes of the Cultural Ecology of Young Children (CEYC) study, on which much of this book focuses. The children are from the United States, Russia, Estonia, Finland, Korea, Kenya, and Brazil; some are from middle-class homes, and some from working-class homes. I doubt that it's possible to guess the country or social-class group of all of the children, although in some cases the names are a useful clue, because in many ways three-year-olds are quite similar. They tend to play a lot with the objects that are available to them, they are often in the company of someone who is responsible for them, they are often asked questions to which the questioner knows the answer, they don't always do what they're told, and so on.

If instead of a sentence or two, however, I gave as detailed a description of the activities and interactions of a number of children over an entire day in each of their lives, the task of guessing the children's society and, perhaps their social-class background, would be far easier. Instead of the verbal equivalent of a photograph, we would have then the equivalent of a feature film! Despite all that three-year-olds have in common, the settings in which they are situated, the values and beliefs to which they are exposed in the course of their everyday activities, the types of interactions to which they become accustomed, the activities in which they are encouraged to participate (and in which they are discouraged from participating), and so on are all linked to the culture in which they are raised.

The goal of this book is to illustrate both the impact of culture on children and the ways in which children help to change the culture of which they are a part. I'll thus show how culture is implicated in development because of the types of settings, partners, activities, and interactions that it considers possible and appropriate. If members of a culture make certain opportunities available to its young and discourage others, we can gain some insight into what it is that this group values. However, these opportunities are not necessarily chosen freely from a wide array that is equally available to all; different cultures, both within and across different societies, have access to different resources and power. Moreover, the children's personal characteristics, preferences, abilities, and so on also affect the activities, interactions, and settings in which they are involved, thereby helping to change their culture while at the same time being changed by it.

"Culture" is a word that has proven extremely difficult to define to everyone's liking, leading to a proliferation of definitions (see, for example, Matsumoto, 2006; Rogoff, 2003). In part, this difficulty exists because some scholars define culture primarily in terms of material artifacts or as "collective problem solving toolkits of individual social groups in response to their historical and ecological circumstances" and "as the entire pool of artifacts accumulated by the social group in the course of its historical experience" (Cole, 2005b, pp. 2–3) whereas others (see, for example, Super & Harkness, 2002) define it in terms of customs, practices, and parental ethnotheories (that is, their values and beliefs about raising children) or as shared cultural models, expressed in the course of everyday routines (Holland & Quinn, 1987; Weisner, 1997).

I find most useful a definition that includes the notion of a group of people who share a set of values, beliefs, and practices; who have access to the same institutions, resources, and technologies; who have a sense of identity of themselves as constituting a group; and who attempt to communicate those values, beliefs, and practices to the following generation. Such a definition clearly does not specify the nature of the group; it can refer both to an entire nation, country, or society and to a group within any given society. One clear inference, then, is that individuals should, with rare exceptions, be thought of as members of several cultures, rather than just one. It's also the case that the degree of sharing may not be evenly distributed and that within any culture may be found competing or conflicting values, particularly where power differentials are concerned. However, as an initial working definition it will serve current purposes, and I'll provide a more critical discussion in the final chapter.

That culture is deeply implicated in children's development cannot be doubted. We thus have scholars such as Tom Weisner (1996) declaring that the single most important thing to know about a person is his or her culture and Barbara Rogoff titling her 2003 book *The Cultural Nature of Human Development*. The question of greatest interest is this: *How* is culture related to human development? As Weisner, Rogoff, and a wide variety of other scholars (for example, Michael Cole, Patricia Greenfield, Mary Gauvain, Beatrice Whiting, Carolyn Edwards) have noted, culture is important as a provider of settings, by specifying the types of environments in which members of the culture are likely to spend their time. Culture is important because it specifies the types of roles occupied and communication patterns used by high- and low-status individuals, by adults and children, and by females and males. Culture is important as a provider of resources, both material and intangible. At the most general level, culture is important as a specifier of the types of activities and modes of interaction that are considered appropriate and inappropriate.

Cultures clearly have powerful influences on how individuals develop. This is seen most easily in the case of children who, as newborns, come into the world with the potential to become a competent and successful member of any human culture but quickly become easily recognizable as members of a specific culture. However, cultures are always in the process of change. Some of that change, particularly in a world in which various technologies have made contact between widely distant societies far easier than ever before, is because of the influence of ideas and practices from other cultures.

Regardless of the extent of contact, however, cultures continually undergo change because the members of each new generation never simply adopt the totality of ideas and practices of the preceding generation. Sometimes they invent new technologies, undreamed of by their parents. Sometimes they object to the ways their parents do or say things and find new ways of achieving the same goals. Sometimes they pursue different goals. Whether in the process of learning to do things that their parents do or doing things differently, however, it is what they do on a regular basis that matters for their development. It is by engaging in practices – activities and interactions in which we engage alone and with others – that we both recreate the culture of which we are a part and help to change that culture. To see this process, it is thus important to examine how people, particularly young children, engage in their typically occurring activities and interactions with others.

It is therefore somewhat surprising that so little is known about how young children spend their time in the various settings that are made available to them, the people with whom they typically interact, and the ways in which they engage in activities and interactions. Or, to be more accurate, little is known about children's regularly occurring activities in the United States and Europe; rather more is known about children's lives in parts of Africa and Asia. The research that I'll describe in the course of this book was designed in part to fill that gap by examining children's daily experiences in the United States, Russia, Estonia, Finland, South Korea, Kenya, and Brazil.

First, though, I'd like to discuss some of the reasons we know so much more about children's everyday lives in non- and semi-industrialized societies than in those that are industrialized. A little discussion about terminology might be helpful. Many terms have been used to describe these types of societies, including "developed" versus "developing," "Western" versus "non-Western," and "First World" versus "Third World." Rather than use terms that define some societies by an absence of what others have (implying either envy or a linear "progression" of societal development), I borrow from Çiğdem Kağitçibaşi (1996) who prefers to refer to the industrialized world on the one hand and to those societies sometimes referred to as the developing world, the non-Western world, or the nonindustrialized world as constituting the "majority world" (given that the majority of the world's children live in these societies).

The fact that we know more about how children spend their time, the company they keep, and the settings they frequent in the majority world than we do about children in industrialized societies in part is a consequence of researchers' different disciplinary backgrounds and the different types of methods they use. I'll examine each of these disciplinary approaches and methods in more detail in the pages that follow, as a way of explaining why it is that my own study may fill an important gap in what we know about young children's everyday lives. What I think will become clear is that the types of data derived from each of these literatures do not fit well together.

It does not fit primarily because those who study children's everyday lives approach their studies from differing theoretical perspectives or without any foundational theory and use different methods to collect their data.

In some cases, mostly when studying children in the majority world, researchers spend a good deal of time with children, observing where they are, with whom they are interacting, and the activities in which they are involved. In other cases (typically when studying children from the industrialized world), the children are either observed briefly, and under controlled conditions, or are not observed at all because their parents or other caregivers are either interviewed or asked to complete reports of how their children spent their time. This lack of consistency in the methods used means that it is difficult to compare the experiences of children from the majority and industrialized worlds. The research that I present in this volume uses exactly the same methods to examine how and with whom children spend their time in diverse societies around the world.

A further problem that my research addresses is the fact that too often scholars who have studied children's daily lives in two or more societies have not paid enough attention to the heterogeneity that exists within any society. Studies contrasting the lives of White middle-class children from a Western European or U.S. urban center with the lives of rural and minimally schooled children from some part of the majority world are useful in showing the wide diversity of child-rearing practices in different parts of the world. However, they tend to downplay the fact that the lives of White middle-class children in the United States or in Europe may be different in important ways from the lives of middle-class children from other racial or ethnic groups and from the lives of White children growing up in poverty in the same countries. Scholars also typically ignore the fact that even in a society that is part of the majority world, children's experiences vary greatly by virtue of urban and rural dwelling, by extent of parents' schooling, and by relative wealth.

The research presented in this volume therefore accomplishes three major goals. The first is to describe the activities and interactions of young children from a variety of societies, using the same methods to gather, analyze, and interpret the data. The second is to show both the variations that exist across societies and, at the same time, some of the variation that exists within each society. I'm able to do this because in each place where we observed children, we chose half the children from middle-class backgrounds and half whose parents were working class. In addition, in the United States, half of the families were of African American descent, and the other half were European American. The third is both to show the influence of culture on children's development and to describe the ways in which young children play a role in changing their culture.

First, however, I want to provide more detail about the ways in which children have been studied, grouping the research into three types: those stemming from developmental psychology, those from sociology, and those from cultural anthropology. I accept that there is some degree of overlap because scholars are influenced by a variety of disciplinary backgrounds, but this is a convenient way to show the type of diversity in method that I mentioned earlier.

STUDIES IN THE DEVELOPMENTAL PSYCHOLOGY MODE

The first literature is that of child development and developmental psychology. We can find a wealth of data in this literature, from thousands of studies of children and their parents in the industrialized world, primarily from the United States and primarily featuring White middle-class children (Graham, 1992; Hagen & Conley, 1994; Hill, 1999; Rogoff, 2003; Scott-Jones, 2005). The vast majority of these studies are conducted in controlled laboratory settings or rely on parents completing questionnaires that feature a set of possible responses from which to choose. The reason for the emphasis on control, whether in the laboratory or via multiple choice–type questionnaires, is to remove the influence of "extraneous" contextual factors that could reduce the impact of whatever experimental factor is being studied or to restrict the responses to a predetermined set.

Not all of the studies that fit into this body of literature are conducted in laboratories, of course. Recognizing that the child-development laboratory is just one type of context, many researchers have chosen to collect their data within one or other of the contexts in which children naturally are to be found. In most cases, however, researchers are interested in imposing some control even within the home to ensure that variations in children's interactions with a parent or caregiver, or play with another child, are due to variations within the child or the interacting dyad and not to events that pertain simply to one or other household. For example, if in one house the mother spends the entire observational time talking with a friend on the phone rather than interacting with her child, most researchers would be loath to use these data to talk about the quality of mother–child interaction.

Thus observation of child–child or adult–child activity in the home is often structured to ensure a minimum of interruption and the maximum of adult–child interaction; mealtimes and bedtimes are thus thought of as optimal opportunities, and observations are more likely to occur then than at other times of the day. Observations are far less likely to take place when the adult (typically the mother) intends to cook dinner, go shopping, entertain friends, clean the house, watch television, or do any of the myriad activities that are a feature of everyday life. However, not only are these more adult-oriented activities common in children's lives, they are also precisely those areas in which children are most likely to be exposed to and participate in adult life in that family. Moreover, the implicit message given to the mother, when the observer arrives, is that she should interact with, or at least be available to, her child. Researchers might well gain an understanding of how mother and child interact under such circumstances but have no idea of the extent to which such interactions typically occur in this family. By restricting the "disruptions," developmental psychologists may thus have presented a misleading picture of the types of activities in which children engage and the extent to which adults engage with them. Not surprisingly, then, "we are still far from understanding the daily lives of children and how these experiences fit with development" (Gauvain, 1999, p. 184). Moreover, as various scholars have noted over the past 30 years (e.g., Bloch, 1989; Corsaro, 1997; Dunn, 1988; Richards, 1977), this is particularly true of the naturally occurring activities of children from the industrialized world.

Moreover, child or developmental psychologists have typically been far more interested in the epistemic child than in actual children; that is, they are interested in general aspects of development – those that affect children in general – rather than in the specifics of any one child or particular groups of children (Hogan, 2005). This concern with the epistemic child is reflected in the titles of many introductory texts on this topic, with names such as *Child Development* or *Adolescent Development*. The exception that proves the rule is Cole, Cole, and Lightfoot's *The Development of Children* (2005), a book that takes a decidedly different approach, featuring a good deal of the variations in children's development in different cultural contexts.

An alternative approach that has been taken by many developmentalists, at least those in the United States and other industrialized societies, involves an indirect approach to children's experiences; parents are asked to respond to questionnaires or are interviewed about their values and beliefs about how to raise their children, either verbally or in written form. There is a large and growing literature on parental beliefs about child rearing (see, for example, Bornstein, 2002; Bornstein et al., 1998; Chao, 2000; Goodnow & Collins, 1990; Harkness & Super, 2002; Holden, 1995; Sigel, McGillicuddy, & Goodnow, 1992), as well as a literature that discusses the cultural models related to those beliefs (D'Andrade & Strauss, 1992; Holland & Quinn, 1987; Lewis & Watson-Gegeo, 2005; Weisner, 1997).

In the United States at least, the views of Baumrind (1989, 1996) on parenting styles have been highly influential, seeking to understand the ways in which beliefs and behavior are interrelated. However, all too often behavior is asked about rather than observed, although presumably there should be a relationship between parental beliefs and attitudes on the one hand, and what they actually do with their children, on the other. Luster, Rhoades, and Haas (1989) provide a good illustration of how the connection between values, beliefs, and practices may occur. For example, a mother who wishes her child to be obedient and to follow the rules that she imposes (a value) may believe that she should not overly express her feelings of love and affection for her baby (a belief) for fear of spoiling or making the child disobedient therefore does not often hold or rock him or her when he or she is crying (a practice or behavior).

STUDIES IN THE SOCIOLOGICAL MODE

Although sociologists have long been interested in children, this interest was, until the 1980s or '90s, limited to studies of the ways in which the various institutions of society (primarily family and school) have treated children. Children, in other words, were typically relegated to a passive role as the objects of socialization and given the status of a minority group (see, for example, Christensen & Prout, 2005; Corsaro, 1997; James, 2004; James & Prout, 1997). From the 1950s in the United States, structural–functionalist theorists focused primarily on the ways in which children had to be socialized to fit into their social group. Critical theorists argued against this traditional view of socialization, focusing instead on the ways in which more powerful and richer groups in any society worked hard to ensure that their children would inherit their status along with their wealth. In both cases, however, children were viewed as essentially passive in the process of socialization.

Some researchers, from both sociology and family studies, made more explicit attempts to treat children and adolescents as important actors in their own right, for the most part by studying the types of activities in which they were involved. The method that was predominantly used also focused mostly on the presumed agents of socialization, with parents (mostly mothers) responding via questionnaires and interviews. In some cases, however, adolescents were asked to report on their own activities (Savin-Williams, 1982). Developmental psychologists have also used the same types of methods, asking people to record diaries or respond in various ways to an electronic signal (Bolger, Davis, & Rafaeli, 2003; Larson, Moneta, Richards, & Wilson, 2002; Larson & Verma, 1999). For obvious reasons, this work is not done with young children, and the typical method is to ask parents to report on themselves and their children. Thus Hofferth, Sandberg, and their colleagues (Hofferth & Sandberg, 2001; Yeung, Sandberg, Davis-Kean, & Hofferth, 2001) use parent (and parent-with-child) 24-hour diaries that attempt to list everything that the respondents did, collected from a representative sample from across the United States. Robinson and his colleagues have made similar assessments of time use by Americans (Robinson, 1977; Robinson & Godbey, 1997) and Russians (Robinson, Andreyenkov, & Patrushev, 1989), relying on questionnaires designed to elicit recollections of the approximate time that adults and children spend engaging in various types of activities. I'll describe this work in more detail in the next chapter.

STUDIES IN THE ANTHROPOLOGICAL MODE

The final literature is that of cultural anthropology in which I'm including some culturally oriented developmental psychologists, including those whose work is placed in the sociocultural or cultural historical traditions (for example, Cole, 2005b; Farver, 1999; Gaskins, 1999; Gauvain, 2001; Göncü et al., 1999; Rogoff, 1990, 2003). There is in this literature a great deal of information on how children are socialized in societies from the majority world. This information, primarily based on extensive observational or ethnographic work, is more likely to portray, in rich detail, the everyday lives of children, the settings they inhabit, their social partners, the various activities in which they engage, and so on. For example, there are books on specific cultural groups in Liberia, Kenya, Zambia, and India (Lancy, 1996; LeVine et al., 1994; Serpell, 1993; Seymour, 1999) and a number of books on language and literacy, for example, in Samoa and New Guinea (Ochs, 1988; Schieffelin, 1990).

This anthropologically based research has its intellectual forebears in the pioneering work of Margaret Mead (1928/1961), Bronislaw Malinowski (1966), and Ruth Benedict (1959). The purpose of these studies was to try to provide an emic, or insider's, perspective on the varied approaches to child rearing that could be found in different parts of the world. They therefore spent a good deal of time carrying out fieldwork with the groups being studied, so that they could understand not only how members of these groups raised their children but the reasoning behind their different practices. As I mentioned with regard to structural–functionalist sociology, however, much of the research in cultural anthropology treats children as the "recipients" of culture, being socialized in such a way that they learn how to fit into their cultural group.

Not surprisingly, most of this early anthropological research is based on studies of a single community, although occasionally there have been collections of linked studies, most notably those of the Whitings and their colleagues (Minturn & Lambert, 1964; Whiting, 1963; Whiting & Whiting, 1975) and, in its most recent form, Whiting and Edwards's (1988) extension of the original "Six Cultures" study, titled *Children of different worlds*. These volumes feature the results of observational studies in India, Okinawa, the Philippines, Mexico, Kenya, Liberia, and "Orchard Town" (a small community situated in the northeastern United States).   *Concord, MA ?*

The goal of this large collaborative study was to observe, in each of the original six communities, approximately 20 children, aged 3 to 11, and their social partners in the natural settings they typically inhabited. The focus was on the children's social behavior – in particular on "a number of transcultural categories that could be presumed to describe social interaction" (Whiting & Whiting, 1975, p. 40). The particular categories of social interaction they examined were nurturance, succor, sociability, achievement, dominance, submission, aggression, responsibility, and self-reliance. In each of the communities chosen as the six research sites, observers first obtained a sense of the daily routines of the children by following them around in the various settings, and then spent approximately five minutes noting the activity in which the target child and his or her social partners were engaged and the way in which the child interacted with others. Only one observation was taken of any child on a given day, and at least 14 observations were taken of each child across the six communities. This led to an average of between 74 and 135 minutes per child in each community. Although no attempt was made to document the various activities in which the children were involved, the observers grouped activities into three main types (play, work, and learning) and classified all other activities as "casual social interaction" (Whiting & Whiting, 1975).

The extension of this original work (Whiting & Edwards, 1988) added samples from six new areas (one from Liberia, one from India, and four from different parts of Kenya) from which the data were collected in similar ways to those described earlier, although typically with more children. For example, as part of the later Kenyan samples, Weisner (1979) observed 68 Abaluyia two- to eight-year-olds from 24 rural and 24 urban families for two hours each, and Harkness and Super (1985) observed 64 Kipsigis 3- to 10-year-olds, also for a total of two hours each. In addition, "spot-observation" samples were drawn from a further six communities (three from Kenya, and one each from Guatemala, Peru, and Claremont in the United States). The spot observations, on approximately 20 children in all places except for Guatemala, where 53 children were involved, were observed between 8 and 16 times each, so as to describe the setting, the activities in which the children were involved, and the children's social partners at specific points of time.

There have been other, more recent, examinations of the differing ways in which parents think about raising children, some of which have included observation of children's activities. However, the focus of attention is typically on mother–child interactional patterns (see, for example, Bornstein & Cote, 2001, 2004; Bornstein et al., 1996, 1998). Harkness and Super (1992, 1999, 2002; Harkness et al., 1999) and Heidi Keller and her colleagues (e.g., Keller, 2003; Keller et al., 2004) have linked parental ethnotheories, or ideas about how to raise children that are based both on the parents' personal views and the cultural customs of the group of which the parents are a part, and parent–child interactions. Their focus, however, has been almost exclusively on the mother and on a restricted range of young children's activities, rather than on the full range of activities in which children are involved, which was the focus of the earlier work by Whiting and her colleagues.

DISCIPLINES AND PARADIGMS

The study of young children has thus taken different forms, using different methods and approaches, by members of different disciplines. The situation is more complicated, however, because even within disciplines there are different ways of thinking about the nature of reality and how best to try to study it. I'll discuss this issue in more detail in Chapter 3 and return to it in the final chapter, but for now I'll simply mention that the main theories scholars use as the guiding rationale for their research can be situated within one of three major paradigms, or ways of viewing the world (Pepper, 1942). The dominant paradigm, at least within the United States, in both psychology and sociology, is mechanism in which a neo-positivist position is taken on the nature of reality (reality exists, and although it is not possible to prove that reality, science advances by accepting as real what has yet to be disproved), on the relationship between the researcher and the phenomena to be researched (it is important to maintain a separation of the two), and on the manner of conducting research (researchers should use methods that allow for careful control of the variables of interest to allow for clear cause–effect relations to be established).

Although mechanism has been dominant for the last century or more, theories that fit into one of the other two main paradigms (organicism and contextualism) have also played a role, albeit one that is subordinate (Tudge, Gray, & Hogan, 1997). Both paradigms differ from mechanism in that they hold that variables, such as the individual and context, cannot be treated as independent but as necessarily interrelated. They also do not try to impose a separation of researcher and participants in research. Where the two paradigms differ is in terms of their position on universals and a defined endpoint to development, with contextualists believing that what is significant about human development is the way in which it proceeds differently in different contexts and with adaptive development needing to be defined by reference to culture rather than something that can be applied to all humans. By contrast, organicists hold that cultural variations may speed up or slow down the pace of development but otherwise have rather superficial effects; the same developmental phenomena apply to all normally developing children, and endpoints to development can be clearly defined (even if not all individuals attain them).

Scholars who work within the contextualist framework often appear to be interdisciplinary in their approach. Contextualists are likely to talk about the simultaneous role of both the active individual and the changing context, with context being considered at the local level (children in families, or in peer groups, an approach common to psychology), at the social structural level (the interrelated role of ethnicity, race, or social class, the province of sociology), and at the cultural level (the domain of anthropology). As I'll discuss in Chapter 3, however, there are a number of contextualist theories that require study at each of these levels.

Within sociology, the clearest example of contextualist approaches are those that fall into the emerging field known as the sociology of childhood – a field that is quite explicit about the need to study children, as actors in their own right, in the different contexts in which they find themselves. Key proponents include Bill Corsaro in the United States (1985, 1992, 1997; Corsaro & Molinari, 2000), and Alison James and Alan Prout (James, 2004; James, Jenks, & Prout, 1998; James & Prout, 1997; Prout & James, 1997) in Britain.

Within the fields of psychology, human development, and cultural anthropology, there are not only different definitions of culture but also competing views on the relation between culture and human development (see, for example, Cole, 1996, 1998; Donald, 2000). However, the easiest way in which to show the distinction between mechanistic and contextualist approaches is to describe two of the ways in which scholars have approached the study of culture and development, one termed a "cross-cultural" approach and the other termed "cultural."

Scholars who have labeled themselves as cross-cultural psychologists typically fit within the mechanist paradigm. They have generally conducted their research as a means of testing the generalizability of the data that have been gathered within their own society. For example, cross-cultural psychologists interested in issues of children's development have compared child rearing in an industrialized society (typically the United States) with equivalent practices in societies from the majority world in which the parent generation has had little or no schooling (as in many parts of rural Africa or South America). Because of this research, it is clear that behaviors, beliefs, practices, and so on that are considered competent in one cultural group are not necessarily seen as competent in another. For example, cultural groups differ widely in terms of such things as the appropriate age to wean the child from the breast, the age at which children should not be sleeping with parents, when it is worth trying to communicate with babies, and so on. As Adamopoulos and Lonner (2001) have argued, in the dominant (mechanistic) approach culture is treated as an independent variable, and studying cultures that differ across many dimensions allow a type of "natural experiment" that helps us to understand "how and why cultural . . . factors serve to mask, mediate, or modify an otherwise common core of regularities in human thought and behavior" (p. 8). These authors went on to point out that "cross-cultural psychologists have proposed the adoption of classical [i.e., mechanistic] scientific methodology to investigate human behavior comparatively" (p. 28). Cross-cultural psychologists are therefore likely to use methods such as questionnaires (translated into the language of the other culture(s) and back-translated into the original language to ensure equivalence) or experimental tests that can be applied in all cultures in which the research is taking place.

By contrast, scholars who term themselves "cultural psychologists" fit within the contextualist paradigm, given their belief that culture is inextricably intertwined with individual activity and interaction (see, for example, Gauvain, 2001; Greenfield, 1997; Miller, 1997; Rogoff, 2003; Shweder, 1990). Greenfield, for example, pointed out not only that the typical (i.e., mechanistic) methods used in psychology could not be used to serve cultural psychology but that the methods that could be used in one culture would by no means necessarily work in another culture. "The procedures and methods of cultural psychology arise from the culture itself, not from the methodological cupboard of psychology" (1997, p. 321). The reason for the different methodological stance taken by cross-cultural and cultural psychology stems directly from their different paradigmatic foundations (Miller, 1997). Cultural psychologists are therefore likely to collect data in an ethnographic manner, trying to understand the practices of a culture from the culture's own perspective by spending a good deal of time in the culture, observing naturally occurring activities, and interviewing members of the group. However, far more research on cultural variations fits within the mechanistic paradigm and features cross-cultural than cultural psychology.

We thus have the situation that, for reasons both disciplinary and paradigmatic, we have relatively little research that tries to understand the ways in which children actually live, act, and interact in different cultural groups. Instead, for the most part we have short-lived observations of children in relatively controlled or limited settings from the industrialized world; we have comparisons across different cultures that primarily feature experimental methods, questionnaires, or some type of diary method; and we have lengthy observational and ethnographic accounts of young children's everyday lives in the majority world.

There are, of course, some exceptions to this general tendency; some good ethnographic and observational research has been conducted in parts of the industrialized world, including the United States. Most of these studies, however, have focused on cultural groups that are comparatively small and that are studied precisely because they are seen as being different from groups that are more or less in the mainstream of society. There are studies of Native American groups, for example, including those reported by Deyhle and Swisher (1997) and research by scholars such as Suina and Smolkin (1994), Tharp (1989, 1994), and Weisner and his colleagues (Weisner, Gallimore, & Jordan, 1993). Rather more work has been conducted by cultural anthropologists interested in the development of language and literacy (for example, Heath, 1983, who is unique in that she studied the literacy development of middle- and working-class White children and working-class Black children from three communities in the South), but anthropologists have for the most part not studied the everyday activities of children in the mainstream. Fischer and Fischer's (1966) work in Orchard Town as part of the Six Cultures study stands almost alone in its focus on all typically occurring activities rather than a restricted subset, such as schooling or language use. The pioneering work of the ecological psychologists Barker and Wright featured intense observational study of *One Boy's Day* (1951) in which every behavior from morning to night was faithfully documented by a team of observers. They also provided a detailed accounting of the typical activities in one Midwestern city in the United States (Barker & Wright, 1954).

In Britain, the closest equivalent study is the work of John and Elizabeth Newson in Nottingham, whose work I cover in some detail in Chapter 2. This ambitious project followed approximately 700 children and their families from infancy until the children reached seven years of age (Newson & Newson, 1963, 1968, 1976). Other important and relatively lengthy (an hour or more over several visits) studies of everyday activities have been undertaken that aim for unstructured naturalistic observations, derived from ethology (Bateson & Hinde, 1976; Blurton-Jones, 1972), applying the same type of method to the observation of young children as would often be used to study the behavior of nonhuman species.

In the United States, too, these types of shorter observational studies, in which observers try to make sense of children's regularly occurring activities and interactions, have also been done, generally either in a restricted setting such as a child-care center (for example, by Clarke-Stewart, 1973; Corsaro, 1985; Corsaro & Molinari, 2000; Corsaro, Molinari, & Rosier, 2002; Lubeck, 1985; Lubeck, Jessup, deVries, & Post, 2001; Smith & Connolly, 1972), in the home (Carew, Chan, & Halfar, 1976; Richards & Bernal, 1972) or, occasionally, in both settings (Carew, 1980; Tizard & Hughes, 1984). There have also been some excellent observational studies of young children's naturally occurring play – the work of Haight (Haight, 1999; Haight & Miller, 1993), Farver (Farver, 1999; Farver, Kim, & Lee, 1995; Farver & Shin, 1997) and Göncü (Göncü, Mistry, & Mosier, 2000; Göncü, Tuermer, Jain, & Johnson, 1999) stands out in this regard. Similarly, studies of children's language and literacy development have used observations in the home and school to excellent effect (see, for example, Dickinson & Tabors, 2001; Dunn, 1988, 2005; Hart & Risley, 1995, 1999; Heath, 1983, 1986; Wells, 1981, 1985), about which I'll write more in Chapter 2.

Despite these exceptions, however, the situation is clear: there are lengthy observational and ethnographic accounts of young children's everyday lives in the majority world, with the goal of understanding how culture is implicated in children's development. By contrast, in the industrialized world, we have a huge number of short-lived observations of children in controlled or limited settings in industrialized groups. What we have extremely little of is research that has focused on the full range of activities in which young children in the industrialized world typically engage and the types of interactions in which they typically participate. Moreover, on the few occasions in which similar methods are used to collect data on everyday life among a community in the United States or Western Europe and a community from the majority world, the researchers for the most part concentrate on between-group differences among groups that are deliberately chosen to be maximally different and tend to ignore the within-group variation that can be found within any cultural group.

For example, middle-class families in Boston have been compared with Kipsigis families in Kenya and Efe hunter-gatherers in Zaire (as the Democratic Republic of the Congo was called when this research was done); middle-class families in Salt Lake City and in an urban area in Turkey with rural Mayan families in Guatemala and a peasant community in India; and middle-class families in Wisconsin compared with rural families in Senegal (Bloch, 1989; Dixon, LeVine, Richman, & Brazelton, 1984; Morelli, Rogoff, & Angelillo, 1992; Morelli, Rogoff, Oppenheim, & Goldsmith, 1992; Rogoff, Mistry, Göncü, & Mosier, 1991; Super & Harkness, 1982). Similarly, Keller's (2003; Keller et al., 2004) research contrasts models of child rearing and associated parenting practices among middle-class mothers in Germany and rural Nso mothers from Cameroon, although her most recent publication (Keller et al., 2006) also includes child-rearing models and practices from a variety of different cultural groups.

Although this research has been valuable in pointing up the great differences in child-rearing practices, everyday activities, and so on, two problems have arisen as a result. The first is that we come to view cross-cultural comparisons as being important only when the cultures to be studied are maximally dissimilar. As Bornstein, Tal, and Tamis-LeMonda pointed out:

Cross-cultural research is often geared to evaluate the distinctiveness of some phenomenon in a setting that is exotic or unique; frequently, it is undertaken to compare samples from contrastive settings in order to maximize the potential of uncovering differences. However, such a strategy potentially confounds childrearing aspects of culture with other factors. (1991, p. 73)

Although access to technology, industry, institutions such as schools, and the extent of city dwelling are among the markers of culture, we should be careful not to conflate them with culture itself. It is thus important to examine cultural variations in children's experiences that are not confounded with such things as the degree of industrialization. As Hallpike (2004) expressed it, the "failure to compare like with like inevitably produces an exaggerated sense of cultural difference" (p. 14).

The second, and related, problem is that researchers interested in cultural issues have paid too little attention to heterogeneity within societies. Middle-class White children and their families in the United States are, by default, taken to be representative of the whole United States, if not of the entire industrialized world (Rogoff, 2003). Cross-societal research should always recognize the within-society heterogeneity that is a function of social class, race, ethnicity, and so on.

I don't wish to imply that the scholars engaging in research into the cultural practices of one or more small group, or "community of practice" (Rogoff, 2003), believe that their findings can be generalized beyond the particular group being studied or that there is an assumption of within-society homogeneity. In fact, the richly contextualized descriptions of practices in these groups are meant to indicate their specific ecocultural niche. In this sense, their work is a conceptual world away from traditional research in developmental psychology as practiced in North America, where generalizability is the explicit goal and thus the impact of context is, supposedly, reduced to a minimum. Nonetheless, without any explicit discussion of within-society heterogeneity, problems in interpretation may occur. For example, by virtue of the fact that the families of "Orchard Town" were the only ones drawn from the industrialized world in the Six Cultures study (Whiting & Whiting, 1963, 1975), they have come to serve as representative of families far beyond the confines of the small New England village where the data were collected. This is partly because of the lack of good-quality observational data of everyday lives in families from the industrialized world. But it is also the result of the absence of any explicit attention to the heterogeneous nature of industrialized societies or to the changes in social relationships over historical time. Readers of reports of the Six Cultures study may thus be left with the understanding that, compared with mothers in Kenya, India, the Philippines, Mexico, and so on, mothers in the United States are more likely to be the social partners of their children. Even in the most recent report (Whiting & Edwards, 1988), no mention is made of possible variations across historical time (the 1950s, when the data were gathered, and the 1980s), across social class (the families were all middle class or self-employed working class), across race (the families were all White), or area (the families all lived in a small New England village).

The issue of heterogeneity has long been recognized, of course, but principally by those with a sociological background who explore racial, ethnic, or social-class variability within societies or by psychologists who include these terms as independent variables of interest but who go little beyond using what Bronfenbrenner and Crouter (1983) termed "social address" models (that is, they remain content with showing that racial, ethnic, or socioeconomic groups vary in terms of some domain of interest rather than trying to understand what might account for those variations). Moreover, even when scholars examine within-society heterogeneity, they also tend to maximize the differences between the groups. In the United States, for example, although most of the developmental research conducted in the United States has focused on White middle-class children, as noted earlier, studies of Black children have concentrated overwhelmingly on those who live in poverty (Abell, Clawson, Washington, Bost, & Vaughn, 1996; Billingsley, 1988; Boykin & Allen, 2004; Bradley, Corwyn, McAdoo, & Coll, 2001; Chase-Lansdale, Gordon, Coley, Wakschlag, & Brooks-Gunn, 1999; Hill, 1999; Kelley, Power, & Wimbush, 1992; Luster & McAdoo, 1994; McLoyd, 1990; McLoyd,

Cauce, Takeuchi, & Wilson, 2000; Taylor, Chatters, Tucker, & Lewis, 1990). It may be the case that a greater proportion of Blacks than Whites live in poverty in the United States, but that does not mean that poor Black children's experiences should be conflated with those of all Black children. Instead, greater attention needs to be given to the early experiences of Black children from middle-class or wealthy families.

OVERVIEW OF THE BOOK

My reason for writing this book stemmed in large part from the types of issues and concerns that I've discussed so far in this chapter. Specifically, I wanted to use the same methods to explore the everyday activities and interactions of children from a range of different societies in such a way that like could be compared with like while taking into account within-society heterogeneity. I also wanted the research to have a clear theoretical foundation and to ensure that the methods that I used were explicitly linked to the theory. I therefore decided to study the everyday activities and typical social partners of three-year-olds in a variety of cultural groups.

As mentioned earlier, the definition of culture that I use means that different societies may qualify as being different cultures (although this by no means precludes within-society cultural groups from existing). The societies from which we collected the data were chosen for several reasons. A number of scholars (see, for example, Hofstede, 1980, 1991; Kim, Triandis, Kagitçibasi, Choi, & Yoon, 1994; Schwartz, 1994; Triandis, 1995) have distinguished between individualistic/independent and collectivistic/interdependent societies, and although I think that these ways of classifying societies is overly simplistic (see, for example, Strauss, 2000), it influenced my thinking as I started preparing for this study. So, if the United States may be considered an individualistic society, Russia and Korea may be viewed as relatively collectivist and interdependent, although with completely different histories and ideologies. Estonia and Finland provide interesting variations; the Estonian parents who participated in this study were raised in the Soviet Union and so were clearly influenced by a collectivist ideology. However, culturally and linguistically, Estonia is far closer to Finland than to Russia, and Finland has been viewed as an individualistic society. Realo and her colleagues (Realo, 2003; Realo & Allik, 1999) argue, in fact, that Estonia in many ways should be thought of as an individualistic society, despite its having been incorporated into the former Soviet Union for many years. Kenya and Brazil are two examples of societies that have not industrialized to the level of the other societies.

One of the reasons for choosing these particular societies was therefore that they allowed for interesting contrasts. Another reason relates to my background. Although English by nationality, I lived in the former Soviet Union for two years in the 1970s and did research there during the 1980s, and I have lived and worked mostly in the United States since the early 1980s. It therefore made sense for me to plan a research project that would involve American, Russian, and Estonian families. I recruited, and trained, the people who have become my colleagues in this project, in Russia, Estonia, and Finland (to allow the Russia–Estonia–Finland comparison), and trained American, Korean, and Kenyan graduate students who were interested in collecting data in their own societies. The Brazilian part of the project began for different reasons. I was interested in collecting data from a second society that does not consider itself part of the "First World" and have spent periods of up to a year living in southern Brazil. Therefore, with the help of colleagues there and thanks to my speaking Portuguese, I was able to recruit and train, in Brazil, the people who collected the data there.

Each of these societies is, of course, large and complex. My goal was not to try to recruit a random sample of three-year-olds from each society but rather to choose a single city from each of them. Each city was selected because it was similar in some ways to the city – Greensboro, North Carolina – in which I currently work. Each city but one is considered medium sized by the standards of the society, ranging from 100,000 to 700,000 inhabitants, and is several hours' drive from each country's capital city. Moreover, each city has at least one institution of higher education and a large range of occupations from professions with high status in the society to more traditional working-class jobs. The Brazilian city is an exception; it is larger than the others, with more than a million inhabitants; is much farther from the capital than is true in the other societies; and is itself the capital city of its state. Each of the cities involved in this project is described in more detail in Chapter 5.

In each city, we chose families from a minimum of two groups – those in which the parents had higher education and an occupation considered professional (families that I refer to here as "middle class") and those in which the parents did not have higher education and whose work would be considered blue collar (families that I call "working class"). In Greensboro, moreover, we examined ethnic variation; half of our families, equally divided by social class, were Black, and half were White. I'll describe the recruitment strategies for the families we selected in Chapter 5.

The reasoning behind the choices of these particular groups was to allow me to examine one or two aspects of heterogeneity. As I mentioned earlier, there are many sources of heterogeneity in any given society – social class, race, ethnicity, recency of arrival in the society, region, city dweller or inhabitant of a rural region, and so on. I wanted to choose just one source of heterogeneity that could be found in each of the societies, and social class was the chosen candidate. In addition, race (a term I am using as a proxy for skin color rather than to imply genetic differences) was another important candidate in Greensboro. What this meant was that we could examine the extent to which heterogeneity, in terms of children's activities and interactions, could be found even within a single city from each of the societies.

In the chapters that follow, I first (Chapter 2) describe what is known about the everyday lives of young children in the United States and United Kingdom, as examples of the most studied groups of children in the industrialized world, and in Kenya, the most studied part of the majority world. My goal in this chapter is to show both the major differences that can be found when looking at cultures in societies that have industrialized to a greater or lesser extent but also the differences within societies – differences that are also cultural in nature. I describe the theoretical framework for this study in Chapter 3 and the methods my colleagues and I used to gather our data in Chapter 4. In Chapter 5, I describe the cities themselves and how we recruited the families who participated in this research. Chapter 6 is devoted to an exploration of the different activities in which the children were engaged, examining similarities and differences in the types of activities both at the level of each city and also showing class and race variations. This chapter also features individual variations in activities, together with some of the reasons for and consequence of those variations. In Chapter 7, I show the impact of the various settings (for example, in and around the home or in a formal child-care center) in which the children were situated and the partners with whom the children were engaged in their various and sundry activities. These two chapters, for purely heuristic reasons, divide up aspects of children's lives that are, in reality, not divisible. Therefore, in Chapter 8, I provide some vignettes of the daily lives of children from each of the cities to capture more of the feel of their everyday activities and interactions. Finally, in Chapter 9, I draw the various strands together, examining the relation between culture and human development, and showing how the theory on which this work is based can help us make better sense of the similarities and variations in young children's typically occurring activities and interactions in different cultural groups around the world.

2   The Daily Lives of Toddlers

Our deeds still travel with us from afar, and what we have been makes us what we are.

George Eliot, *Middlemarch*, 1872/1988, p. 575

As I pointed out in the previous chapter, in many ways we know a great deal about young children. The pages of the leading North American journals are filled with studies featuring children of preschool age, and textbooks provide great detail about various aspects of young children's cognitive, moral, and socioemotional development. What we don't know a great deal about is how young children spend their time, with whom, doing what, in what types of settings. My goal in this chapter is not to try to provide a comprehensive account of what we know about young children's development in different parts of the world; to achieve that goal would take rather more space than this volume provides. My aims are rather more limited. First, I want to show that there are indeed major differences in children's lives in industrialized societies and in societies that form part of the majority world. Second, I want to describe some of the heterogeneity that exists within any society, whether from the industrialized or majority world.

As I argue in Chapter 3, what really matters for development is what one does on a regular basis, with those people and objects one spends time with. This is hardly a new thought; Aristotle wrote in the fourth century B.C. that "virtue of character results from habit" (1985, p. 33), and in the 1870s George Eliot wrote much the same thing in the epigraph at the start of this chapter. However, what one does can only be understood by examining the individual who is doing and what there is to be done in the immediate context. What there is to be done depends on the things that are available, the people who are available, and notions about what it is that is appropriate to be done (whether in general or by the particular individual being considered). These types of things, termed "ecocultural conditions" by Tom Weisner, produce differences in the everyday *activity settings* around children. Activity settings are defined as the personnel, goals, motives, tasks, and culturally appropriate scripts for conduct that constitute children's daily routines. . . . These activity settings are both the instantiation of ecocultural presses on the family and child, and the framework within which meaningful behavior occurs and is constituted by culture members. (Weisner, 1989, pp. 76–77)

For this reason, I'm going to concentrate my attention on those studies that have tried to examine what young children do in their everyday lives, rather than on the wealth of research that shows what children can do in certain circumstances or in particular settings. I thus do not deal with quasi-experimental or observational studies that take place either in the laboratory or in the "real world" but under highly constrained conditions. Moreover, recognizing the impossibility of trying to do justice to the myriad types of societies in the world, I focus on children's lives in two of the industrialized countries (the United States and England) where we have some reasonable data on how children spend their time and in one society from the majority world (Kenya) that has yielded a large number of studies of young children's everyday activities. I don't wish to imply that one can generalize from either the United States or England to other societies from the industrialized world or that Kenya somehow "represents" the majority world. It should become clear from this chapter, however, that different types of societies have very different approaches to raising children and that within any society it is impossible to ignore the within-society cultural diversity that exists and that also influences child-rearing practices.

YOUNG CHILDREN'S EXPERIENCES IN THE INDUSTRIALIZED WORLD: EXAMPLES FROM THE UNITED STATES AND ENGLAND

As I laid out in Chapter 1, because child developmentalists in the industrialized world have concentrated on controlled studies under constrained conditions, whereas cultural anthropologists and cultural psychologists have spent much more of their time observing the ways in which people's lives are lived in the majority world, we know less about the naturally occurring activities of children from the industrialized world than about the activities of their counterparts in the majority world. However, efforts have been made to understand how young children occupy themselves in some industrialized societies. For example, some researchers have asked parents about how much time they spend with their children, their sense of how much time their children spend in various activities, and so on. Other researchers have tried to get at the meaning of the activities in which the children are engaged by either interviewing parents or observing in the settings in which the children are situated.

Time-Use Studies

Time-use studies are primarily conducted by sociologists, who ask respondents to use a type of daily diary in which they note what they were doing, with whom, and where every hour of the day. These studies also provide an estimate of the amount of time parents spend doing various child-care tasks or actually engaging with the child in play or watching TV. One of the first of these studies, conducted in the early 1960s, was a cross-national study using a similar methodology in the United States and in various countries in both Western and Eastern Europe (Szalai, 1972). As part of this volume, Stone (1972) reported on the patterns of child care in 12 countries and showed that fathers in Eastern Europe spent about twice as much time on "child-related activities" on workdays (and one third more time on weekends) as did fathers in Western countries. The amount of time was not great, however (about 30 minutes in Eastern Europe, 17 minutes in Western Europe) and much less than the time spent both by employed mothers (almost an hour in the East, and 50 minutes in the West) and by women who did not work outside the home (75 minutes and 84 minutes, respectively). Robinson (1977), using the U.S. data, showed that mothers of children four years of age and under reported spending about two hours per day on various types of child-care activities (cleaning, dressing, reading, putting to bed, etc.), compared with about 20 minutes for fathers. The amount of time varied by whether the mother was employed outside the home, and parents also noted that more time was spent doing some other activity with the child as a social partner. Interestingly, a later study (Robinson, Andreyenkov, & Patrushev, 1989) using the same methodology in a U.S. and Soviet city in the mid-1980s, had similar findings to those in the 1960s (Szalai, 1972); in both the American and Russian samples, mothers in full-time employment reported spending about twice as much time on the care and upbringing of children as did fathers. As in the earlier study (Szalai, 1972), American parents, however, reported that they spent about half as much time (fathers) to two thirds as much time (mothers) looking after their children as did the Russian parents.

Other research, using a similar time-use methodology, conducted by the University of Michigan Survey Research Center in 1975–6 and 1981–2 (Juster & Stafford, 1985) included data on children's use of time, with children as young as three years of age participating (Timmer, Eccles, & O'Brien, 1985). Children younger than six were not asked to fill out diaries, and neither were they interviewed; instead, their parents were asked to estimate how much time these young children were involved in various activities. The results suggested that, in their waking hours, three- to five-year-olds spent about three and a half hours a day in play during the weekday, about an hour longer at the weekends, a little over two hours in some type of formal child-care or preschool setting, almost two hours watching TV, and almost an hour and a half eating. They spent about seven minutes looking at books or being read to, two minutes a day in other school-related activities, and were involved in some type of household work about 15 minutes a day. However, Timmer and her colleagues pointed out the limitations of using the same type of diary for children of all ages and adults. "If we want to know what young children do when they play, or what parents and children do when they are together, it might be better to tailor a diary to these activities, getting detailed reports of time the children spend with their parents or of a child's activities during a typical play period" (Timmer et al., 1985, pp. 356–357).

Hofferth and Sandberg (2001) used part of the 1997 Panel Study of Income Dynamics to get similar information on children from birth to 12 years. The main activities of the three- to five-year-olds in this nationally representative sample look fairly similar to those reported by Timmer and her colleagues. During their waking hours, they spent, on average, about two and a half hours a day in play, almost two hours a day watching TV, almost one and a half hours eating, and a little over an hour being cared for. Eighty-one percent of these children were involved in some type of household work, for an hour a day, on average, although 20% of the children were never involved in any type of work. The children, on average, spent almost three hours of their time in some type of formal child-care arrangement (with half of the children going to preschool and 25% of them in a child-care center). The children, on average, spent about seven minutes a day in conversation and 12 minutes a day looking at books, but these were activities that between 40% and 50% of the children were reported as never doing. About five minutes a day, on average, were spent in other types of school-related activities, but more than 80% of the children were reported never to be involved in these types of activities.

The most recent report of how North American children spend their time was published by the U.S. Department of Commerce and titled "A Child's Day: 2000" (Lugaila, 2003). Data were collected from the parents of more than 22,300 children under six years of age (with approximately equal numbers from each of two other groups of older children). Fifty-five percent of children aged six or younger ate breakfast with at least one of their parents seven days a week, and almost 77% ate dinner with at least one parent each day. Seventy-three percent of the children were praised at least three times a day by at least one parent, and 75% of the children were reported to be talked to or played with, for fun, three or more times a day. Approximately half the children were read to at least once per day, and fewer than 10% were never read to, but these percentages varied by both race/ethnicity and parents' educational level. More than 60% of non-Hispanic Whites reported reading at least once a day to their one- and two-year-olds, compared with less than 35% of Hispanics, and more than 60% of parents with a college degree reported reading with their children at least once a day, compared with less than 45% of those who completed their education with a high school diploma or less. When both mother and father were in the household, regardless of marital status, mothers were approximately 50% more likely to read to the children than were fathers.

Efforts have been made to get finer-grained information on how children spend their time by requesting information about specific activities. For example, researchers in England used a time-budget approach to assess the extent to which English five- to six-year-olds were involved in school-related activities at home (Plewis, Mooney, & Creeser, 1990). Parents of almost 200 children from London responded to questions about the previous 24 hours. The average (median) child was reported to have spent two and a half minutes a day reading to a parent, less than two minutes reading to him or herself, one and a half minutes being read to, 13 minutes a day looking at books, no minutes writing, and no minutes a day involved in any type of mathematical activity. Some children (but fewer than 50% of the sample) engaged in writing (and did so, on average, almost five and a half minutes a day), and some (30%) were reported as having done some mathematical activity in the previous 24 hours but only for about two minutes on average.

As I mentioned in Chapter 1, there's often a lack of consistency between the methods used to collect data on children's lives in the industrialized and majority worlds. Telling examples can be found in the research conducted by Marianne Bloch (1989) on children's play and by Harkness and Super (1992) on fathers' involvement with their children. Both studies clearly illustrate the propensity to rely on reports from parents, often by telephone, survey, or interview, when gathering data about children's use of time in the United States but real-time observations to gather similar data in a majority culture. Bloch used this hybrid methodological approach to study young children's activities in Wisconsin, where she relied on telephone calls to caretakers who were asked to report on the children's activities, and in Senegal, where she trained Senegalese women to observe and write short narratives about daily activities. The American two- to four-year-olds spent about 30% of their time in play, 10% of the time watching television, 3% of their time involved in work, about 9% of their time in "sociable interaction" (10% for girls, 8% for boys), about 4% of their time either in preschool or engaged in "school-related" activities, and the remaining time being cared for, eating, sleeping, and so on. Few differences were noted for boys and girls. By contrast, Senegalese children of the same age were less likely to spend time in play (21% for boys, 27% for girls) and more likely to spend time in school (12% for boys, 6% for girls). Girls were also slightly more likely to be involved in work than were boys (5% vs. 3%) and in sociable interaction (10% vs. 8%).

Bloch (1989) was most interested in the types of play in which the children were involved and noted that in both societies children were involved in play about 25% of the time that they were awake and not in school and that in both societies children played alone about half of the time. However, in the U.S. group, the child's mother (but not the father) was a partner in play about half as often as were other children; in Senegal, partners in play were always other children.

Harkness and Super (1992) also used a hybrid method to gather data on the extent to which fathers were involved with their young children. They used interviews, primarily with mothers but sometimes with the fathers them-selves, to describe the involvement of middle- or upper-middle-class fathers in Cambridge, Massachusetts. These parents reported that the fathers spent a good deal of "quality" time playing or reading with their children and how important it was for them, as fathers, to have this time with them. By contrast, Harkness and Super relied on observations in Kokwet, a Kipsigis community in western Kenya, to assess paternal involvement there and found that fathers spent little time (by comparison with those in the U.S. sample) with their children and that their engagement primarily involved discipline. I don't doubt that Cambridge and Kipsigis fathers engage to different extents with their young children and are involved in different types of activities, but given the fact that the former obviously value the time that they spend with their children, it is at least possible that they may overestimate the amount of their involvement.

These studies give us some sense of how young children in the industrial-ized world spend their time, and with whom. Drawing primarily on the two U.S. national data sets (Hofferth & Sandburg, 2001; Timmer et al., 1985) and Bloch's (1989) study of children in Wisconsin, the range and extent of activ-ities in which American three- to five-year-olds participate are as follows: If we assume that three- to five-year-olds are awake for about 14 hours a day, most of their time is estimated to be spent playing (18% to 30%, depending on the study), a lot of time watching television (10% to 14%), not much time involved in some type of household work (2% to 7%), and even less of their time looking at books or doing some other type of school-related activity (1% to 2%) and in conversation (1%) (although Bloch reported that the Wisconsin children on whom she gathered data spent 9% of their time in "sociable interaction"). The two national data sets noted that the children spent between 14% and 21% of their time in some type of child-care center, although in Bloch's data the children engaged in school-related activities, including preschool, only 4% of the time. The remaining 30% to 50% of the children's time was spent doing something else, including eating and sleeping. Drawing on Lugaila's (2003) data, most of the children would be likely to spend some of their eating time in the company of at least one parent, mostly the mother, and most of them would be likely to be played with or talked to at least three times by their mother (although we don't know for how long), and half of the children would be read to, again most likely by the mother.

It's reasonable to question the accuracy with which parents, or other people involved with young children, can judge how much time young children spend in their everyday activities. Robinson and Godbey (1997) argued that such types of retrospective accounts of time spent in activities is reasonably accurate, drawing on studies comparing parent reports with actual video observations of television watching (Anderson, Field, Collins, Lorch, & Nathan, 1985; Robinson, 1985). However, because TV programs have specified times and people often watch from beginning to end of any specific program, it is likely to be far easier to estimate how long one watches TV than how long one spends doing virtually anything else. Estimates of time spent in different types of play, looking at books, or in conversation are likely to be less accurate; close observation of young children's naturally occurring involvement in mathematical experiences, for example, reveals far more involvement than parents report (Tudge, Li, & Stanley, in press). As I'll show in Chapter 6, although time-use studies' estimates of television watching matched closely our own observations of American children, we found wide discrepancies with their estimates of other types of activities. Estimates of time spent by young children also do not provide a rich sense of what actually goes on in children's everyday lives.

Observations and Interviews

Studies of all Activities
Fortunately, there have been studies of young children's everyday lives in both the United States and England that have aimed at providing a "thick

description" (Geertz, 1973, 1977) and which, as a result, provide a fuller portrayal of young children's lives, either through interviews with the parents or in the course of lengthy observations. In one of the earliest such studies, conceived in conjunction with the Six Cultures research, John and Ann Fischer observed "Orchard Town" (1963), where children "spend much of their time during the day tagging along after their mothers around the house" (p. 957). Supporting the results provided by the time-use studies, mothers served as the "sociable partner" (Whiting & Edwards, 1988) to their children, because of the amount of time spent in each other's company. Although most of the children's time was spent in play and chatting with the mother, children also became involved in tasks around the house, not so much because the work was considered to be of any great help or because it was viewed as important training for the future, but more for the child's own amusement. They may have had some chores at this age, such as helping to put away toys they had taken out, but these types of tasks were never considered the child's sole responsibility.

By contrast, early childhood in Orchard Town was viewed as a time for play, and all of the children observed there had lots of toys to play with, as well as different types of games – such as simple board games, drawing in coloring books, looking at books, and so on. Fischer and Fischer (1963) also noted that watching television, "which is new with this generation of children" (p. 960) had become important in the lives of many children. The children's movements outside the house were free within fairly strict limits; they could play in the yard, or in a neighbor's yard, with a few other children, but all of the children of this age had clear restrictions on which roads they could not cross.

Occasionally an older sibling was asked to look after a three-year-old, but this was not typically seen as appropriate, at least for long periods of time. For this reason, young children were far more likely to be found in the company of their mothers or children of the same age (or both). The families observed by the Fischers did not use any type of formal child-care arrangements (apart from Sunday school when the parents attended church), but on occasion a grandmother or aunt was asked to look after a child, and when close relatives were not available, a babysitter was used. Babysitters (almost entirely girls) had to be at least 12 years old, and preferably older than that. Fathers all worked outside the home and typically did not spend much time with their young children; when they did, it was more often than not to "roughhouse" with them, although occasionally they agreed to act as a babysitter while the mother went shopping.

Approximately 10 years after the data were being gathered in Orchard Town, John and Elizabeth Newson were interviewing 700 mothers in

Nottingham, England, about their four-year-old children as part of a longitudinal study of child rearing. Although the children in Orchard Town were all from families in which the parents were either middle class or self-employed working class, those in Nottingham were from England's full social-class range. The Newsons were careful to point out the existence of contemporary cultural variations in child rearing in different parts of the world and about the changes in England over historical time. The focus of their attention was therefore "not what these children might do, but what they do in fact do in the circumstances in which they variously find themselves" (Newson & Newson, 1968, p. 49).

As was true for the Orchard Town children, the fathers were typically at work, older siblings at school, and so the Nottingham children were in the company of their mothers and sometimes younger siblings. They endured the same types of restrictions as their counterparts in the Fischers' northeastern U.S. village, being relatively free to wander only within the home, the garden or backyard, and perhaps a short distance away from the house.

> Many children make a constant companion of their mother, following her round the house as she cleans and tidies, helping her in her housework or using her continually as an adjunct to their own play. . . . Perhaps the major demand made by the four-year-old upon his mother is that she should talk to him. (Newson & Newson, 1968, p. 52)

Children also had small chores to do, such as tidying their room or play area, and occasionally were asked to run an errand, perhaps going to a local shop for something that the mother had forgotten, and sometimes simply going into a shop to get something while their mother waited outside. But in no sense were these types of chores considered the children's primary responsibility. More often than not, a task was done because a child had pestered to help washing dishes or dusting rather than because the mother saw it as useful. However, working-class children were more likely than their middle-class peers to get sent on short errands. During one interview, for example, a four-year-old was sent on three separate occasions to buy something for his mother, each time receiving a penny for his services, which involved three more visits to the same shop. One might wonder, of course, whether the volume of errands was an aberration in this child's life, perhaps designed to allow the mother an easier time conversing with the interviewer! The children got to see more work than the typical housework that their mother did, however, because workers would come to the house, and they also saw people doing jobs when out on trips with their mothers. As the Newsons humorously expressed it:

"Men down holes and up ladders are usually prepared to pass on a little specialized knowledge to the inquisitive onlooker" (1968, p. 61).

These children also welcomed social contacts with peers, but most spent far less time with a peer than with their mother, their primary source of social interaction. Some of the children (about 11% of the sample) spent some time in a formal child-care setting – some all day long, some in a half-day program, and others in a play group for just a few hours a week.

How did these children spend their time? Just as in Orchard Town, many of them watched television. "Indeed, for some children the pattern of family life in the early evening seems to be geared more closely to the television schedule than to the clock" (1968, p. 64). But the dominant activity in their lives was play, and the children in Nottingham clearly had many toys with which to play. The Newsons pointed to the newfound affluence of postwar British society, and many of the mothers talked about the fact that they were able to buy their children the types of toys that they themselves had never had as children. "The parents' wish and ability to indulge and the children's own acquisitiveness are not the only factors behind the growing accumulation of toys in nearly every home" (p. 137), but clearly they were important factors.

Much of the children's time was spent in play, and a large majority of the mothers in the Newsons' sample valued it and saw in it educational possibilities. The mothers often talked about their children's fantasy or role-playing games, and most of them (66%) engaged in a "wholehearted" way (i.e., a "willingness to join in on equal terms") with their children in those games. As one mother said: "'Course, you have to join in if you have the time. We do try to take an interest in that sort of thing, because we know that it's his mind at work all the while and he's learning all the while" (p. 165). The rest of the mothers, almost without exception, talked about being involved with their children in other types of play, particularly those with some obviously school-related focus, although a small number of mothers said that their children preferred to play alone or with other children. Perhaps not surprisingly, mothers were more likely to play with their children when they only had one or two than when they had three or more. Mothers from the lowest social-class group (unskilled laborers, cleaners, and the chronically unemployed) were much less likely to be involved in play with their children than were mothers from any of the other social classes. The Newsons argued that this difference could not be explained by the fact that these families tended to be larger (mothers were equally unlikely to participate in their children's play when they only had one or two) but may have been because "these mothers often have a somewhat more formal and tradition-oriented conception of the maternal role, which does not include coming down to the child's own level in play" (1968, p. 172).

Mothers also tended to be the main conversational partners for their children, particularly (but by no means exclusively) in the course of their joint play. As the Newsons pointed out:

> Most mothers seem to appreciate their role of conversationalist, even if they sometimes find it wearing; and for many, the child offers a *quid pro quo* in his readiness to listen to them, which for the housebound woman can answer a real need. (1968, p. 430)
>
> bored, lonely

The importance of considering historical time is obviously relevant in this case, as in Orchard Town, because although in the 1950s and 1960s, in both England and among Whites in the United States, women were "housebound" and tended not to work outside the home, this is no longer the case in either society.

I have focused primarily on the mothers' role because the Newsons' interviews were with the mothers. However, the interviewers also asked about the fathers' roles, and about half of the fathers were said to have a "high" amount of participation in the raising of their children, with a further 40% "fair" participation, and 9% "little or none" (1968, p. 514). Middle-class fathers tended to be more likely to be involved than were working-class fathers, or at least this was the perception of the mothers. Many of the mothers talked about the fathers' role as authority figures, but they also talked about the ways in which fathers would put the children to bed, read stories with them, engage in little rituals, and so on. As one mother said, "If Daddy's not here when he goes to bed, Andrew blows him a kiss, and then his Daddy has to give it back to him in a bag in the morning" (pp. 289–290). By and large, however, these mothers did not have a lot to say about fathers playing with their children, although one father, who was present during part of the interview, did talk about the fact that he loved to go upstairs to the bedroom with his daughter, encouraging her to jump on the bed, turn somersaults, and so on.

These two studies, with data gathered in the northeastern United States (Orchard Town) and in the north Midlands city of Nottingham, were conducted in the 1950s, and it's reasonable to suppose that, if nothing else, one thing that has probably changed in the past half century is the availability of the children's mothers as their play and conversational partners, as has the likelihood of the children spending more of their time in some type of child-care center. Fortunately, there are a few more up-to-date studies of children's everyday activities in parts of the industrialized world, even though there is still a propensity, as we'll see, to focus on what children are doing either at home when their mothers are with them or when they are in child care.

The most recent example of observations of naturally occurring activities in the United States is the research of Morelli, Rogoff, and Angelillo (2003), who compared the activities of three-year-olds in two middle-class communities in the United States (in Boston and Salt Lake City) with those in one cultural group in what had been called Zaire during data collection and another in Guatemala. Morelli and her colleagues noted that children in the U.S. communities were little involved in work (in perhaps 4% of the observations) and were involved in relatively didactic, school-related, lessons about the same amount. The children were much more involved in play, and in 16% of the observations were observed playing with at least one adult. The children were also far less involved in lessons or work than in conversations, about 70% of which featured one or more adult. These data provide a picture of children who are little involved in the work that is going on around them and who are as likely to receive didactic lessons as they are to work. However, they participate a good deal with adults in both their play and, most clearly, conversations about things not related to the here-and-now activity. As Morelli and her colleagues pointed out, this pattern of activities looks very different from that observed in the two communities from the majority world, in which adults were little involved with their young children in these types of activities.

Studies of Children's Play and Conversation

The work that I have discussed so far in this chapter gives us a reasonable idea of the wide range of activities in which young children are involved. However, a good deal more observational research in both the United States and England has a rather more limited goal, namely, to focus on one or two different activities – primarily play or literacy, including conversation. This research has also found that toddlers' parents are highly involved with them, confirming what the Fischers (1963) and the Newsons (1968) had earlier found. It's worth noting that these data do not accord well with the time-use data, which suggested that neither mothers nor fathers were greatly involved with their young children.

Judy Dunn (1988, 2005) found that mothers were highly likely to be involved with their young children in both play and conversation, with English mothers more likely than those from the United States to be involved in their children's pretend play (Dunn & Brown, 1991). Dunn (1988) also saw many examples of children engaging in play with their siblings (see also Miller & Garvey, 1984), when children become drawn into the imaginative world created by an older sibling even as young as 18 months of age. Dunn found interesting differences in the children's play when with an older sibling compared to when they were with the mother. In the latter case, the mothers were generally attentive and supportive of their children's play but rarely took a lead role. By contrast, siblings were highly directive, informing the younger child what he or she was supposed to be and how to take on the role appropriately. This was not only true of pretend play; Dunn described an 18-month-old who regularly engaged in soccer games with her six-year-old brother, with sequences of play lasting from 20 to 40 minutes. The little girl repeatedly (and mostly carefully) followed his instructions on where to stand, how to kick, when to praise a good goal, and so on.

Wendy Haight and Peggy Miller (1993) focused exclusively on children's naturally occurring pretend play. They studied nine children, all from middle-class backgrounds in and around Chicago, and they did so on seven occasions, from 12 to 48 months of age, with each observational period lasting several hours (1.6 to 4.2 hours), with most observations lasting more than three hours during weekday mornings or afternoons. Observations took place primarily in (or close to) home and allowed the authors to study the development of the children's pretend play. The study had been originally designed to examine language use, and so neither the observers nor the parents were initially aware of the study focus, thereby making it less likely that the children or parents would deliberately increase the extent to which they engaged in pretend. At 12 months of age, as Piaget (1951/1962) argued should be expected, almost no pretend play was seen, but by 24 months these children were engaging in a little over two minutes of such play every hour; by 36 months, about eight minutes per hour; and by 48 months, when the study stopped, about 12 minutes of pretend play every hour. As I show in Chapter 6, Haight and Miller saw far more examples of pretend play than we did in our observations. However, this may well have been because they observed the children only when they were at home with their mothers.

Consistently, at each age studied, children were less likely to engage in solitary pretend play (less than 30% of the time), and mothers were the main social partners of their children in their pretend (90% of the time at 12 and 24 months, dropping to around 70% at 36 months, and falling to 50% of the time at 48 months). Other children were the main other social partners, although for one child, another adult featured as a significant social partner. The mothers of these children obviously valued this type of play; within their own homes "all mothers directed pretend play to their children at twelve months of age, although pretend play had emerged barely in some children and not at all in others" (p. 42). A year later, however, mothers and children were equally likely to initiate this type of play and were equally responsive to the other's leads. As Haight and Miller (1993) pointed out, it is not surprising that the mothers were the main social partners; these children were in homes in which the fathers were out at work, and the mothers, who did not work outside the home, were their primary caregivers. The other children who were involved as partners in play were predominantly the target children's own siblings.

Most of the children's play (60%–70%) at 36 and 48 months involved what Haight and Miller (1993) termed "replica" objects, namely, "a realistic minia-ture of an object that is used conventionally during play" (p. 87). Children had requested and parents had bought various types of stuffed animals, dolls with accessories (both "Barbie" or "Ken" adult dolls and child or baby dolls), action figures, cars, trucks, train sets, other vehicles, puppets, a shopping cart, and sets of dishes. Probably most important, then, is the parents' belief that children's play is something to be encouraged and something in which the parents themselves can and should be involved.

When mothers weren't playing with their young children, they were often talking with them. Dunn (1988) found that mothers with children as young as 14 months were likely to engage them in conversation even before the children could do much in the way of talking themselves, filling in the appropriate conversational spaces for their children. Many of these conversations related to what had been going on at the present time (and therefore would not constitute conversation as I defined it, as we'll see later on), but many of them referred to situations that were separate from the here-and-now of everyday activities, such as "to the feelings of others, and to the consequences of the children's actions" (Dunn, 1988, p. 38). "Parents and siblings talk to [young children] about the social world from their infancy; they also talk to each other about such matters, and young children . . . monitor and often comment on these interactions" (1988, p. 185).

Other observational research in the United States confirms the extent to which American parents, particularly mothers, treat their children as con-versational partners. Hart and Risley were explicit about the advantages of observations in the home compared with studies conducted in structured settings when trying to understand what typically occurs:

Laboratory settings have the advantage of constraining the variability in what people do by presenting the same situation to them all. But people are likely to show what they *can* do when given the perhaps enriched materials and unin-terrupted opportunities presented in a laboratory setting rather than what they actually *do* do on a routine basis in ordinary circumstances. (Hart & Risley, 1999, p. 17)

For this reason, they collected one hour of natural observations every month for two and a half years, from 42 families from a range of socioeconomic and ethnic backgrounds. The children observed by Hart and Risley (1999) were described as having a great deal of freedom to choose what they wanted to do, wear, eat, and so on, living "in a social world that fostered independence" (p. 31) and were given few responsibilities, apart from occasionally being asked to bring things or put things into the trash. This independence, however, occurred within relatively clear limits, specifically by all manner of structures designed to prevent them from putting fingers into sockets, falling down stairs, getting into cupboards, and so on.

An amazing amount of talk was recorded; on average 700 to 800 utterances an hour within the children's hearing, about half of which were addressed to the children themselves. All of the parents talked more to their own children than they did to others', approximately 300 to 400 utterances per hour. Interestingly, Gordon Wells (1981, 1985) found that English parents talked almost as much as did these American families, averaging close to 300 utterances per hour. The American children in Hart and Risley's study were actually likely to initiate most (59%) of the interactions, by touching, babbling, or offering the parents something, as early as 12 to 19 months.

Hart and Risley (1999) observed that children do not always need other people around to engage in conversation about the future. They quoted one 35-month-old girl, sitting on her bed with three dolls, explaining to them what's going to happen, as she decides what to put into her bag.

Here I gonna get this out 'cause we going camping. . . . Going camping today. Lots of toys and my horn and this and . . . going camping today. Like my car go camping. Oh, my barrettes. This, put in. And some gloves go with me and Alice and him and her and him. Every people can go along. Oh, me take kitty cat and my babies. (p. 137)

It is important to note that, even by three years of age, the vast majority of what the children in Hart and Risley's (1995, 1999) study were saying we would not have coded as conversation. More than 40% of the children's utterances were descriptions of what they had just done or were currently doing, and about one third were simple phrases such as "Hi" or were simple answers to someone's questions. However, "all of the children were telling readily about past events and happenings beyond the visible referents of home and the immediate surroundings and about connections between events" (1999, p. 131), talking that in my study would be coded as conversation. By three years of age, on average, the children produced about 17 utterances per hour that used some sort of future tense and 19 involving some description about the past. Of these, it is reasonable to suppose that at least some of them would have involved interaction on the part of an interlocutor, in which case we would have coded it as conversation.

David Dickinson and his colleagues (Dickinson & Tabors, 2001; Dickinson, St. Pierre, & Pettengill, 2004) argued convincingly that this type of more sophisticated talk is likely to be helpful to children's development. They followed a group of 74 children, three-years-old at the start of the study, for two years. They paid a one- to three-hour home visit to each child, once a year, and audiotaped the language used during storytelling, playing, and eating. They also interviewed the mothers about the types of activities the family participated in. What Dickinson and his colleagues found was that those children who engaged in more "extended discourse," who participated in conversations using more "rare words" (words that were likely to be outside a preschooler's typical range), and who participated with an adult in literacy activities (looking at books, writing letters, etc.) were significantly more likely to do well on measures of literacy in kindergarten. Specifically, they were better able to tell a story based on pictures, knew more concepts related to print, had some awareness of beginning and ending sounds of words, had some knowledge of writing, and had a broader vocabulary. These advantages were found for children over and above anything that could be explained by the children's social-class background, race background, mother's education, and even by the child's complexity of language use as measured at the start of the study (Dickinson & Tabors, 2001). These gains held up through the early years of elementary school (Dickinson et al., 2004).

Do these examples provide a good sense of how young children spend their time in at least two examples of societies from the industrialized world? Well, yes and no. They do indeed give us insight into some of the experiences of young children who are viewed in and around the home, but almost exclusively with mothers who are not working outside the home. These descriptions do not give us any insight into the lives of children whose mothers are in full-time employment, they do not tell us anything about children's experiences with adults outside the nuclear family (whether an aunt, grandparent, or a child-care provider, whether in a formal or informal setting). Moreover, I have so far made almost no reference to variation either by social class (although the Newsons did comment on some class differences) or ethnicity. And it's clear that children's experiences vary a great deal as a function of each of these within-society factors.

Variations by Setting, Race, and Social Class

One of the most striking examples of social-class variations is gained from Hart and Risley's work on young children's language experiences. These authors devoted much of their 1995 book *Meaningful Differences in the Everyday Experience of Young American Children* to a discussion of the different amounts and type of talking that goes on with children from middle-class and working-class backgrounds, although it is clear that there were also large individual differences in the age at which the children in their study started to talk and the extent to which they did so. Nonetheless, parents in the 13 professional families addressed more than 2,000 utterances per hour to their children, those in the 23 working-class families used only 1,200 each hour, and those in the six families living on welfare on average addressed only 600 utterances per hour.

In part, this can be explained by the fact that the parents in the professional families spent twice as much of their time interacting with their children as did the parents on welfare, and the professional parents gave their children positive feedback when they talked twice as often as did the working-class parents and five times as often as did the parents using welfare. Not surprisingly, the use of vocabulary and its growth rate was far higher in the case of children from professional homes compared with the children from the other two backgrounds. As the authors pointed out, if one can extrapolate from the 25 hours each child was observed between 11 and 36 months of age, that

the average child in a welfare family would have had 13 million fewer words of cumulative language experience than the average child in a working-class family. . . . [Moreover, the] extra talk of the parents in the professional families and that of the most talkative parents in the working-class families contained more of the varied vocabulary, complex ideas, subtle guidance, and positive feedback thought to be important to cognitive development. (Hart & Risley, 1999, p. 170)

These differences were clearly expressed in the differences in IQ scores and children's intellectual competence once they had reached school (Hart & Risley, 1995).

Why might we expect to find these types of differences in children's experiences as a function of their social-class background? Part of the answer has to do with parents' values and beliefs about how to deal with their children and what's important for them. As early as the 1920s in the United States, the Lynds (1929, 1937) showed how working-class mothers in "Middletown" valued obedience in their children, whereas mothers of the "business class" were far more likely to value their children's independence. Mel Kohn, from the 1960s onward, argued that the reason stems from differences in the parents' experiences, both during their own schooling and subsequently in the workplace, with working-class parents more likely to achieve success by conforming to rules established by others and middle-class parents' success more likely to stem from their being able to exercise greater independence of thought and action (Kohn, 1977, 1979, 1995). As Tom Luster and his colleagues (Luster & Rhoades, 1989; Luster, Rhoades, & Haas, 1989) were able to show, these differences in values translate into different ways of dealing with young children. They also relate to different ways of using language (Bernstein, 1971; Hoff, 2002; Hoff, Laursen, & Tardif, 2002).

Social class is just one source of within-society variation, however, and just as social class is related to differences in the experiences of young children, so, too, are racial/ethnic differences. It is worth pointing out that most of the research within the United States has focused on White middle-class children (Graham, 1992; Hagen & Conley, 1994; Rogoff, 2003), not simply to point out the obvious lacunae but to stress that generalization to other groups is not appropriate. Clearly there is a danger in equating the practices of a single group within any society with the practices of the society as a whole, particularly when there are plenty of studies that show great variations among different groups. Here I discuss only differences between African American children's experiences and those of children of European American background. This is not because I believe that the experiences of Black youngsters in the United States are the same as those of Black children in England or France or anywhere else in the world, or that African American experiences are like those of Cuban Americans, Mexican Americans, or members of any other minority group in the United States. My sole point is to show that even when families come from a similar social-class background, ethnic/racial variations in activities and interactions can easily be found.

Heath (1983, 1986), for example, showed clearly the ways in which young children used language in the course of conversation and looking at books differently if they grew up in White middle-class or working-class homes and that these "ways with words" were in turn quite different from those found in working-class Black homes. Heath argued convincingly that the different approaches used with children from these three groups were differentially related to teachers' expectations once the children entered school, with the approaches of the middle-class children lending themselves more easily to success with reading and writing.

Heath (1986) described how the middle-class White children that she studied inhabited a world in which literacy was stressed from six months of age, when they were in rooms that had bookcases, and had mobiles, bedspreads, and stuffed animals that featured characters from books. Not only were they read to, but their parents often alluded to characters in books while talking to them, and by two years of age the children were encouraged to make up their own booklike stories. By age three, they were expected to (and themselves looked forward to) listen to stories and to "read" their favorite stories to their parents. The world of the working-class White children was in many ways similar; babies had cribs decorated with story or nursery-rhyme characters, and two-year-olds had either simple cloth books or "books that provide sounds, smells, and different textures or opportunities for practicing small motor skills" (1986, p. 106). Just like their middle-class counterparts, these young children were provided the opportunity to participate in the telling of the story or to respond to what the word or letter "says." By age three, however, reading had become something rather different, with children being expected to stay quiet during reading, and before they had started school, they had had a lot of practice in recognizing letters and some words. However, unlike the middle-class children, they had had few possibilities to explore the imaginative power of books.

The world of the Black working-class children studied by Heath was entirely different, with children's books (apart from some Sunday school material) almost entirely absent and virtually no attempts made to read to the children, apart from their older siblings occasionally treating them as "schoolchildren" in play. Not that their lives were bereft of language, however; on the contrary, "they eat and sleep in the midst of human talk and noise from the television, stereo, and radio. Encapsulated in an almost totally human world, they are in the midst of constant human communication, verbal and nonverbal" (1986, p. 112). By the age of three or so, however, the children were becoming adept at holding their own both in conversation and in storytelling.

The children's play materials and partners were also quite different in these communities. In the working-class White community, for example, children were routinely given lots of toys although, by the time the children were two years of age, the toys were highly sex-typed. Girls were given dolls, doll houses, doll furniture, tea sets, and books about little girls, cuddly animals, and babies. Boys, on the other hand, were given toy trucks, tractors, plastic soldiers, and jeeps, and their books featured boys and their animals, ballgames, and so on. These children also got toys that had some educational purpose, but again these were differentiated by sex: "Girls are given educational toys which stress girls' and women's activities; boys are given those which emphasize the activities of boys and men" (Heath, 1983, p. 133). Parents appeared more than happy to participate in their children's play, although Heath noted that most of the time they did so with the help of toys rather than joining in with the children's pretend play. By the time the boys were four years old, their fathers would teach them how to play ball games and would tussle with them to teach them "toughness" and the importance of standing up for themselves. "Little girls are increasingly left to their tea sets, dolls, and doll houses" (p. 138).

By contrast, the playthings of a child in the Black working-class community were far more likely to be

the household objects deemed safe for him or her – pot lids, spoons, plastic food containers. Only at Christmastime are there special toys for very young children; these are usually trucks, balls, doll babies, or plastic cars, but rarely blocks, puzzles, or books. (Heath, 1986, p. 113)

Toys that were designed to have some educational value did not feature prominently in these children's lives. Their parents did not play with them, or at least not in the sense in which the White working-class children's parents played with their children. As I mentioned earlier, the Black children were immersed in a world of talk, playful challenge, and verbal games, and they could often play these types of games with adults as well as with their older siblings and the other children of the community.

Young children in the industrialized world do not only spend their time at and around the home in the years prior to school; many of them attend some type of preschool institution, although here, too, there are major differences in the types of institutions attended even in a single society, such as the United States. Not only are there clear differences in the quality of different institutions (National Institute of Child Health and Human Development [NICHD], 2003), but those that cater to working-class children (traditionally termed day-care centers) have entirely different roots than "preschools" that cater to children from middle-class families (Freitas & Shelton, 2005; Freitas, Shelton, & Tudge, in press; Scarr & Weinberg, 1986). Many children, moreover, are in the care of someone who is an unlicensed child minder, in what is known as "family care" in the United States. Not surprisingly, then, some clear differences should be seen in the children's experiences depending on the type of child-care arrangement.

It would be impossible to do justice to the myriad experiences that children have in child-care settings prior to attending formal school. Here I settle for a taste of the variation possible, drawing from ethnographic studies in which children's activities are carefully observed. Sally Lubeck (1985) spent a year studying children in two child-care classrooms just a mile apart in a single Midwestern city in the United States. One of the classrooms was a Head Start center that catered to poor Black children, the other a classroom in a preschool attended by middle-class White children. Children in each classroom were four years old and spent three hours a day in the class.

From the start, it became clear to Lubeck that the two classrooms saw themselves as providing different things – the preschool trying to be an extension of the home, where children could play and develop through their play, and the center seeing itself as a prelude to school. The center thus allotted 25% of the child's time to group sessions in which children were expected to learn to recognize their printed names; know the day, month, and year; and memorize their address and phone number. During this time, the children also listened to stories being read or to music. As Lubeck noted,

> the head teacher believes that group time is the time when children learn. . . . She believes that what children really need is to know something. . . . This concern encompasses the children's general behavior as well, for she likewise sees group time as "getting the children ready to listen to the teacher." (1985, p. 74)

By contrast, only about 12% of the children's time in the preschool was spent in group sessions, also with a focus on learning but learning more varied things such as the colors and names of vegetables, information about insects, and listening to stories.

Most (75%) of the preschool children's time was spent in free play, in various activity areas set up around the room. The teachers moved around these areas and talked with children about what they were doing, sometimes encouraging a different activity but for the most part following the lead of the children. "The free play time is, in effect, the purpose of the morning, a time for children to freely choose from a variety of activities that the teachers value and therefore provide" (p. 73). The center children also had free play but for only about 12% of the time, and typically the children did not get to choose the activity but were sent to one of several areas around the room. The teachers did not interact with the children at these times but caught up on paperwork or prepared for the group session. Approximately the same amount of the children's time at the center was spent resting, lying on small rugs with the lights dimmed.

One of the important differences in these two classrooms has to do with the type and amount of language that was used, echoing the work I presented early by Hart and Risley (1995). In the center, children almost never conversed with a teacher; any talking was with one or more other children, and the teachers intervened only when the noise level became too great. The children had opportunities to interact with the teachers during group time but were restricted for the most part to providing answers to the questions the teachers raised or to chanting in unison things such as the days of the week. The children in the preschool classroom were far more likely to engage in conversation with the teachers about the specific activities in which they were involved, to raise questions themselves, and to express their own individuality. The two groups were, in effect, repeatedly getting the types of experiences that led them into different worlds, with the middle-class White children being encouraged to explore their worlds as relatively autonomous beings, learning through their play and conversation, and the working-class Black children being encouraged to follow the rules, being trained to sit and listen to their teachers, and not to converse with adults.

Note that I am not saying, by any means, that all White middle-class children have the same experiences and that they are different from the experiences of all Black working-class children. There is good evidence that this is not the case. Bill Corsaro, for example, has also done ethnographic observations with White middle-class children in a preschool classroom (Corsaro, 1992) and with Black children who attend a Head Start classroom (Corsaro & Rosier, 1992), as well as with Italian preschoolers (Corsaro, Molinari, & Rosier, 2002). By immersing himself into the children's world (becoming, in the process, "Big Bill"), Corsaro was able to see what Lubeck had not, namely, the typical play, conflict, and discourse that seems to be widespread among groups of children, particularly those given time to play. Where Lubeck (1985) noted the limited conversation between the Head Start children, Corsaro was able to listen in on all sorts of language exploration, including the type of "playful banter" that typified the language of the children Heath (1983) observed.

Dickinson and his colleagues (Dickinson & Tabors, 2001; Dickinson et al., 2004), in the study I discussed a few pages ago, went beyond collecting data on children's language use in the home. All but 10 of the 74 children in the study were visited both in the home and also once each year at preschool, and their language was audiotaped for about 90 minutes. The researchers also gathered data on literacy use in each classroom and interviewed the children's teachers. The results were similar to those obtained in the home. The extent to which children engaged in extended discourse with the teacher during free play and at mealtimes and the use of words not commonly found in preschool-aged children's vocabularies was relevant to the children's abilities to tell stories, their knowledge of things relevant to reading and writing (emergent literacy), and their vocabulary. Both social class and race were related to these growing abilities (not surprisingly, given Heath's and Lubeck's earlier work), but, as Dickinson and his group found when focusing on language use at home, the benefits of extended discourse with teachers were independent of the children's gender, race, and class, as well as the child's use of words at the start of the study.

The main point that I want to stress, from this discussion of some of the variation in experiences that exists in any society, is that we need to be cautious indeed in focusing on the everyday activities of any one group and imagine that this somehow stands for the experiences of any other group from the same society. I should also mention here that experiences in any group, even at the classroom level, do not stay constant. Teachers come and go, values and beliefs change over time and practices change concurrently, and the children themselves change, in part because of their experiences in the home.

Nonetheless, I hope that by now I have provided sufficient detail for an adequate, albeit imprecise, sense of children's everyday lives in at least two societies drawn from the industrialized world. It should be clear that there are some major problems, not least that much of the observational work focusing on children's everyday activities conducted in the United States was done decades ago, that the vast majority of it has been done with a preponderance of White and middle-class families, and that the major study from England relied on interviews rather than observations. The more recent observational research focuses on one or two specific types of activities – play and conversation, typically – or activities in a single setting out of the many that children frequent.

CHILDREN'S EXPERIENCES IN THE MAJORITY WORLD: EXAMPLES FROM KENYA

Because comparatively few scholars have tried to document what young children in the industrialized world typically do, the settings they inhabit, and their interactions with the full range of other people they spend their time with, we have much richer information about young children's experiences in many parts of the majority world. In this chapter, I concentrate on just one society, Kenya, in part because of the large number of observational studies that have been conducted there. Let me stress that I in no way wish to imply that Kenyan experiences are similar to those in other parts of the majority world – any cross-cultural handbook should be sufficient to debunk that idea, with Whiting and Edwards's (1988) *Children of Different Worlds* the clearest illustration of just how different children's experiences can be.

In the earlier sections of this chapter, I showed that in many communities in the United States and England, young children spend a large proportion of their time playing, mostly with toys, and quite often with their mothers whether in pretend play or play that the mothers view as having some educational value. They also engage her in conversation, particularly when there's no one else around to play with. They may have some chores to do, such as tidying away their toys, but nothing that they do is considered essential, or even helpful, to the smooth running of the household. The situation is far different in Kenya or, to be more accurate, in any of the tribal groups in Kenya that have been studied by cultural anthropologists.

Engaging in Work

How do young children in Kenya spend their time? By comparison to the children from the United States and England, a good deal more of their time is spent in work. As Martha Wenger pointed out, the amount of time children in Kenya spend "contributing to the household economy" is "one of the most striking differences" (1989, p. 92) between them and American children. Wenger conducted her work in the Giriama community called Kaloleni, in southeastern Kenya close to the Indian Ocean, where the very name given to children in the two- to three-year-old age range translates as "a youngster who can be sent to fetch a cup of water," and children of this age group often were engaged in this type of little errand (Wenger, 1989).

Elsewhere, the same situation was found. For example, in Ngecha, a Kikuyu community about 20 miles from Nairobi, children's tasks also started early in life, often soon after a new sibling was born. Very young children could be asked to carry food from a neighboring house within the homestead or to bring a coal from the fire if an adult wanted to light a cigarette, bring a stool for a visitor, or tell neighbors that there is to be a beer party and borrow cups and mugs. Three-year-old girls were trained to carry small pans of water on their heads so that they could be sent to the river for water. As they got older, so the pots got larger. "An adult will never get something for himself if he can order a child to do it, even if the child is farther from the object than he is himself" (Whiting, 1996, p. 181). Older siblings treated younger siblings in much the same way. Similarly, when Robert and Barbara LeVine were collecting their observational data in Nyansongo, a Gusii community in the western highlands, they saw that by the age of three, girls might already be expected to help their mothers in the fields, and by five years of age could be seen looking after a younger sibling. Given their usefulness, it is understandable that their mothers did not let them wander too far from the home, although there was still a great deal of opportunity for spending time with others, both siblings and other children in the homestead (LeVine & LeVine, 1963).

Whiting and Whiting (1975) discussed five types of tasks that were potentially available to all children in the Six Cultures study, namely, carrying water
and wood, preparing food, gardening, cleaning, and taking care of animals.
Children as young as three years were observed doing each of these tasks
in Nyansongo, and by the time they were five, their mothers believed that
they were capable of looking after a baby. Given these expectations, it is not
surprising that the Whitings found that Nyansongo children were the most
nurturant of any in the various cultures:

Since few of the children were in school at the time of the study, these child
nurses were available all day long. They were observed feeding, bathing, and
caring for the infants while their mothers worked in nearby gardens or went to
the market. . . . A child nurse must be able to guess the needs and motivations
of his or her small charge and learn what behavior is required to satisfy these
needs, the essence of nurturance as we have defined it. (Whiting & Whiting, 1975,
pp. 95–96)

Each of the chores in which the Nyansongo children were involved was important – without wood to burn, water in which to cook things, and the vegetables picked from the gardens, the family would be hungry. Insufficient care
in looking after animals or attending to a younger sibling could lead to loss,
injury, or death. It is not surprising that these children developed a sense of
responsibility early in life.

Not all of the tasks are assigned equally to boys and girls; the children who
are doing most of the care of younger siblings are primarily girls. This type
of child care, in Kenya, is viewed as girls' work. This is in part because girls
are considered more nurturant than are boys (Whiting & Edwards, 1988), but
simply by virtue of having more experience around infants and toddlers, girls
may develop more nurturance. Ember's research among the Luo of western
Kenya supports the view that children's activities foster nurturance, at least
as much as do biologically based propensities. When the Luo boys were
assigned traditionally "girl" work (because of an imbalance in the number of
boys and girls), they exhibited "less overall egoism, more prosocial behavior,
less egoistic aggression, and less egoistic dependency compared with boys
low on feminine work" (Ember, 1981, p. 432). And those boys who did the
most "girllike" work, specifically looking after younger children and other
"inside" work, were most likely to show prosocial behavior. However, the
situation of boys looking after younger children is not the norm.

In the Gusii area in and around Nyansongo, child-rearing duties are explicitly assigned. A specific person, generally an older sister, is given the role of
the newborn's main babysitter, at least until the baby is weaned, and this is

her main chore (LeVine et al., 1994). The expectation is that these girls will do all that mothers would typically do, breast-feeding apart, and although they are not instructed to play with the infant, there is some expectation that they will do so. Nonetheless, "our observations indicate that Gusii children are often remarkably quiet as infant caregivers and that they go for long periods of time without talking to, playing with, or otherwise stimulating their charges" (p. 155).

The type of work and, therefore, in many cases the setting for the work, is not only differentiated in many cases for boys and girls but has an impact on the opportunities for play and social interaction. Wenger's (1989) spot observations in Kaloleni allowed her to note the activities young children were engaged in with their social partners. Some of their work, such as pounding maize, took a good deal of time and did not allow for much in the way of social interaction. They were also asked to run errands, however, and while doing that task they could work, play, and socialize at the same time. As Wenger noted, girls worked more than did boys and tended to have chores that limited their opportunities for social interaction. By four to five years of age, the Giriama girls in Kaloleni were seen spending about 10% of their time in work, about twice as much time as were boys. After about eight years of age, girls were observed spending about half of their time in work, twice as much as were the boys of this age, and the tasks that they were given varied dramatically. Girls had responsibility for most of the child care, gardening, housework, collecting and carrying firewood, water, and so on, whereas boys were expected to run errands.

Play, Often while Working

In part because the Giriama boys studied by Wenger (1989) had more unstructured time than did girls and also because their work generally occurred outside the household area, they had more opportunities for social play with their peers; girls, as might be expected, were more often found playing with infants or toddlers. Boys of four to five were observed spending about half of their time with peers, although by eight years of age that had dropped to about 25% of the time. Girls, however, were most likely to be in the company of peers when they were two to three years of age, but this high of about 23% of the time dropped in half to about 12% by age eight. By contrast, girls of four to five were seen in the company of infants in about 20% of the observations (almost twice as often as were boys), and by age eight, this figure had increased to 25%, compared with 5% for boys. As might be expected, by age eight boys were much more likely to spend time with same-sex companions than were girls, who looked after infants and toddlers of either sex. Harkness and Super (1985) found similar results in their observational study of the social partners of boys and girls in a Kipsigis community from the west of Kenya.

Adults are conspicuous by the absence from the play of these children from different groups in Kenya. As LeVine and LeVine (1963) reported about Gusii families in Nyansongo, "Mothers do not play with their children, fondle them, or display affection for them openly" (p. 165). Although mother–child relationships were described as "relatively informal," mothers did not typically reward their children, even verbally, and were far more likely to use fear to control their children's behavior. Giriama children also learned early not to expect their mothers or other adults to engage with them in play. In fact, children "are reluctant to attract adult attention, since this often incurs an undesirable consequence, such as the assignment of some task" (Wenger, 1989, p. 96). The LeVines also noted very little in the way of fantasy play among Nyansongo children, whether boys (who were frequently observed looking after the cattle) or girls, often in charge of younger siblings. "The girls cuddle, play with, and carry about some of the others' infant charges; they whisper secrets about one another and giggle; they watch and comment on activity on the road, particularly the buses and who is going into town; they rarely fight" (1963, p. 174).

The type of play in which the children engaged is primarily with household objects or natural objects. In one example provided by Edwards and Whiting (1993), for example, a three-year-old girl is observed playing with an empty teapot, pretending to pour tea for herself after her mother has given her some. She then sees her five-year-old sister playing with a corncob and whines when her sister doesn't let her play with it. Her grandmother and aunt intervene, and her sister gives her the corncob, and "she begins to play with it, covering it with green corn husks. She throws a husk at [her sister] in a playful, teasing way" (p. 314).

Sibling Care and Interaction

Siblings, as we know from the work of Weisner and Gallimore (1977), play a key role in the development of young children in all parts of the world, but do so particularly in communities in which play and conversation between young children and adults are not considered appropriate. This has certainly been the case in many Kenyan communities, as documented by Edwards and Whiting (1993) in Ngecha, the Embu children studied by Marion Sigman and her colleagues (1988), as well as the Gusii (LeVine et al., 1994), Kipsigis (Harkness & Super, 1985), and Giriama children (Wenger, 1989).

The practice of sibling care for young children is more easily followed, of course, when there are plenty of siblings and cousins who are available to care for toddlers. In rural communities or in small towns in which many marriages are polygynous, where families have many children, and where closely related families live nearby there are many more children of the appropriate age to look after toddlers than is true in larger cities (Edwards & Whiting, 1993; Weisner, 1979). In a situation such as this, for example, in Ngecha, mothers were much more likely to scold, comfort, and provide food or basic caretaking to two-year-olds than were siblings (Whiting & Edwards, 1993). Mothers were also more likely to require the child to do simple chores or get them to behave appropriately. However, siblings were much more likely than mothers to play with these toddlers, be sociable with them, tease them (in play or not), or simply hang out with them. As the authors noted, "For the mothers, 90 percent of their acts were of the 'mother role' type, versus 10 percent of the 'peer role' type. For the siblings, 73 percent of their acts were of the 'peer role' type and 27 percent of the 'mother role' type" (Whiting & Edwards, 1993, p. 318). The two-year-olds, similarly, were more likely to try to get food or drink from their mother than they were from their siblings and were also more likely to seek help, comfort, attention, approval, and permission from her. By contrast, these youngsters were more likely to play with, tease or insult (generally in a playful way) or try to dominate in some way their siblings than they were their mothers.

Heterogeneity, by Space and Time

The studies done in different parts of Kenya, featuring children from different tribes, reveal a good deal of similarity in the types of activities and typical social partners. This should not be taken to mean that there is homogeneity of experience. Much of what we know about children's activities in the various parts of Kenya comes from studies in rural areas of the country. That's perhaps not surprising, given that at the end of the 20th century only about 20% of the population was living in urban centers (Odero, 2004). Fortunately, we do have some data from Nairobi, the capital, which reveals a pattern that is quite different from what has been reported from Kenyan villages, with children engaged in far less work than their counterparts in rural regions, and different types of interactions with adults, particularly their mothers (Weisner, 1979).

Weisner gathered his data from a matched sample of Abaluyia who either lived in Nairobi or who came from a rural community about 200 miles away. All men had had minimal education themselves and had unskilled or semiskilled jobs. As Weisner mentioned, few of the typical chores mentioned earlier, so helpful in a rural setting, were needed in the city, and rural children were observed doing twice as many chores as were those who lived in the city. Weisner also found differences in the extent to which the children engaged in social behavior, with rural children, including those in the two- to four-year-old group, being somewhat more likely to engage in social interaction and, when they were engaged in social interaction, in more friendly and sociable interactions than those who lived in Nairobi. In part, this was because the rural children were often engaged with others (particularly other children) in their various tasks and could talk with them. By contrast, the children in Nairobi, much like their counterparts in Orchard Town or Nottingham, were more likely to seek interaction from their mother and were more likely to want attention or praise from them.

The other major source of heterogeneity has to do with the passage of time. Most of what we know about young children's lives in Kenya comes from the observational studies conducted as part of the Six Cultures research, started in the 1950s with additional research in different parts of Kenya in the 1970s. These data are somewhat misleading, however, because they have mostly failed to address the issue of the huge changes that have occurred in Kenya since independence in 1963. I provide a little more detail about this in Chapter 5, but suffice it to say that immediately after independence, the first president, Jomo Kenyatta, promised free and universal primary education, believing that education was going to be the means to modernize the society. Within two decades, 80% of preschool-aged children were enrolled in school, and parents viewed education as the key to their children's (and their own) future (Buchmann, 2000). Even in rural areas, such as the Giriami community studied by Wenger, "the most traditional [heads of household] tend to view education as a good investment at least for their sons" (1989, p. 94).

Participation in formal schooling, and preparation for formal schooling (in child-care centers), still coexists with children's work, although it is increasingly clear that children in urban areas engage in less work than do those who live in rural regions, in part because of the need for them to attend school (Buchmann, 2000). Moreover, because increasing numbers of children attend school, girls are no longer as available to look after their younger siblings. In the 1970s, for example, Gusii families with sufficient resources sometimes had to hire and pay an unrelated child to care for an infant (LeVine et al., 1994). As noted by Edwards and Whiting (1993), when the Ngecha study began in 1968 children (primarily girls) who were aged five to ten were the ones primarily responsible for looking after toddlers. A few years later, because children of this age were primarily attending school, the responsibility for looking after toddlers had fallen to children as young as four. The recognition of the impact of these types of historical changes was highlighted by Edwards and Whiting (2004) in the title of their most recent book, *Ngecha: A Kenyan Village in a Time of Rapid Social Change.*

In Ngecha, Beatrice Whiting found that as early as the late 1960s the traditional ways of life were beginning to be influenced by the perception that the most rewarding jobs, at least for men, were those that required literacy, and once it became more common for girls to go to school, they were no longer as available as they had traditionally been to look after their younger siblings and other toddlers (Whiting, 1996). "All the mothers we interviewed wanted their children to finish at least primary school. . . . Mothers who had formerly taught farming, housekeeping, and childcare skills now wanted to help their children be successful in school" (1996, p. 8). Whiting asked the mothers what it meant to be a "good" child. Without specific reference to school, mothers typically viewed good children as obedient children, children who were responsible for their chores (particularly when their job was to look after younger children). But they had to be prompted to come up with adjectives that described children who were likely to be successful in school; clever, self-confident, brave, and inquisitive are not terms that would traditionally be used to describe valued qualities of children, but mothers (particularly those who had had some schooling themselves and who were married to a man who had been to school) felt that these were qualities more likely to lead to success in school than was obedience.

Interestingly, however, these mothers viewed only curiosity as something that they, as mothers, could influence. "Allowing children to ask questions and exposing them to new experiences were mentioned by the mothers as prerequisites for the development of this characteristic" (Whiting, 1996, p. 23). These mothers viewed preparing children to learn most of the traditional skills that would serve them well in their adult life (such as weeding crops, preparing a meal, or looking after a baby) as far more likely to be under their control than are the skills likely to lead to success in school. They also believed that they were able to influence their children's obedience and respectfulness. Not surprisingly, then, when these mothers were observed interacting with their four- and five-year-old children, Whiting found that close to half of the mothers' interactions involved training, stressing appropriate behavior, and reprimanding. However, those mothers with more education and whose husbands had also been to school were less likely to spend their time getting their youngsters to perform chores than those mothers with little or no education.

As we can imagine from the fact that two- to four-year-old children spend so much time with their older siblings and other children, particularly girls, Kenyan mothers do not spend a lot of time trying to inculcate obedience and respect once the children have reached the age of 18 months or two years of age. As LeVine and his colleagues pointed out:

the Gusii mother does not assume responsibility for teaching the desirable forms of competence and virtue but rather for managing a household organization of production and consumption from which its youngest member, her children, can learn skills and virtuous behavior through their participation. . . . The mother assumes the young child will learn what is necessary from its older siblings. (1994, p. 265)

Again, schooling has wrought some changes in the traditional customs. Boys, able to be out in the fields or with the cattle, had always been more free than were girls, but with girls increasingly likely to go to school by the 1970s, they, too, had more opportunity to escape the supervision of parents and older siblings.

The Role of Fathers

To this point Kenyan fathers have been conspicuous by their absence, in part because of cultural beliefs that the raising of children is primarily the work of females, whereas the male role is that of providing food, clothing, and (in more recent times) the money for school fees for the children. However, just as mothers often needed to delegate the role of primary caregiver to an older sibling (preferably female) because of their own work needs, men, too, were largely unavailable to be with their young children, even had they wished to be.

Kokwet, the Kipsigis community in which Harkness and Super gathered their data, was one in which few men needed to work far away from the home. Although fathers were typically observed in the presence of their young children (newborns to four-year-olds), in between 25% and 33% of the observations, they were never the designated caretaker. That's not surprising, given the fact that men are barred from even viewing the child for a minimum of one week after birth, and close contact is actively discouraged within the first year – for the protection of both newborn and father (Harkness & Super, 1992). Kipsigis fathers' roles with toddlers are restricted to verbally disciplining them and occasionally teaching them chores. Among the Gusii, too, contact with the father occurs far less frequently than it does with the mother. The LeVines pointed out that "The Nyansongo father is viewed by his child as an awesome and frightening person, and with some justification. Fathers do not play, fondle, or praise their children, and, unlike mothers, they do not feed them or comfort them when hurt" (1963, p. 178).

The Munroes, who collected data using the same methodology in a Logoli community in Kenya close to Lake Victoria, found a similar pattern, with men involved in the caretaking of their infants in only 1% of their observations (Munroe & Munroe, 1992). Fathers were present in 69% of the homes in which there were children aged from three to nine but were only involved in 5% of the "social environment" of their children (defined as within the same space or participating in the same activity).

CONCLUSION

This brief examination of the study of young children's everyday lives, focusing primarily on ethnographic work from the United States, England, and Kenya reveals some striking differences in the experiences of young children. This can constitute a problem, however, when straightforward comparisons are made from one group to another. In this case, we have the situation in which children from middle-class families (i.e., well educated and with professional occupations) in a city (Boston, for example, or Salt Lake City) in an industrialized society (the United States) are compared with children from a majority-world rural community in which parents have little or no education. These types of studies are excellent for showing us the wide range of approaches to child rearing or the markedly different types of activities in which children are involved, or the clear differences in the extent to which adults (particularly fathers) are involved in the daily lives of their children. These studies are less sound, however, in that they do not allow us to see the interrelations among culture, urbanicity, and education.

The fact that children's lives in the industrialized and majority worlds are different should not be a cause for much surprise; what should also be made clear is that within each of these societies, children are likely to have significantly different experiences as a function of their social class and ethnic/racial group and whether they live in an urban or rural setting. It should also be clear that the passage of historical time makes a great difference in children's experiences. We should be cautious about accepting too readily the notion of mothers in the industrialized world being sociable mothers to their children when that judgment comes from a time when mothers, at least in the White middle class in the United States, did not customarily work outside the home. But we should also take seriously the profound impact of the growth of schooling and urbanization in many parts of the majority world and be careful not to confuse the "Kenyan" experience with the lives of Kenyan children growing up in rural areas at a time when schooling was not so important.

Two further issues need to be raised before moving on. The first is that there is not a lot of methodological consistency among the various studies I have discussed. Even in the research reported by Whiting and Edwards (1988, based on the Six Cultures research and the follow-up work in additional cultures) in which the goal was to gather data in the same way from different groups, there was considerable variation in the amounts of time spent observing children. As I mentioned in Chapter 1, some of the children participated in just eight "spot observations," whereas others were observed for a little over an hour and others for more than two hours. The situation in the other studies I've discussed is far more variable, with some scholars relying on surveys (Robinson, etc.), others interviewing mothers (the Newsons), yet others trying to do "spot observations" or gather time-use data by telephone (Bloch; Plewis et al.). Even where observations in children's own environments have taken place, some have occurred for relatively short periods of time but spread over months or years (Dunn; Haight & Miller; Hart & Risley), others have followed children for longer stretches of time but not involved follow-ups in later months (the Fischers), and yet others have involved actual participation in children's lives (Corsaro).

I'm by no means trying to argue that only one method is appropriate when trying to find out about young children's everyday lives or that nothing can be gained from a process of triangulation in which different methods are used to get a more complete sense of how children spend their time. However, it seems to me that we are on dangerous grounds when we try to compare the experiences among two or more different groups but have used very different methods to gather data on those groups.

It is in this sense that the work of Barbara Rogoff and her colleagues is so useful, for they have used identical methods to study the type of work that children become involved in (Morelli et al., 2003), as well as the ways in which mothers and toddlers deal with one another in the context of being introduced to novel objects (Rogoff, Mistry, Göncü, & Mosier, 1991). The same concern with using the same methods in different cultures is found among scholars who have studied patterns of infant care (see, for example, Bornstein & Cote, 2004; Bornstein et al., 1998; Harkness et al., 2001; Keller, 2003; Keller et al., 2004, 2006).

The second issue is a related one, namely, that the lack of methodological consistency across the myriad attempts to understand young children's everyday lives stems from the fact that the methods used have not been explicitly grounded in theory. That's not to say that theory is absent; Rogoff (1993, 1995, 2003) has written about the importance of studying development across three interrelated planes of development, Weisner (1996, 2002) has written about ecocultural theory, and Harkness and Super (2002; Super & Harkness, 1997) have given us developmental niche theory. What is needed, however, is a clear theoretical underpinning to the research and a set of methods that are closely linked to the theory. So that, over the course of the next two chapters, is what I attempt to provide.

3 Cultural–Ecological Theory and Its Implications for Research

I have always been in favour of a little theory: we must have Thought; else we shall be landed back in the dark ages.

(George Eliot, *Middlemarch*, 1872/1988, p. 15)

In the previous two chapters, I talked about what is currently known about the everyday activities of young children in societies from the industrialized and majority worlds. In this chapter, before describing a theory that's relevant to the study of everyday lives, I argue for the necessity of theoretically driven research, with links between our basic assumptions about the world (our meta-theory), the theory we use, the methodology employed, and the way we analyze our data (see, for example, Richters, 1997; Tudge & Hogan, 2005; Winegar, 1997). I begin by discussing two of the most important metatheories or paradigms, namely, mechanism and contextualism, as a way of illustrating the differences between a positivist (or neo-positivist) and a nonpositivist position. The two currently most influential contextualist theories are those of Vygotsky and Bronfenbrenner, and I present summaries of their theories. Both theories have weaknesses, from the contextualist perspective, however, and I present cultural–ecological theory as a contextualist theory that builds on Vygotsky's and Bronfenbrenner's theories in a way that I find useful for my research. I end the chapter by talking about some of the implications for using this type of contextualist theory in doing both what is often referred to as cross-cultural research as well as research on within-society heterogeneity.

Let me begin by drawing on the ideas of Terry Winegar (1997), who has made a persuasive case for the necessity of ensuring a tight connection among one's theory, the methods that one uses, and one's analytic strategy. Winegar makes clear that the initial step in the process is considering what he terms "metatheory." One way to define metatheory is that it is a theory of theories, or a way of thinking at the level of theory, and for Winegar, this means considering the paradigmatic nature of theory or the ways in which different types of theory fit within different paradigms or views of the world.

What is crucial to know about the paradigms that we use in psychology is that they each comes with a different set of ontological, epistemological, and methodological assumptions about reality, about the ways in which we can understand reality, and about the means that we should use in describing reality. Part of the process of ensuring a good fit among theory, method, and analyses is to consider their paradigmatic nature. In this way, we can guard against working within a theory that fits within one paradigm but using methods or analyses that fit within another paradigm. The problems that ensue when not following this metatheoretical advice can be seen most easily when considering the ways in which North American researchers have tried to test Piaget's theory (a theory that fits within the organicist paradigm) with methods and analytic strategies drawn from the mechanist paradigm.

Not only are these various paradigms incommensurate, but critiques based in one are not appropriate as attacks on another. In other words, as Pepper (1942), Winegar (1997), and Goldhaber (2000) have argued, the case for or against one or another paradigm cannot be made by reference to a different paradigm. What is supportive of a worldview from the perspective of one paradigm may be viewed as an attack from the perspective of another paradigm. In this sense, paradigms are not falsifiable. Our reasons for choosing one or another therefore cannot be based on a comparison of their relative merits; what is meretricious for one will be problematic for another. As Winegar (1997) put it, paradigms (or metatheories, in his terms) have an aesthetic quality. We find one or another paradigm appealing; the one that we choose feels right to us. What feels right can change, of course; our reading and thinking can make us less comfortable with one paradigm, and another may begin to become more appealing. Moreover, as the questions we want to answer within psychology or human development change, so one of the paradigms might be more helpful than the others to answer these new questions.

Before continuing, I should point out that the paradigm with which I feel most comfortable is contextualism. Why should this paradigm "feel right" to me, rather than mechanism or organicism? The answer probably lies in my background. My undergraduate degree was in history and my master's degree in sociology, before I moved into the area of education and taught young children for several years. My Ph.D. was in developmental psychology, gained in a department of human development. Not surprisingly, given this type of background, a view of the world that takes seriously the interconnections among history, culture, social institutions, and individual development is one that I would find appealing. Contextualism constitutes such a paradigm, as I now show.

PARADIGMS IN THE STUDY OF HUMAN DEVELOPMENT

As Guba and Lincoln (1994) argued, a paradigm refers to "the basic belief system or worldview that guides the investigator, not only in choices of method but in ontologically and epistemologically fundamental ways" (p. 105). Pepper (1942) discussed four worldviews that he titled mechanism, organicism, contextualism, and formism, each of which has its own position on the nature of reality, how that reality (or realities) can be known, and its appropriate methodological stance. Each worldview also has its own root metaphor – that of the machine for mechanism, the living organism for organicism, the historical event for contextualism, and similarity in the case of formism.

Deriving from Pepper's initial discussion of different worldviews or from Thomas Kuhn's (1962) view of paradigms and paradigm shifts, a number of scholars (Eckensberger, 1979, 2002; Goldhaber, 2000; Guba & Lincoln, 1994; Kuczynski & Daly, 2003; Overton, 1984; Overton & Reese, 1973; Winegar, 1997) have discussed the ontological, epistemological, and methodological consequences of taking seriously these different paradigms, focusing primarily on mechanism, organicism, and contextualism. I won't go into great detail about these different paradigms, although it will be important for my argument to link two of these paradigms (mechanism and contextualism) to two basic perspectives in psychology – positivism and nonpositivism. Such a distinction is overly simplistic; as Guba and Lincoln (1994) have shown, classic positivism has been superseded by what these authors call "post-positivism" (and which I'll term "neo-positivism") and there is not a single nonpositivistic perspective, but a variety, including critical theory, constructivism, feminism, and postmodernism.

The neo-positivist mechanist ontology involves the position that reality is not directly knowable but that methods are available that can allow us to "disprove" incorrect views of reality, by subjecting different claims to careful and critical examination. (This position on the nature of reality constitutes the main difference, at least according to Guba and Lincoln, between this "critical realist" view and the "naïve realism" espoused by positivists, who argue that reality not only exists but also is directly knowable.) The relevant epistemological and methodological positions are that careful experimental control is necessary to ensure that we can make appropriate (and generalizable) claims about reality. Not surprisingly, the dominant methods are quantitative, although some use of qualitative methods is encouraged as a way of generating new hypotheses to be tested (the tests themselves are almost always quantitative) and allowing some consideration of meaning for individual subjects of the research. When researchers talk about using "mixed methods," they typically have in mind this neo-positivistic conjunction of quantitative and qualitative approaches, rather than a mixing of paradigms, something that may be difficult, perhaps impossible, to achieve (Goldhaber, 2000; Guba & Lincoln, 1994; Pepper, 1942).

By contrast, a contextualist ontology, or view of reality, is one that sees a multiplicity of realities, rather than a single reality. Or perhaps there may be just one reality, but people's perceptions of reality are necessarily constrained and shaped by their specific circumstances. These circumstances change with time, power, and local situations. From a contextualist perspective, one should expect a different sense of "reality" from those who have power compared with those who do not (those with power expend a good deal of effort trying to convince those without power that their view of reality is the correct one). Similarly, people in different historical periods would subscribe to different notions of reality, and the same would be true for people in different cultural groups (whether culture is considered at the level of society or as different groups within society, such as racial/ethnic groups), in different socioeconomic positions, and people of different sexes and age groups, in addition to any other source of power differences.

In the contextualist paradigm, even things as apparently tangible as this book that I have written and you are currently holding may be viewed as entirely different things – for me an object of pride and for you perhaps a source of irritation at the price you had to pay, perhaps a paperweight, perhaps an object with which you intend to squash a spider, or perhaps something convenient on which to prop a data projector. And things become even more complex and varied when we start to consider the words themselves, objects of meaning for me, a possible source of ideas for you, strange or incomprehensible black marks on white paper for those who cannot read, who have mislaid their glasses, or who do not understand the language in which this book is written.

As for the ideas I am trying to express, from a contextualist perspective, no matter how clearly I manage to write, the sense that you will glean will necessarily be influenced by your past experiences (both with reading and with these ideas), your reasons for reading this text, the interest with which you are doing so, and the attention you are paying. And a book, when written, is at least a finished product, changing only as it decays, and from the marks in the margins, underlinings, and other physical evidence of a dialogical experience with it.

When one thinks about a relationship between two people, in which both are developing while the relationship itself is also developing, the situation is yet more complex. Even when both have experienced the same event, each person's perception of what transpired can differ markedly. Perceptions of the other person rarely manage to keep up with the developments the other is undergoing. Parents are particularly aware of this phenomenon, especially during their children's childhood and adolescence, but the differing views of reality continue throughout development – throughout life, in other words. Even within the same family, experiences are necessarily different, and from a contextualist perspective, differing experiences mean differing perceptions of reality. Family members, however, at least tend to share the same cultural background, although this is not the case for immigrants whose children know the "new" culture better than they know their parents' culture of origin, or those who have experienced significant social mobility. Differing perceptions of reality are that much greater for those whose social and cultural backgrounds are entirely different.

Two arguments can be raised against this contextualist position. The first is that all I have been talking about so far are perceptions of reality, and not reality itself. From a neo-positivist perspective, although our hypotheses can never be proved but only disproved, the goal is to use methods designed to show that some views of reality are incorrect (the falsification of hypotheses). From this neo-positivist perspective, careful control of variables and every effort to ensure an objective accounting for reality are crucial. From the contextualist position neither approach makes sense, for this type of careful control may give us access to one reality, but a reality controlled by scientists for the purposes of furthering their views of the scientific enterprise is still just one among many alternative realities.

The second argument has to do with communication. How is communication possible, if no two people share the same view of reality? The response to this is that perceptions of reality do not have to be the same for communication to occur – they either have to be close enough so that the communicating partners are not working at total cross-purposes or one of the communicating partners has to have the power to ensure that his (and here I use this personal pronoun for obvious reasons, given prevailing power relations in most if not all societies) view of reality is the one that carries the weight. Families and societies are likely to function best when the varying perceptions of reality are sufficiently similar (Berger & Luckmann, 1966), but both can also exist for a long time when one person, or one group, ensures that one single view of reality is dominant.

These differing views of reality have their counterparts in different epistemological positions, and these are related to different methodologies for doing research. From the perspective of research in human development and related disciplines, perhaps the most interesting discussion is about the relationship between the knower and what is known, or between the researcher and what is "out there" to be known. From a neo-positivist perspective, although there is a recognition that perfect objectivity is impossible to attain, the goal of researchers should be to do all that can be done to get as close to objectivity as possible. Insofar as is possible, a clear separation should be kept between the researcher and the subjects of research, attained in the laboratory when the researcher and subjects are in separate rooms or out of sight or, if in sight, by trying to ensure that the way each subject is treated by the researcher varies as little as possible. Outside the laboratory, carefully designed questionnaires serve this purpose well because the influence of the researcher, clearly present in the form of the questions, is at least identical for each respondent. If interviews are required, there should be as little variability on the part of the interviewer as is possible; if follow-up probes are required, they should be carefully scripted in advance, to avoid the interviewee being influenced by variations in wording.

From a contextualist perspective, these careful attempts at control make little sense. From a contextualist's epistemological standpoint, there never can be the type of separation of researcher and researched for which neo-positivists strive. When the "objects" of research are human beings, and therefore makers of meaning, the researcher is always present, always exerting an influence, if for no other reason than he or she has designed or is now using the particular questionnaire, or has set up the controlled experimental situation, or is currently interviewing and/or observing. From the contextualist perspective, the goal is not to try to make the researcher invisible but rather, having accepted her or his necessary visibility, to treat the information gained as a co-construction of researcher and participant in research. The goal of the co-construction is to create an understanding that both acknowledge to be as currently "real" as possible. As in any ethnographic research (see, for example, Weisner, 1996), this goal is best attained by spending sufficient time with the participants of the research so that they are comfortable doing what they would typically do even without the ethnographer being present. The various vignettes scattered throughout Chapters 6 and 7, and the descriptions of everyday lives (Chapter 8) give every appearance of being real in this contextualist sense.

According to Pepper (1942), each of the paradigms or worldviews has its own root metaphor. The metaphor related to mechanism is the machine, in which clear cause and effect mechanisms can be laid bare. The root metaphor for organicism is the human body; what emerges in development cannot be ascribed simply to biological factors or to the environment but is an emergent phenomenon. Pepper's root metaphor for contextualism is the "historic event," a metaphor that implies that the historical context is key in theories that fit into the contextualist paradigm. The metaphor, however, is somewhat misleading; it becomes clear when one reads Pepper's description that the historic event refers to "the event alive in its present" (1942, p. 232). Accordingly, he argued, it is what is *currently* happening that is most important. Historic events "are like incidents in the plot of a novel of drama. They are literally the incidents of life" (p. 233).

Acts, defined this way, preclude a separation of individual and the context in which that individual is acting. In other words, people's experiences can only be understood by situating them in their context, examining them in the course of their very experiencing. The vignettes to be found in later chapters thus have an important role to play by describing as carefully as possible, albeit from the perspective of the observer, the children in their everyday contexts.

Paradigms or worldviews are not, in themselves, theories. They are better thought of as ways of thinking about the world. A mechanist, for example, would be likely to view the world as operating in terms of causes and effects; her daughter misbehaves, and a punishment will help ensure that the behavior occurs less frequently. The same behavior, viewed by someone who sees the world in organicist terms, might simply be considered typical for a nine-year-old. These views of how the world works are of course malleable, perhaps as we come upon examples that don't fit our views so well, or perhaps as we read about theories of human development. However, these views of the world also make us find some theories of development more comfortable (they fit better with our current worldview) than others.

Theories of human development that fit within the mechanist perspective, according to Goldhaber (2000), include learning theory, social cognitive theory, information processing theory, and behavior genetics. The theories of Piaget, Freud, and Erikson fit within organicism, as does developmental genetic theory. And the ecological and sociocultural theories of Vygotsky and Bronfenbrenner, as well as those of postmodern theorists, fit into the contextual paradigm. I therefore devote the next few pages to a brief discussion of the theories of these two contextualists.

CONTEXTUALIST THEORIES

Vygotsky's Theory

Vygotsky's theory, as my colleagues and I have written elsewhere (Hogan & Tudge, 1999; Tudge, Putnam, & Valsiner, 1996; Tudge & Scrimsher, 2003), involves the mutual consideration of individual characteristics, interpersonal factors, and the broader historical and cultural context. Most commentators on Vygotsky's theory have focused their attention on the interpersonal level, on what goes on between individuals. However, there are problems with the way in which Vygotsky's theory has been interpreted, or perhaps "appropriated" is a better word to be used, because the theory, as typically portrayed, bears little resemblance to the complex theoretical position that Vygotsky laid out in the late 1920s and early 1930s.

Interpersonal Factors

Most attention has been paid to the interactions that occur between individuals (typically children) and other people (typically adults) who are more competent, interactions involving what Vygotsky termed the "zone of proximal development." One problem with the focus on the concept of zone of proximal development as something that goes on between a child and a more competent adult, often a teacher, is that the concept has come to be used as if it were synonymous with "scaffolding." The term scaffolding was first used by Wood and his colleagues (Wood, Bruner, & Ross, 1976) but focuses to a far greater extent than Vygotsky intended on the role of the more competent person – the one whose job it is to provide the scaffolding (Tudge & Scrimsher, 2003). For Vygotsky, by contrast, the concept was essentially one that focused on the interactions between people, and in which both people (more and less competent) could learn in the process of creating a zone of proximal development. The type of dialectic relationship that Vygotsky intended is captured in the use of the word *obuchenie*, a Russian word that translators have rendered either as "instruction" or "learning" in the same text, rather than as "teaching/learning," a far more appropriate translation (Bodrova & Leong, 1996; Tudge & Scrimsher, 2003; Valsiner, 1998b; van der Veer & Valsiner, 1991).

Rather than think about a teacher's role as being one of working out each child's zone of proximal development and providing the right sort of information or assistance to help the child move to the next level of understanding (as is meant by scaffolding), Vygotsky had in mind a process in which the zone itself is a creation in the course of joint activity.

We propose that an essential feature of [teaching/learning] is that it creates the zone of proximal development; that is, [teaching/learning] awakens a variety of developmental processes that are able to operate only when the child is interacting with people in his environment and in collaboration with his peers. (Vygotsky, 1935/1978, p. 90)

As such, the other individuals (teachers included) learn in the process of teaching; a zone of proximal development is created for them as well as the children (Scrimsher & Tudge, 2003).

Cultural–Historical Factors

Another problem with the way in which most commentators have appropriated Vygotsky's theory is that they have not only treated the concept of zone of proximal development as the key concept in the entire theory but have ignored completely the concept's connection to culture and history. It is not for nothing that Vygotsky's theory is termed a "cultural–historical" theory; interpretations of the theory that minimize the role that Vygotsky paid to the role of history and culture in development fail to do justice to the theory. "History," not only in the sense in which that term is usually used to describe things that happened in the past but capturing both ontogenetic development (the history of an individual) and microgenetic development (the development over a relatively short period of time of an activity or set of interactions), is crucial to the theory (Scribner, 1985; Tudge & Scrimsher, 2003; Wertsch & Tulviste, 1992).

"In the process of historical development, social man changes the methods and devices of his behavior, transforms natural instincts and functions, and develops and creates new forms of behavior – specifically cultural" (Vygotsky, 1931/1997b, p. 18). When applied to ontogenetic development, Vygotsky's approach "seeks to present the history of how the child in the process of education accomplishes what mankind accomplished in the course of the long history of labor" (1930/1997a, p. 88). In both cases (societies over historical time and children over ontogenetic time), the significance of the change is that relations with the external world become characterized by conscious (or self-conscious) awareness, that is, the ability to reflect on what one is doing or seeing, rather than simply reacting in a nonconscious way.

"Cultural" forms of behavior are thus of critical importance to Vygotsky – in fact he defined the word "social" as "everything cultural, in the broadest sense of the word. Culture is the product of man's social life and his public activity" (1928/1993, p. 164). Involvement in the sociocultural world is what makes children human, by ensuring that they develop higher mental processes. "The higher functions of intellectual activity arise out of collective behavior, out of cooperation with the surrounding people, and from social experience" (1931/1993, p. 196). Vygotsky made clear the profound impact of culture on children's development:

Educators are beginning to understand that on entering a culture a child not only gets something from culture, assimilating it, inculcating something from the outside, but that culture itself reworks all the child's natural behavior and carves anew his entire course of development. The distinction between the two paths of development (natural and cultural) becomes the fulcrum for a new theory of education. (1928/1993, p. 166)

This view of social development makes clear that the zone of proximal development is a concept far broader than its portrayal by most commentators implies. It is not simply something that occurs in school contexts between teacher and child but deals with the development of new forms of awareness that are created as societies develop new social organizations, such as systems of schooling.

Individual Factors

The third leg of Vygotsky's theory, in addition to the cultural–historical and interpersonal, is that of the individual, including the "natural" (biological) path referred to in the quotation above.

So, our first task consists in following the influence of heredity on child development through all its intermediate links, so that any developmental occurrences and any inherited factors are placed in genetically clear interrelationships. . . . Contemporary genetic research – which deals with both constitutional problems and with research on twins – offers a researcher an enormous amount of material for the deepest constitutional analysis of a child's personality with respect to heredity. (1931/1993, pp. 279–280)

Interestingly, in light of current debates involving behavior geneticists, Vygotsky's position was clear regarding the interrelations of genes and environment:

Development is not a simple function which can be wholly determined by adding X units of heredity to Y units of environment. It is a historical complex which, at every stage, reveals the past which is a part of it. . . . Development, according to a well-known definition, is precisely the struggle of opposites. This view alone can support truly dialectical research on the process of children's development. (1931/1993, pp. 282–283)

The role of individual factors encompasses far more than biological influences on development, however. Vygotsky discussed the interrelations of individual and environment in one of the last lectures he gave before his death, in which he argued that social influences can only be understood in relation to the child.

The same environmental factors which may have one meaning and play a certain role during a given age, two years on begin to have a different meaning and to play a different role because the child has changed; in other words, the child's relation to these particular environmental factors has altered. (1935/1994, p. 338)

In the course of development, children change by virtue of the experiences that they previously had, as well as the meaning those experiences have had for them. Those experiences, although involving them in different social situations, have become "their personal property" (ibid, p. 352), influencing the ways in which they deal with other experiences. As a result, the meaning of any given social or environmental influence (such as a teacher trying to "scaffold" a group's understanding of some concept) will necessarily also be different for each child in that group. In other words, the impact of some social event is determined by "how a child becomes aware of, interprets, [and] emotionally relates to [that] certain event" (ibid, p. 341). The event, by itself, is meaningless without consideration of the individuals involved in it. "This *dynamic and relative interpretation of environment* is the most important source of information for [child development] when environment is under discussion" (ibid, p. 346, italics in the original).

This complex, dialectical, and systemic interweaving of individual, inter-personal, and cultural–historical aspects of development clearly qualifies the theory as one that fits within the contextualist paradigm. Nonetheless, there are, from my perspective, some shortcomings, not surprisingly given that Vygotsky died so young and without having time to refine the theory adequately. Somewhat strangely for a cultural–historical theory, there is no definition of culture and no sense of how exactly cultural differences among groups translate into variations in the developmental experiences of the members of those groups. Second, Vygotsky did not pay a great deal of attention to the "natural" line of development (including what the individual brings to the developmental process).

Bronfenbrenner's Theory

Urie Bronfenbrenner, building in part on Vygotsky's theory, in many ways rectified these weaknesses. His bioecological theory, like that of Vygotsky, requires that we pay simultaneous attention to aspects of individuals, inter-actions, and the broader context, both spatial and temporal. Where Vygotsky wrote in general terms about culture, Bronfenbrenner constructed a theory that included a much more variegated view of context, distinguishing four different "systems," from the immediate (the microsystem, in which the developing person spends a good deal of time engaging in activities and interactions) to the distant (the macrosystem, the equivalent of culture). Bronfenbrenner also wrote about the interrelations among the various microsystems (such as home, school, peer group, and so on) in which individuals spend significant amounts of time (the mesosystem) and about those contexts in which the individuals whose development is being considered are not actually situated, but which have important indirect influences on their development (the exosystem). I'll provide, later, more details about the ways in which these systems relate.

At the time that Bronfenbrenner wrote his first book devoted entirely to this concept, *The Ecology of Human Development* (1979), most North American psychologists were concerned far more with individual factors in development than with contextual influences on development. As a counter to this prevailing trend, Bronfenbrenner focused largely on these various aspects of context, and probably for this reason those who cite his work for the most part continue to write as though he is a theorist of contextual influences on development, rather than a theorist working within the contextualist paradigm. Bronfenbrenner was never a contextualist in the former sense, however, as was made explicit by his use of the word "ecology" to capture the sense of individual–context interrelatedness that is the hallmark of his theory (Tudge, Gray, & Hogan, 1997). Contrary to the views of some who cite him as a proponent of contextual determinants, he has never held that development could be explained by the unidirectional influence of context on individuals.

In the years following the publication of his 1979 book, during which Bronfenbrenner was expanding his theoretical perspective, the theory has come to consist of the application of what he has termed a "PPCT model" of development. This model requires one to consider the interrelations among four key concepts: Process, the Person, Context, and Time.

Proximal Processes

Of these the first, or "proximal processes," plays the crucial role in development, being the "primary mechanisms producing human development" (Bronfenbrenner & Morris, 1998, p. 994). Proximal processes feature in two central "propositions" that appear in several of Bronfenbrenner's later publications. The first states that

human development takes place through processes of progressively more complex reciprocal interaction between an active, evolving biopsychological human organism and the persons, objects, and symbols in its immediate external environment. To be effective, the interaction must occur on a fairly regular basis over extended periods of *time*. Such enduring forms of interaction in the immediate environment are referred to as *proximal processes*. (Bronfenbrenner & Morris, 1998, p. 996, italics in the original)

The examples that he provided ("playing with a young child; child–child activities; group or solitary play, reading, learning new skills," and so on) are precisely the types of things that I wrote about in the previous chapter as the everyday activities in which individuals participate. They constitute the engines of development for precisely the same reasons that I said that engaging in activities and interacting with others is the way in which all individuals come to make sense of their world, understand their place in it, and both play their part in changing the prevailing order while fitting into the existing one.

As Bronfenbrenner made increasingly explicit, perhaps responding to the fact that he continued to be cited as a theorist of context, proximal processes are key to the theory, but their nature varies according to aspects of the individual and to the context (Bronfenbrenner, 1995, 1999, 2001/2005; Bronfenbrener & Evans, 2000; Bronfenbrenner & Morris, 1998). As he explained in the second of the two central propositions:

The form, power, content, and direction of the proximal processes effecting development vary systematically as a joint function of the characteristics of the *developing person*; of the *environment* – both immediate and more remote – in which the processes are taking place; the nature of the *developmental outcomes* under consideration; and the social continuities and changes occurring over *time* through the life course and the historical period during which the person has lived. (Bronfenbrenner & Morris, 1998, p. 996, italics in the original)

Bronfenbrenner stated that these two propositions "are theoretically interdependent and subject to empirical test. An operational research design that permits their simultaneous investigation is referred to as a *Process-Person-Context-Time model* (PPCT for short)" (Bronfenbrenner & Morris, 1998, p. 996).

Context
The environment, or context, as I earlier mentioned, involves four interrelated systems, from micro to macro. Rather than use the traditional but flawed concentric ring representation of context, Figure 3.1 shows that proximal processes involve a developing person (P) interacting with other individuals, objects, and symbols within a given microsystem. The mesosystem involves the relations among two or more microsystems. The other two systems are

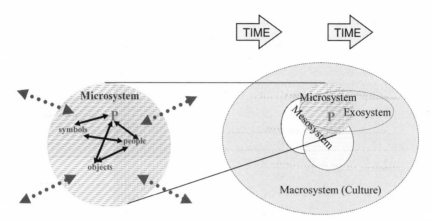

Figure 3.1. Urie Bronfenbrenner's PPCT (Process, the Person, Context, and Time) model. The active *Person* (P) engaging in *Proximal Processes* with people, symbols, and objects within a microsystem, in interaction with other *Contexts*, involving both continuity and change over *Time*.

displayed with dotted lines to indicate that the influences on the developing person are indirect. Thinking about a mother and her son (the developing person of interest), one example of an exosystem influence is when the mother, who's been particularly stressed at work (an exosystem for the child) behaves more irritably with her son when she gets home. Bronfenbrenner defined the macrosystem as a context encompassing any group ("culture, subculture, or other extended social structure") whose members share value or belief systems, "resources, hazards, lifestyles, opportunity structures, life course options and patterns of social interchange" (1993, p. 25). The macrosystem envelops the remaining systems, influencing (and being influenced by) all of them. A particular cultural group may share a set of values about who should or should not be allowed to sleep by himself or herself (an example that I'll return to later), but for that particular value system to have any influence on a developing person, it has to be experienced within one or more of the microsystems in which that person is situated.

The Person

As for the person (P), Bronfenbrenner (like Vygotsky) acknowledged the relevance of biological and genetic factors (Bronfenbrenner, 2001/2005; Bronfenbrenner & Ceci, 1994), although he devoted more attention to the personal characteristics that individuals bring with them into any social situation in his papers up to 1998 (Bronfenbrenner, 1993, 1995; Bronfenbrenner & Morris, 1998) than in his final papers (Bronfenbrenner, 1999, 2001/2005;

Bronfenbrenner & Evans, 2000). He divided these characteristics into three types, which he termed demand, resource, and force characteristics. *Demand characteristics* are those to which he had referred in earlier writings as "personal stimulus" characteristics, those that act as an immediate stimulus to another person. Think about the first time that you meet another person – those characteristics that are initially obvious to you (age, gender, skin color, physical appearance, and so on) may influence you to act in a certain way toward that person. The other person has already altered your view of the situation, simply by the stimuli that you have picked up. (At the same time, although Bronfenbrenner did not write about this, the other person has reacted to the same type of stimulus characteristics that you carry with you – your age, gender, appearance, etc.).

Resource characteristics, by contrast, are not immediately apparent, although sometimes we induce them, with differing degrees of success, from the demand characteristics that we see. These are characteristics that relate partly to mental and emotional resources such as past experiences, skills, and intelligence and also to social and material resources (access to good food, housing, caring parents, educational opportunities appropriate to the needs of the particular society, and so on). *Force characteristics* are those that have to do with differences of temperament, motivation, persistence, and the like. According to Bronfenbrenner, two children may have equal resource characteristics, but their developmental trajectories will be quite different if one is motivated to succeed and persists in tasks and the other is not motivated and does not persist.

Thus, unlike Vygotsky, who did not specify the ways in which individuals are implicated in their own development, Bronfenbrenner provided a much richer sense of individuals' roles, from the relatively passive (we change the environment simply by being in it, to the extent that others react to us differently based on our age, gender, skin color, and so on), to the more active (the ways in which we change the environment is linked to the types of physical, mental, and emotional resources we have available to us), to the most active (the extent to which we change the environment is linked to our motivation to do so).

Time
The final element of the PPCT model is time. As befits any theory of human development, time plays a crucial role in the theory. In the same way that both context and individual factors are divided into subfactors, Bronfenbrenner and Morris (1998) wrote about time as constituting micro-time (the equivalent of Vygotsky's notion of microgenetic development, or what is

occurring during the course of some specific activity or interaction), meso-time, or the extent to which activities and interactions occur with some consistency in the developing person's environment, and macro-time.

Macro-time includes the historical level of Vygotsky's theory but also carries with it the sense that developmental processes are likely to vary according to the specific historical events that are occurring as the developing individuals are at one age or another. This latter sense is captured best in research such as that of Glen Elder (1974, 1996), who was able to demonstrate significant variation in the developmental trajectories of people from two cohorts, cohorts that experienced the effects of the Great Depression in the United States (and subsequent historical events) differently as a function of having been born about a decade apart. More important, and as represented by time's arrow in Figure 3.1, all aspects of the model can be thought of in terms of relative constancy and change. This is true whether we're talking about the developing individuals themselves, the various microsystems in which they are situated, and those broader contexts (exosystem and macrosystem) that have indirect influences. Cultures do not stay the same, although at some periods of historical time the rates of change are much faster than at others. And as with all contextualist theories, the influences are multidirectional.

Bronfenbrenner thus filled in some of the holes that I think can be found in Vygotsky's theory, with much more attention paid to what it is that the individual brings to bear, and a more refined sense of the variation that exists in layers of context. Bronfenbrenner's theory is also, in my mind, far easier to apply in research. Neither Vygotsky nor Bronfenbrenner were greatly involved in the collection of empirical data that could serve to support (or cast doubt on) their theories, but the latter has at least commented on the research of others that approximates the type of studies that he believes should be conducted. For example, in various papers (1993, 1995, 1999; Bronfenbrenner & Morris, 1998), Bronfenbrenner approvingly discussed the work of Drillien, Small and Luster, Langer and Rodin, Tulkin, Steinberg and colleagues, Elder, and others.

However, from the perspective of a contextualist paradigm, weaknesses are apparent in Bronfenbrenner's theory. A rigorous application of such a paradigm should involve interactions at all levels of the system, from cultural to genetic. Bronfenbrenner's theory falls short at the genetic level, for he wrote as if genes determine a range of reaction, which is then influenced by the environment. Genes in fact exist in an interactional state, influencing and being influenced by the cellular environment in which they exist (Johnston & Edwards, 2002), and the cellular environment is itself influenced by and exerts an influence on each surrounding level (Gottlieb, 1996, 2000). A view of gene-environment interaction that includes interactions at each and every level of the system is closer to a contextualist theory than the "reaction range" understanding of genes that can be found in Bronfenbrenner's theory.

A second area of weakness (at least from a contextualist perspective), is that although Bronfenbrenner talked a good deal about the importance of proximal processes, the research that he cited as exemplifying, to a reasonable extent, the PPCT model is not research that allows a rich sense of these processes themselves. The studies tend to be large scale, with proximal processes evoked primarily through parental or adolescent reports, as opposed to the type of "thick" observation (to refer again to Geertz's 1973 term) of ethnographic research that would allow us to see the ways in which individuals actually engage in activities with their main social partners, the ways in which the individuals concerned initiate the activities and their partners' involvement, the ways in which the roles are negotiated, and the meaning that the activities and interactions have for the individuals concerned. In fact, although ethnographic studies would seem to be an optimal way of examining proximal processes in context, Bronfenbrenner never cited any such research.

A third area in which Bronfenbrenner's theory cannot fully exemplify a truly contextualist position is, in another way, one of the theory's major strengths. Bronfenbrenner was always intensely concerned with the policy implications of his (and others') research, and he was very much interested in making a difference in people's lives. He thus always had in mind what needs to happen for *positive* development to occur. Further, in common with most developmental psychologists, he clearly viewed positive development from a Western (primarily North American) and middle-class perspective. He thus wrote about how proximal processes need to become "progressively more complex" (Bronfenbrenner & Morris, 1998, p. 996) if they are to be "effective" (see also Bronfenbrenner, 1999, 2001/2005; Bronfenbrenner & Evans, 2000). Development, however, will occur even if a parent continues to behave in the same manner toward the child or in a progressively less complex fashion. What matters for development is the way in which people typically act and interact with objects, symbols, and the social world, without any regard for the apparent appropriateness of that development.

This raises the fourth weakness of the theory from a contextualist perspective – the fact that it does not deal adequately with issues of culture. I'm not bothered by the fact that the term "culture" rarely appears within Bronfenbrenner's writings because his definition of macrosystem encompasses culture, as I mentioned earlier. What is missing is that there is no sense in his writings that cultural groups with values, beliefs, lifestyles, and patterns of social interchange different from those found in North American middle-class communities would necessarily value different types of proximal processes or that what counts as more complex to one group might be viewed as less complex by another. Nowhere is this more apparent than when Bronfenbrenner (1995, 1999; Bronfenbrenner & Morris, 1998) cited the research of Steinberg, Darling, and Fletcher (1995). Steinberg and his colleagues' research examined the nature and impact of parenting among different ethnic groups in the United States, but Bronfenbrenner discussed it from the point of view of mesosystem effects (home–school linkages) rather than as providing insight into the ways in which different macrosystems (or subcultures) are related to different, and equally effective, proximal processes.

Having identified what I, at least, view as weaknesses in these two theories, I will now discuss the type of theory that I believe to be adequately contextualist – a theory that I'll refer to as cultural–ecological theory. It is this theory, clearly based on both Vygotsky and Bronfenbrenner, on which I have based the research that is described in the remainder of this volume.

Cultural–Ecological Theory

As I have already pointed out, contextualist theories are *not* theories that hold that context is the main explanatory variable. Instead, they are theories that have at their heart the "stuff" of everyday life, the everyday dramas, events, and activities in which individuals participate, by themselves and with others. Necessarily, these dramas, events, and activities are intertwined within the contexts in which they take place, but that does not mean that development is a simple function of context, any more than development is the result of individual competences, innate characteristics, and the like, important though these competences and characteristics are. Theories that fit within a contextualist paradigm are those that take seriously the complex interconnections among individual, interpersonal, and contextual aspects of development.

Cultural–ecological theory is a theory that has at its heart the typical everyday activities that take place between developing individuals and the people with whom they commonly interact. As Bronfenbrenner wrote about proximal processes, these typically occurring activities are the "engines of development" in that it is here where individuals learn what is expected of them, the types of activities considered appropriate or inappropriate for them, how they are expected to engage in these activities, the ways other people will deal with them, and the ways in which they are expected to deal with others. People initiate activities themselves, and try to draw others into those activities, and it is in the course of these activities that we try out different roles and observe the roles of others, both with regard to themselves and with others.

By way of an example, let's consider some apparently simple activity like going to bed. It's an activity that occurs regularly, and the way in which it occurs will vary greatly according to the age of the person being considered, the other people who play important roles in the life of this person, the immediate context, and the overarching context. If the person is a child, how this event occurs is likely to be quite different than if the person is an adult, and of course the age of the child will also have an impact. However, the wishes and feelings not only of the child but also of those around will influence the ways in which going to bed takes place. Some children of any given age get tired and are ready for bed much before other children. Some parents have strict views about when bedtime should occur, whereas others are less strict. In some families, there is a routine surrounding bedtime, with a fixed order of events, culminating in a bedtime story while the child drops off to sleep. In other families, parents are much more likely just to wait for the child to become tired and fall to sleep wherever he or she is.

Culture is of course necessarily connected to the ways in which children (and adults) go to bed; in some cultures, soon after children are born, they sleep in their own space, often in their own bedroom, whereas in other cultures children are never allowed to sleep separately. What's important in this example, as in any example I could have provided, is that in the course of participating in whatever bedtime practices are routine children come to view those practices as the appropriate ones, even as moral practices, as I'll discuss shortly. That's not to say that many children don't argue with the person who is trying to put them to bed, and might very well wish that the situation were different. Nonetheless, the notions that children of a certain age are expected to go to bed at a certain time, that the older that children and adolescents are the later they should go to bed, that it is the mother's job to put the child to bed and read a story, that it is appropriate for children to have a room to themselves, that there are acceptable reasons to disturb parents' sleep but also unacceptable reasons – these are all notions that, being gained by children in the course of participating in this particular practice, allow children to become competent members of the cultural group in which they are growing up. Needless to say, growing up in a different culture, one that engages in different sleep-time practices, leads children to develop a different set of notions.

I don't wish to imply that events that only occur sporadically or even just once have no impact on someone's development. Obviously the death of a parent, a serious accident, the winning of the lottery, and a host of other events that do not occur on a regular basis may have a profound impact. However, I suspect that it is the ongoing, everyday, reactions to these sporadic or one-off events that are at least as important for development as the events themselves. It seems clear that engagement in everyday activities with other members of the cultural group, particularly those who are more experienced in the ways of that group, plays a powerful role in helping children become more competent in the ways of that group.

As is the case with any theory that fits within the contextualist paradigm, although we can think or write separately about the roles played in an activity by any individual, the influence of the immediate setting on that activity, and the impact of the cultural context on the individuals and the context, this separation is only possible for heuristic purposes. Activities only are possible within contexts, and the contexts themselves are transformed in the course of those activities. Activities are only possible with individuals to do them, and the activities are necessarily transformed depending on the characteristics of the individuals who are engaged in them. Age, gender, temperament, motivation, experience with the activity, experience with the other or others who are also engaged in the activity – all are implicated in the processes by which any activity is altered by the characteristics of the individuals involved. At the same time, as I have illustrated, individuals themselves are transformed in the course of engaging repeatedly in activities.

This can be illustrated by a simple example involving an activity in which many people are involved in Western industrialized societies – looking at a book. The activity, apparently identical in form, is completely different depending on whether the individual can read; whether the inability to read is normative (the individual is too young to read by herself) or non-normative (an adolescent or adult struggling to read in a society in which people are expected to learn to read in childhood); whether the activity is being engaged in for its intrinsic interest or because someone else (a parent or teacher, perhaps) has required it; whether the book is being looked at to extract some particular information, is a novel the individual is desperate to finish, is being used as a teething object, or is being evaluated for its likelihood of being able to prop open a door.

Moreover, as in the example given earlier in this chapter, if this is the book under consideration, the way in which I am currently reading it while writing has only partial resemblance to the way in which you, the reader, will be reading it at some time in my current future. My hope, of course, is that while engaged in the activity of reading it, you will come to think differently about the way in which development occurs. Similarly, as children engage repeatedly in the activity of looking at books, particularly with others who are more competent in the process, their ways of looking change dramatically, and most become readers, who then move on to longer books which they can read without needing another person to help them. What they read about, as well as what they do, also helps them to better function in the culture in which they are living.

The way in which a child looks at a book is thus in large part a function of her particular characteristics. (This is of course true for any activity.) She brings to any book her own reasons for looking at it, her past experiences, her motivation, and so on. No other child will bring precisely the same set of characteristics to the same book, because the past experiences will have been different. In this sense, the child brings her "personal culture" (Valsiner & Litvinovich, 1996) or "personal property" (Vygotsky, 1935/1994) to any activity and any interaction. Part of what makes every individual unique is biology, including one's own unique genetic inheritance. From the contextualist point of view, however, genes do not, as the behavior geneticists would argue, set the limits within which context can operate; rather, genes themselves are a part of a complex set of multidirectional influences (Gottlieb, 2000; Johnston & Edwards, 2003).

Individuals, then, are unique. However, as is the case for any contextualist theory, what is individual is at one and the same time a social creation. Use of the term "social creation" may appear to imply a unidirectional flow, from social world to the individual. Similarly, because Vygotsky stated that the social world "is a source of development" (1935/1994, p. 351) many who have invoked Vygotsky have argued that his theory involves a view of culture and context that acts in a unidirectional fashion on the individual. However, one has to take a strictly dichotomous view of "social" and "individual" to accept this unidirectional position, and theories that fit within the contextualist paradigm are anything but dichotomous. The social world is not separate from but is inclusive of the individual; individuals are always, even when alone, embedded within a social world. Thus, when I wrote that individuals are "social creations" this merely means that the social settings of which the individuals themselves are a part are responsible for development. This is not individual as separate from social but an interweaving of individual and social. Further, because the individuals themselves are necessarily a part of their social world they necessarily, because of their very presence within it, change that world. Individuals, activities, and social settings, although conceptually distinct, are empirically enmeshed while any individual is engaged in some activity in a particular setting. I return to this notion of the embeddedness of individual and context in the final chapter.

In any contextualist theory, context is only partially represented by the setting in which individuals engage in activities. The physical setting is important, as are the objects with which individuals can be active and the other individuals who are involved with them in activities. But why is it that the particular setting, the hut, house, tent, street, or apartment in which the individual lives, is set up in the way it is? Why is it that in some living spaces children are allowed into some areas and not others, are allowed to play with some things but not others, are allowed to sleep next to some people but not next to others? Why is it that parents encourage some activities, discourage others, and never even consider the possibility of yet other activities? The answer partly relates to the specific characteristics (values, beliefs, resources, etc.) that individuals possess, but it also relates to the social group of which the individuals are a part. Culture, in other words, is inextricably a part of any contextualist theory.

As Tom Weisner (1996) argued, if you want to know how a child will develop, the most important single thing to know about that child is the cultural group of which he or she is a part. Knowing a person's cultural group allows us to make inferences about that person's values, beliefs, range of activities, access to resources, institutions with which he or she will interact, social relationships and a whole range more. From a contextualist perspective, however, culture can never be viewed as a determinant of those values, beliefs, and so on, even though it is heavily implicated in them. As Marx wrote in *The 18th Brumaire of Louis Napoleon*: "Men make their own history, but they do not make it just as they please; they do not make it under circumstances chosen by themselves, but under circumstances directly found, given and transmitted from the past" (1852/1978, p. 595).

How is this possible? Culture clearly influences our development; if this were not the case, it would be difficult to explain why it is that cultural groups differ from one another in terms of values, practices, and so on. Yet what is the mechanism of influence? Once again, we have to return to the everyday activities in which individuals are engaged, the interactions in which they participate, and the settings in which they are situated. On one hand, these are clearly constructed at the local level by the individuals concerned, a response to local and current constraints, needs, desires and so on. On the other hand, they are also reflective of culture. I discussed the activity of going to bed before, mentioning that how one is raised helps determine one's view about appropriate sleeping arrangements. This was illustrated nicely in a study of Indian and North American families.

All Indian parents studied by Rick Shweder and his colleagues (Shweder, Jensen, & Goldstein, 1995) made a personal decision, whether explicit or not, that neither their young child nor their adolescent female could sleep alone. When making this decision, they did not refer explicitly to their cultural group or to culture-wide values. However, the fact that no members of their group made a different decision whereas members of another group, from the United States, made a completely different judgment about this practice implicates the power of culture. Simply in the course of engaging in the activity of going to bed, in the company of some people but not others, has led members of both cultures to develop ways of thinking about sleeping arrangements that are in some important ways quite different. I should also point out that there were some sleeping arrangements that members of neither group considered morally acceptable and other arrangements that members of both groups might accept – it is not the case that the two groups developed entirely different notions about acceptable and unacceptable sleeping arrangements. It also has to be said that these notions about sleeping arrangements do not stay constant, partly because members of one culture come into contact with the ideas and practices of other cultures, but also because members of one generation never simply accept all aspects of all practices of an earlier generation. Practices, rules, activities, as well as values and beliefs, are not simply copied wholesale but are transformed in the course of being appropriated by the members of the new generation, particularly as cultures undergo change.

   Activities, relationships, and settings are thus at one and the same time an individual and a cultural matter. Individuals make the decisions (consciously or not) about what they will do, with whom, and where depending on their personal views, needs, desires, and values but what it is that they view, need, desire, value and so on also depends on the group in which they have been raised. The Indian families to whom I just referred make their decisions about who may or may not sleep alone without referring to others in their group, but the reason that they make these decisions in the way they do stems from the fact that their parents made the same decisions as do their friends and neighbors. From a sociological point of view, one could say that they have been socialized to think and act in this way, but socialization implies a more passive role on the part of these parents. Instead, they have been acting and interacting in a world in which these are the things one does. If one is to fit into this world, one should do the same.

   Because both individuals and the group of which those individuals are a part are implicated in the process of development, cultural change is guaranteed from a contextualist's perspective and culture can never be thought of as a single determinant of development. As I mentioned earlier, individuals are not simply representatives of groups – they are unique members, all of whom bring their own personal peculiarities to any situation. The cultural messages to which they are exposed, communications in the form of conversations, or from the media, or from the objects and symbols in their settings are not simply "transmitted" in some unidirectional fashion from the group to the individual but instead are interpreted and thus transformed by the "recipients" of those messages. Individual differences, or individual variability, should therefore be viewed not as standing in opposition to group values, beliefs, practices, and so on but are a necessary component of those aspects of the group. From a contextualist perspective, the contrast between group and individual differences is a type of false dichotomy that a dialectical position must eschew. Jackie Goodnow nicely articulated this position:

It must be recognized that young children do not merely adopt understandings and modes of response that constitute adult endpoints in a given culture, but they develop outlooks that are not communicated in the culture or that may even be in conflict with those that are emphasized in the culture. (Goodnow & Collins, 1990, p. 113)

Cultures change, sometimes quickly and sometimes slowly, and on occasion because of interaction between members of different cultural groups. However, cultures always change because of the tension between the current prevailing ideas, values, beliefs, and so forth within the group, the specific ways of understanding and putting into practice those ideas by parents, and the particular ways in which those ideas are experienced, reinterpreted, and transformed by the children. This process of differentiation is likely to be magnified in cultures in which adolescents are expected, at least by some members of their peer group, to take on ideas, roles, values, practices that run counter to those of the parents.

To this point I have written about individuals being members of specific cultural groups, but now I need to go back to the definition of culture that I presented in Chapter 1. Implicit in what I have written so far in this chapter is the notion that cultures consist of groups that share a general set of values, beliefs, practices, institutions, and access to resources. The group may have a sense of shared identity or the recognition that people are in some way connected and feel themselves to be part of the group, and the adults of the group should attempt to pass on to the young of the group the same values, beliefs, practices, and so on. This attempt to pass on values does not have to be made explicit. For example, in the case of the Indian and North American families' views about sleeping arrangements, I doubt very much that any parent thought explicitly about the fact that he or she was trying to pass on specific cultural values to the next generation by arranging particular sleeping arrangements. Nonetheless, the effect is the same whether the attempt is explicit or implicit, because by continuing to participate in a specific cultural practice, that practice attains some degree of longevity.

By this definition of culture, members of different countries or societies constitute different cultural groups. Or rather, if we are able to show that members of a given country or society identify with that country or society, have a particular set of values, beliefs, practices, and institutions, and share a commitment to pass on those values and so forth to the next generation, we should feel comfortable referring to them as members of a cultural group. However, precisely the same point could be made about different groups within any given society or country. Any group for whom the earlier cited definition holds may in this case be considered a cultural group. Within a given society's politically defined borders may be found many cultural groups, and people thus have to be considered members of more than a single cultural group. Different ethnic groups, different socioeconomic groups, regional groups, and groups that are more locally constituted may all constitute cultural groups, so long as they conform to this definition. (The social class and racial/ethnic differences in children's activities described in Chapter 2 are clear manifestations of the relevance of within-society cultural variations.) Whether any particular individual considers himself, at any given time, to be a member of one or other of those groups would depend on the current point of reference.

For example, someone currently living in the United States might consider herself American (when comparing herself with Japanese visitors), as a Southerner (when thinking about people from the North or West), as working class (when comparing herself with people with different educational backgrounds and a different type of occupation), or as Black (when thinking about herself with reference to Hispanics or Whites). This fluid sense of cultural identity is built on the assumption that each of these groups is in fact differentiable in terms of the facets of culture I have included in my definition, and the individual has reason to think about other groups. If so, this woman might identify with other Americans, regardless of their ethnicity, social class, or region when traveling in Japan but might focus at work on the differences between herself as a Southerner and the brash Northerners who are in the same office.

However, the types of cultural differences I have mentioned do not determine the interactions that this woman has with others. As always from a contextualist perspective, actions and interactions are a complex amalgam of individual characteristics, the particularities of the setting, and the broader contextual aspects such as the interacting individuals' various cultural groups.

What I have done to this point is to describe the cultural–ecological theory that I have found helpful when thinking about development, and to show how it fits within the contextualist paradigm. The theory obviously owes a great deal to the theories of Vygotsky and Bronfenbrenner, but there are other theories that are also related. For example, there are obvious points of comparison with theories such as Weisner's concept of the "ecocultural niche," Harkness and Super's "developmental niche" theory, and Rogoff's view of the interrelations among three planes of sociocultural activity, mentioned in Chapter 2. Before moving on to consider the types of methods that fit within cultural–ecological theory, I want to consider some of the implications of cultural–ecological theory for the ways in which cultural groups can be studied.

IMPLICATIONS OF CULTURAL–ECOLOGICAL THEORY FOR THE STUDY OF CULTURAL GROUPS

Cross-Cultural Psychology Versus Cultural Psychology

As I pointed out in Chapter 1, there is a split among developmentalists interested in issues of culture between those who call themselves cross-cultural psychologists and those who term themselves cultural psychologists. The split occurs at the paradigmatic level but has, necessarily I would argue, important implications both theoretically and methodologically. Cross-cultural psychologists fit well within a neo-positivistic framework in which culture serves almost exclusively as an independent variable (Adamopoulos & Lonner, 2001; Lonner & Berry, 1986). One of the important reasons for conducting cross-cultural psychology is to "extend the range of variation" permitted by monocultural research and thus to "investigate the robustness of generalizability of psychological findings that many . . . consider to be true and invariant" (Adamopoulos & Lonner, 2001, p. 15). Adamopoulos and Lonner made a strong argument for the use of "classical scientific methodology" to accomplish this goal.

The purpose of using this type of methodology, as Shweder (1990) pointed out, is to uncover the "psychic unity" that is presumed to exist. However, because large variations in performance have been demonstrated when tests developed for use in one or more group from the industrialized world have been used with groups from the majority world, the goal of many cross-culturalists has been, at a minimum, to show the conditions under which such unity can be most easily revealed. Cross-cultural psychologists might thus "search for the most 'natural' or 'realistic' settings, activities, and institutions in everyday life" to show that basic unity in ways that might be obscured by more traditional psychological tests (p. 85).

This neo-positivistic approach to culture and development has been dominant for a long time (Jahoda, 1993; Super & Harkness, 1997) within the fields of psychology and human development, although less so within some branches of anthropology. However, its challenge by those who fall within cultural psychology is a challenge from theories within the contextualist paradigm, entailing a belief that culture and mind are not independent of one another but are intertwined and therefore cannot be parsed into independent and dependent variables. As Shweder (1990) argued, "Intentional persons [mind] and intentional worlds [cultures] are interdependent things that get dialectically constituted and reconstituted through the intentional activities and practices that are their products, yet make them up" (p. 101). From this perspective, cultural psychologists should not waste time searching for universals, part of the psychic unity that cross-culturalists assume to exist. Sawyer (2002a) referred to this position as "emergentist," alluding to the view that complex phenomena cannot be simply reduced to the sum of a set of independent causal phenomena (such as culture or an essential psychic unity) but instead emerge from the interplay of culture and mind to form something that is qualitatively different from them. This view has a long history in both psychology and sociology, going back to Durkheim, James, and Bergson (Sawyer, 2002a) and is clearly related to the theories I have described as contextualist.

Some scholars (see, for example, Adamopoulos & Lonner, 2001; Super & Harkness, 1997, 2003; Van der Vijver & Poortinga, 2002) have taken the position that the existence of various methods and analytic strategies, cutting across paradigmatic boundaries, can only help our understanding of complex phenomena by getting a more complete picture than could be obtained by reliance on methods and analyses based in a single paradigm. Goldhaber (2000) recognized that the different paradigms work at different levels of analysis, but argued that studying human development will prosper when we learn how to conduct research incorporating each level. Rogoff and Angelillo (2002) stated that they "agree with Pepper (1942) that it is valuable to have a diversity of approaches in the portfolio of research – including mechanistic as well as contextual world hypotheses" (p. 221). Their position is in keeping with Pepper's notion of "postrational eclecticism" that requires "the recognition of the equal or nearly equal adequacy of a number of world theories and a recommendation that we do not fall into the dogmatism of neglecting any one of them" (p. 342).

However, this postrational eclecticism should not be confused with the type of "irrational eclecticism" that involves mixing, within the same study, concepts, methods, or analytical techniques from different paradigms. Pepper asked the question: "Can [these] interpretations of truth, which are supported by relatively adequate world theories, be harmonized or amalgamated into one interpretation that will do justice to them all?" (1942, p. 344). His answer is clear: "No, not in a manner that will be acceptable to them all" (loc cit). This is the position that I take; I find compelling Pepper's (1942) position that the four worldviews about which he wrote are incommensurate, given that they incorporate different ontological, epistemological, and methodological assumptions about the nature of reality and knowledge, and thus about how we can study reality (see also Eckensberger, 1979; Goldhaber, 2000; Guba & Lincoln, 1994; Winegar, 1997).

Given the paradigmatic basis for the differences between cross-cultural psychologists and cultural psychologists I see no possibility for there to be the type of rapprochement that some have looked (or hoped) for. Indeed, although the dialectic approach embodied in the contextualist paradigm argues that syntheses emerge from the clash of apparently contrary positions, it is hard to imagine the synthesis that can emerge out of the conflict between, on one hand, the position that culture and development are independent of one another and, on the other, the view that they are inseparable.

The Study of Race/Ethnicity and Social Class

The second major implication for the study of culture from a cultural–ecological perspective that I want to discuss here has to do with the ways in which we study different cultural groups within a single society. The neo-positivist approach is to treat such groups in effect as independent variables in a statistical sense, just as any cultural group is treated by many cross-cultural psychologists. Two or more groups are the focus of the research, and the goal is to determine whether one group scores higher on some measure than another. As Bronfenbrenner (1988) described it, these approaches to research constitute "social address" studies, with no possibility of understanding the processes that relate membership in one or other group to the results that are obtained. More sophisticated approaches, such as including moderating factors (Do performances of Blacks and Whites differ by their social-class membership?) or "controlling for" one factor (class, for example) while examining the other (race), equally employ the neo-positivistic attempt to separate the different factors to show their supposedly unique effects. Not surprisingly, the results are often interpreted in such a way that one group is viewed as having an advantage, the other a deficit (LeVine, 1989; Ogbu, 1981). Implicit in these approaches is the idea that a single measuring stick is appropriate for all groups; those groups that score higher are "better" and those who score lower are worse. As Hill (1999) argued, if one group has a deficit, it's easy to interpret it as being of genetic cause (such a position was taken as recently as the mid-1990s; see Herrnstein & Murray, 1994), learning style (Willis, 1989), or sociocultural deprivation (Moynihan, 1965).

By contrast, a contextualist approach requires that one takes seriously the idea of multiple realities, different measuring sticks even within the same society. Different cultural groups have different values, beliefs, practices, access to resources, and so on – a fact that is relevant whether we're considering culture at the level of society or a within-society cultural group. In either case, one has to consider not simply that one group does better than another on some measure, but why the two groups differ. In other words, a focus on the explanatory processes is essential to explain different outcomes. I first discuss social-class differences, drawing on some of the work that I wrote about in Chapter 2.

Mel Kohn and his colleagues (1979, 1995; Kohn & Slomczynski, 1990) built on an early paper by Bronfenbrenner (1958) to try to explain why it might be that middle-class and working-class parents raise their children in somewhat different ways, something that many researchers had found. Kohn wanted to explore the underlying processes that might be involved and focused on parents' child-rearing values. Kohn and his colleagues reported, from a variety of countries from the industrialized world, that middle-class parents were more likely to value independence in their children, whereas working-class parents were more likely to value conformity.

Why should there be these class-related differences? Kohn's answer was found in the different conditions of life experienced by the two groups – specifically the educational practices while the parents themselves were at school and, even more important, the parents' current workplace experiences. In both their education and at work, middle-class parents in the course of their everyday experiences are more likely to be encouraged to exercise self-direction and come to see that as helpful for success. By contrast, working-class parents are more likely to view following the rules as the key to success both at school and at work because that accords with their own experiences.

Precisely the same argument about the role of experiences can be made for the study of groups that differ, in any given society, in terms or race or ethnicity. (I should make clear that I consider "race" an important social category, marked by a particular range of shades of color, but not one for which there is any genetic marker. Unless explicitly stating otherwise, when discussing Blacks and Whites in this book, I mean people of African heritage or primarily European heritage, respectively, and who are currently living in the United States.) As with any cultural analysis, everyday practices, beliefs, and values need to be linked to the prevailing conditions of life. I'll restrict my discussion here to the situation of Blacks and Whites within the United States. It's the same country, all are Americans, but, by virtue of skin color, have histories that are totally different. Despite the passage of time since the ending of slavery, notwithstanding the Civil Rights movement, these two histories, linked in conflict, continue to exert their powerful effect.

It's impossible to think about the cultures of Black and White America without considering the impact of their separate, but interlocked, histories. Yet one also cannot ignore the role of Blacks' West African heritage (Asante, 1987; Boykin, 1994; Boykin & Allen, 2004, Hale, 1986; Nobles, 1974). Research on Black families' child rearing was typified, for much of the previous century, by a focus on deficits – the weaknesses of Black families, compared with Whites, and the poorer performance of Black children in school. Regardless of the extent to which the "cause" of the deficit was held to be genetic, the result of slavery and the apparent destruction of the Black family as a consequence, or cultural deprivation, few questioned the neo-positivist idea that a single measuring stick was appropriate. This is particularly a problem when so much of the relevant research, as is clear from the discussion in Chapter 2, compares middle-class Whites and working-class or very poor Blacks. The fact that so many researchers have concentrated on Black families living in poverty has thus fostered the unwarranted idea of a linkage between Black culture and poverty. By contrast, scholars who have focused on the differences between working-class and middle-class Blacks have noted major differences in the child-rearing approaches adopted by the two groups (Busse & Busse, 1972; Hill, 1999, 2001; Hill & Sprague, 1999; Kamii & Radin, 1967; Lareau, 2002; McLoyd, 2004; Ogbu, 1981; Willie & Reddick, 2003).

Cultural–ecological theory, however, can help us to understand Black approaches to child rearing not in terms of a comparison with White approaches but as necessarily linked to Black history, including the African heritage, and the current situation. The current situation is related to contemporary Black–White relations, differential access to resources, living conditions, the necessity to prepare children for living in a society in which skin color is apparently a sufficient cause for differential treatment, and so on. As Boykin and Allen (2004) argued, we don't need to choose between a deficit or deprivation model on one hand or a strengths-based model of Black families on the other if we think about African Americans' "cultural integrity," which they define in much the same way that I define culture, as a constellation of values, beliefs, practices, access to resources, and so on. However, as McLoyd (2004) wrote: "Empirical verification of how culture is implicated in race differences in developmental outcomes and their antecedents has lagged far behind conceptual work on this issue" (p. 188).

Taking this type of cultural approach is not to accept that one group behaves as it does because of its culture – that would be tantamount to accepting a cultural deterministic view that fits with a neo-positivist, not a contextualist, paradigm. Cultures do, of course, influence values, beliefs, practices and so on, but so are cultures influenced by both the new members of each culture (new generations, who never simply accept the cultural pre-scriptions of the previous generation but transform them in the process of appropriation) and by members of other cultural groups with whom there is contact. In the case of within-society racial/ethnic variation, other cultural groups include both individuals of the same racial/ethnic background but of a different class as well as individuals of a different racial and/or ethnic background.

It's for this reason that we have to think more carefully about the "inter-section of race and class" (Hill, 2001). Given what I have written, the question to address is not whether race or class has more influence on young Black or White children's experiences or their parents' child-rearing values and beliefs but how to understand the ways in which class has a different meaning in the two racial groups. One should expect, from a cultural–ecological per-spective, that social class might be expressed differently in any two groups, whether they are in the same society or different societies. For example, middle-class Black parents, working in professional occupations, are as likely as middle-class Whites to raise their children to think for themselves and be self-directing. On the other hand, unlike their White counterparts, middle-class Blacks in the United States, in common with their working-class peers, have to deal with prejudice, whether real, implied, or perceived and, to raise their children for success, need to teach racial socialization.

The situation is more complex for members of two or more cultural groups that exist within a single society, however, than for two or more cultures that constitute different societies. In any society in which the members of one group have a dominant role and in effect set the rules for what sorts of behaviors or activities are to count as appropriate for the society as a whole, groups within that society that encourage different activities (or the same activities to a different extent) are likely to be at a disadvantage. By contrast, there are no such difficulties for members of other societies who have established different sets of norms for what is to count as appropriate behavior for their children.

CONCLUSION

What I have tried to do in this chapter is to describe cultural–ecological theory, showing how it fits within the contextualist paradigm and how it has been developed from two other contextualist theories. I've also discussed the ways in which such a theory has implications both for how we think about studying cultural groups outside the society in which we live (often described as cross-cultural psychology) and the study of different cultural groups within a single society.

There is a danger, however, in imagining that a cultural–ecological position precludes one from comparing groups. The problem is not so much in comparisons as it is in the use of a single measuring stick, as though two or more groups can be evaluated as being in some way better or worse on a single set of measures. Comparisons cannot be avoided; an ethnographic account of a single cultural group is of interest to its readers in part because of the implicit comparison with the situation in the readers' own cultural group. Explicit comparisons are helpful in that they can inform us about the different values, beliefs, and practices of different groups, and can make explicit the historical, cultural, or social reasons for those different values, beliefs, and practices. In the following chapter, I describe the methods I developed for applying cultural–ecological theory, and this will lead us to the comparisons of different cultural groups' engagement in their everyday activities.

4   Methods

There must be a systole and diastole in all inquiry, . . . a man's mind must be continually expanding and shrinking between the whole human horizon and the horizon of a [magnifying]-glass.

(George Eliot, *Middlemarch*, 1872/1988, p. 524).

In the previous chapter, I talked about the theoretical foundation for the research that is the focus for this book, explaining how it fits within the contextualist paradigm. In this chapter, I want to draw the connections between theory and method and describe the method that we use to gather our data. When people say that something or other is "fine in theory," they typically mean that whatever it is will not work well in practice. In other words, sometimes people make an implicit distinction between theory and practice. What I want to do is make the opposite argument – namely, that what we do in practice is to a very large extent determined by our theory, if by "theory" we mean a way of making sense of the world, either implicitly or explicitly. In research this has to be the case – there needs to be a clear and firm connection between theory and method, as Vygotsky specified more than three quarters of a century ago: "Every basically new approach to scientific problems leads inevitably to new methods and ways of research" (Vygotsky, 1931/1997, p. 27).

If one accepts this as true, it means that we can't really talk about how worthwhile one method is vis-à-vis another without considering the theoretical purposes for which the method is to be employed. Books devoted to research methods are fine for informing us how to employ a particular method and how to use it well, but they miss the central issue of the connection between theory and method. One can like the experimental method, devise a tightly controlled research design, pay great attention to issues of validity and reliability, and collect an impressive amount of data, but if the theory on which one is building is contextualist, systemic, or ecological, there is a clear mismatch between theory and methods. In such a case, the data can neither support nor cast doubt on the theory itself.

So, before talking at any length about the methods themselves, it is necessary to do some preparatory work – to discuss the connections between theory and method. Drawing on the insights of Winegar (1997), among others, I'm going to use the term "meta-method" for the explicit consideration of the types of methods that need to be used given the theory of choice. Use of this terminology mirrors the earlier discussion of metatheory, or ways of thinking about theory, discussed in Chapter 3. Researchers whose theories can generally be described as neo-positivist appropriately use methods that involve at least some degree of control over the situation. It's important, for example, for neo-positivists to be able to manipulate one specific part of the context in order to test causal relationships between that context and the outcome of interest. Neo-positivists are also, for similar reasons, far more likely to use surveys with forced-choice responses to gather their data than to use open-ended interviews, in an attempt to keep the information-gathering process as "clean" (i.e., uncontaminated by unaccounted-for interviewer influence) as possible.

What, then, should be the methods that are used by those whose worldview is contextualist? They have to be methods that do not artificially separate the individuals from the contexts in which they are situated or the researcher from the individuals who are participating in the research. It would thus make little sense to attempt to try to understand individuals better by carefully controlling everything except the one variable to be manipulated, whether that control were to occur in a laboratory or in a "naturalistic" setting. Instead, as I have argued elsewhere (Tudge, 2000; Tudge, Doucet, & Hayes, 2001; Tudge & Hogan, 2005), use of a cultural–ecological theory requires use of cultural–ecological methods.

As I showed in the previous chapter, cultural–ecological theory forces researchers to pay simultaneous attention to aspects of the individuals who are the focus of the study, aspects of the context (immediate, cultural, and historical), and (most important) to the actions and interactions going on between these individuals and the social partners, objects, and symbols that play important roles in their development. Weisner persuasively argued that the ethnographic method is "the most important method in the study of human development because it ensures that the cultural place will be incorporated into understanding development" (1996, p. 306). Although there are multiple interpretations of what constitutes ethnography (Atkinson, Coffey, Delamont, Lofland, & Lofland, 2001), all interpretations share the view that it involves "the study of people in naturally occurring settings, or 'fields' by means of methods which capture their social meanings and ordinary activities" (Brewer, 2000, p. 10). Ethnographic methods, broadly construed, thus share a determination to focus on what occurs naturally in cultural context and to try to understand the cultural relevance of those things that occur.

In this chapter, I discuss the observational methods that I use, explaining first why I think that they fit within a contextualist paradigm, and within cultural–ecological theory in particular. If my description of ethnographic methods is accepted as reasonable, then I would argue that my methods qualify as ethnographic, although some ethnographers might be concerned by the fact that the observations take place over hours rather than weeks or months. Nevertheless, as I explain, the intention is to focus on the naturally occurring actions and interactions that can only be made sense of by understanding both what the participating individuals bring to those actions and interactions and the culture that provides the meaning. I try to get a sense of the values and beliefs of the children's parents not simply by observing the settings and materials that they provide and the encouragement that they give to children to engage in some activities and not others, but also through interviews, although they will not feature in this book.

A FOCUS ON TYPICAL EVERYDAY ACTIVITIES

Because of the grounding in contextualist theory, at the heart of the methods is an emphasis on the "historical event," defined by Pepper as "the event alive in its present" (1942, p. 232). In the Cultural Ecology of Young Children project, we are interested in the typical everyday experiences of children. The goal is simply to follow the children who are the focus of attention, putting no restrictions on where they go or on the people who interact with them. The reason is simple and derives from the theoretical framework laid out in the previous chapter. One of the most important factors in anyone's development, children included, is their typically occurring engagement in everyday activities with the people who spend a good deal of time with them.

There are many ways in which researchers have tried to find out how children spend their time, the activities they engage in, and the company that they keep, all discussed in Chapter 2. Given that the children in my study are all between 28 and 48 months old when the study starts, direct observation is probably the best way to get a good sense of children's typical activities and partners. (There are, admittedly, some drawbacks to this method of gathering data, the most obvious being the fact that people's behaviors might well change while being observed, but I discuss this issue, and other potential drawbacks, toward the end of the chapter.)

Because we're interested in knowing the full range of activities in which children can be involved, we do not limit our observations to any particular time of the day. We do not, therefore, only focus on times when we can be reasonably sure of observing some parent–child interaction, such as mealtime or bedtime. Instead, we follow each of the children in our study for 20 hours over the course of a week. We do this in such a way that we cover the equivalent of a complete day in their lives, observing on one day when the child wakes up, another day the hours before he or she goes to bed, and on other days during the hours in between. Using this technique, we try to get a good sense of the types of activities in which the child is typically involved, the partners in those activities, the roles taken, and so on.

Our aim is to gather data over periods of time long enough to ensure, as much as possible, that the participants in the research behave as naturally as they can. We therefore collect the data in blocks of two and four hours. During the first two days of observation, we collect data for just two hours each day. This is a time to allow the participants to become acclimatized to the observer's presence and we are prepared, if we see major changes in behavior, to discard these four hours of data. Data are gathered on the remaining days during four-hour sessions.

Although each observer observes for 20 hours, data are only gathered during a 30-second period (a "window" of observation) every six minutes. The remainder of the time is spent coding and writing field notes, while continually tracking what the participants are doing. Time is signaled in such a way that the participants are unaware of when their behaviors are being coded, and the child who is the focus of attention wears a wireless mike so that the observer can hear what is being said without having to be too close to the activity.

The observer spends several minutes before each observation session talking with the child and with the other people who are around, and fitting the child with the wireless mike. The microphone itself is placed on the child's shoulder, close enough to his or her head to pick up easily not only what he or she says but also others' voices, but in such a place that it is unlikely to be damaged. The transmitter is small and light enough to fit easily into a little pack that goes around the child's waist. The earphone connecting to the receiver goes into one of the observer's ears, and a second earphone, connected to a tape recording that keeps track of the time, goes into the other. The observer also carries a clipboard, ready to write the codes for the various activities as well as the field notes. The observer is thus easily believable when she says (most of the observers were female) that she can no longer talk with the child but has to do her work. She does not appear in any way to be available for play or conversation.

The observer's job is to keep track of the various activities going on around the child (activities that the child could potentially become involved in), paying particular attention to those in which the child is actually involved. For these activities, she has to know how they began and how the child became involved in them. It is partly for this reason that she has to observe throughout the six minutes, not simply during the 30-second observational window. After the window has closed (signaled by the tape that keeps track of the time), she writes the codes and field notes.

Only the final 2 of the 20 hours of observation are videotaped. We video-tape for a number of reasons, the most important of which is that the live coding every six minutes does not allow us to study closely the ways in which children are drawn into activities (or how they draw in others) or how the activities and roles change over time. The videotapes allow us to attend to these processes of initiation and engagement. A second reason for filming is to give the parents a two-hour tape of their child engaged in typical activities (quite unlike the typical videotape of special occasions, such as birthdays). The third reason is that we are able to use the tapes for training purposes. As observers are being trained, they are given specific segments of tape to code that will be compared with the established codes as a way to ascertain reliability.

Although videotapes clearly have their uses, we do not film the entire 20 hours and base our codes on the taped activities. There are a number of reasons for this. One is that the presence of a camera is likely to change people's behavior more than does the simple presence of an observer. Equally important, however, is the fact that the camera's field of vision is so much more limited than the human eye. As I just mentioned, although our focus is on the child, we also need to know what activities are going on in which the child is not currently involved (activities that are as yet simply available to him or her). We also need to know whether others are watching the child, either closely observing him or her or looking at the child from a distance (eavesdropping) or whether the child is eavesdropping on an activity out of the camera's field of view. All of these things are accomplished much more easily without a camera.

This approach is thus designed to capture children's activities in an eco-logically appropriate way (children are not separated from the contexts in which they are active), and it does so over enough time to give, we believe,

Table 4.1. Definitions of Focal Activities

Lessons	Deliberate attempts to impart or elicit information relating to the following:
Academic	School (spelling, counting, learning shapes, comparing quantities, colors, etc.)
World	How things work, why things happen, safety
Interpersonal	Appropriate behavior with others, etiquette etc.
Religious	Religious or spiritual matters
Work	Household activities (cooking, cleaning, repairing, etc.), shopping, etc.
Play, Entertainment	Activities engaged in for their own enjoyment, including
Toys	Play with objects designed specifically for play or manipulation by children
Natural objects	Play with objects from the natural world, such as rocks, mud, leaves, sand, sticks, etc.
No object	Play that does not feature any type of object, such as rough and tumble play, chase, word games, singing, etc.
Adult objects	Play with objects that were not designed for children, such as household objects, games designed for adolescents, etc.
Pretend play	Play involving evidence that a role is being assumed, whether part of the normal adult world (a mother shopping, a teacher) or purely fantasy (being a superhero, fantasy figure, or baby)
Academic object	Play with an object designed with school in mind, such as looking at a book, playing with shapes or numbers, etc., with no lesson involved
Entertainment	Listening to radio, going to a ball-game, circus, etc.
TV	Watching television, video, or DVD, whether school-related, child-focused, or not designed with children in mind
Conversation	Talk with a sustained or focused topic about things not the current focus of engagement
Other	Activities such as sleeping, eating, bathing, etc. and those that were uncodable

a reasonable sense of the types of activities that typically occur in these children's lives. The approach also allows us to examine the types of activities that are going on in which the children do not participate or those in which they would like to participate but are discouraged from so doing. The specific activities in which we are interested are displayed in Table 4.1 and divided into four major groups (each of which is subdivided into numerous subgroups), comprising lessons, work, play, conversation, and "other" (sleeping, idleness, eating, bathing, etc.).

The division between "major" and "other" activities reflects the way in which we chose to view children's world through the "lens" of our observational methods – the major groups of activities were those that we termed "focal" activities, those that were the main focus of our attention, or "activities of interest." Whenever the child was involved in any of the focal activities, we coded the activity, how the activity started, how the child became involved in it, the child's role in the activity, any partners who were also involved in the activity, their roles in the activity, and whether the partners appeared to be giving their undivided attention to the activity or were simultaneously involved in something else. The remaining activities were termed "nonfocal" activities to reflect the fact that we did not focus the same degree of attention on them. What this meant in practice was that although we coded whenever the child was eating, sleeping, being bathed, and so on, we only coded how the activity started, the role played by the child and partners, and so on when no focal activities were occurring at the same time.

ACTIVITIES OF INTEREST

Lessons

Lessons involve the deliberate attempt to impart or receive information in four areas: *academic* (relevant to school, such as spelling, counting, learning shapes and colors, etc.); *interpersonal* (teaching appropriate, nice, or "proper" behavior); *world* (how things work and why things happen in the world); and *religious or spiritual.* As an example of an academic lesson, a mother is reading with her son when she asks him how many birds are in the picture and helps him to count them. Reading, by itself, does not count as an academic lesson, but the attempt to help him learn his numbers does count. Similarly, if her son asks her what a particular word says, he is asking for information about something that is relevant to school, and this also would be coded as an academic lesson.

A mother's attempts to help her son tie his shoelaces or to answer her son's questions about why it is that leaves fall from trees, or her explanations of why it's dangerous to drink water from a contaminated well would all be coded as examples of lessons about the world. Explaining to her son the importance of saying "please" or "thank you," about why it's important to take off shoes when entering the house, or about being nice to the other children at school are examples of interpersonal lessons. Asking for information about some aspect of the spiritual world or trying to provide information about it was coded as the final type of lesson, but because so few examples of the latter were observed, I've included them in the interpersonal category.

All lessons thus have to involve either the attempt to provide information in an explicit way or an explicit request for information. The idea here is *not* that children only learn about the way in which the world works through this relatively didactic means of imparting information. As I pointed out in Chapter 2, this particular approach to helping children learn seems to be found far more often in industrialized societies in which children are expected to learn via formal schooling than in the rest of the world. In all societies, moreover, an enormous amount of learning about the world occurs in non-didactic ways, simply by engaging in work, play, and general conversation, as well as by observing others engage in these activities. However, we were interested to know the extent to which children are provided information, or request information, in this relatively didactic way.

Work

Another way in which children learn about their world and learn to become competent within it is by observing and participating in the types of work that goes on. We defined work as "activities that either have economic importance or contribute to the maintenance of life" (Tudge, Sidden, & Putnam, 1990). Because of this definition of work, we were able to distinguish between a child playing with a small broom (or an object designed to represent a broom) while engaging in pretend play, and a child helping a parent or sibling clean the house, or being required to do the work herself. As is clear from Chapter 2, cultural groups differ greatly in terms of the extent to which young children are expected to contribute to the family, but we did not restrict the coding of work to those cases in which the child was making a real contribution. Even if the child were not particularly competent at the task (and his father later on had to redo the work), if the intent of the task were to help do something designed to contribute to the maintenance of life, even if for no other reason than to help the child learn that these types of tasks are important to do, the activity would be coded as work.

Play

Play was defined as engagement in any type of activity simply for fun or for its own sake, with no apparent curriculum (which would constitute a lesson) or sense that the activity had economic importance (work). This was the single largest category, with 16 subcategories. Types of play include pretend or role play, in which the child acts out some type of role, whether from the "real" world (playing at being a mother, or being in school, or pretending to gather crops) or pretending to be a dinosaur, a lion, or one or other superhero. We were also interested in play with an academic object (such as looking at a book, playing with a calculator, or manipulating magnetized letters found on some fridges), playing with toys or other objects typically designed for children, and play with objects that had not been designed specifically for children. A child beating on a pan, for example, would be coded as playing with an object from the adult world, whereas another child, beating on a toy drum, would be coded as playing with a toy. We also coded play that involves no object at all (such as chase or rough and tumble), as well as playing with objects from the natural world (with sticks, leaves, or with and in the mud). We were also interested in the types of entertainment children are involved in, whether watching television, listening to the radio, being a spectator at an organized game, going to the cinema, or watching some type of ceremony.

Conversation

Conversation, the final major category of activity, was defined deliberately to allow us to focus on the relatively sophisticated talk that involves distance from the here-and-now. In other words, we only coded as conversation talk that was not related to the ongoing activity and which had a sustained or focused topic. Talking that was simply an accompaniment to play, work, or a lesson was therefore not coded as conversation. However, if a child were talking with a friend or sibling about what she had been doing the night before or with her mother about visiting the grandfather the following week, these exchanges would be coded as conversation.

During any 30-second window, more than one activity could occur and be coded. Generally speaking, several activities occurred at the same time, depending on the number of people in the setting with the child. For example, while observing in the home during the evening, it is possible that the father was preparing the meal, the mother and a sibling were talking about the child's day at school, and the television was on. In this case, three activities were available to the child, assuming that they were all going on within the child's easy earshot and within sight. Each of the activities would be coded, but if the child were only involved with her father in cooking, she would be coded as having no role in either the conversation or the entertainment (play) but would have a role in the work she was doing. It is also possible that, during the course of the 30 seconds, she stopped helping her father and started watching television. In this case, she would have a role in both activities.

To this point, I have primarily talked about the activities in which children could be engaged. They are important because they are the "stuff" of everyday life, the things that children (and the rest of us) spend our time doing. When Bronfenbrenner wrote about proximal processes, it is precisely this type of engagement in everyday, typically occurring, activities that he had in mind. When Cole discusses practices, what he is thinking about are these types of regular activities in which individuals engage. From a cultural–ecological point of view as well, they are, of course, essential. The focus on activities is necessarily ecological, because there is no attempt to separate the child from the things that the child is doing. However, context is also represented by the places where children spend their time, by the other people who are there with the child (or the absence of others, when children spend a good part of their time alone), and by the roles that they take with the child. For our work to be truly ecological, we clearly have to include in our observational system these aspects of the children's context.

SETTINGS

We therefore observed in any of the settings in which the children were situated, and observed any of the social partners with whom the children interacted. This means that we observed in the home, child-care center if a child went to one, with friends or relatives, at the park, in the streets, yard, or community, or at the shops if the child went there. For ease of coding, we grouped the various settings into four major types: in and around the home (including the garden, yard, compound, play area attached to an apartment complex); in and around someone else's home (including the homes of extended family, friends, or a child-minder); in a formal child-care setting; in any public space (parks or public play areas, shops, restaurants, and streets or spaces available for anyone to use).

The data were gathered in any setting in which the child spent time because we believe that it is important to know more than what goes on in the home or child-care center, the most usual locations where observational data are gathered, at least in the industrialized world. We therefore not only followed the child wherever he or she went during the observational session, but also found out where the child was scheduled to be for the next session, so as to be in that place at the appointed time. The goal was not to change, apart from the presence of the observer, what would have been happening in the child's life had the observer not been there.

PARTNERS AND ROLES

The child's social partners are clearly one major component of the context in which the child is situated. It is therefore important to note the people who are potentially available as partners for the children, as well as those who are actively involved with them. For example, the everyday context for some children involves many other children of the same age – most typically when a good deal of time is spent in some type of preschool or school setting. For other children, children of different ages (their siblings or other children from the neighborhood) are more important, and for yet others it may be one or more adult (often a mother or mother substitute, and more rarely a father or father-substitute) who is most available to be a partner. Availability of partners thus occupies as important a place in the child's context as does the availability of activities.

The coding scheme that we use allowed us to record the number and age of available partners, and also to note the presence of both the mother and father (or their substitutes). This is important if we want to be able to report not only on whether the mother or father was more involved with the child but whether they were more involved even when taking into account the different amounts of time that they spent together. It may be the case, for example, that mothers in some cultural groups were more involved in the various activities with their child than were the fathers. However, if it's the case that the mothers were more often in the child's company because they either did not work outside the home or worked fewer hours outside the home than did the fathers, it is also important to be able to answer the further question: did mothers or fathers spend more time involved with their child, or engaged in different types of activities with him or her, when they were actually in the presence of the child?

Clearly, it is not simply the availability of social partners that is important, but the extent of involvement with the child and the roles taken. We therefore also coded both the role played by the child in the activity and the role played by any partners who were involved, even if they were simply watching the child. In the example given earlier of Dad cooking and his daughter helping, we might imagine that the child is helping to cook by stirring the contents of the frying pan while her father helps by holding the pan steady. In this case, the child is *participating* in cooking and the father is *facilitating* the child's engagement. Other roles included trying to *manage or direct* the activity (actively trying to make the activity occur in a certain way, for example, if the father is telling his daughter exactly what she has to do at every step of the way), trying to *resist or stop* the activity (telling the child that she can no longer help cooking because of the mess she's making or the child resisting being put to bed), and *observing* the activity (if the child were closely watching what her father was doing but not involved in a more active way, or if the child were playing, and her mother was close by, watching her at play). We also include as a role *eavesdropping*, similar to observing but from a greater distance and with no assumption that the person being watched is aware of being watched.

No matter what role the other person is taking while interacting with or observing the child, that person can give either full or partial attention to the activity in which the child is engaged. For example, if while the father was helping his daughter cook, he also had his eye on a game on TV (perhaps the reason why the child made as much mess as she did in the example given earlier!), we coded that his attention was only partially on the activity in which the child is engaged.

THE CHILD AS ACTIVE AGENT

By including, as a major part of our observations, the role played by the child in these various activities, we are already acknowledging the fact that the child is actively involved in the activities. For theoretical reasons this is, of course, extremely important. In cultural–ecological theory it is the intersection of individual and environment that should be the center of attention, not either the individual or the environment considered as having an influence that can be separated from the other.

There are other ways as well that we were able to examine the active role of the children on whom we focused. The most important has to do with our consideration of the ways in which activities began (how they were initiated, in other words). Specifically, children are involved in activities not simply because others get them involved; they initiate activities themselves and try to recruit others to be their social partners.

If a child were involved in a specific activity during our coding 30-second "window," we coded whether the child (alone or with someone else) initiated the activity, and whether the child or another person got the child involved in the activity. Think back to the earlier example of the father helping his daughter to cook. If the father had started the cooking and asked her to help, we would have coded the father initiating both the activity and his daughter's involvement in that activity. However, if she had come over and asked to help, we would have coded that the father initiated the activity and the child initiated her involvement in it.

This is one of the main ways in which we capture what it is that the individual brings to any situation. When Bronfenbrenner wrote about "developmentally instigative" characteristics, he had in mind precisely the fact that some children are far more likely than others to try to take the lead in getting new activities started and seem to find it easier to involve others in them. We are also able to examine differences in other types of individual characteristics, such as gender. We can examine, for example, whether girls are involved in different types of activities than boys and, if so, whether that stems from differences in encouragement to get involved in different activities or differences in the extent of initiation. We are thus able to see, for example, the extent to which boys and girls differentially initiate the activities themselves, and draw others into those activities, compared with the extent to which the boys and girls are drawn into activities that others start.

Each of these aspects (the activities, the child's role in each activity, who initiated the activity and the child's involvement in it, the various partners and their roles, and where the activities occurred) was coded immediately after each coding window closes. We also noted the time and the presence of other people in the setting (these are the people who are the child's potential partners) and whether the mother (or mother-substitute) and father (or father-substitute) were in the setting. A copy of the coding sheet that we use in the project is provided in Figure 4.1.

CULTURE AND HISTORICAL TIME

So far in this chapter, I have tried to show the ways in which the methods that we used to gather our data fit well with cultural–ecological theory, which requires that our research allows us to examine the interwoven effects of aspects of the individual, aspects of the setting in which the individual is situated, and the typically occurring everyday activities and interactions that go on between the individual and the other objects, symbols, and people who are in the environment in which the individual of interest is to be found. The environment, however, is far more than the immediate setting (the home, apartment, preschool, park, yard, or shops) where the current activities are taking place but also includes the broader sociocultural context at some given period of historical time.

Culture, as I made clear in Chapters 1 and 3, has to be significant in any ecological approach. Children are raised to become competent members of the cultural group into which they have been born. Different cultural groups value different objects, have different sets of social, economic, and political institutions, expect different things of their children, provide different

Child ID _____ Case no. _____ Day _____ Time _____ Observer _____ Weather, temp _____

	Lessons	Work	Play	Conv	Other
Continues					
Available					
Ch. Role					
Init of Act.					
Init of Inv.					
Partner #1					
P #1 Role					
Divided Attn.					
Partner #2					
P #2 Role					
Divided Attn.					
Partner #3					
P #3 Role					
Divided Attn.					
Partner #4					
P #4 Role					
Divided Attn.					
Partner #5					
P #5 Role					
Divided Attn.					
Avail. adults		Window notes here			
Avail. yths					
Avail. child					
Avail. peer					
Avail. inf.					
Location					
Mother loc.					
Father loc.					

Figure 4.1. Coding Sheet for a Single Observational "Window."
Child ID __ Case no. _ Day __Time _ Observer ___Weather and Temp. ____

types of opportunities for their children to become competent members of their group, have different values and beliefs about how best to raise their children, and so on. Cultures, of course, are not static phenomena, and so it's also important to take into account the influences of recent or current socioeconomic or political factors, something I discuss in more detail in the next chapter.

It is thus important to gather data in different cultural groups to examine the extent to which those who are already competent members of the group (adults, in other words) value different things for their children, have different beliefs about how to attain those valued goals, make available different activities for their children to engage in, encourage their children to engage in some activities, discourage involvement in others, and so on.

How do we instantiate culture using this methodology? Given my earlier definition of culture (see Chapters 1 and 3), different societies constitute different cultural groups, and we accordingly gather data in different societies. As I wrote in Chapter 1, data were initially collected in the United States, where I have lived since the early 1980s. However, I have also lived in the former Soviet Union and spent at least some time there almost every year between 1976 and 2001. It therefore made sense to gather comparative data in Russia and Estonia, two distinct cultures but ones in which the parents of the children in whom I was interested had been raised in a single society. I was also able to gather data in Finland, culturally and linguistically similar to Estonia, but without the Soviet connection. I didn't want to restrict the research to just two areas of the industrialized world, however, but wanted to explore children's activities in a more diverse range of societies, including from parts of the majority world. I was helped to achieve this goal by two graduate students, one from South Korea and one from Kenya. It is thanks to them that we were able to gather data in the same way from those two societies. The last of the societies where we have done this research is Brazil, another country that I know well, having spent significant amounts of time there since 1993.

These societies, of course, vary on many dimensions, and I wanted to avoid the type of problem caused by gathering data in a major urban area in one society, a small town in another, and a rural community in a third. I therefore chose a single city in each society, of medium size by the standards of that society, with a range of cultural, educational, and professional possibilities. (Each of the cities in which we collected data is described in much more detail in the following chapter.)

However, as I argued in Chapters 1 and 3, culture and society are not synonymous, and too much of the cultural and cross-cultural literature has ignored issues of within-society heterogeneity. A variety of cultural groups can be found within any society, given my definition of culture. Different ethnic groups may therefore constitute separate cultural groups, and so may different social classes. As discussed in Chapter 3, a cultural–ecological approach helps us, I believe, to think more clearly about how to deal with within-society variation, in particular to avoid thinking about differences in children's experiences in terms of advantages or deficits. This is true whether looking across different societies, or within any society. Regional differences, rural–urban differences, ethnic differences are all examples of the types of within-society heterogeneity that we could have examined, but given the types of cities that we chose, it was easiest to look at social-class differences.

As I pointed out in the previous chapter, my position, based on Kohn's work (e.g., Kohn, 1995), is that the most critical aspects of social class for children's development are their parents' education and their occupation, because parents' experiences during their schooling and currently while working seem more likely to influence the ways in which they raise their children than does income, one of the other best-known markers of class (Ensminger & Fothergill, 2003; Hauser, 1994; Kohn, 1979). In this study, I therefore wanted to examine, in each of the cities, children from two groups – those who were defined as either working or middle class on the grounds of their parents' education and occupation. In the city in the United States, we also examined children from Black and White families, equally divided by social class.

It's probably worth reiterating the point made in the previous chapter that my intention is not to use a single measuring stick against which to compare these different groups; for the children of one group to be more involved in one type of activity than are the children of another group, or to have more interactions with a certain type of social partner, or to watch more or less television carries no implication of being higher or lower on a set scale of values. The goal, instead, as I pointed out in Chapter 1, is to show the ways in which culture is implicated in development by the types of settings, partners, activities, and interactions that it considers possible and appropriate; for one group to make available certain opportunities and discourage others is an indication of what that group considers (implicitly or explicitly) to be valuable.

Of course, from a cultural–ecological perspective, this apparently top-down position is moderated by the fact that individual characteristics, preferences, abilities, and so on also play a large role in the types of activities and interactions children have and also on the types of settings they inhabit. It is also important to recognize, of course, that children's settings, activities, interactions, and so on are not chosen freely from some set that is available to all; different groups, both across societies and within a single society, have access to different resources, power, opportunities, and so on.

METHODOLOGICAL CHALLENGES

I devoted much of this chapter to showing that this method of collecting data fits well within a contextualist paradigm in general, within cultural–ecological theory in particular. The method allows us to treat children as active initiators of and participants in the activities and interactions that are everyday parts of their lives. In effect, they are engaged in a process of joint construction of reality with others, in a world that provides sociocultural meaning, which has been developed over historical time.

I'm not trying to argue that this particular method is the only appropriate ecological or contextual one. Ethnographic approaches, including participant observation, use of "beepers" with adolescents, and interviews, particularly with the children themselves (rather than relying on others to interpret their experiences for them), also qualify to the extent that they are able to deal adequately with the interrelations among individual, interpersonal, and cultural–historical factors. None of these alternative approaches, however, is likely to be successful when the most important participants in the research are only three years old.

I also don't wish to argue that this method is problem-free; in fact, there are a number of challenges that I should address. One is that this method is extremely time-consuming, not simply because each child is observed for 20 hours. Learning to observe in this way also takes a good deal of time and effort; observers have to be able to identify the various activities going on around the child, how the activities were started, how the child became involved, the various partners involved with the child, and the roles of the various individuals involved. The process takes well over a month of daily training sessions, using a mixture of live observation and observation of previously coded videotapes of naturally occurring activities. This is a somewhat daunting prospect but one that, I believe, is well worth the expenditure of time and effort.

Given that this research occurs in different cultural groups, a second challenge should immediately come to mind. To be able to observe children in their natural settings, understand what they are saying (and what is being said to them), and appropriately interpret the subtle cues that indicate that something is being said or done for fun rather than seriously requires that one has an intimate knowledge of the culture in which observations are taking place. I used to speak pretty good Russian and am close to fluent in Portuguese, but knowledge of the language is not the same as being one with the culture. I've lived in the United States for almost half my life, but no one listening to me would ever confuse me with an American, not only because of my accent but because of the ways in which I see the world. Although anthropologists learn, as well as one is able, how to become a part of a cultural group different from their own, my approach was to train people from the cultures of interest. Each of the people who collected the data is thus from the local culture. Some of my former graduate students from the relevant cultural backgrounds were therefore trained to collect the data from the White and Black children in the U.S. city, the Korean children, and those in Kenya. In the case of the data from Russia, Estonia, Finland, and Brazil, I recruited and trained people to do these observations, with training taking place both in their home cities and (except for the Brazilian observers) in Greensboro.

Then there is the issue of the time of observation itself. Are 20 hours sufficient to get an adequate sense of the typically occurring daily activities and interactions? I can't deny that the longer the observers spend with the participants, the more likely they are to be accepted, the more they know about the relevant contexts and the participants' roles in those contexts, and the more they are likely to understand the meaning to the participants of the experiences in which they engage. The best response that I can provide is simply to say that 20 hours allows observers to follow children over the equivalent of one complete day in the child's life and this may be sufficient to get a reasonable sense of the types of activities and interactions that are important in children's lives. *what if it's a weird day?*

Another challenge has to do with the extent to which observations of children necessarily treat children as passive objects, specimens under the scrutiny of the scientist (Greene, 1997; Hogan, 2005; Hogan, Etz, & Tudge, 1999; Woodhead & Faulkner, 2000). I believe that what is important in the determination of whether the child is treated as object is the position that the researcher takes vis-à-vis the child and context. Putting the child into a contrived situation to see how he or she responds to that particular variation in context may indeed imply that the child is simply the object of investigation. However, observing children engaging, in as natural a way as can be arranged, in the types of activities that would be a typical part of their everyday lives, is surely a way for those children to be active and involved participants in the study rather than objects of study. They, after all, control what it is that they do, when they do it, and with whom – at least to the extent that they are allowed by the children's social partners and the preexisting constraints of the setting.

Nonetheless, the children themselves are clearly not the people who are constructing the meaning of their experiences. Instead, the observer, using a coding scheme that has already been developed, in essence provides the meaning from what it is that the children and their social partners are doing. In this sense, there is not only a distancing of observer and children but a privileging of the former. This separation is something that may only be (partially?) overcome by participant observation or completely free and open-ended interviews. I have to acknowledge that the use of preset coding categories might disenfranchise children because experiences important to them might not fit within the established categories and therefore be excluded. In the CEYC project, this potential does exist but is dealt with through the use of field notes that always accompany the more formal coding of activities. These notes allow for the inductive creation of codes (we were able to expand our codes for types of work, for example, from the field notes), as well as for analysis in their own right.

A related argument sometimes used against observation as a method of gathering data is that the only valid route to understanding children's experiences is to study the language that they themselves use to describe and explain them, usually in direct conversation with the researcher. I'm not at all sure, however, why interviews should necessarily be viewed as being a more valid way of understanding children's experiences than observations. Interviewing children, particularly young children, involves a host of difficulties, not least of which is the fact that talking about what one does is not the same as the doing thereof. Although when observed children are not being given a voice through language directed at researchers, it is my view that they are given a voice – a means of conveying a description of their lives and how they live them – through action observed.

Some believe, however, that interviewing children themselves is the only way to learn about the inner world of children, to find out what they are thinking and feeling. Interviews can certainly focus on these things in a way that observations never can. Gifted interviewers who have established the trust of the interviewees, whether children or adults, can certainly gain remarkable insights (Bearison, 1991; Graue & Walsh, 1998; Westcott & Littleton, 2005). However, most of us (and here I mean "us" not simply as researchers but as people) do not spend our time interviewing children as a way to find out what they're thinking and feeling. We talk to them, listen to them, watch them, engage with them, listen to them talking to other people, and so on. As people, we make sense of others around us by attending to both verbal and nonverbal cues, and if our interpretations are incorrect we are likely to get clear feedback when we act on those interpretations.

Observers do not lose these skills when observing young children. More important, by observing children in their natural settings with their typical social partners, we (as researchers) can be privy to the understandings and misunderstandings demonstrated by those we are observing. Interviews about experiences require a removal from engagement in the very experiences in which we are interested; observations of children experiencing allow us, as observers, to get insight into the minds and feelings of those we are observing via the children themselves and via the behaviors of those with whom they are engaged.

A further criticism of the type of observations I have discussed in this chapter is that the presence of the observer is conveniently forgotten, or deemed to be irrelevant. For example, Woodhead and Faulkner criticized observational approaches in which the aim of the observers is to render themselves invisible to the immature members of the human species they want to observe. Observers may be found backed-up against the corner of the classroom or playground, trying to ignore children's invitations to join in the game, and kidding themselves that they can appear like the metaphoric "fly on the wall." (2000, p. 15)

The aim may not be invisibility, however, but a desire to change children's regularly occurring behavior in as minimal a way as is possible – to allow them the freedom to behave without the expectation that the observer will intervene to change what they are doing (which is not quite the same as doing exactly as they would were the observer not present). Corsaro's (1985, 1997) participant observations with preschoolers (in which the children define him as "Big Bill" an "untypical adult") similarly allow the children the freedom to behave without concern that Corsaro will act like a teacher. If we are interested in not separating children from context (the essence of a cultural–ecological approach), it is surely important to gather data in a way that does not involve such separation – and that means observing the child in context.

As with any ethnographic approach, time is important to help children know that the adult's role is *not* to alter, in any deliberate fashion, what they might otherwise do. This is the main reason that we observe for 20 hours over the course of a week, in lengthy blocks of time. Because the children are approximately three years of age, they appear to adapt quickly to the observer. For the most part, they do not treat the observer as someone with whom they could interact (as mentioned earlier, the observer has earphones in both ears and often is writing on a clipboard), and to help ensure this, the observer chats with the child before the start of the observational session and then says that it is now time to "work," and puts on the earphones. The length of time of observation makes it easier for the children to ignore the observer's presence and to behave as normally as possible.

I am under no illusions that the other participants (particularly adults) can "forget" the observer's presence so easily. Indeed, as children become more self-aware, observations may become more problematic; I don't think, for example, that we could have observed adolescents and expected them to have gone about their typical activities with as little evidence of influence as with young children. However, there are reasons to believe that even the behaviors of the adults that we observed with the children were not totally untypical. First, with observational sessions lasting so long, typically occurring activities (getting the child up, preparing meals, taking the child to a child-care provider, for example) have to happen. Second, if the parents behaved in ways that were not at all typical, it seems reasonable to suppose that their children might signal that fact. Finally, if parents behave differently from their normal behaviors, it is likely that they do so in the direction of the things that they value. In other words, if they think that it is important to help their children behave independently, they may do so more often than is typical; if they believe that it is important to discipline their children, they might do this more often. Because we assume that parents' activities may bear some relation to their values, their exaggerated behaviors, if this was what we were observing, were interesting in themselves.

The final criticism that I want to address goes back to the theoretical underpinnings of this research. Cultural–ecological theory is a theory of human *development*. If one wishes to study development, one has to study individuals over time, and to this point I have yet to discuss the type of longitudinal data that are necessary if we are interested in development.

The reason for this lack of attention is that I have yet to complete collection of the longitudinal data that will make this research not only ecological but also developmental. Discussion of the developmental data must therefore wait for a follow-up to this book. However, I can at least describe what it is that we do. As is clear by now, we gather the types of observational data discussed earlier when the children are of preschool age but then gather follow-up data once the children have entered school. Parents and teachers are interviewed and complete questionnaires that examine, among other things, their views of the children's social, behavioral, and academic competence. We are interested in examining the relations, if any, between three-year-old children's initiation of and engagement in different types of activities and their parents' and teachers' perceptions of them during the early years of school. (For a taste of the follow-up data, see Tudge, Odero, Hogan, & Etz, 2003; Tudge, Tammeveski, Meltsas, Kulakova, & Snezhkova, 2001).

Conducting a longitudinal study, however, is not the only way in which the passage of time can be captured in research. As I mentioned earlier, in any contextual approach, it is important to situate our children not simply in their physical context but also in their temporal context. The way in which even young children experience their environments depends in part on what is happening, during that period of historical time, in the culture of which that child is a part. This is true for children in a society that is rapidly industrializing, in an industrialized society in the midst of recession or boom or, as in the case of our research, in societies struggling to adapt to the changes wrought by the collapse of the Soviet Union.

Moreover, even if one does not want, or is unable, to collect longitudinal data but is more interested in trying to capture a sense of children's experiences, one should not ignore time. The beauty of observations, rather than interviews or questionnaires, is that researchers are necessarily examining those experiences as they happen, over time, rather than getting a retrospective accounting of what has already happened. Only with observations is it possible to examine the ways in which a child draws a friend into an activity with her or examine the changes in roles as a father first insists that his daughter reads with him, only to have her completely take over the process.

In summary, this approach to naturalistic observations has a number of methodological challenges, but I do not believe that any of them are sufficient to discredit this method as an important way in which to understand children's experiences and development from a contextualist and ecological perspective.

5   Life in the Cities

What is the city but the people?

> William Shakespeare, *Coriolanus*, Act 3, Scene 1, 1623/1954, p. 719

In this chapter, I want to introduce you to the places where we collected the data. As I mentioned in the previous chapter, just a single city was chosen from each of the societies where I wanted to conduct the research. I should be clear about the fact that I don't believe children living in any single city can in any way "represent" children across the entire society, or children from different regions of the country, different ethnic groups, or different social classes. This is no more appropriate than to imagine that an ethnography of a single hunter-gatherer tribe in the Congo can be generalized either to other hunter-gatherer groups in other parts of the world or to the experiences of other groups within the Congo. We already know, from the literature discussed in Chapter 2, that there are large differences in the everyday lives of young children who live in cities in the industrialized world and those who live in predominantly rural regions in the majority world. We have much less evidence about cultural diversity in children's experiences in cities in different parts of the world, whether thinking exclusively about cross-societal variation or about within-society heterogeneity.

However, cultural–ecological theory's concern with context should not be interpreted to mean simply the geographical, social, or cultural context but also the temporal context. As I pointed out in Chapter 3, contextual and cultural variations can only be explained by referring to how those contexts or cultures developed over historical time. Scholars in human development have become increasingly aware of the dangers of generalizing across space or social grouping. However, we have not yet taken sufficiently to heart the insights of Glen Elder (e.g., 1996) and others who have studied the developmental processes of growing up at different time periods, as in cohort analysis. Three-year-olds developing during historical periods of great stress, such as in times of famine, war, or epidemic, are likely to develop differently from their counterparts in the same culture who are developing during times of peace and prosperity. Even in less obvious ways time matters, as is most obviously clear in the case of Russian or Estonian children who were raised either before or after the collapse of the Soviet Union or in the case of Kenyan children who were raised before or after schooling became considered necessary (although not sufficient) for a successful future. Context, in other words, is as much a temporal as a spatial phenomenon. So as well as writing a little about the physical aspects of life in the different cities where we collected data, I give here a sense of what was occurring during the historical period during which the data were being collected.

I consider the cities in three groups, corresponding to the way in which I describe the children's activities, partners, and so on in subsequent chapters. The first group is from a single city in the United States, where we collected data on both White and Black children, equally divided by social class.

GREENSBORO, NORTH CAROLINA, UNITED STATES

This city is home to about 230,000 inhabitants, and is located approximately 250 miles (400 kilometers) south of Washington, D.C. The city was founded early in the 19th century and by the end of the century was an important textile manufacturing center (Putnam, 1995). The city's economy is still based in manufacturing, primarily of textiles, furniture, and tobacco products, but a good deal of employment is also to be found in the banking and insurance industries, as well as in the five colleges and universities within the city borders. Although the city also has rapidly growing Latino (4.4%) and Asian (2.6%) populations, those classifying themselves as White (53%) and Black (36%) constitute the two major groups in the city (The City of Greensboro Data Book, 2003).

The city's history is heavily linked with issues of race and the civil rights movement. Because of the influence of the many Quakers who settled in Greensboro, one branch of the Underground Railroad, the network of anti-slavery activists who helped slaves escape from the South, was established in Greensboro. Greensboro, during the buildup to the Civil War, voted against secession from the Union just weeks before the state of North Carolina joined the Confederacy. In 1960, one of the first civil rights acts, the sit-in at Woolworth's lunch counter, started in downtown Greensboro. In 1979, members of the Ku Klux Klan murdered five people demonstrating for justice in one of the Black neighborhoods of the city, and although the negative attention this drew the city from across the country forced a reexamination of race relations in the city (Putnam, 1995) and established a Truth and Reconciliation Commission to try to deal with the issues, it is impossible to spend much time in Greensboro without becoming aware of the racial divide that still exists.

This divide is most easily seen in the city neighborhoods. As is common in many cities in the United States, Greensboro is divided into several distinct areas. To a visitor, the most obvious distinction is between the areas that lie east and west of the railway lines that bisect the city. In the east, the population is almost entirely Black, whereas in the west, although there is much greater evidence of integrated neighborhoods, the majority of the population is White.

Social class also divides the city, at least in the White areas. This, too, has its historical roots. Textile work, a major part of the Greensboro economy, was restricted almost exclusively to working-class Whites. During slavery, there were both economic and racial objections to training slaves to do this work, and after Emancipation jobs in the textile mills went to the poor Whites who came to the city to escape the poverty of life on small farms. In Greensboro, as in many other similar Southern cities, the mill owners established small "villages" around their mills, and the workers lived there. The practice of mill-owned houses and stores gradually declined over the middle part of the 20th century, but the legacy continues to the present, with the areas around the primary textile mill in Greensboro consisting predominantly of small homes occupied for the most part by working-class Whites. Other areas of the city consist of far larger and grander-looking homes, with wide expanses of lawn, many trees and bushes. It is here that the middle-class and upper-middle-class families of Greensboro are to be found. Although some middle-class Black families are to be found in these areas, most of the families are White.

The White participants were recruited from birth records if they lived in one of two areas (each 2–3 square kilometers) that appeared to be relatively homogeneous in terms of housing and racial background. One of the areas, that we termed "Summit" was around the largest textile mill in the city and was bounded by two major roads and a railway line. The second area, bounded on three sides by major roads, termed "Holden," was one of the clearly middle-class areas. A total of 20 families with young children were recruited from these two communities. In Holden, all of the 11 families that were recruited were middle class, featuring parents with higher education who worked in professional occupations. From Summit we recruited nine working-class families in which none of the parents had a college degree and who worked in the nonprofessional sphere. Acceptance rates from those initially contacted were reasonably high (64% in the middle-class community and 78% in the working-class area).

Data were gathered from the middle-class and working-class White children between 1991 and 1993 by two graduate students, Sarah Putnam and Judy Sidden. This was the time of the first Gulf War, with George H. W. Bush as president and the country experiencing economic difficulties and an increase in poverty, particularly among Black families with young children, in part a result of the economic policies of the preceding Reagan years.

We tried to use the same strategy for recruiting our Black participants, but this proved to be impossible. For reasons mentioned earlier, the vast majority of the Black population of Greensboro is found on the east side of the city. There are some small areas that consist entirely of large and well-appointed houses, but these are not areas in which young children can be found. Middle-class Black families with young children are essentially required to make a choice. They can choose to live in a middle-class neighborhood and mostly have White families for neighbors, or they can choose to live in a Black neighborhood. If they choose the latter, they'll find a variety of types of houses, as well as apartments, but unless they are either wealthy or come from long-established middle-class backgrounds, they will have ethnically homogeneous but socioeconomically diverse neighbors.

We chose two areas from the Black part of town, each between one and two square miles (2–3 square kilometers) in size. Although we were able to draw primarily middle-class families from one neighborhood and primarily working-class families from the other, neither neighborhood could be described as homogeneous by social class. As in the White communities, however, the Black middle-class homes were typically larger, two-story, homes with more spacious yards, whereas the homes of the working-class families were generally smaller one-story structures (Doucet, 2000). The acceptance rate was similar to that for the White families. Of the 50 families we contacted, 15 did not meet our requirements (in each of these families, one parent was middle class by education and occupation and the other parent was working class), and 16 declined to participate (a 68% acceptance rate). Nine of the families were middle class, by our definition, and ten of the families were working class, and, just as in the White community, the two groups were quite different in terms of their levels of education and occupational status. The data were collected by two Black graduate students, Fabienne Doucet and Nicole Talley.

It is important to point out, however, that the apparent similarities between White and Black families in terms of the social-class variations in each ethnic/racial group are misleading. The fact that Blacks are far less likely than Whites in Greensboro to live in neighborhoods that are homogeneous by social class means that they are less likely to interact on a daily basis with neighbors who share similar class-linked values, beliefs, and practices. Moreover, for historical reasons, Blacks on average receive less income than do Whites across all levels of education (Smith & Horton, 1997), and the same may well be true for Blacks and Whites who share the same job title. For example, a small business owner in a predominantly or exclusively Black neighborhood may make a good deal less money than the equivalent person who caters to Whites. Thus, even when a middle-class Black family might wish to live in closer proximity to other middle-class families (Blacks or Whites), they may be unable to for purely economic reasons.

I should also note that we collected the data from the White and Black children in Greensboro at different times. We were observing the middle-class White children during the first Gulf War, and this (in at least one case) was the cause of some conversation and perhaps concern. The working-class White families were all observed after the war was over, and the Black families were observed during the economic upswing that accompanied the first years of the Clinton presidency in the 1990s in the United States. We have no way of knowing whether the types of activities in which children were involved would have changed markedly if we had been observing during times of greater economic or political stress, but we should not simply assume that these types of broad historical events and changes have no impact on developing children.

It is also worth mentioning that children of preschool age in Greensboro, in common with the rest of the country, are fairly likely to be put into some type of child-care setting. For some children, particularly from families in which both parents work and who have sufficient income, this means full-time child care; for others, generally families in which the mother does not work outside the home, this means either no time spent in a child-care center or part-time presence. For other children, a good deal of time is spent during the day with someone other than a parent – perhaps a grandmother or a child-minder, someone who is paid to look after the children, often in company of a few others. Because publicly funded child care is relatively rare, and primarily for those considered to be most at risk (Freitas et al., in press), child care in Greensboro is fairly expensive, particularly for those centers that are considered to be of higher quality (Cassidy, Hestenes, Hegde, Hestenes, & Mims, 2005).

CITIES IN THE NORTHEAST OF EUROPE

The next three cities about which I write are from a part of the world very different from that of Greensboro, in the southern United States. Although Greensboro was selected as a city in which to observe children because I happen to work there, I'll provide a little more detail than I gave in Chapters 1 and 4 to explain the reasons for the selection of cities in Russia, Estonia, and Finland. I worked in the former Soviet Union in the 1970s, as a teacher of young children in the Anglo-American school in Moscow, and spent at least some time in that country every year until it ceased to exist. My knowledge of Estonia was less well formed than that of Russia; although I had visited Tallinn, I had never set foot in Tartu (a city that was "closed" to foreigners in the Soviet era) until my initial attempts to recruit people whom I could train as observers. I knew little about Finland, apart from a few visits to Helsinki, and also first set foot in Oulu when hoping to recruit observers.

The reasons for finding a Russian city to compare with Greensboro should be fairly obvious. I knew a lot about the history and culture, spoke the language, and I thought that it would make a nice comparison with a U.S. city, given (at least at the ideological level, although less obviously in practice) a clear distinction between people living in a collectivist society and those from one that has been termed individualistic. I wanted to find a city that was somewhat similar to Greensboro and so, with my Russian collaborators and observers Irina Snezhkova and Natalya Kulakova, searched for a city of medium size, with at least one institution of higher education within reasonable distance of Moscow.

Estonia seemed to constitute a fascinating contrast with Russia. Estonians had been a part of the Soviet Union since 1940, and all of the parents of the children in our study had been raised in the Soviet Union. Being raised in the Soviet system is not the same as being raised Soviet, however, and each of the 15 republics that formed a part of the USSR has a distinctive culture, history, and language. Estonian parents were, of course, exposed to precisely the same media, the same types of schools, the same restrictions, and the same opportunities as members of all other Soviet republics. However, Estonian culture and language are far closer to their Finnish neighbors to the north than to their Russian neighbors to the east. Moreover, all Estonians had access, either through personal memories or through oral history, to the period of independence from Russia from 1919 to 1940. Perhaps more telling is that many Estonians have a family member or close friend who had been forced into exile or to Siberia by the Soviet regime.

We thus have a situation in which both Russian and Estonian parents had been raised within the Soviet system but who had markedly different reactions to that system. Similarity of socializing agencies but differences of history, culture, and language allow a wonderful comparison of similarities and differences in the ways in which children are raised. Again, I wanted to find a medium-sized city, one with a range of educational, cultural, and work options, that was reasonably close to the capital city. Thanks to Jaan Valsiner, a colleague in North Carolina at the time, I met Tiia and Peeter Tulviste, who were, in the early 1990s, both teaching in the psychology department of Tartu University. Tiia arranged for me to give a talk there, and thanks to her I met Marika Meltsas and Peeter Tammeveski, who became my collaborators and observers in Tartu.

Finland is the obvious candidate for the location of a third northeastern European city. Finland's links with Estonia are more linguistic than political, for during the past 1,000 years Estonia was controlled by Danes, Germans, Swedes, and Russians. Connections with Finland were primarily due to that country's incorporation first into Sweden and then, at the start of the nineteenth century, Russia. Estonian, however, is a Finno-Ugrik language, one that shares many (although not all) words with Finnish, and that meant that Estonians, certainly those who lived in the north of the country, could tune in to Finnish television during the Soviet period. Culturally speaking, if Russians have a history of collectivism that far predates the Soviet period, both Estonians and Finns are more individualistic in orientation (Bardi & Schwartz, 1996; Realo, 1998, 2003; Schwartz, 1994; Schwartz & Bardi, 1997; Triandis, 1995).

The University of North Carolina at Greensboro has an extensive range of exchange programs. For reasons unnecessary to go into here, for many years the greatest number of exchanges was with the Scandinavian Studies program at the University of Oulu. I took advantage of this connection, and with the great help of Dean Jaakko Luukkonen of the School of Education and Leena Syrjälä, chair of the Department of Early Childhood Education, I met Marikaisa Kontio, a student who was starting on her master's work, and she became my collaborator and observer in Oulu. Oulu, to be sure, is much farther from Helsinki than are any of the other four cities I have so far discussed from their respective capitals. In other ways, however, Oulu fit my requirements nicely. It is a similarly sized city to Obninsk and Tartu, has a range of cultural and educational possibilities, and a similarly wide range of occupational possibilities.

Obninsk, Russia

Leaving central Moscow by Leninsky Prospekt, going beneath the underpass of the massive ring road that circles Moscow and defines its borders, and the road turns into the Kaluga and Kiev road. Soon after leaving the Moscow ring road the countryside begins, with some heavily wooded areas and large stands of silver birches alongside the road. The road starts out as a two-lane highway but fairly quickly becomes a single wide lane, which has become, unofficially, two lanes. In Soviet times, when relatively few people had cars, the road was of a reasonable size. Currently, however, the road is very busy, with a number of older Zhigulis, Ladas, and Moskviches dating from the Soviet period, as well as a lot of shiny new Russian-made cars, and a fair sprinkling of foreign cars – BMWs, Mercedes, Hondas, and the like. Obninsk is about 100 kilometers south of Moscow. It takes about two hours to reach, passing half a dozen small towns and villages along the way, some with evidence of new buildings being erected, and people selling things along the side of the road, from rocks and stones to potatoes, sugar, and kitchen utensils.

Turning off the Kiev highway at the large stone sign that announces the city, it takes about five minutes to get to the center, now dominated by a recently built church. Obninsk is a new town, built in the 1950s around a nuclear power plant, no longer in use, and is home to about 120,000 inhabitants. Because of the need for scientists and skilled technical workers two institutions of higher education were established, as well as a number of polytechnical institutes of lesser standing. The town was named after Viktor Petrovich Obninskii, the owner of a *dacha* (summer house) in the nearby village of Belkino. Obninskii had been a member of the Russian Duma or parliament in the first few years of the 20th century, who had worked on the agrarian commission looking at ways to provide more land for the peasants, and who was sentenced to three months' solitary confinement in prison for his opposition to the tsar (Chernykh, 2000).

Perhaps because of its recent birth and perhaps because of the demand for skilled workers, when we began the study Obninsk appeared more prosperous than equivalent sized cities in Russia. Compared with the large and stolid apartment complexes that are typical of many larger Russian cities, those in Obninsk were relatively stylish, using color and architectural features to enhance the buildings' appearance. They are still stylish but are now showing their age to some degree. But if most of the apartment complexes are aging, new ones are being put up that rival many new buildings in Moscow. The city also has a number of small wood and plaster houses, mostly located in the older part of the city, and which are more typical of towns the size of Obninsk in the region.

We chose Obninsk as the setting for the Russian part of the study for a number of reasons. It was a medium-sized city with institutes of higher education and the chance to find families with higher education and professional employment, as well as working-class families. It was also a reasonable distance from Moscow, where my colleagues were situated. Most important, however, was the long-standing friendship between Natasha and Nelli, and the link to Nelli's sister-in-law, Sveta. It's thanks to Sveta that we were able to do the study in Obninsk, because she opened her apartment to Ira and Natasha, during their long weeks of data collection, and to *Dyadya Dzhon* (Uncle Jon), the name I soon came to be given during my yearly visits to Obninsk.

Nowadays, when we arrive, the first thing that happens is that we all sit around Sveta's kitchen table while she pours a little tea into our cups and tops it up with water heated in the electric samovar. While she prepares some food for us, the phone calls start, from Ira or Natasha to the families or from a parent to Sveta, asking whether we've arrived yet. Sveta's apartment is the hub of all activity, and so it's been since the beginning of our data collection.

It proved impossible to locate families with children of the appropriate age using the methods I had used in Greensboro – birth records were not available to us. We therefore relied on "snowballing" starting with Sveta, one of whose two children was of the right age for our purposes. Several of the families live in or close to Sveta's apartment complex. Entrance to the block is by a code, which changes every few months for security purposes. There are typically one or two elevators, although some of the blocks have only stairs. Having got out on the correct floor, there are usually four apartments, entrance to which is by a common door, leading to a corridor off which are the apartments themselves.

Most of the apartments are of a similar size, small by American standards but the norm in Russia since the 1950s and 1960s, when mass construction of such apartments began. (Before that families typically occupied one or perhaps two rooms in a communal apartment, sharing access to kitchen and bathroom.) Sveta's apartment complex was newer, dating from the 1980s, and she and her husband actually helped in the construction of it, as part of a *molodezhnyi zhilishchnyi cooperativ,* or youth housing cooperative. It therefore featured an "improved layout" of larger kitchen and bathroom, and more storage space. Immediately after entrance to an apartment, shoes are removed, to be replaced by *tapochki* (flat slippers, of leather or cloth, often with flat backs, that are only ever used within the apartment). A corridor has kitchen, bathroom, living room, and bedroom leading from it. Most apartments are known as "two-room" apartments, meaning one room that to a guest appears like a living room and another that is a bedroom. However, rooms do not have any single function; within that space the families live, with children often sharing a bedroom and the parents sleeping on a sofa bed in the living room. Sveta's apartment is a three-room apartment, one that allows her and her husband, two children, and as many as five guests to stay.

One common "living room" arrangement is the sofa bed against one wall, a carpet above it that covers most of the wall. Against the other wall is a large cupboard that stretches most of the room length, with a mixture of glass-plated sections, where precious things are displayed, whether photos of the children, books, glass and china, examples of children's work, souvenirs of trips, items of religious significance, and so on. Another, smaller sofa or chair might be against a third wall, and in a corner, near the window, the TV is often found. Sometimes the television is left on when we arrive, other times turned off or was not on. Hidden from view are children's toys, books, clothes, and many other necessities of life.

This basic pattern disguises the great variety that lies behind it: for example, one living room divided into smaller areas, a piano, a place for children to climb and swing, and books in every conceivable place; in another, there's a full-scale wooden xylophone along with a mass of computer equipment; in another, a small area devoted to a ham radio office, complete with radio, computer, maps of the world, and much more. In some apartments there are dogs, both large and small, or a cat that could be found on top of a cupboard in the corridor, on a visitor's lap, or being scared into its home in a cabinet under the TV by a free-flying budgie.

None of our Obninsk families live in the most modern apartment complexes, although a number of them are hoping to move into one or other of them. In many cases, their apartment complex is situated among large spaces, with many trees, sometimes just a small climbing frame or two for children, but in others are more elaborate play structures. In some cases the complex is surrounded by so many trees that you could be excused for thinking that you're in a little wood, with birches, oaks, maples, elms, and pines as well as tall grasses and little shrubs. Some of these areas include neatly planned gardens, but most appear to be left pretty much to grow as they will.

Unlike the situation in Greensboro, at least for the European American families, Suwon (Korea) and Kisumu (Kenya), in Obninsk, as is true of other cities in the former Soviet Union, it is not possible to find areas of the city that are differentiated by social class, type of occupation, and so on. Well-educated professional families are likely to live next door to less-educated workers. Although there are some small single-family dwellings around the outskirts, the vast majority of the city's population lives in the type of apartment complexes that I just described. Half of our Obninsk families consisted of parents who had the equivalent of a U.S. college education or higher and whose primary occupation was judged to be professional (many parents held more than one job, as a way of supplementing their income). The other half had no more than the equivalent of high school in the United States and worked in the nonprofessional sphere. In the middle-class group, all the fathers and all but two of the mothers had completed a higher education degree (typically a five-year program involving completion of a thesis), whereas in the working-class group, no one had more than the equivalent of a high school education or "incomplete secondary education" sometimes followed by courses in a technical college.

In other respects, these two groups of families were similar. For example, they lived in similar apartment complexes in the same areas of town. In terms of total family income, the group of parents with higher education earned, on average, only slightly more than their counterparts without higher education. It is thus clear that although in terms of education and occupation, the two groups in Obninsk differed from each other in a way similar to those in the United States, in terms of income and housing they did not differ at all. This was in marked contrast to the European American, Kenyan, and Korean families.

According to the tenets of cultural–ecological theory, it is impossible to consider development without placing it in the context of what is happening historically. In the case of cities such as Obninsk and Tartu, the collapse of the Soviet Union was a historical event that had immediate and direct effects on families in both cities. Russians, at a stroke, became members of a society much reduced both economically and politically, whereas Estonians were delighted to be members of an independent state once more.

For our families in Obninsk, the changes were pretty immediate. The old certainties of life in the Soviet Union had vanished, and now people had to find a way to help their children successfully negotiate a very different landscape. In the country at large, rampant inflation had destroyed most people's savings, reducing many to a life that was far harder than before the collapse of the USSR. In the first decade of the "new" Russia, the country's GDP shrank by almost threefold, and spending on education fell even more (Elliott, Hufton, Willis, & Illushin, 2005). The infant mortality rate was high, life expectancy dropped, and the health care system was in a terrible shape. Although food was plentiful in the shops, many people simply did not have the money to buy more than the basics (Shiraev & Gradskova, 2005).

One of the most obvious changes for the Obninsk parents was that they no longer had access to plentiful and virtually free child care for their children, something that had been taken for granted during the Soviet period. For some families, it was difficult to find money to enroll their children in the new private preschools that had sprung up by the mid-1990s, even though they often valued the variety of new options that were now available. In the light of these changes, it is perhaps not surprising that we observed so few of the children in formal child-care settings, although even in Soviet times many children did not attend preschool during the summer months (part of the time during which we collected data in Obninsk). It is also necessary to point out that, particularly by comparison with Greensboro, the ease of access to safe play areas and the fact that grandmothers (whether the child's own or someone else's) often kept an eye on the children meant that many families did not feel the need to have their children in child care.

In 1999, about four years after observing the children, we asked many of the parents about their views on the changes. Fyodor's mother (names are all pseudonyms), a working-class woman, expressed herself forcefully: "School has become dirtier, laxer, less responsible. . . . Everything should be changed, both in school and in the country. Chaos in the country, chaos in school. Our school needs repairing; they should replace some of the teachers, as well as improve discipline." On the other hand, she had been able to set up her own small business, making paint (she had studied chemistry for two years at a technical college, before dropping out) and she hoped that that would lead to financial independence. Unfortunately, at the time of the interview, she was making only enough money to pay the utility bills and the tuition costs of a private teacher who was teaching Fyodor English. Zhenya's mother, an engineer at a medical radiological center, whose job it was to teach the personnel how to use the equipment, was also clear about the impact of the changes. When she was asked if there was anything she worried about, she immediately replied: "Of course there is, in this abnormal country. One doesn't know how to get the child educated, where to get money."

Liuba's mother, a middle-class woman, on the other hand, was delighted with at least some of the changes in possibilities for school. She had been able to enroll Liuba into a school that allowed children to have a variety of programs, including the opportunity for children to learn by responding to questions, rather than being told what to do or think. This was something unheard of in Soviet times, and currently only found in three schools in Obninsk. The downside, however, was that the school was private, and charged fees, again something that was not the case in the Soviet Union. She believed that the advantages of the new approach to teaching far outweighed the disadvantages of cost, however. Vera's mother, a working-class woman, was also delighted by the changes, insofar as they affected Vera's schooling. She really liked the fact that the school had "modernized." She continued:

There are very many new programs, teaching aids, textbooks. We used to have one textbook in each subject, one for all the schools in the whole country. Few additional aids could be bought in bookstores. Now we have bought tons of aids and are using them all the time.

However, when asked what she worried about, she replied:

We are worried about the rampancy of crime. Drug addiction, AIDS are so widely spread now. We keep warning her about all this, tell her about such things, tell her about real incidents, so that she understands well all kinds of dangers.

Tartu, Estonia

The main way to get to Tartu is by road, a journey of a little less than two and a half hours by express bus from Tallinn, 180 kilometers to the northwest. It used to be possible to arrive there also by rail, either from Tallinn or from Moscow (an overnight journey of about 16 hours), but in 2000, the rail link was halted. Nowadays the journey is exclusively by bus, car, or truck, and the road is typically busy, with many new cars of Western manufacture, as well as older cars, both from the West and Soviet-made.

About five minutes after leaving the bus station in Tallinn, you're already in open countryside, and for about 20 kilometers the bus speeds along a new two-lane road, before it becomes just a single lane in each direction. You go past small copses, as well as more heavily wooded areas, a lot of agricultural land with small settlements, most with two-story buildings, made of wood, concrete, or cinder block with steeply pointed roofs covered with *eternit* (a type of tile that comes in large corrugated slabs, recently declared by the European Union to be bad for the health, as it's made partially with asbestos). Cows, sheep, and the occasional pairs of storks can be seen along the way. The earth looks good; it's black, unlike the red soil of Greensboro or Obninsk. You go past a few small villages, as well as the larger towns of Paide, about half way to Tartu, and Põltsamaa, the ancient capital of Estonia, about 60 kilometers from Tartu.

After crossing the old Tallinn–Tartu railway line, you are almost immediately in Tartu, with the agricultural university on the right. On the left, just outside the city boundary, is an ironic reminder of Soviet times; there's a high wall, rather more attractive than the one that used to be there, behind which are no longer the houses reserved exclusively for the Soviet military. Instead, there are large and opulent homes, the property of those who have become very wealthy since Estonian independence.

The city, of approximately 100,000 inhabitants, is an old one (the first recorded reference stemming from 1030), founded on the banks of the Emajögi River. The University of Tartu was founded in 1632 and is the pre-eminent institution of higher education in Estonia. Besides the agricultural university, the city also had a teacher training college when we began our research, although this has since been incorporated into the university. In addition to education, the main work is primarily in light industry, for the city boasts a brewery, sawmill, the production of furniture, plastics, footwear, and leather goods, as well as enterprises that produce concrete building materials, car parts, and light engineering (primarily in a factory once devoted, during Soviet times, to the making of the "black boxes" for civil and military planes and to other, more secret, components, but now manufacturing mostly telecommunications equipment).

Ethnically, the city is approximately 75% Estonian, with close to 20% being of Russian ethnicity. Middle-class families are found in both groups, although a larger proportion of Russians are working class, many of whom (particularly those who were adults when the Soviet Union collapsed) spoke little or no Estonian at the time of data collection. This is of some significance, because those who don't speak Estonian are not eligible to become Estonian citizens. During the Soviet period, many workers were brought from Russia, partly as a way of "leavening" the population, partly to work in the new factories that were built. In Soviet times, the city also had a large army base, which explains why the city was closed to foreigners.

The city is formally divided into 12 separate areas, but the clearest to distinguish are those in the heart of the city, close to the river, where the town hall and university are situated, and where older single- and joint-family dwellings (many of which are wooden) are to be found. Another area, north of the river, consists almost entirely of large apartment complexes, predominantly either five or nine stories high, built in the Soviet era. There are also a number of areas south of the center that have many old single-family dwellings, as well as new houses that are currently being built. As is the case in Obninsk, and quite unlike the situation in Greensboro in the 1990s, there used to be no clear division between areas of the city in terms of the inhabitants' occupations; factory workers and doctors were likely to live next to one another and were as likely to be found in the rather unattractive apartment complexes as in the architecturally more interesting new houses. Over the past few years, however, during which Estonia has seen education and occupation differences increasingly related to variations in income, many of the wealthier families have moved from the apartment complexes into new homes. These families are predominantly, although not exclusively, middle class, and tend to be ethnically Estonian rather than Russian.

As was the case in Greensboro, two areas of the city were selected, one of which consists solely of apartment complexes and the other from an area of single-family houses, both new and old. Each area is smaller than its Greensboro equivalents, approximately 1 square kilometer, but with a similar or higher density of families. Each area was bounded by large roads or by the river. Families were located from the birth records, as was the case in Greensboro. Workers at the local ministry supplied names and addresses and occasionally some basic demographic details (such as educational level) of families living in the relevant streets and with children of the approximate age. Of the 34 families who were contacted, 67% agreed to participate, from which 20 families were selected, equally divided by social class. All families were of Estonian ethnicity. As was the case in Obninsk, at the time that we observed the children the families were clearly differentiated by educational level and by occupational status, but were not differentiated by income.

Veeriku is an area of the city that has seen the addition of many new houses since the 1980s, in a huge variety of styles. One, for example, has three stories, windows everywhere, light pouring in and making vivid the stained glass work that the man of the house creates. The pale wood floors that have been laid down intensify the impression of brightness. Other houses do not look as attractive from the outside but have been furnished with a lot of care and attention, with large and spacious rooms, children's rooms with places for books, toys, computers, and so on. Some of the houses have little space for gardens, whereas others have more but still comparatively little by U.S. middle-class standards in similarly sized towns. Many of the side roads in Veeriku have been paved during the past decade, but at the turn of the century, there were still several that were unpaved sandy roads, with large puddles during rainy days.

The other area is named Annelinn. Much of the area was built in the 1970s and 1980s and features large apartment complexes around central grassy areas with some metal climbing frames and swings for children, and the occasional sandbox. The Soviet authorities built many of the blocks to house workers, particularly those Russian workers who were brought into Tartu, but others were built as "cooperatives" by Estonians, paid for by themselves, as the easiest way, during the 1980s, to own their own apartment. An alternative was simply to wait to be allotted an apartment, and many Estonians (including the last two rectors of the university) did just that, after having lived for years with parents or in student dormitories. From outside, the appearance cannot be described as attractive; large and rectangular in shape, they have none of the little architectural details (curved buildings, various colored bricks, archways, and so on) that grace many of the blocks in Obninsk.

The insides of the apartments, however, are in many cases attractive. Typically they are small, by comparison to apartments in the United States, two- or three-room apartments, one of which is the main room for entertaining guests and which typically includes a music system, sofas and comfortable chairs, a television, and so on. Some of the apartments feature a large Soviet-style glass- and wood-fronted cupboard, with china, glasses, books, souvenirs, and the like, and some have a computer desk. Many of the apartments have been extensively and nicely renovated inside, with hardwood floors installed, fresh paint, altered so that the straight lines that feature from the outside have been softened by the judicious use of arches and well-placed lighting. In all the homes, the norm is to remove outside shoes; inside the homes people either go barefoot or wear light slippers, as in Obninsk.

The changes that arrived with independence were at least as profound as those affecting the families in Obninsk. In general terms, it is possible to say that Estonia is one of, if not the most, successful of the newly independent states, and economically the changes are clearly noticeable. The successes have not been equally felt by all sections of Estonian society, however. In general, those who live in cities such as Tallinn and Tartu have profited from the changes far more than those living in the countryside, but both urban and rural areas have seen clear divisions into those labeled "winners" and those who are "losers" from the dramatic changes during the 1990s (Narusk & Hansson, 1999). During the early 1990s, when we were collecting our data, no fewer than 75% of the Estonians who participated in the "Estonia 93" survey said that the single biggest problem was the lack of money, perhaps not surprisingly given that consumer prices tripled in the four years following independence while incomes stayed low. During the same period, life expectancy dropped whereas the mortality and divorce rates both rose (Narusk & Hansson, 1999). The situation was most difficult for those with limited education, single parents (or those families in which only one member had a job), and families with large numbers of children. Whereas in the Soviet era, these families felt themselves to be in a secure and stable situation, the change to a free-market economy found them in dire straits.

The same problem that I noted in regard to Obninsk was found in Tartu, where no longer did the parents have access to virtually free child care during all but the summer months. There were countervailing advantages, however, and families that could afford to send their children to private preschools were happy with the changes. Nonetheless, as in Obninsk, only a few of the children attended preschool during the times that we were collecting data. Schools, too, have changed dramatically, and many of the parents commented on the spirit of competitiveness that emerged in the years following independence. This is particularly true for the schools that have come to be "elite" schools, those that accept children only after an interview and that are seen by many as catering only to middle-class families. As Olev's mother, a middle-class woman who worked as a teacher, commented a few years after we observed her son:

I think that the competition, this ranking is totally new for us nowadays. Even in [the] first class everybody already has been ranked. The children knew already for a long time that in spring they have to take tests. Not all the children could tolerate that stress; their results were poor. . . . But there is also another type of ranking. I think that its background or origin is the child's family and the overall ranking in our society.

Tiia's father, a working-class man, was another of many who commented on the newly arrived divisions among groups:

The stratification starts very early, not during the whole life span, but right from the early childhood. Those who have more possibilities can provide to their children more options. In other families children feel already very early, that the family cannot afford them such possibilities. I feel that in these years almost everything has changed quite suddenly. I cannot explain it in word; I have a feeling. . . . This is a label of our time – the whole environment has changed – all those glittering toys. All these items made of artificial material; these are not for me. These are external things, but they are the signs of this changing time.

Growing up in societies such as Russia and Estonia, where profound social changes occurred so rapidly, cannot help but have an impact on how children, and everyone else in the family, develops (Tudge, Tammeveski et al., 2001).

Oulu, Finland

Oulu is situated a little more than 600 kilometers north of Helsinki, close to the northernmost end of the Gulf of Bothnia, about 200 kilometers below the arctic circle. The city was founded in the early 17th century and is now home to 120,000 inhabitants. In the past, the city derived its economic importance from tar, when Oulu was the world's largest producer of the material used to seal the wooden hulls of ships. Its dominance in that area came to an end at the beginning of the 20th century, both as a result of changes in the ship-building business and a disastrous fire in 1901 in which 15,000 barrels of tar burned. A century later the city has a far more "high-tech" feel. Nokia, the telecommunications giant, has its home in Oulu, and there are a host of smaller companies that work in the same field, supporting Nokia, and medical and biotechnological enterprises are also present. Oulu also boasts a major university, with 13,000 students, as well as a polytechnical college where students with a more applied focus can study. Oulu hasn't forgotten its history in basic manufacturing, however, and not far from the city is one of the largest paper mills in Europe, as well as a large chemicals plant.

The trip from the capital takes about an hour by air or slightly more than six and a half hours by train, a more leisurely way to arrive in the city, taking you past innumerable forests, across rivers and by lakes, with occasional views of isolated farms, small settlements, and larger town. Arriving in summer, the sun is still shining as the train pulls into the station after 10:30 at night; during the winter, it's already dark by 3:00 in the afternoon, and as you leave the station, your boots squeak on the dry snow.

The city is a mix of old and new. Brand new apartment blocks have been built facing the small harbor that's at the center of the city, at the mouth of the Oulujoki River. Next to them are beautifully renovated warehouses built more than a century ago, and in many parts of the central area of the city, you can see examples of the old wooden architecture from the same period. Somewhat surprisingly, to an outsider's gaze, despite Oulu's northern location it has thousands of bicycles, and one of the best cycling paths in Finland. Snow on the ground does not seem to stop a proportion of the hardiest souls, but, during the warmer weather, bikes are everywhere.

Unlike the situation in Greensboro, Suwon, and Kisumu, it's not possible to find many clearly defined areas of the city that are homogeneous in terms of social class. Class-based differentials in disposable income are not as great in Finland as in many areas of the world, a feature it shares with Estonia and Russia, although the reason in Finland stems from its approach to taxation rather than Soviet ideology, the effects of which can still be felt in the other two countries. However, we were able to locate two areas of the city that were relatively distinct in terms of the type of housing and the social class background of the families.

Having decided on the areas, the local government records office was able to provide us with the names and addresses of all families in the areas who had a child of the correct age. Following an introductory letter, Marikaisa Kontio conducted the initial phone interview to make sure that the families met our education and occupation requirements. As in the other cities, the participants who lived in the "working-class" area had to consist of parents who had not attended college or university and whose occupation was not professional. By contrast, the participants from the "middle-class" area had to consist of parents who had had a college degree (or higher) and whose occupation had to be professional.

A total of 63 families were initially contacted, of whom 37 did not meet our requirements (not clearly middle class or working class by our definitions). Of the 26 that fit our requirements, 18 agreed to participate, or 69%. The families that refused gave reasons such as not having enough time, that they didn't want someone in their home, that they were just about to move, had just participated or were at the same time participating in a study, or "Our family is not one you want to study!" Of the eight families who refused, seven came from the working-class area.

Koskela is in the north of Oulu and is home to a large number of private houses and some small apartment complexes, just two stories high. Most of the houses have several trees close by, and the overall impression is one of trees with houses scattered among them, rather than the other way around. The apartment complexes also have lots of trees, and large open spaces with flowers. We found our middle-class families in this area.

The other area from which we recruited is called Rajakylä and is also in the north of the city. Unlike many areas of the city, this one is dominated by a number of large apartment complexes, although there are also some small private houses as well as the type of low-rise apartments found in Koskela. The apartments also have large open spaces between them, equipped with climbing frames, sand pits, and other things for children. The overall impression is less favorable than that seen in Koskela, with its many trees, flowers, and more generous space. We recruited our working-class families from this area.

The main difference between the two sets of homes was that the majority of the working-class families lived in apartments in one of several high-rise apartment complexes. The remainder lived in small "low-rise" complexes. In the middle-class area, some families lived in similar low-rise apartment buildings, although the remainder lived in private houses. This sense of privacy, of space between your family and those around, is important to Finns, and it is thus not surprising that in the few years since the observations were completed, all of our working-class families have moved to other areas of the city, primarily because this enabled them to move into their own house. Several of the middle-class families have also moved, also either into a larger house or one with more space around it.

No matter how much space a family has, connection with the outdoors is of great importance. In a high-rise building, this means having plants on the balcony and windows open whenever possible. A garden is always valued, whether outside an apartment or house, and generally it's clear that a great deal of care and attention has been paid to the choice and placement of flowers, bushes, and even (in a few cases) a small pond. In all the houses, the flooring is made either of wood or linoleum with the appearance of wood, and the furniture made of birch or some other light-colored wood, typically with a rug or two.

As is also the case in Tartu and Obninsk, shoes are removed at the door, and inside the home people go barefoot or wear light slippers. The homes themselves are larger than those in the other two cities, typically ranging from 50 to 80 square meters, and have to conform to a minimum standard, established in the late 1940s. Most of the homes thus had two or three bedrooms, as well as a living room and kitchen. All of the homes had a television, and it's typical for the kitchens to be equipped with a regular oven, microwave, refrigerator–freezer, and often a dishwasher. In common with the homes in Tartu and Obninsk, they also have a special cupboard above the sink, where freshly washed dishes are put to drip-dry. Finally, and unlike the other northeastern European homes, all families have access to a sauna, either in their house or apartment or, in the case of the families living in the high-rise complexes, a communal sauna in the basement.

For Finland, the collapse of the Soviet Union has had an impact unlike that experienced in either Obninsk or Tartu. There were, of course, concerns about what would happen in a country with which they share a long border. By 1996, however, when we were observing the children in Oulu, no dramatic changes in Finnish society had occurred. Estonia, no longer a part of the Soviet Union, had come to be viewed, at the political and economic level, as a new trading partner. The same is true, of course, for Russia, but immediately after the collapse of the Soviet Union there was a sharp decline in trade with Russia, which led to economic difficulties in Finland and an increase in the unemployment level, to about 15%. On the other hand, Nokia, based in Oulu, was starting to take on more workers as its business rapidly expanded, and the price of apartments was still relatively cheap. On the political front, the Social Democratic Party had won power in 1995 and Finland had recently become a member of the European Union.

Another difference between Oulu and the other two cities from this part of the world is the fact that Finns have more disposable income and, particularly given the prevailing standard of living, child care was relatively affordable.

It also, particularly by comparison with the situation in Greensboro, was far more uniform in quality.

THE "DIVERSITY" SOCIETIES

The remaining three cities are from societies that were included in this study to move away from just two regions of the world and provide a sense of the diversity of children's experiences, including one Asian city and two from the majority world. However, I should also note again that the choices of South Korea and Kenya occurred at least in part because I had graduate students from those two countries who were interested in collecting comparative data.

South Korea, to be sure, allows a comparison with another country (Russia) that, at least ideologically, stressed an interdependent (collectivist) approach to life rather than the individualistic approach that, at least ideologically, is one of the hallmarks of the United States. But I have to admit that it's a bit of a stretch to view Korea's interdependent view of life as something as simplistic as collectivism minus the Soviet ideological overlay. If it had not been for Soeun Lee, my doctoral student from Seoul, I would not have gathered equivalent data in Suwon.

The same was true for Kenya. I was happy to be able to have equivalent data from a city there, primarily because it allowed me to look at one side of Kenyan life, specifically urban, featuring both middle-class and working-class families, that has not featured greatly in reports of how children are raised in that country. Had it not been for another doctoral student, Dolphine Odero, however, I would not have had this opportunity. I should stress that I had not visited either of these two countries at the time of writing and rely for these descriptions of the cities and the families on Soeun and Dolphine. In all cases, interpretations of the observations have been greatly informed by discussions with my collaborators, but I am more reliant on their expertise in the cases of Suwon and Kisumu.

Having collected data in one developing society in the Southern Hemisphere, I planned to do the same in one other. Brazil is one other country where I have a good deal of personal experience, having been there at least once a year since 1993, teaching in Brasília, Ribeirão Preto, and Porto Alegre, and I have become close to fluent in Portuguese. I was able to collect data in Porto Alegre thanks to my colleagues Tania Sperb, Cesar Piccinini, and Rita Lopes of the Institute of Psychology that is part of the Federal University of Rio Grande do Sul. I trained Giana Frizzo, a doctoral student, and two recent graduates of the program (Fernanda Marques and Rafael Spinelli) to collect the data from the three-year-olds in that city.

Suwon, South Korea

This town of almost 1 million inhabitants (as of 2003, and approximately 700,000 in 1993 when the data were gathered) is located approximately 70 kilometers from Seoul and is one of the satellite cities around the capital. It has four universities situated within its borders, including the agricultural branch of Seoul National University, and two 2-year colleges. The city has some major industry, including Samsung Electronics and a range of smaller electronics firms. It is an attractive city, situated in and around a range of hills, with its main tourist attraction being Hwaseong Fortress, named a United Nations Educational, Scientific and Cultural Organization (UNESCO) world cultural heritage site in 1997. Because of the tourist trade, the city is home to many hotels, inns, and restaurants. The city has an ancient history and has undergone various name changes since A.D. 475, when it was known as Maehol-Gun; it has been known as Suwon (with varying additions, such as Suwon-Gun) since the early 15th century. It was designated a city in 1949 and the provincial capital in 1967.

As was the case with each of the non-U.S. cities, our intention was to locate families that were the closest equivalent to "middle-class" and "working-class" families in U.S. terms. This translated into choosing two groups of families that were distinguishable in terms of education and occupation in the same manner as in the U.S. groups. This proved to be relatively straightforward in Suwon, where we located two communities. Metan-Dong, from where we recruited our middle-class families, is a newly developed residential area in the east part of the city, with a river running through it and several parks; it is overlooked by a mountain from which the area received its name. Metan-Dong is partitioned into four regions, namely, Metan-1Dong, 2Dong, 3Dong, and 4Dong, and each of these regions is clearly separated from the others by major and minor roads. Samsung Electronics has a large plant in Metan-3Dong, where our middle-class families were observed, but for the most part this area consists of large apartment complexes, and large parks.

Each of the apartment buildings are at least five stories high, and the apartments themselves are large, with three bedrooms, one living room, one combined kitchen and dining area, and one bathroom. They are well furnished with modern household conveniences such as microwave oven, washer, audio and video systems, and so on. When family members enter the apartment they, like their counterparts in the northeastern European cities, remove their outside shoes and walk either barefoot or wear light slippers inside. The children and their families spend most of their leisure time within the apartment complex, each of which has one or two playgrounds featuring slides, swings, seesaws, and jungle gyms.

Wonchen River is close to the apartment complex, and Metan Park is just a 10-minute walk away. The industrial complex that includes Samsung Electronics, Samsung SDI, and Samsung Corning is about a thirty-minute walk from the complex, toward the southeast. Many of the adults who live in these apartments work at Samsung-related factories, and they are highly educated. Others own small businesses or work professionally as engineers, bankers, architects, and so on. Most of the mothers do not work outside of the home, and those who have young children spend much of their time in the company of their children.

The Seryu-Dong area is a working-class area in the south of the city, cut through by a major expressway and also by the Suwon River. Like Metan-Dong, Seryu-Dong is divided into three regions (Seryu-1Dong, 2Dong, and 3Dong), each of which is divided from the others by major roads. The families were all chosen from Seryu-3Dong, where most of the houses are old three- or four-story buildings, many of which are in row-house form. Typically at least 3, but sometimes as many as 10, families share a house. These families are generally low income, and the head of the household usually is a skilled or semiskilled worker who is employed as a taxi or truck driver, salesman, delivery person, heavy equipment operator at construction sites, and so on. All mothers are housewives, but for additional income some also work at home. Doll-making, knitting, and jewelry assembling are some of the work they bring home. The largest employers in the Seryu-Dong area were, at the time of the study, the Daehan transportation and clothing companies.

The homes in Seryu-dong were smaller than those in Matan-dong, usually with only one or two bedrooms and generally without a living room. However, each household usually had a TV at the time we collected the data, as well as a refrigerator, washer, audio, and a microwave oven. In most of the homes, the bathroom and kitchen facilities were well equipped, although small. People went barefooted or wore slippers in the home. There were no parks or playgrounds in the neighborhood, and children often played in the streets without adult guidance, although there was a public playground some three or four blocks away from the area.

A small agricultural field still exists in Seryu-dong, called Andognae, where farmers grow organic vegetables. Daehan Tongwoon, a major moving and transportation company in Korea, and the Suwon factory of Daehan Clothing Company were located nearby, but there was no other major industrial complex like those in Matan-dong. A local Korean Air Force airport was situated toward the southeast.

Inspection of birth records was not possible in Suwon, and so we contacted community representatives who had detailed information about the people residing in the community. They helped us to locate potential participants, and screening calls were then made to gain information about parental education and occupation. Families had to meet the same educational and occupational criteria as was the case in Greensboro. Twelve families participated in Suwon, divided equally by community and gender. However, recruitment was far more difficult in Suwon than in the other cities. Of 36 families who were contacted in the middle-class community, 13 (36%) were willing to participate, but seven of the children were enrolled in preschools that did not permit observations. All had college degrees and, as noted above, all fathers worked in the professional sphere. In the working-class community, 16 families were contacted, of whom 7 (44%) were willing to participate, but one was enrolled in a preschool that did not permit observations. None of the working-class parents had completed a college education, and all fathers had traditional working-class jobs.

In the past, Korean families did not commonly use child care, although this has changed somewhat in the past decade or so, and Korean children are now more likely to spend at least some time in a child-care setting. The fact that so few of our children were observed in preschool was not, however, because children were not enrolled but, as noted earlier, because we were not given permission to observe eight children who were enrolled in preschool. Suwon, therefore, is one city in which we are likely to have misrepresented children's experiences, given that we would have had far more observations in preschool if these eight children had been able to participate in the study.

Kisumu, Kenya

Kisumu obtained the status of a city in 2001, is the third largest urban area in Kenya (with a population of a little over 200,000), and is situated about 300 miles (500 kilometers) from Nairobi on the shores of Lake Victoria. The town was founded in 1901, originally with the name Port Florence, and achieved the status of Municipal Council in 1960. It is the major administrative, commercial, and industrial center for Western Kenya. Agriculture is the primary industry, with textiles, sugar and molasses production, and fishing also found in the region. Tourist attractions in the area include the wild life (hippos, leopards, hyenas, and impalas can all be found), and Lake Victoria is also a draw for tourists (Odero, 1998). The town is also home to Moseno University, one of five State universities in Kenya. Close to Lake Victoria, the city has asphalt roads and six- or eight-story buildings, with a bustle of cars and bicycles, but in other areas the roads are gravel or dirt, and one of the main modes of transport is the bicycle taxi.

A number of different ethnic groups live in Kisumu, but the large majority is Luo, the second largest ethnic group (of a total of almost 50) in Kenya. They are descended from pastoralists who had originally moved from Sudan, several centuries ago, and who settled primarily in the area of Lake Victoria. The Luo, traditionally, worshipped their ancestors, and although many were converted to Christianity their religious beliefs still combine both traditional and Christian practices. There is a similar duality of marriage arrangements, with "statutory" (monogamous) marriage going hand-in-hand with "customary" (polygamous) marriage and both are recognized by the Kenyan government (Odero, 1998).

Kenya, as I mentioned in Chapter 2, has been the source for a good deal of the observational data on young children's everyday life. Nyansongo featured as one of the original "Six Cultures," and four other Kenyan communities were included in the "new" samples described by Whiting and Edwards (1988). Of these five communities, however, only one (studied by Weisner) was partially set within an urban setting, another (Ngecha) close to Nairobi, and the remaining three were rural. This has contributed to the view of children's development in Kenya as having little to do with schooling and much more to do with learning traditional tasks (primarily agricultural) alongside siblings or mothers.

However, Kenya has changed a great deal since the LeVines (1963) gathered data in Nyansongo. Following independence in 1963, the Kenyan state promised free primary education to all, a decade later abolished all school fees for the first four years of school, and by the mid-1970s almost 80% of the children were enrolled in primary school. This is particularly impressive when we realize that not until the 1940s was it considered appropriate for girls to attend school (Whiting, 1996). The number who move on to secondary school is currently far less and is partially based on examination results in primary school (although girls are far less likely than boys to move on to secondary school regardless of examination scores). "The result is a highly expanded educational system that rivals those in the most industrialized countries in terms of its complexity and competitiveness" (Buchmann, 2000, p. 1350). Schooling is seen as the path to success, although there is as much evidence of unemployed or poorly employed school graduates as there is of those who have attained employment appropriate to their level of education, thanks to the rather slow economic growth. Kenya, in other words, cannot be thought of as an exclusively rural setting in which either parents or children have no schooling.

During the period in which we gathered data in Kisumu, Kenya was going through a difficult time economically, in part because of demands placed on the country by the International Monetary Fund and the World Bank. When Daniel Arap Moi's government did not meet those demands, funding was stopped. Other donors had also cut or withdrawn funding because of the perception of rampant corruption. For these reasons, unemployment increased dramatically at the same time that utilities increased in price. The situation was further hurt by the drought and famine that was occurring in parts of the country.

Kisumu is divided into "estates," each of which are approximately 1 square kilometer in size. The estates are differentiated by social class, with some estates having larger and better-appointed houses or apartments and being home primarily to families with college education and professional occupations, whereas other estates feature smaller and simpler residences and are occupied by working-class or poor families.

Families were recruited primarily through the local office of birth records. We initially tried to contact the parents of all 30 children who had been born two to three years earlier in five estates (three middle-class estates and two working-class estates). In the middle-class community 7 of 16 families had relocated; of the remaining 9 families, 6 agreed to participate (67% acceptance). In the working-class community, 9 of the 14 families who had had a child three years earlier had already left the area, but the remaining five families agreed to participate (100% acceptance). Eleven other families (four middle class and seven working class) were contacted by "snowball" methods, with information on the presence of these families being provided by families who had already agreed to participate. Two of the working-class families that were approached in this manner declined to participate, but the remainder was happy to do so. A total of 20 families, equally divided by social class, were thus included in the study.

In the middle-class group, all mothers and fathers had had at least some college education, and some had a graduate degree. Fathers' occupations included university lecturer, sales manager, public administrator, and owner of a travel agency. All of the middle-class mothers worked outside the home, with occupations such as high school teacher, registered nurse, and nutritionist. The houses in which they lived were much larger than those of the working-class families, having between three and five bedrooms, two or more bathrooms, in addition to a living room and kitchen. The rooms have a mixture of carpets and tiles on the floors, and paintings of scenic views are most likely to be found on the walls. The houses were on their own lots of between a quarter acre and 1 acre, typically behind a fence. The children thus had a lot of room to play, but it was not easy for them to interact with children from neighboring houses because of the fences between them. Mostly, then, the children played with their siblings or with friends who had been invited over to play. Of the 10 middle-class families, 5 rented their homes and 5 had purchased the land and built the houses.

The working-class fathers were primarily skilled and semiskilled manual laborers, and had jobs such as plumber, pipe fitter, store clerk, and messenger. None of the mothers worked outside the home, with the exception of one who had a job as clerk, but all of them engaged in some type of subsistence selling (vegetables, fruit, bread, etc.) to supplement the family income. One of the fathers had had some college education, but in the remainder of cases the level of education ranged from primary education to the completion of high school.

The working-class families who participated in our study mostly lived in houses that had one or two bedrooms, a living room, and bathroom. Larger families in these estates often have the older children sleeping in the living room (or sometimes in the kitchen), whereas the younger ones sleep with their parents in the bedroom. The floors tend to be of cement, with no covering, and the walls feature family pictures, calendars, and sometimes cuttings from the newspapers (Odero, 1998). Eight of the ten working-class families shared bathrooms that were built outside the houses, and they also had to fetch water from a well in the center of the estate. Three of the families did not have electricity and relied on lanterns. These families shared compounds with their neighbors, and only in two cases did houses have any type of fence. This meant that children were free to mingle with the other children in the compound, playing one minute in and around their own home, and the next in another child's home.

All families were ethnic Luo, and all but two were monogamous. The two children who were from polygamous families were both working class and lived in different sections of town with their mothers. Fathers in polygamous families divided their time between the wives' households, although one of these fathers spent the majority of his time with the family that included the child who was being observed, because this child was the only male child that he had with either wife. The middle-class families tended to be smaller (one–four children) than were those of working-class background (two–seven children).

The experiences of the two groups of children were also different in that the middle-class children all attended some type of private preschool, which were well equipped with commercially made learning and play equipment.

These children spent their weekends going to the lake, a museum, shopping with parents, or taking swimming lessons (seven of them did that). Most of the working-class children did not attend any preschool, and those who did went to community schools in which the play things were made from locally available materials (for example, a doll made from banana leaves, a car made from cans of juice with bottle tops for wheels). These children also went shopping, but they, unlike their middle-class peers, went alone or with other children, to buy something for the family.

Porto Alegre, Brazil

Porto Alegre is the largest of the cities in which we have collected data. It has close to 1.4 million inhabitants and is the capital city of the southernmost state in Brazil, Rio Grande do Sul. The first inhabitants of the area on which the city now stands were indigenous, but the first known village at the current site was founded in 1742 by the Portuguese, who encouraged settlers from the Azores Islands to come to southern Brazil to help secure the area for the Portuguese, who were fighting for control with the Spanish. The village grew and went through a series of name changes until people decided on Porto Alegre ("Happy Port") because it is situated on the banks of what is referred to as the river Guaíba although it is in fact part of a huge lake. Porto Alegre soon became the capital of the state and was named a city in 1822 following Brazilian independence.

Immigrants were eagerly sought after in the 19th century, and as a result, the city is now home to descendents of Portuguese, Italians, and Germans, although most people in the city are now a complex blend of different racial/ethnic groups. The state has sometimes had mixed feelings about being a part of Brazil, fighting for a decade during the late 19th century to be independent. The population of Porto Alegre was strongly opposed to the military dictatorship, imposed in 1964 and lasting a little over 20 years, and was the first major city in Brazil to have a Workers Party (PT) government. However, in the years in which Brazil first elected and then reelected a PT candidate to be president (Luiz Inácio Lula da Silva, universally known simply as Lula), Porto Alegre chose candidates from center-right parties.

Descendents of the indigenous population are found in Porto Alegre, but they constitute an extremely small minority, and people who, in the United States, would be considered Black are only a small minority, although skin color encompasses a large variety of shades in Brazil. As in Kisumu, however, the city features a wide range of contrasts. Many people are wealthy enough to frequent the large shopping centers filled with fine restaurants and boutiques with fashionable clothes. They drive to these centers in expensive cars – but encounter the poor of the city along the way, passing horse-drawn carts that collect recyclable trash and sometimes encountering at traffic lights children who juggle or offer to wash windshields and then ask for money. The city is clearly divided by social class, with communities of middle-class apartment complexes (all enclosed within tall metal fences and securely locked gates, typically patrolled by security guards) situated in fairly close proximity to much poorer neighborhoods and slums (known as *vilas*), mostly with small houses in close proximity. However, Porto Alegre is in a state that, in common with its neighbors in the south and southeast of the country, is economically advanced by the standards of the rest of the country, and the differences between rich and poor in Porto Alegre are not as marked as they are elsewhere (Rebhun, 2005).

Not only is the city considerably larger than the other cities from which we have gathered data, but the way in which the families were recruited for the study was also different. In Porto Alegre, working with colleagues who had interest and expertise in the transition to parenthood and infancy, we planned a longitudinal study starting before the birth of the parents' first child, and designed to follow the families at least until the children reached three years of age, when the observational part of the study could begin (Piccinini, Tudge, Lopes, & Sperb, 1998).

A total of 81 families were originally recruited from Porto Alegre, with expectant mothers contacted at hospitals and prenatal clinics in their third trimester of pregnancy. All parents who wished to participate were interviewed before the birth of their child. Unlike the recruitment from other cities, no effort was made to recruit from areas of this city that were exclusively middle class or working class but rather to recruit from a variety of families, including those who were very poor and those who were extremely well-off.

Most of the families were interviewed and observed (although only briefly, to examine mother–baby and father–baby interaction styles) again when the child was 3 months, 8 months, and at 12, 18, and 24 months. By the time that we were ready to start data collection at three years, nine of the families had decided that they no longer wanted to participate in the study. One child died soon after birth, and we lost a further 14 families because they moved and left no details of their new address or phone number (in Brazil, when a person moves, even within the same neighborhood, he or she is assigned a different phone number).

We were therefore left with 57 families with a child of three years of whom some families fit the same educational and occupational criteria as the middle-class families from the other cities, many families who fit the same criteria as the working-class families from the other cities, and a smaller number of families whose educational and occupational situation did not fall easily into either category. From this group we selected 9 of the middle-class families, 11 of the clearly working-class families, and 5 of the mixed families for the typical intensive observation and subsequent interviews (although the data from families that were neither clearly middle nor working class will not be included in the chapters that follow). The remaining families were interviewed but only observed for 2 hours, and their data also do not feature in this book.

Families in the study came from many areas of the city, and one family from an adjoining town. As is true for all cities apart from Obninsk, Tartu, and Oulu, Porto Alegre has some clearly defined middle-class areas, as well as some areas that consist almost entirely of places where much poorer families live. However, many areas of the city are mixed, featuring a mixture of large and expensive houses, apartment complexes (some clearly designed for middle-class families and others for working-class families), small wooden or concrete-block houses for working-class families, and various and sundry shops and businesses. The city is hilly, with many families, both the rich and the poor, having access to some beautiful views, particularly over the river.

The middle-class participants were fairly evenly divided between those who lived in apartment complexes or condominiums and those who lived in houses. Each of their homes featured two to three bedrooms, as well as a large living room with dining area, kitchen, and laundry area, often a separate room for a maid (all families employed a maid, at least on a part-time basis, and in some cases the maid lived with the family). As is typical in contemporary Brazilian cities, these middle-class homes and apartments were surrounded by large fences, kept locked at all times, and many with a porter or guard to ensure that only residents or people invited in gain admittance. Most complexes have swimming pools or a place for children to play, as well as communal areas for social events.

Almost all of our working-class families lived in small houses that were completely lacking the tight security of the middle-class homes, although generally with a small wall that provided some privacy. Some of the houses were clustered together behind a wall or fence. They typically consisted of just a single room for sleeping – in one house, for example, the mother and child slept together in a single bed, with the father's mother sleeping on a small sofa in the living room. The father worked at night, and so used the bed during the day. The remaining rooms are the kitchen and bathroom with shower and toilet. The floors of these houses are typically made of concrete, finished with wood, and the concrete or wooden walls generally are painted and with few if any pictures.

Despite the clear differences in the physical settings inhabited by our middle- and working-class children every home, without exception, had a large television set, most with cable and videocassette deck and CD player. All of the children had large numbers of toys with which to play, and although the middle-class homes had more books, each working-class home featured a number of children's books, as well as child-oriented videos (including the omnipresent Xuxa, doyen of children's television).

CONCLUSION

It should be clear, then, that each of these cities is different in many ways, and there are also some obvious differences in the types of homes in which our families lived. Nonetheless, there are also some marked similarities – far more than would be found if we had done what many others have done, namely, compare a cultural group from an urban center from some part of the industrialized world with one or more other groups living in rural areas in the majority world. As I've mentioned before, such research is fine for showing the wide range of different ways in which children can be raised, the values, beliefs, and practices of the parents, and so on. However, as Hallpike (2004), Bornstein and his colleagues (Bornstein, Tal, & Tamis-LeMonda, 1991; Bornstein et al., 1998), and others have pointed out this process of "maximizing the differences" leads both to exaggerating some types of cultural differences and also to a failure to recognize the cultural differences that exist even when "like is compared with like" (Hallpike, 2004, p. 14).

The next question to turn to is thus the extent to which we found cultural differences in the types of settings and activities to which the children in our study were exposed, in the types of activities and interactions the children engaged, and in the types of partners with whom they interacted. These questions are answered in the following two chapters.

6   Everyday Activities

Our deeds determine us, as much as we determine our deeds.

George Eliot, *Adam Bede*, 1859/1981, p. 359

Over the course of Chapters 3 and 4, I discussed the nature of cultural–ecological theory and the associated methods that my colleagues and I used to collect our data on young children's everyday activities. The goal of this chapter is to describe the main activities in which the children were involved (play, lessons, conversation, and work), describing various types of each of these activities, how they varied both across the different cities and by social class within each city, and race and class in the case of Greensboro. It will also become apparent that at least some of the variation in the extent to which the children were involved in activities can only be explained by individual differences among the children themselves; in each group, some of the children were far more involved in certain of the activities than were others. In part, as I'll show, this can be explained by the children taking a more or less active lead in starting particular activities.

FOCAL AND NONFOCAL ACTIVITIES

As I pointed out in Chapter 4, we distinguished between the activities on which we wanted to focus our attention (focal activities) and those that were less important to us, and which we termed "nonfocal activities." In all societies children spend a good part of the time in these nonfocal activities, sleeping, eating, being cared for, and so on. Almost one third of the observations, across all groups, featured one or other of these nonfocal activities, with the children sleeping in about 8% of the observations, eating on almost 12% of the occasions, and being dressed or bathed in about 7% of the observations. On a further 5% of our observations, the children were either observed apparently doing nothing at all, or we were not able to code what it was that they were doing (interacting with the observer, out of sight, and so on). I won't discuss these activities further but concentrate on those activities that were the focus of attention.

As discussed in Chapter 4, we chose to break down these focal activities into four major categories, with numerous subcategories. There are, of course, other ways in which children's activities can be divided, but we thought that it made sense to examine separately lessons, work, play, and conversation. This division allows us to look at deliberate attempts to impart (or request) information about the world and how it works – the lessons that children may receive or ask for. Watching someone else work, or being involved in work, is a wonderful way in which to learn skills, but it is conceptually important to be able to distinguish between the deliberate attempt to provide information in a verbal form (a lesson, as we defined it) and learning the same skill in the course of engaging in work without any explicit lesson. Charlie, for example, helping his mother lay the table, may well be learning one-to-one correspondence, but in a manner quite different from Nadia being given a lesson on counting. A good deal of previous research, some of which I discussed in Chapter 2, strongly suggested that cultures in which there is a lot of verbal interaction between adult and child are likely to see a good deal more didactic lessons, whereas other cultures (particularly those in the majority world) should exhibit more in the way of children's observation and participation with little or no verbal interaction. It will be interesting to see whether this type of variation is found in our data.

Similarly, children learn a great deal about the world in the course of their play. However, there's a difference between engaging in some activity that is designed to be helpful (making things to sell, helping to clean the house, repairing things, and so on) and pretending to "clean house" in the dressing-up area of a child-care center or using a child's set of tools to "build a house." The distinguishing characteristic between work and play is not a matter of whether the activity is enjoyable; both children and adults may enjoy helping to cook, repairing something, or going shopping. Play, for children and adults alike, can be a terribly serious business. However, we wanted to distinguish between activities that were being engaged in primarily for fun (those that we called play) and those whose primary intent appeared to be to contribute in some way to the running of the house (work).

As I mentioned in Chapter 4, I also thought it helpful to pay particular attention to the type of language that involves distancing from the here and now, given that in some societies at least, this type of language is viewed as being more sophisticated and more helpful to children's subsequent performance in school than is talk that is simply an accompaniment to the current activity. It's this more sophisticated type of language use that we termed conversation.

We will thus be able to gauge whether, as many authors (e.g., Rogoff, 2003) have argued, White middle-class children in the United States engage to a greater extent than other children in activities that involve a good deal of language (lessons and conversations) or whether their engagement in this type of language is relatively common in many schooled societies. Similarly, we will see whether children in Kenya, as discussed in Chapter 2, spend far more of their time engaged in work and far less of their time conversing with adults than is the case in various countries from the industrialized world.

AVAILABILITY OF AND PARTICIPATION IN ACTIVITIES

I first examine variations in the extent to which these activities were available to the children in each city. I think that participation in activities is of far more consequence than simple availability, because children become drawn into their cultural group because of the activities in which they participate. However, their participation depends in part on the activities that are going on around them; it's difficult to watch television in a culture that does not use electricity, and it's difficult to develop much expertise in looking after crops if one lives in an apartment complex in the middle of a metropolis.

Members of cultures try to draw their children into those activities that they feel are appropriate for them and therefore make some activities more available than others. If members of one group think that it's important for children to see their parents working at the tasks that the children themselves will be expected to do once they have become adults themselves, it should not surprise anyone to find that the adults expose their children to these types of jobs and encourage their children to attend to them. On the other hand, activities can be available to children without the children paying any attention to them. Alternatively, an activity can be available and of interest to a child, but the people engaging in that activity might not want the child to participate in it.

It is also the case that activities become available to children because they themselves start the activities. For example, Sandra (all names, have, of course, been changed), one of the working-class African American children in Greensboro, was often around other adults in her mother's beauty salon but was involved in many conversations because she initiated contact with those adults. As we'll see later on, a great deal of the play that was going on around the children occurred because the children themselves initiated it, and many lessons occurred because a child asked a question about how something functioned or what a particular word meant. The extent to which children are engaged in different types of activities is thus related to the cultural group of which they are a part, but they are also clearly involved in changing that context, by initiating many of the activities in which they are involved and engaging others in those activities.

When examining children's development in many parts of the majority world, it's clear that exposure to activities is particularly important, because children get to see the types of activities in which they'll be expected to engage when older. Daughters thus observe mothers weaving long before they're expected to weave, and sons might observe other males herd cows or hunt for small game before they can participate in any more active way in either activity. By contrast, in the industrialized world, children generally do not get to see those activities in which they'll be expected to engage when they have become productive members of society. Instead, they are expected to go to school to learn the skills that will help prepare them for the types of jobs they will eventually take.

This means that there's a separation in the industrialized world between productive work and the skills that children are expected to learn, the major exception being those children who eventually become teachers themselves. Most adult work, at least that work that brings in an income, occurs out of sight of children. What, then, are children in the industrialized world exposed to? What types of activities are available to them on a regular basis, and who do they observe engaging in them? Even if children do not participate in some of the activities that are available to them, they may come to view them as important in the cultural group in which they are being raised. For example, a boy and a girl may see their mother, but not their father, working in the kitchen. In this case, whether either of them participates in that work, they may well be learning that such tasks are women's work. However, more is likely to be learned when they are engaged in that work, either as an active participant or as a close observer of the work that is being performed. Although most of our attention was paid to those activities in which the children were engaged, either as participant or observer, I first discuss the relation between availability of and engagement in each of the four focal activities.

Play

I start with play, which was the activity that was most often available to the children (in approximately two thirds of all of our observations) and,

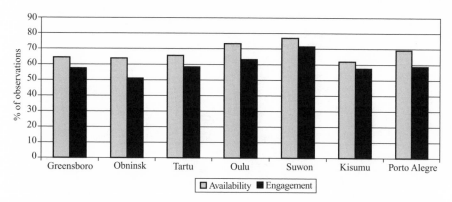

Figure 6.1. Availability of and engagement in play.

not surprisingly given the age of the children, the activity that they were most often involved in (almost 60% of all observations, across all groups). When children were playing, by definition play was available to them, but because sometimes play occurred without the children being involved in it, availability is always higher than involvement. What is particularly striking about Figure 6.1 is the relative similarity across all groups in the extent of both availability of and engagement in play, although children in Obninsk were least likely (51%) to be observed in play and those in Suwon the most (71%). By contrast, children were less likely to have available to them, or be involved in, each of the other activities of interest.

Lessons

Across all groups, lessons were only available to the children in about 7% of the observations, and children were involved in them in almost 6% of our observations. However, not only were the children far less involved in lessons than in play, but there was also far greater variability in the different cities. Children in the former Soviet cities of Obninsk and Tartu were exposed to and involved in lessons more than three times more than those in Oulu and Porto Alegre (see Figure 6.2).

Conversation

We also observed a fair amount of variation in the extent to which children were exposed to and involved in conversation. Compared with lessons, in each of the cities, conversations were going on far more often around the children

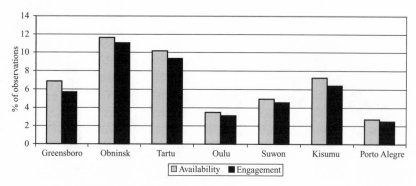

Figure 6.2. Availability of and engagement in lessons.

without any evidence that the children were involved in them, either as active participants or even in the sense of appearing to listen to the conversation that was occurring around them. However, it would be dangerous to be too categorical here; if a child were actively participating in a conversation, this was obviously easy to code. It was more difficult in the case of a child who may or may not have been listening in on a conversation between others. We only coded the latter situation when children showed evidence of attending – looking in the direction of the people speaking, for example – and so it's likely that we have underestimated the extent to which the children were involved. We all know examples of having a conversation around a child who appeared to be paying no attention whatsoever but who later made clear that she had listened to every word.

Be that as it may, the children in Oulu were exposed to conversations far more than were children in the other cities (almost 25% of the observations in Oulu featured some conversation), and they were also the most likely to engage in conversation with others. They were involved in more than twice as many conversations (17% of their observations), as were the children in Suwon and Kisumu (6%–7% of their observations), and almost twice as many as children in Greensboro, Obninsk, Tartu, and Porto Alegre (see Figure 6.3).

Work

The final activity on which we focused was work. Here, as might be expected, we saw the biggest discrepancy between availability and involvement, with work going in many observations around the children when the children were not involved, even to the extent of observing it. Parents cooked, swept the

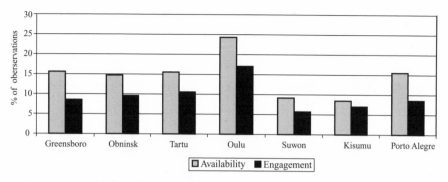

Figure 6.3. Availability of and engagement in conversation.

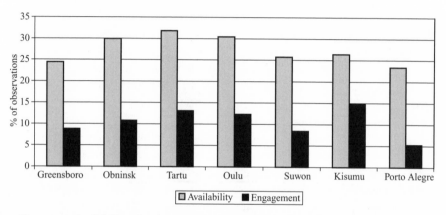

Figure 6.4. Availability of and engagement in work.

floor, mended clothes, and repaired broken objects in easy earshot or eyeshot of the children, and in many instances, the children paid no obvious attention. In all cities except Kisumu, children were involved in work in only about a third of the cases in which work was going on around them. Interestingly, there was not a great deal of variation across the cities in terms of availability of work (between 23% and 32% of the observations), but children in Kisumu were three times more likely to be observed engaging in work than were children in Porto Alegre (see Figure 6.4).

Summary

One clear advantage of the approach that my colleagues and I have taken is that, having used precisely the same methods to collect our data in each of these communities, we can call into question some of the assumptions that have been made in the literature about children's engagement in activities. For example, American children are thought to be exposed to a lot of relatively didactic lessons, certainly in comparison to majority-world children, such as those in Kenya. However, what we saw, by simply following children around and noting the activities going on around them and in which they were involved, is that the children in Greensboro were, if anything, slightly less likely to be involved in these types of lessons than were their counterparts in Kisumu, and far less than their peers in Obninsk and Tartu.

It also is not the case that the American children were clearly more involved in conversation than children in the other cities; although they were somewhat more likely to converse than were their counterparts in Suwon and Kisumu, they were far less likely to be involved in conversation than were their Finnish peers in Oulu. Finally, and contrary to what other researchers have suggested, the children in Kisumu were not more likely to be exposed to work than were children in the other cities, but actually less so than their peers in the three northern European cities. True, they were more likely than children in the other cities to be involved in work, but the differences are far less striking than would have been expected given what appears in the literature.

At this point I want to broaden the discussion, moving beyond simple availability of and engagement in activities, and talk instead about the types of lessons or play in which the children were involved. I'm also going to deal with ethnic and class variations. For reasons discussed in Chapter 4, I chose to study children from a single city in each of the societies in which we conducted this research. In each of the cities, however, we recruited two groups of families, one that I have labeled middle class and one working class (based on education and occupation criteria). In Greensboro, moreover, families from two racial/ethnic groups participated, one in which the families are of European American background and one in which families are of African American background, divided by social class. This attention to within-city heterogeneity allows us to assess the extent to which it is misleading to use White middle-class samples as the source of comparison with the other "cross-cultural" sample or samples, which is the tradition, at least in the United States, among cross-cultural child developmentalists.

To make the discussion of within-activity and within-city variations easier to follow, I'll present the findings separately for the four Greensboro groups (children from middle- and working-class White and Black families), the children from the northeastern European cities of Obninsk, Tartu, and Oulu, and those children from the "diverse" cities of Suwon, Kisumu, and Porto Alegre. I'll continue to provide graphs for each group, because they allow us to see both similarities and variations across the groups. However, it's also important, both for theoretical reasons and to put a human face on the activities, to look at individual children engaged in activities. As one should expect from cultural–ecological theory, development is not a top-down phenomenon in which membership in one or other cultural group determines how children spend their time. Rather, development is a complex interaction of cultural opportunities and children's active desires to make sense of the world in which they find themselves.

ENGAGEMENT IN PLAY (INCLUDING EXPLORATION AND ENTERTAINMENT)

We observed eight types of play, but for ease of graphic representation, I'll split them into two groups. For each group of cities, I'll first talk about playing with toys (objects designed with children in mind, without a clear intent to teach them anything that might be relevant to school), playing with natural objects (sticks, leaves, mud, and so on), playing with no objects (chasing one another, singing, rough-and-tumble play, etc.), and playing with objects that were not designed specifically with children in mind (objects from the world of adults or adolescents). Second, I'll discuss pretend play, playing with academic objects (for example, looking at a book or playing with geometrical shapes), watching television, and engaging in other types of entertainment (listening to the radio, watching some organized sport, etc.).

Greensboro

The clearest differences in the first graph show that these children, in each of the four groups, were much more likely to play with toys (22% of their observations, on average) than be engaged in other types of play. It was also the case that the Black children were more than twice as likely as the White children to play with no objects – that is, to engage in rough-and-tumble play, chase one another, and so on. White middle-class children were also far less likely than the other groups of children to play with objects that were not specifically designed for children (see Figure 6.5).

Focusing on the remaining types of play and entertainment, it is clear that watching television was the activity that the children in Greensboro were observed in second-most frequently (after playing with toys); on average, these children were observed watching TV in almost 12% of the observations. Class differences were also fairly striking, with children from middle-class homes somewhat more likely than those from working-class homes to engage

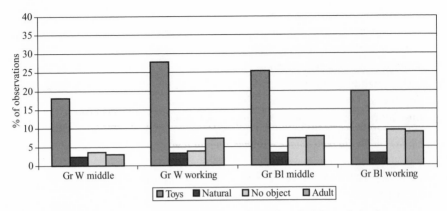

Figure 6.5. Engagement in types of play, Greensboro (by ethnicity and class).

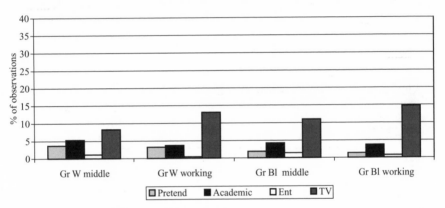

Figure 6.6. Engagement in types of play (continued), Greensboro (by ethnicity and class).

in pretend play and play with academic objects. Working-class children from both White and Black homes were also more likely to watch television than were children from middle-class backgrounds but were less likely to be involved in other types of entertainment (see Figure 6.6).

Averages across groups are somewhat misleading, however, because they disguise the extent of variation within any group. For example, in the White working-class community in Greensboro, Leslie was observed watching television just nine times, whereas another girl, Patty, watched television in a total of 52 of our observations of her (almost one third of the total).

On Thursday morning, when the first observations began, Patty had watched Sesame Street *with her mother for about 30 minutes, and on Friday afternoon is watching cartoons, again with her mother, when the observations start, and the two of them continue watching for about an hour. Patty's mother sews part of the time while they are watching, and Patty points out toys that she'd like during commercial breaks. After a snack, mother and child continue to watch cartoons, until it's time for Patty's bath. On Saturday and Sunday, while we are observing, the TV is on continually, with her mother, father, and grandparents watching various programs (mostly sports, including golf and car racing). Patty watches from time to time, but also plays with her cousins. On Monday morning, as soon as she wakes up Patty begins to watch cartoons with her mother. However, while the TV is still on, Patty asks her mother to read a book with her, and for a while her mother reads and asks Patty about the puppies that are shown in the pictures.*

In the White middle-class community, Brian and Irene only watched TV on two occasions, whereas Georgina and John both were observed watching on 27 occasions. Similar variations were seen in the other types of play; in the middle-class Black community, Brianna played with academic objects on 25 occasions and engaged in pretend play 13 times, whereas Andrew was only twice observed playing with academic objects and was never observed in pretend play.

Brianna is at her child care center, looking at a book and trying to stop a boy from continually handing her other books. A girl comes over and says: "Let's get in the car." Brianna responds: "You have to put on your seatbelts first. Let me go get some money at the money store." A boy tries to sit in her chair and she tries to get him up, and when a girl says that she's going to be the mommy, Brianna tells her "No, I'm the mommy." Then the children start "driving" their car.

Northeastern European Cities

Within this group of cities, children were again far more likely to have been observed playing with toys than any other type of play. It is also clear that children in Tartu and Oulu were more frequently observed engaging in play with objects from the adult world than were those in Obninsk (see Figure 6.7).

Sometimes playing with objects from the adult world occurred when being transported somewhere.

Anneli, a girl from a working-class family in Oulu, went with her mother to collect a friend and the new baby. Anneli, apparently, hadn't brought anything of her own to play or look at, and spends much of the drive playing with a reflecting mirror – at least until the baby's carriage is placed next to her, when she divides her time between playing with the baby and singing along with songs on the car radio.

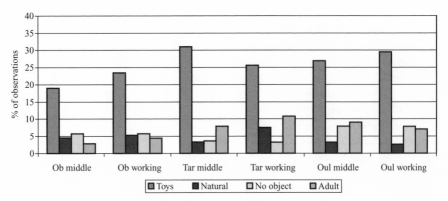

Figure 6.7. Engagement in types of play, northeastern Europe (by class).

On other occasions children played with games that had not been developed with young children in mind but which they found around the home, the property either of a much older sibling or of the parents themselves.

Natasha, from a working-class family in Obninsk, one day found a game of lotto and started playing with it. She asked her mother how to play it, and her mother explained how she had to match the number and the space. Natasha continued to play, on and off, for about 30 minutes, often interrupting her mother to ask whether she had the correct number.

Natasha was observed on one other occasion playing this game, which she appeared to find more interesting than her own toys, and she was eventually observed playing with objects from the adult world on 20 occasions, only slightly less than our observations of her playing with toys.

Children from middle-class homes in each city were more often observed in pretend play than were children from working-class backgrounds, and this social-class difference was also found for playing with academic objects in Tartu and Oulu, though not in Obninsk (see Figure 6.8). The class differences in television watching that were found in most of the other cities were not found in these three. Although the extent of TV watching was not as low as in Kisumu, in each of these cities the children were observed watching much less than in Greensboro, Suwon, and Porto Alegre.

Cities for Diversity

The patterns seen in Greensboro were somewhat similar to those in Suwon and Porto Alegre, with Kisumu providing a different picture. The children in Suwon and Porto Alegre were most likely to have been observed playing

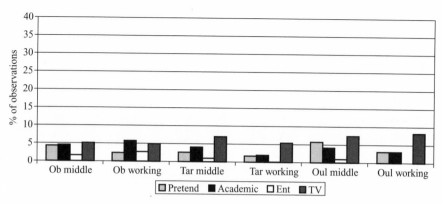

Figure 6.8. Engagement in types of play (continued), northeastern Europe (by class).

with toys far more than with any other type of object. The Luo children in Kisumu were far less likely than children from the other cities to be observed playing with objects that had been designed for use by children (just 12% of the observations). By contrast, they were far more likely than children in the other cities to play with objects from the adult world, and were observed doing so in 16% of the observations (see Figure 6.9).

Luo children were observed playing with Vaseline containers, bottle tops, an old oil bottle, a tube of toothpaste, old cassette tapes, a spice container (Bobbie fought with another child about who would get to play with that), a box of cookies (without eating any of them!), a walking stick, climbing on the fence, and with innumerable other objects from the adult world.

A middle-class boy, Brandon, and another child of roughly the same age move from playing with a car tire (at times Brandon gets to sit, while his friend pulls him around), to swinging around various types of poles, and back to the old tire, pretending to drive a car. But when they start playing with the mirror of Brandon's parents' car an adult appears and tells them to stop. Gesila, a working-class girl, spent approximately 25 minutes playing with her brother, and the things they were playing with were batteries taken from a radio. During one observation Gisela was arranging and ordering the batteries, and in another (during the same period) was counting them.

The objects may have been from the world of adults, but children don't need objects designed either for them or for school to learn mathematical principles!

The children in Kisumu were also far more likely to be observed playing either with objects from the natural world (leaves, branches, clay) or with no objects at all than were the children in the other cities.

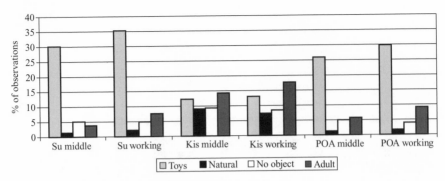

Figure 6.9. Engagement in types of play, diverse cities (by class).

Gisela was playing in her yard with a group of other children. They were climbing a small tree, and invited Gisela to join them. She did so, but between two observation "windows" one of the other children explained to her that they had to take turns, and when she refused the other children left. In the following observation Gisela was still climbing the tree, but alone.

These findings should not come as a surprise, given the findings from earlier research reported in Chapter 2. However, as always, we should examine carefully the within-city data, to see whether the different patterns in types of play were primarily found among the working-class children in Kisumu. We wondered whether the Luo children from different social-class backgrounds in Kisumu might play with different types of objects, but there was little indication that this was the case. Working-class children were slightly more likely to be observed playing with toys (13% vs. 12% of their observations), and although working-class children were more likely than those from middle-class families to be observed playing with objects from the adult world (17.7% vs. 14.3%), they were less likely to be observed playing with natural objects or with nothing at all.

Looking at the remaining types of play, watching television was the second most observed activity in Porto Alegre and among the working-class children in Suwon (see Figure 6.10). Their middle-class Korean counterparts, however, were somewhat more likely to have been observed playing with academic objects – something that in each city middle-class children were more likely to have done than working-class children. Children in Kisumu were much less likely to have been observed watching television than children in the other cities, although this finding cannot be explained simply by the relative absence of television sets in the working-class Kenyan families we observed,

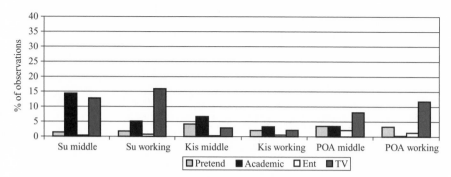

Figure 6.10. Engagement in types of play (continued), diverse cities (by class).

as the middle-class children in Kisumu also watched very little television, despite the fact that their families owned televisions.

As in Greensboro, at least in the White community, and in the northeastern European cities, there were large individual differences in the types of play in which these children engaged. In the middle-class community in Suwon, for example, Sangmin was observed 17 times playing with academic objects, the fewest of all the middle-class Korean children.

In Suwon, Sangmin's mother is reading to him. It's a book about insects, and she's talking about the different types of bugs there are. He'd like to go outside to play, but she tells him: "You can't go outside until you've finished reading the book." They continue reading for the next 10 minutes or so, and during this time some lessons (academic and about the natural world) occur, as for example when she asks her son if he can find the letters in the book that correspond to those in his name and when she explains the difference between a mosquito and a dragonfly. Two older boys come by to play with Sangmin, and one makes a nice link from the book to their intended play, suggesting that they go catch some dragonflies. Interestingly, an hour later, having watched a video and played with some toys, the three boys are outside, trying to catch first a dragonfly and then a butterfly. When he goes back inside, at little later, his mother says: "Now it's time to teach you how to read."

Soeun, a middle-class girl, engaged most often in this type of play (38 times, about 20% of the observations). By contrast, in the working-class community in Suwon, the range was between just one observation and a maximum of 16 (both were boys). In the two other cities in this group, there was also a good deal of variation in these types of play. In the middle-class community in Kisumu, for example, Kenneth was observed in pretend play 23 times and 14 times playing with academic objects, whereas Jeremy was never observed in pretend play, and only seven times with academic objects. In Porto Alegre, in the working-class community, two girls engaged in pretend play on 14 and 28 occasions each, but another eight children were observed only five times or fewer.

Rita, a working-class girl in Porto Alegre, is playing with her younger sister, pretending that she (Rita) is the mother and her sister is her baby. She smacks her, then embraces her tenderly, and offers her a "bottle" to feed from. She's also looking after her pretend dog, cleaning the chair, and putting shoes on her baby. She tries to get her cousin, who lives next door, involved in the play, but her parents, who are in the kitchen, tells the children that they have to stay inside. So instead Rita puts a diaper on her head and says that she's now got long hair.

Summary

It's worth reflecting, at this point, on the fact that although the extent to which the children were engaged in play was rather similar across each of the cities (see Figure 6.1), there were some clear differences in the objects with which children played (or with which they entertained themselves) in the various cities, as well as some interesting social-class differences. The play experiences of the Luo children were different from those of the other children; they were observed far less playing with toys and far more with objects from the natural and adult world than was the case for children in the other cities. Children in Greensboro, Suwon, and Porto Alegre were far more likely than children from the other cities to watch television, and in each case those from working-class backgrounds were more likely to do so than were their middle-class peers. By contrast, middle-class children from each city were more likely to engage in pretend play and to play with academic objects (looking at books, playing with things designed to help them learn about numbers, shapes, etc.) than were their working-class counterparts; this was particularly striking in the case of the middle-class children from Suwon.

It's worth noting, however, that the extent to which the children in our study engaged in pretend play was far less than that reported by Haight and Miller (1993) and described in Chapter 2 (between 8 and 12 minutes per hour, or between 13% and 20% of the time). This may well reflect the fact that these scholars only observed children at home during times when they were not expected to be doing anything other than playing. It's also worth mentioning the fact that social-class differences within a city (Suwon children playing with academic objects, for example) were sometimes far greater than differences across cities. We are thus starting to show the clear importance of examining differences and similarities both across and within societies; within-society heterogeneity, as a function of either class or ethnicity, cannot be ignored.

As noted earlier, the type of play in which children were involved can't be explained simply by reference to the group of which they are a part and to the role of adult members trying to get children to engage in activities considered appropriate, although the example of Sangmin's mother working hard to get her son to look at books is a clear example of this. Instead, many of the brief vignettes show the ways in which the children actively changed the setting, getting their mothers to do things that they may not have otherwise done. Patty, for example, got her mother to read to her, and Natasha interrupted her mother to ask whether she has the correct number. There are also examples of what Corsaro (1992) called "interpretive reproduction," such as Brianna making sure that the children put on their seatbelts before going to the "money store" to get money and Rita caring for her "baby" in ingenious ways. Just to illustrate the fact that sometimes children are more "interpretive" than "reproductive" of cultural norms, we see Rita putting a diaper on her head and saying that she's now got long hair.

ENGAGEMENT IN LESSONS

What sort of lessons were the children involved in? As discussed in Chapter 4, we were interested in three types of lessons – those involving the types of things that children might be expected to know once they get to school (academic lessons); those involving dealing with other people, good behavior, manners, and so on (interpersonal lessons); and lessons about the workings of the natural or mechanical world or about safety (world lessons). (The children on rare occasions participated in religious lessons, and these have been included in the category of interpersonal lessons.) To constitute a lesson, a person either had to request information or had to try to teach someone else about any of these things.

Greensboro

What is immediately clear is that within both ethnic groups, middle-class children were involved in more lessons, overall, than were working-class children (see Figure 6.11). Moreover, middle-class children from each ethnic group were about twice as likely to engage both in academic lessons and in lessons about the world as were working-class children. The White children were about twice as likely to have interpersonal lessons as were the Black

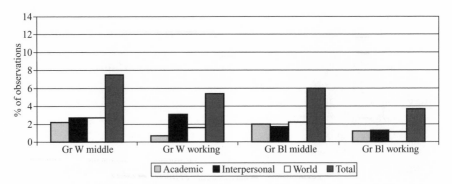

Figure 6.11. Engagement in types of lessons, Greensboro (by class and ethnicity).

children. In no case, however, were children likely to have many such lessons; across the various groups the children were engaged in lessons between 1% and 3% of our observations.

Averages, as I mentioned earlier, are somewhat misleading, particularly if there is a good deal of variability. Some children in these cities engaged in far more of all types of lessons than did others. For example, in the middle-class European American families, only 4 of the 11 children engaged in more than 2 academic lessons, and three of them were boys, who received 13, 6, and 6 such lessons.

In Greensboro, Andy (a middle-class White boy) is with his mother, in his bedroom at home. They've started to play games together, including one that involves recognizing colors, and another one that's a Sesame Street *dominoes game. As Andy deals the cards he tries to count, and his mother guides him in the process.*

One girl was involved in 10 academic lessons, but the remaining girls in this group received only a few.

Similarly, in the African American middle-class community, two boys (Kevin and Charles) received by far and away more academic lessons than did other children in this group. Kevin was involved in 21 lessons altogether, of which 8 were academic and 11 were lessons about the world, and Charles, although only involved in 12 lessons altogether, participated in no fewer than 10 academic lessons.

Naomi (a Black girl from a middle-class home) and her mother had been playing together, drawing faces on their fingers. In the next observational window, Naomi's father is talking on the phone and her mother is watching television. Naomi has taken a piece of paper and is writing on it. Then she says: "Look, Momma, I spell 'Paul'" and asks her mother what she has written. "Paul" answers her mother and then spells it out for her daughter, who writes each letter while repeating "P-A-U-L."

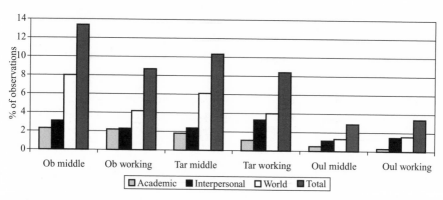

Figure 6.12. Engagement in types of lessons, northeastern Europe (by class).

Northeastern European Cities

In Obninsk and Tartu, as was seen in Greensboro, children from middle-class homes were more likely than those from working-class homes to have been observed engaging in lessons about the world (see Figure 6.12). All children from Obninsk and Tartu were involved in far more of these types of lessons than were children from the other cities. However, the social-class differences found for lessons about the world were not seen for the other two types of lessons.

Why should the children in Obninsk and Tartu receive so many more lessons about the world than the children in other cities? The explanation seems clear; in Russia and Estonia, in both the Soviet period and since independence, many families grow vegetables and sometimes fruits on small plots of land, to have an extra source of fresh produce. Not surprisingly, children are encouraged to know something about growing crops, nature, and so on.

Liuba, a middle-class Russian girl, spent a good deal of her time in the small family-child-care center that her mother ran in her apartment. In an early observation, her mother has brought out books with drawings and painting equipment, and the children are painting. One of the pages had different types of mushrooms, and Liuba's mother was explaining to the children about the difference between edible and poisonous mushrooms. Almost immediately afterwards, the mother moved from a lesson about the natural world to an academic lesson, asking the children to count the mushrooms in the picture.

Kolya, a working-class Russian boy, is with his grandmother in their dacha, a small house in the countryside. She is watering plants that are under some type of covering, and he asks her what the cover is needed for. She explains that the plants have to be kept covered until they're strong enough to withstand the cold and the wind.

In addition, given limited resources, families tend not to throw away broken tools, appliances, and the like but to repair them. Again, the children see parents and friends fixing things, and different sorts of explanations accompany this work.

Marika, an Estonian middle-class girl, is playing outside in the garden while her father and grandfather are welding a new gate. While helping her grandmother wash clothes, she goes to look at the welding and is told not to as the brightness of the welding could damage her eyes.

The children in Tartu received many lessons about health and safety, perhaps because, particularly compared with children in Greensboro, they were given a lot of freedom to be by themselves in the play areas that are close to all apartment complexes. Children living in the Veeriku neighborhood of that city, moreover, were living in an area in which a good deal of construction was happening, and some of the parents were concerned about their safety.

But lest we should imagine that all children were equally exposed to these types of lessons, I should point out that one Estonian middle-class girl (Margit) received only three lessons about the world, and a working-class girl (Anu) from Tartu only received two such lessons. By contrast, two other girls (Ilse, from a middle-class family, and Tiia, a working-class girl) received 18 and 14 lessons about the world. In Obninsk, as well, some children received twice as many such lessons as did others.

Cities for Diversity

A similar pattern as we found in Greensboro can be seen in Suwon, Kisumu, and Porto Alegre, at least with regard to academic lessons; in each case the children from middle-class homes were on average about twice as likely to be involved in them as were children from working-class homes (see Figure 6.13). Unlike the case in Greensboro, however, middle-class children were also more likely to be involved in interpersonal lessons than were their working-class counterparts. In Kisumu, working-class children were more involved in lessons about the workings of the world than were middle-class children.

It is important to recognize the extent of individual variations, however. In Kisumu, for example, two middle-class children (George and Jeremy) were involved in only one academic lesson each (and a total of 3 and 5 lessons), whereas the other eight children in this group were all involved in many more, ranging from 5 to 13 academic lessons, and from 10 to 21 lessons altogether. The

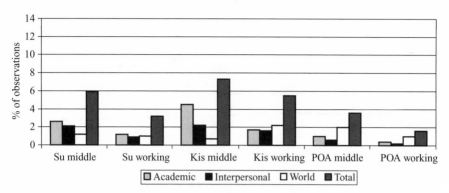

Figure 6.13. Engagement in types of lessons, diverse cities (by class).

same situation was also found in Suwon, where the range for the middle-class children was from seven or eight academic lessons for three of the children but three or fewer for the other three children. In the working-class community of Suwon, the range was from no such lessons to four. In Porto Alegre, Carlos, a middle-class boy, had six academic lessons, whereas none of the other children in that city, from either community, had more than three such lessons, and eight of the children (six from working-class families) had no academic lessons at all.

The children from Porto Alegre also received very few interpersonal lessons. Four children (three from middle-class families) were observed having two such lessons and they were the children who had the most. Of the remainder, 10 (eight from working-class families) did not receive any at all.

Enrique, from a middle-class family, is in child care and sitting at a small table with other children while the teacher gives them juice. The teacher tells Enrique not to put his feet on the table as they're dirty, and will make the table dirty. A few days later, however, when Enrique is back in child care, he and the other children come back into the room after having been playing outside. While the teacher helps some of the children wash their hands, Enrique plays with a little car and then, with some other children, climbs onto the table where they're going to have something to eat, and the teacher tells them why they should not be doing that.

Summary

Recalling the material presented in Chapter 2, one should have expected that children in Greensboro, particularly those from White middle-class families, would have engaged in far more lessons than would their peers from Kisumu. The former, after all, are described in the literature as being far more involved in didactic lessons than are children from the majority world, who apparently learn most of what they need by close observation and participation. What we found, however, runs quite counter to the prevailing literature. The middle-class Luo children, on average, engaged in as many total lessons, and twice as many academic lessons, as did their middle-class counterparts, both White and Black, in Greensboro. The same was true for the working-class children from Kisumu, who were involved in a similar number of total lessons, and twice as many academic lessons, as were their working-class White and Black counterparts in Greensboro.

It should also come as something of a surprise to those who have been accustomed to thinking of White middle-class children in the United States as having far more didactic lessons than all other children to see that children in Obninsk and Tartu, from both middle- and working-class homes, had the same, or more, academic lessons as did their counterparts in Greensboro and far more total lessons. It may well be that when middle-class White children in the United States are compared with other American children living in poverty or with children from rural parts of the majority world, they are indeed more likely to experience more didactic lessons. However, once we examine children living in cities, being raised by parents who are as well educated as middle-class Americans, we find that the American children do not stand out as being particularly different.

It's worth reiterating the fact that membership in one or other cultural group does not explain the differences that we see, although clearly culture plays a role. What is equally clear is the role that the children themselves play; in many of the vignettes provided in this section, we see the children asking questions about numbers or words or about why certain types of technology (covers for plants) are required. They change their worlds by their activities in those worlds although here, in the case of lessons, the vignettes were more likely than was the case of those featuring play to illustrate the ways in which the adults in the setting were more than happy to answer the questions or provide more details.

ENGAGEMENT IN CONVERSATION

American children, particularly those from middle-class homes, are typically described as being highly likely to engage in conversation; the literature comparing them with children from working-class homes and those living in poverty certainly supports this view. What did we find? All of the children were involved in conversation, as we defined it. That is, they talked about things that were not currently going on (things that had occurred or were going to occur), and thus typically involving more sophisticated language than that that occurred as a simple accompaniment to play. We noted whether the conversation was between pairs or groups of children or involved children in conversation with people who were clearly older than they were (adolescents or adults). The children talked a lot – sometimes to themselves, particularly while playing, and they often talked about what they were doing with other children who were their partners in one or other activity. However, they tended to talk much less to other children about things that were distant in time or space (i.e., conversation, as we defined it) than to people who were clearly older than they were (1.5% vs. almost 6% of our observations). We also noted the times when the children appeared to be actively listening to (although not participating in) conversations between adults (we included adolescents who were 10 and older as "adults").

Greensboro

In each of the Greensboro communities, conversation between children and adults occurred far more frequently than did conversations between children. The children also appeared to be listening to conversation between adults more than they conversed with other children. The most striking finding, however, is the large difference in child–adult conversation in the middle-class White families compared with the other three groups (see Figure 6.14), a phenomenon that many scholars have noted (Dickinson & Tabors, 2001; Hart & Risley, 1995; Rogoff, 2003).

In each of the four Greensboro communities, girls were more often observed in conversation than were boys. But it is also clear that some of these mean differences are affected strongly by just a few children. That's

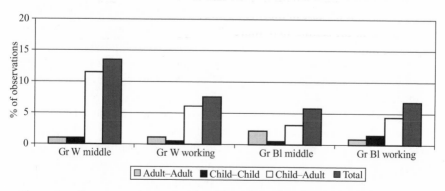

Figure 6.14. Engagement in conversation, Greensboro (by ethnicity and class).

most easily seen in the case of the working-class African American community. As I pointed out at the start of this chapter, one working-class girl, Sandra, was involved in a conversation in no fewer than 41 (21%) of her observations, far more than any other child in this community. Apart from her, the range for conversation among the remaining children in her group was from a single conversation to 17. Sandra not only listened in on conversation between adults but often participated in their conversations (a total of 19 observations), and she was the only child in this group who had more than a single conversation with another child – she was involved in such conversations in 18 of her observations! One girl, Kathy, in the middle-class White community was involved in slightly more conversations (49, or 29% of all her observations), but three other children (two girls and a boy) in that group had 30 conversations or more and so Kathy did not stand out to the same degree as did Sandra.

Sandra spent a lot of her time hanging out at her mother's beauty parlor, watching her mother work on her customers' hair, listening to them talking, and joining in from time to time. It's close to 10 P.M., and her mother, her uncle, and another woman are cleaning up. As Sandra goes into the office to get herself a snack, her mother says to her colleague: "You know it's bad to have kids grow up in a beauty shop, but everyone who works in one does it." When the other woman leaves, Sandra asks her uncle if he's hungry, and says that she wants ice cream. "No ice cream, it's too late," replies her uncle, and her mother suggests that they go to McDonalds, which is what they do.

Northeastern European Cities

The same social-class differences that we observed in the White communities in Greensboro were also found in Obninsk and Tartu, with middle-class children engaging in more conversation than did their working-class counterparts (see Figure 6.15). The children in Oulu were noteworthy not only for the fact that they engaged in more conversations than did children in the other cities but that those from working-class families, on average, were more involved in conversations (19.4% of their observations) than were those from middle-class families (14.5% of their observations). The fact that middle-class children in Obninsk (10.6%) and in Tartu (12.7%) also were involved in conversations almost as frequently as were their White counterparts in Greensboro (13% of their observations) suggests that the latter are far from unique in the industrialized world in terms of extent of conversation.

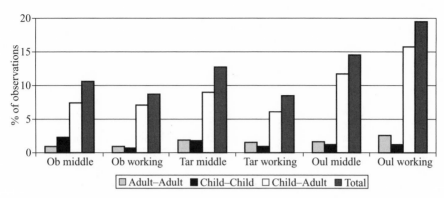

Figure 6.15. Engagement in conversation, northeastern Europe (by class).

Unlike the case in the African American community in Greensboro, however, it was not the case that a single child in Oulu was responsible for the high degree of conversation. Four of the children (three girls and a boy) in this group were engaged in conversations in 40 or more of their observations, averaging more than 45. This means that these four children were observed in conversation in more than a quarter of their observations.

At 6.30 one morning, Jonas, a working-class boy from Oulu, is woken by his mother. The first thing she does is ask him about a dream he had had that night. Shortly after, Jonas' father gets home from his night job, and starts to read the newspaper. Jonas joins him and they talk about what is in the pictures. A bee flies in and the father kills it; Jonas wants to talk to his father about the bee, but his father is more interested in the newspaper and barely responds, and so Jonas talks to himself about the bee. By now Jonas' brother and sister are both in the kitchen, getting themselves something to eat, and their father talks to Jonas about going off to child care (it's his first day), and to Jonas' brother about where he would like to go for their holidays.

The same was true in both Obninsk and Tartu; in both cities, the individuals who stood out as being different did so because they engaged in so few conversations, compared with their peers, and not, as was true in the Black community in Greensboro, because a single child was so heavily involved in conversations. For example, Liuba, a middle-class Russian girl, engaged in only six conversations, less than 4% of her observations; Aivar, an Estonian middle-class boy, was observed in five conversations; and Vahur, an Estonian working-class boy, conversed with someone else only four times (2% of his observations). By comparison, two other Estonian middle-class children (one boy, Toomas, and one girl, Ilse) were observed in conversation in more than

40 of their observations and a working-class boy (Juri) in 31 of his observations. Remember that engagement in a limited number of conversations does not imply that these children were silent; rather, they did not spend very much time talking about things that were not part of the present ongoing activities.

Cities for Diversity

A similar pattern to that found in Greensboro and northeastern Europe was found in Suwon and Porto Alegre, with far more adult–child conversation occurring than either child–child conversation or children listening to adult conversation. Similarly, as in all cities except Oulu, the children from middle-class families engaged in much more conversation than did the children from working-class families. In Kisumu, however, the working-class children were involved in more total conversation than their middle-class counterparts; interestingly, the additional conversation was the result of listening both to more adult conversation, as well as engaging in slightly more child–child conversation than in the other groups. In fact, among the working-class children in Kisumu, all three types of conversation occurred equally frequently (see Figure 6.16).

Only four of the Korean children (all middle class, evenly divided by gender) were observed in conversation on more than 10 occasions, and the other eight children in Suwon were observed in conversation between one and nine occasions. The working-class children, on average, engaged in conversation in about 3% of their observations.

In Kisumu the situation was rather different. Working-class children were observed somewhat more in conversation than were those from middle-class families (8.2% vs. 6%), but there was wide variability in both social-class

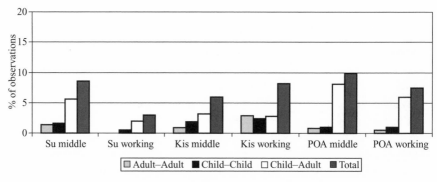

Figure 6.16. Engagement in conversations, diverse cities (by class).

groups. In the middle-class community, half of the children were observed engaging in conversation on 7 or fewer occasions, but one girl and one boy had conversations in more than 20 of their observations.

Bobbie (a girl from the middle-class community), for example, was often observed in conversations, generally quite simple, but which involved her in the sequencing of events. On one occasion, for example, her aunt told her that she won't take her for a walk unless she eats well, and a few minutes later, before an observation window opens, tells her that "You are a good girl because you are eating." That would not constitute a conversation, as we have defined it, but simply a comment on the here-and-now of an ongoing activity. Bobbie asks her, however, during the succeeding observation: "Where will we go when I finish eating?" Her aunt tells her that they'll go to the shops, and that she'll get a reward for eating well!

The same was found in the working-class community, where three of the children had few conversations, whereas one boy (John) was involved in conversations in 26 of his observations, and a girl (Brendah) in 33 (or 18% of her observations). Perhaps more interesting, however, is the fact that in Kisumu a greater proportion (more than 25% in both communities) of children's conversations was with other children, a proportion far higher than in any other group. This was partly because, as we'll see in the next chapter, in Kisumu children spent a lot of their time in the company of other children, and they were able to overhear other children talking and could themselves participate in conversations with other children. It also seems to reflect the fact that, as I pointed out in Chapter 2, in various cultural groups in Kenya it is not considered appropriate for adults to engage in much conversation with their children. This belief appears to be just as true for the well-educated middle-class Luo parents as for their working-class counterparts.

Maggie (a working-class Luo girl) and her older sister are in the small shop where her mother is selling bread and vegetables. They overhear their mother talking to one of the customers about some stolen goods and to another about the fact that this woman was already in debt (to the mother), and needed to pay. Maggie, who has been looking at a book and identifying letters in it during this time, suddenly turns to her sister and says: "You're going to be sent away!" Her sister, not surprisingly, wants to know why, but Maggie doesn't give her any answer and carries on looking at her book.

Almost none of the children from Porto Alegre listened in on conversations between adults, at least in any obvious way; Giana and Gabriela, from middle-class families, did so four and five times, respectively, but 15 other children were observed only one time or not at all listening to adult conversations. On the other hand, almost all of them participated in conversations *with* adults. The range for the children from the middle-class community was from 8 to 20 such conversations, and although Mariana only engaged once in conversation and Gustavo just four times, the remaining working-class children were involved in conversations with adults between 9 and 18 times.

Gabriela is at her child-care center around 6.30 one evening, and is talking to her teacher about the cartoons that she likes watching. Shortly afterwards, Gabriela's mother arrives and talks to the teacher while Gabriela listens to them, before mother and daughter get in the car to go home. About an hour later, when they're at home, Gabriela talks to her father about his trip, and about one of her father's colleagues, and about Gabriela's "boyfriend." Her mother joins in the conversation, and then they all go into the kitchen where Gabriela's mother prepares a fruit juice (made from fresh fruits) for her. They talk about the color of the juice, and then about the bacteria that live on Gabriela's teeth.

Summary

Our data thus clearly support the literature suggesting that White middle-class children from the United States are more likely to engage in conversation than are White working-class or Black children, and we also found that they were more often observed conversing than were their counterparts in Suwon, Kisumu, and Porto Alegre. However, it is again useful to be able to compare the children from Greensboro with children from various cities in different parts of the world and to see that the children in Obninsk, Tartu, and Oulu were as likely (or more so, in the latter city) to engage in conversation as were the middle-class White children in Greensboro.

This finding is particularly interesting, given that middle-class White mothers are often described as being highly talkative with their children, as described in Chapter 2. Finns and Estonians, by contrast, have been labeled as "silent" (Realo, 1998; Tulviste, Mizera, DeGeer, & Tyggvason, 2003). However, as the research into Finnish and Estonian children's and adolescents' propensity to talk has featured recording conversations during mealtimes, the extent to which they engage in conversation at other times of the day may have been misrepresented.

ENGAGEMENT IN WORK

Finally, let's look at the fourth of the major categories of activities that formed the focus of our attention. The type of work that the children were involved in was, not surprisingly, work that took place in and around the home: cooking, cleaning, mending things, doing work in the garden or in small plots of land

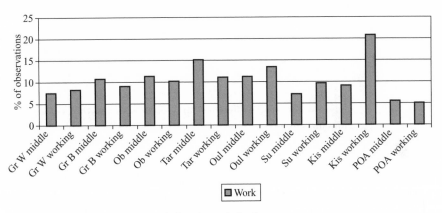

Figure 6.17. Involvement in work (by city and class).

in the vicinity of the home, shopping, and so on. Most of this work involved tasks that someone else had started, and the children became involved either as observers of the work or because they wanted to participate. In some cases they were asked to help out, for example, taking dishes to the table or to clean up.

The clearest finding is the fact that the working-class children in Kisumu were involved in more work than were the children in any other group – almost four times as much as the children in Porto Alegre, for example. However, the middle-class children in Kisumu engaged in less work than did children in many other groups. These findings do not accord well with the widespread view, discussed in Chapter 2, that Kenyan children are heavily involved in work. The children in Porto Alegre were least likely to be involved in work, in only about 5% of their observations (see Figure 6.17).

Nonetheless, these data might be somewhat misleading. As I mentioned earlier, "involvement" means both active participation in an activity and closely observing someone else who is involved in that activity. This distinction may not be so important in the case of lessons, play, or conversation, but in the present case, watching someone else work may be quite different from actually participating in the work itself. For this reason, in the following graph I have provided details about participation alone.

Although the working-class Luo children were still more likely to participate in work (more than 8% of their observations) than were children in any other group, they do not look so different from children in Obninsk and middle-class children in Tartu (see Figure 6.18). What is particularly interesting is the fact that the middle-class Luo children participated so little in work, a finding that should make us pay more attention to class

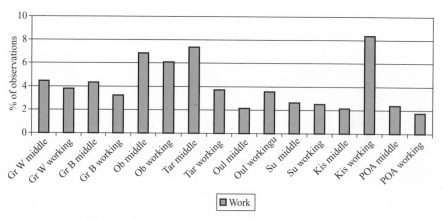

Figure 6.18. Participation in work (by city and class).

differences in that society, particularly given the way in which Kenyan society is changing.

The children in Greensboro were involved in work between 7% and 11% of their observations, with Black children slightly more likely to be involved in work than were their White counterparts. We also saw some interesting sex differences. In the White middle-class community, boys were twice as likely to be involved in work as were girls (10.4% vs. 5% of their observations on average), but this was a somewhat rare situation across all groups. White girls were slightly more likely to be involved in work than were boys in the working-class group (8.7% vs. 7.6%). Girls were also more involved in work than were boys in the Black communities, only slightly more so in the middle-class community (11.6% vs. 10.3%) but more clearly so in the working-class group (11.7% vs. 6.4%).

As always, however, it is important to note individual variations. Among the White middle-class children in Greensboro, two girls were observed in work during only 4 and 5 of their observations, whereas Harry was involved in work in 33 of his observations (more than 17% of his total), and Andy in 22 observations.

Andy spent a good deal of time at home, mostly with his mother and his baby sister. He was obviously very used to participating in the work that she was doing. At the beginning of one observational period, they had just returned from a trip to the vet, and now it was time for the clothes to be washed. Everyone in the family had his or her own laundry basket, and Andy had brought his clothes and was helping his mother to sort them into "whites and colors." He then got his child-sized chair so that he could help his mother load the laundry into the washing machine.

In the working-class group, the situation was much more similar, as noted, with all but Olive (who worked in 23 observations) involved in between 11 and 16 observations. In the African American middle-class community, Andrew was involved in work in no fewer than 45 of his observations (over 23% of his total observations) and Brianna in 40 observations, whereas other members of this group were involved anywhere from 6 times to 28. The situation was not quite so varied in the working-class Black group, with the range between 8 observations for Raymond and 32 for Andrea.

In the northeastern European cities, girls were also more involved in work than were boys, strikingly so among the middle-class children in Tartu (20% vs. 10.2%), somewhat less so among the working-class children in Obninsk (12.6% vs. 7.8%) and among the working class children in Oulu (16.6% vs. 10.9%). However, middle-class girls in Obninsk (like those in the White middle-class Greensboro community) were involved in less work than were boys (10% vs. 12.7%), two of whom (Boris and Zhenya) were involved in more work than any other children in their group, in about 16% of their observations.

Boris is with his mother and baby brother at the doctor's office, where Boris watches the doctor taking notes on what she's seen, and putting the notes in a file. After leaving the clinic, they go to the post office, where Boris' mother has to send a registered letter. His mother and the clerk prepare the letter to be sent, while Boris watches them. When it's time to post the letter, Boris says that he wants to do it, and his mother lifts him up so that he can put the letter into the correct slot. She explains to him where the letter will go.

In each of these northeastern European cities, some children were far more likely to be involved than were others. In Obninsk, for example, Natasha, a working-class girl, engaged in work in more than 18% of her observations, whereas a working-class boy, Fyodor, was involved in less than 6% of his observations. The same variability was found in Tartu, where three children (all girls) from middle-class homes engaged in work in more than 20% of their observations, whereas three others (all male) were involved in work less than half as often. In the working-class community in Tartu, however, only one child (Juri) was involved in work in more than 20% of the observations. Two girls (Tiia and Luule), however, were involved in work in more than 15% of their observations. By contrast, of the three children involved in the least amount of work (approximately 5% of their observations), two were boys and one was a girl.

In Oulu, unfortunately, we did not have even numbers of boys and girls; of the nine children in the middle-class group only two were boys, which makes it impossible to look at variations by gender. However, in the working-class group, where the sexes were evenly divided, one girl (Sari) was involved in a total of 45 (over 25%) observations of work, and another (Piia) was involved in almost 20% of her observations. The least amount of involvement of work (about 7% of observations) featured two boys and a girl.

In Suwon, in the middle-class community, girls were also more involved in work than were boys (9% vs. 5% of their observations), although boys and girls worked similar amounts in the working class community (9.9% vs. 9.4%).

During one observational session, Dongki's mother (from a working-class family) spent a good deal of time washing clothes, folding them, and preparing dinner for Dongki's grandmother while her son watched television. But then she made him put his socks into the laundry basket himself, and later on he watched her as she worked. He was only involved in work during 14 of the observations.

Two middle-class boys were only seen working during 4% to 5% of their observations, whereas a girl (Oksun) was involved in work in 12% of her observations. In the working-class community, although the spread was a little wider (5% to 15% of the observations), girls were not more likely than boys to be involved in it.

In Kisumu, as I already mentioned, the working-class children were more likely to be involved in work than were children from any of the other groups. More than half (six) of the working-class children (equally divided by gender) were involved in work during 37 or more of the observations (more than 20% of their total observations), including one girl (Brendah) who was observed working, or observing work being done, in a total of 70 of the observations (almost 40%). The remaining four children in this group averaged fewer than 25 observations in which they were working or observing others work. In other words, these children were involved in some way in work in about 13% of their total observations, an amount of work not so different from the other children in the study. By contrast, in the middle-class group in Kisumu, none of the children were working in more than 27 (15%) of the observations. In both groups, girls were involved in work slightly more than were boys (9.9% vs. 10.3% among middle class children and 22.8% vs. 18.9% in the working-class community).

Brendah has been watching one of her older sisters prepare a meal, chopping vegetables during the three previous windows. She asks if she can help and is given a blunt bread knife so that she can help to chop. Later on Brendah is watching her mother clean the house when the latter asks Brendah if she would like to help, and sends her to get the dirty clothes, which Brendah first rinses and then brings to her mother for them to be hung.

It's not just household tasks that these young children were involved in, however.

Maggie's older sister sent her to the little grocery store where her mother works to bring back an onion, and Maggie is often sent on little tasks, such as going for water or being asked to get a blanket to cover her baby sister. But she also volunteers to do things such as bring in the dry washing.

Getting water was not always as easy as going into the kitchen, at least for the working-class families; on occasion it meant a trip to a communal water tap and at other times to a neighbor's house.

There was not so great a variation in the extent to which children in Porto Alegre were involved in work, and in general they were involved in work less often than were children in any other group. In the middle-class community, for example, the range was between 3 and 18 and in the working-class group between 4 and 18 observations of work. In both groups, girls were somewhat more likely than were boys to be involved in work, in approximately 7% of their observations versus 4.8% in the middle-class group, 5.7% versus 4.3% in the working-class group.

Summary

To summarize, in the case of the work in which the children were involved, just as was true for the other three major classes of activities, these data should make us cautious about accepting too readily literature suggesting that White middle-class children in the United States have particularly different experiences from children in Kenya, or in other parts of the world. For a long time it has been accepted that children in the majority world are far more involved in work than are those in the industrialized world. Although it is certainly the case that the working-class children in Kisumu were more involved in work than were children in the other communities, they were not that much more involved than were their counterparts in Obninsk and Tartu, although these cities are clearly part of the industrialized world. As for the middle-class Luo children, they were involved in work, on average, less than all other groups except working-class children in Porto Alegre.

Research that has not taken into account the impact of urbanization and education in a society such as Kenya can only provide, at best, an incomplete sense of how young children spend their time there. Similarly, the "special" status of middle-class White children from the United States may most easily be seen when they are compared with working-class Whites or with children in poverty, but our data suggest that their experiences may not be so different from children whose parents are similarly educated and who live in urban areas in different parts of the world.

SOME REMAINING QUESTIONS

Before concluding this examination of children's engagement in their everyday activities, a number of questions are worth pursuing. First, why have I restricted myself to showing similarities and differences among these various groups of children but not conducted any statistical analyses of these data? Second, although the groups differed in terms of the extent to which they were involved in various activities it's also clear that there was a good deal of within-group variability. It's therefore worth asking whether we can see why some children in any group were more or less likely to be involved in these activities. A third question has to do with the possible impact of engaging more or less in one or another type of activity. This question obviously needs data that have been gathered over time, but because the longitudinal data are not yet available, I'll restrict myself here to looking at some of the concurrent effects of watching more or less television. The final question relates to the fact that a huge amount of work has been undertaken to gather these data; would it not have been much simpler to ask parents for their assessment of the extent to which their children were involved in these various activities of interest? Given that we have data, going back over the past 30 years, collected via time-use studies (and discussed in Chapter 2), it's certainly worth considering the extent of overlap between our observational data and the time-use data gathered from parents.

Analyzing the Data

To this point in the chapter, I've written about the different extent to which children in these various groups engaged in the activities of interest, showing group averages, and also discussed some of the individual variation that was found within each of the groups. As noted earlier, you might be wondering why there's been no statistical analysis of these differences, particularly given that the data would lend themselves easily to some type of analysis of variance. Issues of analysis, however, should always be linked to method, theory, and metatheory (or paradigm). As I pointed out in Chapter 3, whereas neo-positivist theories are rightly interested in inferring from samples to the populations from which those samples are randomly drawn contextualist theories are much more focused on the specifics of what is occurring within one or other community of interest. In the case of this particularly study, children and their families from two social-class groups in a single city in each country are not considered to be "representative" of that social class or society, and clearly they were not selected randomly from broader populations of interest. It makes more sense to think of each of these groups as constituting small and carefully selected populations of interest. Inferential statistics, designed to infer from a sample to the population from which the sample was randomly drawn, are clearly neither warranted nor relevant.

However, the question still remains: Are any differences between groups, no matter how tiny, to be treated as worth discussing? (The equivalent question, if I were using inferential statistics, would be: Are these differences statistically significant?) How are we to tell whether these differences in engagement in one or another activity across the various cultural groups are large enough to signify meaningful (rather than significant) differences among them?

I think that a good case can be made for the fact that the differences that I've been discussing in this chapter are large enough to be considered meaningful. To give one example of why I think that this is so, the middle-class White children from Greensboro were observed engaging in lessons in 7.5% of their observations, compared with 3.7% of the observations of their working-class Black counterparts. One way to think about this is that these percentages translate to 13.5 versus 6.7 lessons during 18 hours of observation, an apparently minor difference. However, a more appropriate way to think about this requires remembering the "windows" of observation, which lasted for 30 seconds during each 6-minute period. In effect, therefore, although the observations lasted for 18 hours, we only coded what occurred during a total of 90 minutes.

Given that no one apart from the observer was aware of when the windows opened and closed, it seems reasonable to assume that we can extrapolate (or generalize) from any one set of 90 minutes that occurred during the week in which we observed to any other set. Assuming that the children were awake for 14 hours each day, this would mean a total of 121 lessons for one group of children and 60 for another group over the course of a single day, or 847 versus 420 lessons over the course of a week. I would argue that these differences are indeed meaningful in terms of what it is that the culture makes available to children and to the children's experiences and that this is the case regardless of any claim that more is in some way either better or worse.

To put these differences in wider context, if I extrapolate in a similar way the middle-class children from Kisumu would engage, on average, in a total of 70 academic lessons each day, far more than the equivalent figurers for the middle-class children in Greensboro, whether White (35 per day) or Black (32 per day). Similarly, even though the Luo working-class children would engage, on average, in somewhat fewer academic lessons (28 per day), this is still far more than the number of lessons in which their working-class counterparts in Greensboro would engage, whether White (11 per day) or Black (19 per day).

To take another example, although the differences between middle-class and working-class children in Porto Alegre, in terms of playing with academic objects, were not great when expressed as a percentage of observations (3.5 vs. 0.3), this translates, when extrapolated across an entire day, into a total of 57 such experiences for the former group and only five for the latter. As Dickinson and Tabors (2001) and Hart and Risley (1995) clearly showed, these types of differences in terms of opportunities for looking at books or engaging in conversation can have profound implications for reading and language development; the same should equally be true for learning particular skills, or being involved in work, or what one learns about the world through television. I think that a clear case can thus be made for viewing these apparently small differences in engagement in different activities across the various cultural groups as having a potentially dramatic impact on these children's development.

Reasons for Individual Variation

We did not collect any direct measures of the children's character or personality, but we did examine one way in which children themselves could make a difference in their engagement in activities, namely, the extent to which children themselves initiated the activities in which they were involved. As I described this in Chapter 4, as we were observing we always attempted to see who started each activity that was available to the children. Then, should the child be involved in that activity when the coding window opened, we could note how the activity was started and how the child had become involved in it. We coded the children as the initiator either when they started the activity by themselves or when they did so in conjunction with someone else. Otherwise, we coded either that another person had clearly initiated the activity or that we were not able to tell who had initiated it.

Not surprisingly, not only did the children engage in play far more than they engaged in other activities, but when they played, they were much more likely to have initiated it themselves; across the entire set of participants, they did so a little more than 65% of the time. By contrast, children initiated lessons (by asking questions) or work far less frequently, in approximately 16% of our observations of those activities. Across all groups, the children initiated a little more than 42% of the conversations in which they were involved.

It's worth looking at the activities that the children were less likely to initiate (lessons, work, and conversation) to get a glimpse into why it is that some children were more involved in these activities than were others. In the White middle-class community in Greensboro, for example, some of the children were involved in as many lessons as they were because they asked a lot of questions that led to the provision of information: Andy and Irene, for example, were each involved in a lesson on seven occasions (about 25% and 50% of their total lessons) because of a question that they had asked. Similarly, about one third of the 16 lessons in which Cassandra and Dominic were involved arose because the children themselves took the initiative. By contrast, in the working-class White community the children were involved in far fewer lessons, in part because they asked questions much less often. Olive initiated a lesson on three occasions, but the remaining children did so less frequently. In the Black community, the middle-class children were also involved in far more lessons than were their working-class peers, but the individual variation among the children could not be explained by their differential questioning; only four middle-class children ever initiated lessons (two children twice, two others just once) and only two of the working-class children did so (each on one occasion).

Children from the middle-class community in Obninsk were also more likely than their working-class peers to be involved in lessons, in part because all of them on at least three occasions asked questions, and Boris (who was observed in no fewer than 30 lessons) initiated 10 of them. All but one of the working-class children also initiated lessons, but less frequently than did their middle-class counterparts. The same pattern was seen in Tartu; the middle-class children, overall, were somewhat more likely to be involved in lessons than were the children from working-class homes, but the former initiated almost 30% of those lessons compared with only 20% of the latter's lessons. Annika became involved in a lesson in 65% of her 23 lessons simply because she asked many questions. By contrast, Epp, although from the same group, was involved in 19 lessons, of which she initiated only one. In the remaining northeastern European city, Oulu, the situation was quite different. The Finnish children, in general, were involved in only about one third of the number of lessons of their counterparts from Obninsk and Tartu, and only two middle-class children (once each) initiated a lessons, whereas five of the working-class children from Oulu did so, Anneli and Sini (both girls) two times each.

In Suwon and Kisumu, the situation was similar to all communities except that in Oulu. Children from the middle-class community not only were involved in more lessons than were those from the working-class group but also included the only children who initiated lessons. Sungwhan, for example, asked questions on three occasions, 25% of his total lessons. In Kisumu, as well, the middle-class children were involved in somewhat more lessons than were those from working-class homes, but were much more likely (18% vs. 8%) to ask questions that led to lessons. Richard, for example, was observed on six occasions asking a question, thereby accounting for one third of his lessons, and Frankie, a middle-class girl, did the same thing on 4 of the 11 occasions in which she was involved in a lesson. Brandon, however, although involved in a total of 19 lessons, never initiated any of them, the only middle-class child not to do so. By contrast, in the working-class community, although Gesila was observed three times asking a question that led to a lesson, of the remaining nine children, four never were observed asking a question and five only once each.

In Porto Alegre, as was the case with all other cities except for Oulu, the middle-class children were involved in more lessons than were the working-class children. However, just three children, only one of whom was from a middle-class family, initiated more than one lesson. Renato, a working-class boy, was observed asking questions on three occasions, leading to three of the four lessons in which he was involved.

Some of the variation in activities in which children are involved is thus attributable, at least in part, to characteristics of the children themselves, in this instance the interest in and willingness to ask questions. However, the context has to be such that the environment is receptive to those questions. If by three years of age a child has learned that his or her questions are routinely ignored, the rate at which questions are asked is likely to drop.

It is also worth asking the question about whether these differences in asking questions may signal some degree of regularity, either of temperament (a propensity to be verbal, for example) or of context (a willingness to follow the child's lead). In either case, one might expect to find that children who initiate a lot of questions might also initiate many other activities. There is some evidence to support this position. Across all the children in the study, there were clear relations among the initiation of lessons, conversation, and work but no relation between the initiation of any of these activities and the initiation of play.

Because it's not possible to demonstrate the size of the relation in the way that I did when extrapolating from what occurred in 90 minutes of observation to an entire day, I'll borrow a simple statistical analysis *not* to allow for generalization but rather to let a statistically significant correlation indicate a relation that is large enough to be worth discussing. In these terms, it's possible to argue that those children who started lessons more frequently than did other children were also likely to start more work (.49, $p < .001$) and more conversation (.22, $p < .01$), and children who initiated more conversation were also more likely to initiate more work (.24, $p < .005$). However, because all the children initiated the majority of their play, this was not as susceptible to variation in the extent of initiation.

Impact of Individual Variation

We have seen that the children, within each group, varied in the extent to which they were involved in the activities of interest, and we now know that some of the reason for that variation is that some of the children in each group were more likely to initiate the activities in which they were involved than did other children. It then is interesting to examine the implications for children who spent a good deal of time in one particular activity on their likelihood of engaging in other activities. Given that many people wonder about the effects of television watching on children's likelihood to get involved in other types of activities, I briefly discuss those children who watched a lot of television, examining the extent to which they were more or less likely to engage in lessons, pretend play, play with academic objects, and conversation.

As we've already seen, children in the various cities watched different amounts of television. Children in Kisumu watched less, on average (less than 5% of their observations), than did children in the other cities and children in Greensboro and Suwon did so more, spending between 10% and 15% of their time watching TV. Nonetheless, across all children, watching television was associated with significantly fewer lessons, pretend play, and conversations (as can be seen in Table 6.1). The correlation of television-watching with play with academic objects was also negative, although not significantly so.

There were, however, some interesting variations across the cities. In Greensboro, for example, children who watched more TV were significantly less likely to engage in lessons, but the remaining correlations were all lower and nonsignificant. Patty, a working-class White girl from Greensboro, was observed watching television on 52 occasions and was involved in lessons only eight times (only four White children were involved in fewer lessons). Benjamin, a middle-class Black boy from Greensboro, was watching TV during 55 observations and only engaged in two lessons (the second fewest among all the children in Greensboro).

In both Obninsk and Oulu, however, those who watched more TV did not engage less in lessons or play with academic objects but were less likely

Table 6.1. Is Watching Television Associated with Fewer Activities That Might Be Helpful for Later Development?

	Lessons	Pretend Play	Play with Academic Objects	Conversation
All children	−.25	−.16		−.17
Greensboro	−.36			
Obninsk		−.45		−.62
Tartu	.23			.46
Oulu		−.34		−.27
Suwon		−.37	−.23	−.25
Kisumu				
Porto Alegre	−.26	−.21	−.44	−.44

to engage in pretend play and conversation. Dara and Valya, the two Russian children (both middle-class girls) who watched the least television (3 and 0 observations, respectively) were the most likely to engage in pretend play (14 and 13 observations) and engage in conversation (31 times and 23 times). The two middle-class children (Liuba, a girl, and Zhenya, a boy) who watched the most television (19 and 14 observations) were the least likely to engage in pretend play (5 and 4 observations, respectively). Although Zhenya was involved in conversation on 17 of our observations, Liuba was only observed conversing on 6 occasions.

In Suwon, too, those children who watched more were somewhat less likely to engage in pretend play, play with academic objects, or engage in conversation, and children in Porto Alegre who spent more time watching television were less likely to engage in lessons, pretend play, play with academic objects, and engage in conversation. In Suwon, for example, the middle-class girl and two boys who watched the most television (30–40 of their observations) were less likely than the other middle-class children to engage in either pretend play or to be observed playing with academic objects.

There were exceptions to these patterns, however. In Tartu, the situation was different from anywhere else; children who watched more television there were actually *more* likely to engage in lessons and conversation. In Kisumu, where three of the middle-class children and seven of the working-class children were never observed watching television, all of the correlations were low and nonsignificant. Moreover, although I just mentioned the situation in the middle-class community in Suwon, it is worth nothing that in the working-class community in that city of the two children (Dognki and Jaeyong, both boys) who watched the most television (40 and 51 observations, respectively), one engaged in no pretend play and only once was observed playing with academic objects, whereas the other engaged in more of these types of play than any other child from his group!

Comparisons with the Time-Use Studies

The final question I want to answer is whether it's necessary to spend so much time observing these children so closely to see these variations; are the data that we gathered so different from those that parents report in the various time-use studies I discussed in Chapter 2? It's worth mentioning again my summary of those findings, which were fairly similar across two national U.S. samples (Hofferth & Sandberg, 2001; Timmer et al., 1989) and a study of children's play in Wisconsin (Bloch, 1989), all of which had data on children from three to five years of age.

Although some of the data were expressed as percentages of time during the day and other data as hours during the day, assuming that children of this age are awake for 14 hours per day, then between 18% and 30% of their time is spent in play, 14% to 21% in child care, 10% to 14% watching television, being involved in household chores between 2% and 7% of the time, 1% to 2% of their time looking at books or doing some other type of school-related activity, about 1% of the time in conversation, and the remaining 20% to 30% in other activities, including eating and sleeping.

Our own data from Greensboro (derived from Figures 6.5 and 6.6) reveal some interesting differences with the time-use data. We found that the children were involved in play (not counting television) a good deal more than had been reported (almost 48% of the time, on average) but watched television just as much as the time-use data reported (12% of the time, on average). The children were involved in work a little more than the highest estimate, on the basis of the time-use data (about 9% of the time), and were involved in conversations a good deal more, about 9% of the time, on average. The Greensboro children were also involved in school-relevant activities more than the time-use data suggested (about 6% of the time, including academic lessons 1.5% and play with academic objects 4.5% of the time). Our figure for the extent to which the children spent time in child care was also similar to that reported in the U.S. national studies (16%).

It thus seems clear that parents are able to judge rather accurately the extent to which their children watch television (as Anderson et al., 1985, reported) and how long they spend in child care, although it's important to point out that because the time-use studies rely on parents, what actually occurs in child care is not reported. On the other hand, they apparently underestimate (by comparison with our observations) how much their children play, are involved in school-related activities, and converse (even though we used a highly restricted definition of conversation).

An alternative hypothesis, of course, is that parents may be more likely to involve their children in conversation and school-relevant activities when they are being observed. I obviously can't discount this possibility; however, it's also important to remember that children are not simply involved in activities due to the actions of others but play an active role themselves as I have shown, initiating many of the activities in which they were involved.

CONCLUSION

In Chapter 2, where I laid out what we currently know about how young children spend their time, the most obvious distinction that I drew was between children who were growing up in two countries from the industrialized world (the United States and Great Britain) and children being raised in Kenya, one example of a society from the majority world. However, I also pointed out a number of reasons for being cautious about accepting these differences.

One reason has to do with the ways in which data have been collected in the two types of societies. In the industrialized world, with few exceptions, researchers have tried to find out about the lives of young children by asking their parents to report on what they are doing, whereas in the majority world researchers have actually observed children engaging in activities. Another has to do with the passage of time; data collected in Kenya in the 1950s and 1960s may have little to do with children's current experiences, given the rapid pace of change in that country. A third has to do with the fact that insufficient attention has been paid to within-society variability. This is partly true in the United States, where most of the research has been conducted with middle-class White children and Black children living in poverty, and relatively little with working-class White and middle-class Black children. It's even more true of research conducted in Kenya, where the majority of work has focused on different tribes living in predominantly rural areas but little research conducted with children living in urban areas and none on families that are well educated and have professional occupations, although there is now a sizable number of such families.

The research reported here is entirely different, in that precisely the same methods were used in each of the societies, data were all collected within a 12-year period, and in each city half of the children were from middle-class and half from working-class families. Perhaps not surprisingly, then, the results discussed in this chapter do not fit well with those reported in Chapter 2. Probably the most striking has to do with the Kenyan data. Although previous researchers have shown that young Kenyan children are very much involved in work, we did not find this to be the case. Certainly, the working-class Luo children participated in more work, on average, than children in the other groups, but not greatly more than their counterparts in Obninsk or the middle-class children in Tartu. More surprisingly, the middle-class Luo children participated in less work, on average, than did children from most of the other groups.

Previous researchers have also shown that Kenyan children do not engage in much conversation with adults, certainly by comparison with White middle-class children in the United States. Our data support this position, but we can contextualize this finding in interesting ways. First, the Luo children did not look so different from their counterparts either in Suwon or in the two African American communities in Greensboro in terms of their extent of conversation with adults. Second, although White middle-class children in the United States are held up as the most likely to be involved in both didactic lessons and conversation with adults (see, for example, Morelli et al., 2003; Rogoff, 2003), the extent of middle-class White children's conversation pales by comparison with the conversation engaged in by Finnish children. This finding is particularly interesting, given the fact that Finns have, along with their Estonian compatriots, been described as "silent" (Realo, 1998; Tulviste et al., 2003). This may be because, as I mentioned earlier, they tend not to talk much while being observed eating dinner. On the other hand, I should also stress that our definition of conversation was restrictive, encompassing "distancing" talk (about the past or future) rather than talking about things that were part of the ongoing activity. It could be the case that middle-class White Americans talk about what it is that they're doing far more than do other children, but our data do not reflect that.

It is also interesting to note that children in Obninsk and Tartu engaged in more lessons than did middle-class children in Greensboro, and the Luo children, overall, were more likely to participate in lessons than were their counterparts in Greensboro. There are also some clear differences in children's play, particularly in the extent to which they have different types of objects available to them. In all cities except Kisumu, children clearly had many objects to play with that were designed with children in mind; between around 15% and 35% of our observations featured children playing with toys. By contrast, the Luo children were more likely to play with objects that had not been designed for them, whether objects from the adult world (discarded or not) or objects from the natural world. Middle-class children from Suwon, who were most often observed playing with toys, were also the most likely to play with objects that had been designed to help them with their academic skills, whether looking at books, playing with computer games featuring numbers, and so on. It is also interesting to note that although all of the children except the working-class Luo children had access to televisions, the children in Greensboro (particularly those from working-class backgrounds) were by far the most likely to have been observed watching television.

Clearly, then, our data do not accord well with what previous researchers have reported, particularly in the case of the Kenyan children. One of the reasons for this difference may well be the fact that we collected our data in a city rather than in a rural area of the country, and a related reason may be that all the parents had had at least some schooling, and the middle-class parents in Kisumu had attended university. For these reasons, the children may have been placed into settings different from those inhabited by children from rural areas and may therefore have been in the company of different types of people. I explore the children's settings and their typical partners in their activities in the following chapter.

7   Settings and Partners

I've seen men as are wonderful handy wi' children.

George Eliot, *Silas Marner*, 1861/1985, p. 180

In this chapter, I focus on the various types of settings in which the children were situated during the times that we observed them, their partners during their activities, and variations in the activities because of being with certain types of partners or in one setting rather than another. Remember that when we selected the children for the project, we paid no attention to whether they attended any type of child-care arrangement or where they spent their time, and acceptance to the project was not dependent on the presence or number of siblings, whether the biological father was present, or any other similar factor. The sole concern was that we wanted to recruit all the families with children of the relevant age from the areas that we had selected, the sole criterion being that the families met our requirements for membership in the relevant ethnic and social-class group.

If it were the case that in any group many of the children went to a child-care center, or many of the fathers were absent from the home, or if most of the families had just the one child, we assumed that this simply reflected the prevailing ecology, particularly because of the ways in which we recruited the families and the generally low rejection rates (see Chapter 5). Further, because we followed the children wherever they were situated over every period of the day, this meant that we observed the children when they went shopping, were playing by themselves on a climbing frame outside the apartment, spent the afternoon with a grandparent, or went to visit friends in another area of town. We asked the parents to do all that they could to stick to the children's normal routine. For some, that routine involved spending some time in a formal child-care setting, and for others it did not. For some, this meant a lot

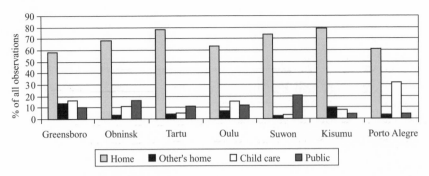

Figure 7.1. Where the children were situated.

of time spent with the father (or father substitute), and for others it meant spending no time with him.

THE SETTINGS

Where were our children situated? As described in Chapter 4, we divided the settings into four main types – in and around the child's home, in and around someone else's home (which could be a grandparent's home, a friend's home, or a home in which children were being cared for during the day, in an informal child-care arrangement), in a formal setting that had been set up specifically for caring for other people's children, and being in a public space, such as a park, public library, shops, and so on.

As might be expected, across the entire sample, children spent around two thirds of their time in and around the home (see Figure 7.1). The amounts varied from city to city, however, from around 60% of the time in Greensboro (United States) to more than 75% of the time in Tartu (Estonia) and Kisumu (Kenya). For some children, it was easier to be outside the house or apartment than for others; the middle-class European American families and middle-class Luo families in Kisumu lived in houses that had large private yards around them, whereas families in other cultural groups lived in smaller houses with small yards or in apartment complexes. Even in the latter case, however, it was often easy to play outside. In Obninsk (Russia) and Tartu, for example, those families who lived in apartment complexes had large areas of land between complexes, with areas of grass, trees, and, in most cases, climbing frames, swings, and other structures that were designed for children to use. This was true also in Porto Alegre, at least for the middle-class children, because many apartment complexes include special play areas for children.

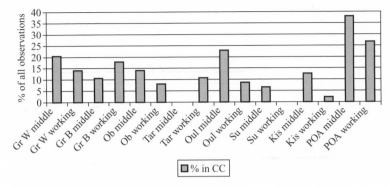

Figure 7.2. Observations in child-care centers.

Whether children were allowed outside to play without adult or older sibling supervision depended mostly on the parents' perceptions of how safe it was to allow the children outside. The typical feeling in the northeastern European cities was that the primary danger was from traffic, and a number of children received explicit lessons on where to play to ensure being relatively safe. Traffic also constituted an important hazard in the other cities, but it was only in Greensboro that a drive-by shooting occurred in the street outside the home in which we were conducting one of the interviews with parents. In Porto Alegre, all of the houses and apartments in which the middle-class children lived were secure behind high metal fences; guards were often present at the apartment complexes.

The children spent some of their time in and around the home belonging to someone else, sometimes at a grandparent's or friend's house, either that of their own friend or the home of one of their parents' friends. Sometimes the children were in the company of someone who was essentially a child-minder, that is, not someone whose home was set up to constitute a child-care center but someone who was there with the child to look after him or her while the parents were at work. We found this type of arrangement most commonly among the African American community in Greensboro, whose children were in someone else's home during more than 20% of our observations, more than double that found in any other community. The Korean children in Suwon and the Brazilian children in Porto Alegre were least likely to spend their time in someone else's home, in only 3% of the observations on average.

Some of the children also spent a good deal of their time in formal child-care centers or in homes that had been modified explicitly for this purpose. The extent to which children were likely to be in such a setting varied widely by both country and social class (see Figure 7.2). The children in Porto Alegre were observed in a child-care center in more than 30% of our observations, whereas their counterparts in Suwon, Kisumu, and Tartu were observed in this type of center in fewer than 7% of their observations. As noted in Chapter 5, however, because child-care centers in Suwon were often unwilling to allow us to observe, our observations of children in that city were largely restricted to those who did not attend child care. In all cases except Black children in Greensboro and children in Tartu, middle-class children were more likely than were their working-class counterparts to spend time in a formal child-care center.

However, these mean variations are not so helpful in the case of time spent in child-care settings, because there was such a good deal of individual variability. In fact, only two children from Suwon, both from middle-class backgrounds, spent any time in formal child care. The same was true of only two children in Tartu, both of whom were from working-class backgrounds, who each were in such a center during a little more than 50% of their observations. In Obninsk, only four children, two from each social-class group, spent any time in a formal child-care setting, and only three of them were observed in that setting in 20% or more of the observations. In Kisumu, 6 of the 10 children from middle-class backgrounds were observed in a child-care center (in each case, in about 20% of the observations), compared with only 1 of the 10 working-class children.

The final setting in which we observed the children was in some type of public space away from the setting in and around the home, such as in a shop or mall, park, museum, religious establishment, restaurant, and so on. Again there was a good deal of variation, from averages of around 20% of the observations in Suwon to less than 5% of all observations in Kisumu.

ACTIVITIES WITHIN FORMAL CHILD-CARE SETTINGS

In this section, I concentrate on the types of activities in which children were involved within formal child-care settings, to find out whether children's experiences there were different from their experiences in the other types of settings in which they were situated. First it's worth thinking about why some children from any given group spent a significant proportion of their time in child care, whereas others did not. There were many reasons why some of the children were placed into some type of child-care environment. Single parents (all of whom were single mothers in our study) working outside the home needed to find somewhere safe for their child, and the most common alternatives were either another person willing to look after the child (grandmothers fairly often filled this role) or to have the child in a child-care setting.

The same situation was true for families in which both parents worked outside the home. In other cases, children were in a child-care center for shorter periods of the day, perhaps to allow the mother to work at a part-time job, to give her some free time during the day, to provide the child with the experience of being with other children, or to give children a "head start" in their schooling.

Whatever the reason, children spending time in a child-care setting are probably experiencing a situation unlike any other. As I pointed out in Chapter 2, in rural areas of Kenya (as in many parts of the majority world), young children are likely to be in the company of many other children of different ages and sex. In industrialized societies or in urban centers such as Kisumu, children are less likely to have that possibility and are more likely to have siblings as play partners than do other children (Weisner, 1979). They are also more likely to engage their mother as a partner in their play, as the Newsons, Judy Dunn, and Wendy Haight have documented (see Chapter 2). In child-care settings, however, children are likely to find themselves in a situation in which they have many other children to be with, typically of the same age as themselves.

Some of the most interesting differences in experiences that children from different societies are likely to have in child care are clearly reflections of cultural variations in the meaning of child care in these societies. As Tobin, Wu, and Davidson (1989) have nicely shown in the case of Japan, China, and the United States, different societies may have different goals for child care; we should also not be surprised to see variations also as a function of within-society cultural factors, whether of social class or ethnicity (Freitas et al., in press). It is also clear that individual parents have differing goals in mind when they provide their children with child-care experiences. Children, as well, vary greatly in not only their interest in and willingness to go to child care but also in their motivations. Some children want little more than an opportunity to play with friends, whereas others use this different setting as providing a new place in which to ask questions, learn new things, and so on.

Comparing Children's Experiences, Within and Outside of Child Care

To what extent do children who are fairly frequently within some type of formal child-care setting experience different activities than they do elsewhere? To answer this question, I present the data in terms of proportions by comparing each set of activities expressed first as a percentage of the number of observations gathered on these children in a formal child-care setting and

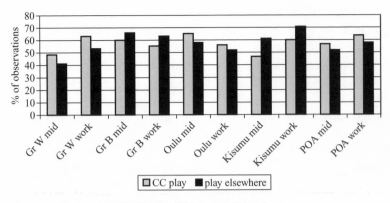

Figure 7.3. Engagement in play, in child care and elsewhere.

second as a percentage of our observations of them in their other settings. This analysis has the effect of putting the children's activities on the same scale; the children spent less time in child care than elsewhere but, as we'll see later, they spent similar percentages of their time in play in child care as elsewhere.

Because some children spent either no time in a child-care center or were observed only occasionally within such a setting, I have restricted these analyses only to those children who spent at least 20% of their time in such a center and only discuss those cities where children who attended child care were from both social-class groups. Of the children who participated in this research, only 48 (approximately one third of the total) were observed this amount in a formal child-care setting, of whom only three were from Obninsk, two from Tartu, and one from Suwon. I'll therefore discuss only the children from the remaining cities.

Not surprisingly, given their age, the activity in which these children spent most of their time, both in and out of child care, was play (45%–65% of their observations within child care, and 40%–70% of their time in other settings). As we can see from Figure 7.3, White children from Greensboro, children in Oulu, and children in Porto Alegre were somewhat more likely to engage in play and entertainment in child-care settings than in the other settings where they spent their time. The situation was the opposite for Black children from Greensboro and for those in Kisumu, children from middle-class and working-class families alike. This is the first indication that child care may have had a somewhat different meaning for the Black children from Greensboro and their counterparts in Kisumu. This is an issue I'll return to later.

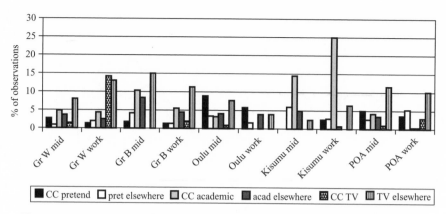

Figure 7.4. Engagement in types of play, in child care and elsewhere.

As I showed in Chapter 6, most of the children's play and entertainment involved toys and other objects designed with children in mind. In the context of child care, it is worth paying particular attention to three types of play – pretend play, because some scholars have noted links between engaging in pretend play and later development (Dansky, 1980; Piaget, 1951/1962; Singer, 1973; Smilansky, 1968), playing with what we termed academic objects (that is, objects designed to help children learn school-relevant things), and watching television, something that seemed to feature relatively frequently in the child-care experiences of working-class White children in Greensboro. As we can see in Figure 7.4, almost 15% of these children's observations in child care featured them watching television, approximately the same amount as they watched in other settings.

The most striking aspect of this figure, however, is the fact that play with academic objects was a common feature of children's child-care experiences in Kisumu, but occurred far less frequently in the other cities. We were somewhat surprised by this, particularly in Greensboro and Porto Alegre, given that one goal of child-care centers is to help children get a good start academically, both in the United States (Tobin et al., 1989) and Brazil (Freitas & Shelton, 2005), and one way in which to do this is to provide school-relevant materials with which the children may play. Middle-class Black children in Greensboro were involved in this type of play in more than 10% of our observations of them in child care, more than twice as many as their White counterparts and their working-class Black counterparts. By contrast, the working-class children in Porto Alegre were almost never seen engaging with these types of materials, whether in child care or outside. It's clear, however, that the Luo children in Kisumu who attended child care spent a good

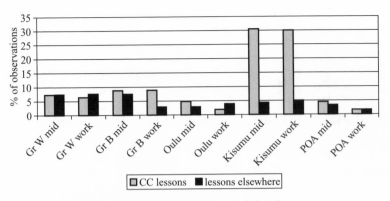

Figure 7.5. Engagement in lessons, in child care and elsewhere.

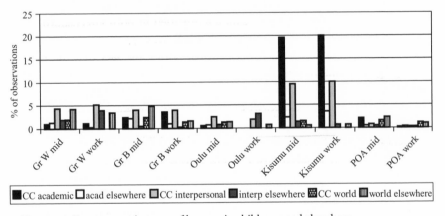

Figure 7.6. Engagement in types of lessons, in child care and elsewhere.

deal more of their time there engaging with objects (books, numbers, letters, shapes, etc.) that had an explicitly school-related focus than was true for children from any other group.

Turning to the lessons in which children engaged (see Figures 7.5 and 7.6), those in Kisumu also clearly differed from the rest, with 30% of their observations in child care featuring lessons, more than three times as many as their counterparts in Greensboro and more than six times as many as the children in Oulu and Porto Alegre. It is also interesting to see that although the children in Greensboro, regardless of ethnic background or social class, were involved in similar percentages of lessons in child care, working-class Black children had far fewer lessons outside child care. Children in Oulu and Porto Alegre were involved in lessons in fewer than 5% of our observations in any setting, and the working-class Brazilian children were involved in almost none. The experiences of the Kenyan children, clearly, were quite different if they attended child care than if they did not.

It is worth looking at the specific lessons (Figure 7.6), however, to see whether children in child care received a greater percentage of school-related lessons (as opposed to interpersonal lessons or lessons about the world) in child care than in other settings. Again, apart from the situation in Kisumu, there was little evidence to support this supposition. In the Kenyan city, the children who spent more than 20% of their time in a child-care setting were far more likely to receive academic lessons there than they were in the other settings in which they spent their time, and far more likely than were any other group of children. Most of the Kisumu children's remaining lessons were interpersonal lessons – lessons, in other words, relating to getting on with others and learning social rules. It is also interesting to note that in the child-care centers that our children attended in both Greensboro and Oulu, interpersonal lessons were the most common type of lesson in which the children were involved. It's also worth noting the fact that the Black working-class children in Greensboro were also likely to get three times as many academic lessons when they were in child care than when they were not, although this difference pales by comparison with the children in Kisumu.

Child-care centers may be good places in which children can engage with others in conversation. There are always other children around, and often a wider selection of adults with whom to converse. Our observations did not support this expectation, however; in virtually all of the groups, those children who were observed more than 20% of the time in a child-care center were far more likely to be involved in conversation in other settings than they were within child care (see Figure 7.7). It's important to remember, however,

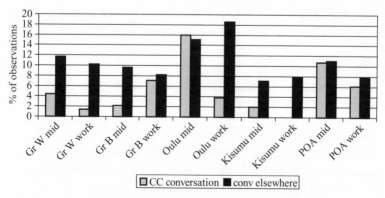

Figure 7.7. Engagement in conversation, in child care and elsewhere.

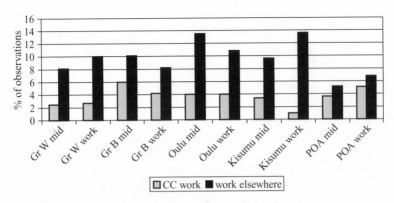

Figure 7.8. Engagement in work, in child care and elsewhere.

that we defined conversation as discourse about things distant in time and space rather than talk that simply was a part of the ongoing activity. The only children for whom the proportions of conversation were similar both in and out of child care were those from middle-class families in Oulu and Porto Alegre, and Black working-class children from Greensboro.

As I'll show shortly, by far the majority of the discourse that we termed conversation involved the child talking with an adult. This was true even in Kisumu, although less clearly than in the remaining cities. It is worth speculating that teachers of the Black working-class children in Greensboro were making a particular effort to engage them in conversation, given the fact that we observed more conversation in this group than in child-care centers attended by children from other groups in Greensboro. (The greater involvement of Black working-class children in conversation in child care mirrors their greater proportion of academic lessons in which they engaged in child care.) Clearly, no such effort was being made for the teachers of our working-class children in Oulu or for teachers of any of the children in Kisumu.

The final activity in which we were interested was work and here, as might be expected, children were typically more likely to be involved in work outside child care than within that setting (see Figure 7.8).

In Figure 7.9, I summarize the various types of activities in which these children engaged in child care. It's important to be aware that in each of the stacked graphs I'm showing the *proportion* of observations of each type of activity in which the various groups of children engaged, as opposed to the *percentage* of observations that have been displayed to this point. It's clear that in each city except Kisumu children spent the bulk of their time in child

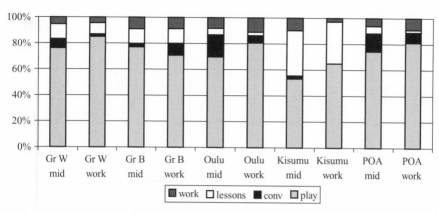

Figure 7.9. Engagement in activities in child care.

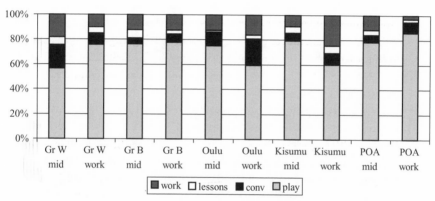

Figure 7.10. Engagement in activities, children who spent no time in child care.

care engaged in play, exploration, and entertainment. Moreover, in each case except among the Black children in Greensboro, middle-class children were more likely than their working-class peers to be involved in lessons while they were in child care. It's also strikingly clear that in Kisumu, children were not in child care to spend the large majority of their time in play and that explicit lessons were far more frequent there than was true for child-care centers in any other city.

It's difficult not to believe that this pattern reflects the current view in Kisumu that the purpose of child care is to prepare children for the entrance exams that they need to pass to gain entrance into what are considered the best schools. Although the Kisumu situation is most clearly different from that of the other cities, it is also worth attending to the fact that the experiences of the Black children in Greensboro, particularly those from working-class

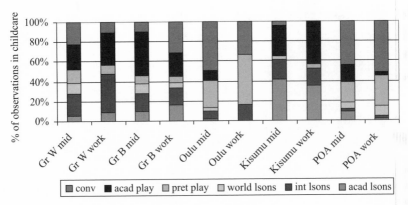

Figure 7.11. Engagement in selected activities in child care.

backgrounds, were also different from their experiences outside child care, perhaps also reflective of prevailing beliefs in this community about the importance of child care as a preparation for the transition to school (Doucet & Tudge 2007).

Comparing Children Attending Child Care with Those Not Attending

Given that I have been focusing so far only on those children who spent 20% or more of their time in a formal child-care setting, it is worth comparing them with those children who spent none of their time in such a setting to assess the extent to which their activities were similar or different. Were the experiences different for children who did not go to child care? In some ways, no; as we've seen, children spent most of their time in play (see Figure 7.10). However, as can be by comparing Figures 7.9 and 7.10, they were far more likely to be involved in work if they did not go to child care – that was most obviously true in the case of the working-class children in Kisumu, who were observed working far more than were any other group. These children were also somewhat more likely to engage in conversation and less likely to be involved in lessons (particularly in the case of the Luo children) than those who spent 20% or more of their time in child care.

A second way of comparing the activities of children who spent time in child care with those who did not attend, is to focus, as I did in Chapter 6, just on those activities that one might expect would be viewed as relevant to later success in school – various types of lessons, pretend play and play with academic objects, and conversation. Examining first just those children who spent time in child care (see Figure 7.11), it is clear just how different the

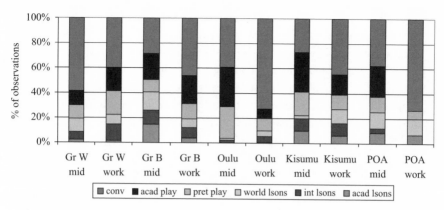

Figure 7.12. Engagement in selected activities, children spending no time in child care.

experiences of Kisumu children were in child-care centers than were those of children in the other cities.

The differences are striking when looking at the same set of selected activities for children who spent no time in child care (Figure 7.12). For example, those children in Kisumu who did not go to child care were involved in a far smaller proportion of lessons and play with academic objects, although a larger proportion of conversation, than did their counterparts who spent a significant amount of time in child care. In Greensboro, in the White community, middle-class and working-class children who did not attend a formal child-care center engaged in a greater proportion of conversation than did their peers who went to child care but were less likely to play with school-related objects. Black children from Greensboro, from both social-class backgrounds, were only half as likely to engage in this set of activities if they did not attend a child care, but working-class children in Oulu were much more likely to be involved in them (particularly conversation) if they did go to child care.

Summary

Among those groups in which some children spent a significant proportion (20% or more) of their time in a formal child-care setting, it thus seems clear that children who attended child care engaged to a somewhat different extent in school-relevant activities than did their peers who did not attend. However, it is also clear that different groups provide different experiences for their children within child care, which may be related to the different functions that child care is expected to fulfill. This is most easy to see in the case of Kisumu, where child care is viewed as a place in which children should be equipped with academic skills. This explains why such a large proportion of the time we observed the Luo children in child-care settings was devoted to lessons or play designed to help children learn school-related skills – far more than these same children received outside of child care. This meant that the experiences of the Luo children who attended child care were significantly different their peers who did not, as can be seen in a comparison of Figures 7.11 and 7.12.

Although Kisumu provided the most obvious example of a clear set of values underlying child care, other cities provided interesting insights into the different functions that child-care centers serve. In Greensboro, for example, we can see differences by both class and race. For working-class White children, the activities in which they engaged within child care in many ways mirrored the activities in which they were involved when they were not in that setting; they even watched the same amount of television in their child-care centers as they did elsewhere. For working-class Black children, however, child care served to involve them in far more lessons (both academic and interpersonal) than they received elsewhere. These children, in fact, received more academic lessons, on average, than did any other group of children except those from Kisumu. Although these working-class Black children were involved, outside of child care, in somewhat fewer conversations with adults than were children in the other groups from Greensboro, they were involved in far more such conversations inside child care than were children in the other groups. Overall, the impression is given that the goals for these children in child care were clearly different from the goals for children from the three other groups.

In neither Oulu nor Porto Alegre was there any evidence that the children who attended formal child-care centers were being encouraged to be involved in a greater extent of school-related activities than they were likely to get elsewhere. The only striking difference was that working-class children in Oulu were far less likely to be involved in conversation in child care than they were elsewhere. In fact, in both of these cities, as was the case for the child-care centers attended by the White children from Greensboro, the centers' primary goal appeared to be to provide a secure place in which children could play with other children. This may reflect the belief that play is what children should be doing at this age and that they learn through their play.

Children in the three remaining cities – Obninsk, Tartu, and Suwon – did not attend child-care centers in sufficient numbers to allow us to make these types of comparisons. In the case of Suwon, one might suppose that this reflected cultural values; in Korea, traditionally, mothers stayed at home with their children and were unlikely to enroll them in preschool institutions.

However, as I mentioned in Chapter 5, Korean views have changed in recent years, and more mothers of young children work outside the home and use some type of formal child-care arrangement. In our study, the lack of data from preschool stems primarily from the fact that eight families that had agreed to participate in the study could not be included because the preschools the children attended did not give us permission to collect data there. In the case of Obninsk and Tartu, however, the situation was different. In those two cities, although there is a tradition of young children attending kindergarten (*detskie sadi* in Russia), some of our families preferred having their children at home until the year before the start of formal schooling, if possible, whereas others simply could not afford the rates charged by the growing number of private preschools.

THE PARTNERS IN ACTIVITIES

Who did the children spend their time with in these various settings? As discussed in Chapter 4, we were able to code an array of categories of partners, as well as indicate when children were involved in an activity by themselves. As described in that chapter, individuals were coded as a partner if they were either engaged in an active way with the child (participating in the activity, or trying to facilitate, direct, or prevent it) or were observing the child engaged in the activity. People who were simply in the same setting as the child were not considered partners but were coded as being "available" to the child. We were able to code up to five partners in any single activity in which the child was engaged. I focus on the following situations: children involved by themselves, with other children, with teachers in child care, grandparents, and the child's mother and father (including men who had taken the role of father, regardless of biological connection).

I'm not going to provide the raw numbers of partners in each activity, because this would be somewhat misleading given that children in these different groups engaged in different numbers of activities. Instead, for each activity, I show the proportion of partners who were other children, a child-care provider, mother, and so on. This type of graphic representation helps us to see, I think, the extent to which children in these different groups were involved with different types of social partners.

Partners in Play

The majority of the children's time, as we already know, was spent engaged in play, and in many of their observations the children played alone, about 25% of the time on average across all the cities (see Figure 7.13). Their most

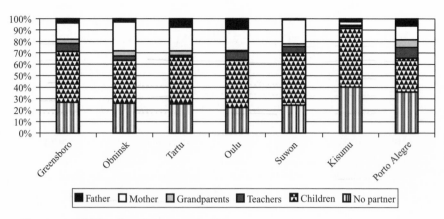

Figure 7.13. Children's main partners in play.

frequent partners were other children (40% on average), with mothers, fathers, grandparents, and child-care providers the other main partners. These percentages somewhat underrepresent the extent of involvement of children and teachers, several of whom could be involved in an observation of a single activity; a mother or father, by contrast, could necessarily be observed no more than once per observation of an activity.

Looking at the situation in the different cities, it is clear from Figure 7.13 that the children in Kisumu had strikingly different experiences from their counterparts in the other cities, with adults much less frequently involved in children's play than was true in the other cities. As I pointed out in Chapter 2, the data from Kenya, predominantly from rural areas, has shown that parents and other adults do not see themselves as children's partners in play. These data, from an urban area and with educated parents, suggest that adults are involved, although less so than adults elsewhere. Whereas in the other cities adults constituted about 30% to 35% of the children's partners in play, in Kisumu adults featured as about 8% of the partners. In each of the cities, we can see that mothers were far more likely to be involved with their children in play than were fathers, and also more than were other adults, whether grandparents (including other extended family members) or teachers.

Unlike the impression provided by many observational studies of young children at play in the United States and England (see Chapter 2) of mothers being the primary partner in the play of their children, our data reveal that these three-year-olds played by themselves as much as they played with their mothers and were far more likely to play with other children than with adults. The results from earlier research may, in part, be an artifact of the prevailing tendency to observe children in and around the home and to recruit families

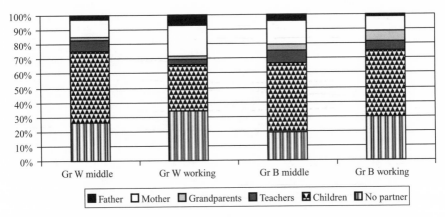

Figure 7.14. Main partners in play (Greensboro, by ethnicity and class).

in which the mother is at home during the periods of observation. By contrast, the time-use data, also presented in Chapter 2, seriously underrepresent mothers' involvement with their children.

To examine the variations by ethnicity and social class, I'll break down the results into the same three clusters as I did in Chapter 6, looking first at the Greensboro families; then at the northeastern European cities of Obninsk, Tartu, and Oulu; and finally at the "diverse" group from Suwon, Kisumu, and Porto Alegre. In Greensboro (see Figure 7.14), middle-class children were less likely to play alone than were their working-class counterparts; by contrast, the former spent more time playing with other children than did the latter, particularly in the White community. In each group, mothers were far more likely to have been observed engaged in play with their children than were fathers, and in the Black community grandparents (primarily the grandmother) were far more likely to be involved than they were in the White community.

It is interesting to note that in each of the northeastern European cities, as in Greensboro, working-class children were more likely than their middle-class counterparts to play by themselves and middle-class children more likely to be observed playing with other children (see Figure 7.15). Other class differences were not particularly noticeable. Children were more likely to be involved in play with their fathers in both Oulu and Tartu than they were in Obninsk, and grandparents were more likely to be involved in their children's play in Obninsk and Tartu than they were in Oulu.

In the final group of cities, it is clear (see Figure 7.16) that city differences were far more striking than were class differences. As I already mentioned,

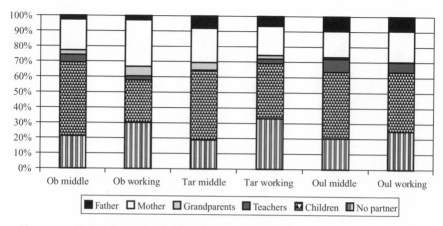

Figure 7.15. Main partners in play (northeastern Europe, by class).

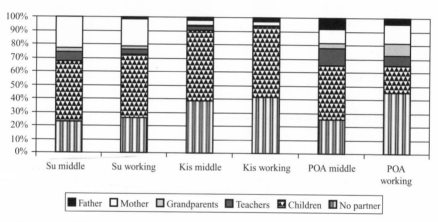

Figure 7.16. Main partners in play (diverse cities, by class).

adults in Kisumu were not often observed engaging with children in the course of their play; these Kenyan children were far more likely to play either alone or in the company of other children. However, adults constituted a little more than 10% of the play partners of the middle-class children and about 6% of the partners of working-class children, more than one might have expected from the literature. In Suwon, fathers were involved with their children even less than they were in Kisumu, but the mothers were at least as likely to be engaged in play with their children as they were in any other city.

Interestingly, as in each of the other cities, children from working-class families were more likely to be observed playing alone than were children from middle-class backgrounds, but the differences were minimal in Suwon and Kisumu. In Porto Alegre, however, the children's social experiences were more similar to those of their counterparts in Greensboro and the north-eastern European cities than they were to those in Suwon and Kisumu, with the middle-class children more likely to play with other children than by themselves, the opposite of the situation for children from working-class backgrounds. The middle-class children from Porto Alegre were also the only group for whom both parents constituted almost 20% of children's play partners and in which the father was as likely as the mother to be involved in play with their children.

Partners in Work

Are the patterns that we found for the predominant partners in children's play also found in the case of the work in which the children were involved, either as participants or close observers? Play, of course, is the sphere of children. Although in some communities mothers were highly likely to be involved in their children's play (middle-class families from Suwon were the clearest examples of this), for the most part children either played alone or had other children as their social partners in their play. In the case of work, however, one might expect that adults would be more likely to be involved. To what extent was this supposition born out?

In most cases, as can be seen in Figure 7.17, adults were indeed the main partners (60%–80%) in the work in which children were involved, with the mother the most likely partner, except in Kisumu, where other children were

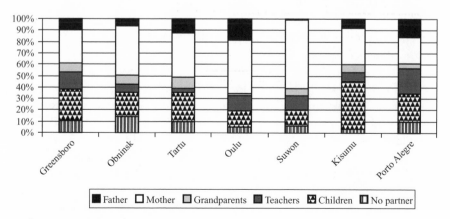

Figure 7.17. Main partners in work.

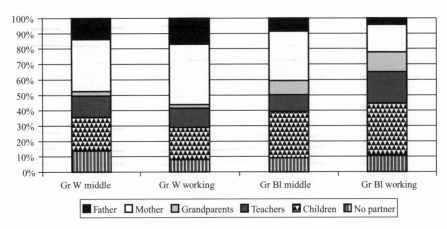

Figure 7.18. Main partners in work (Greensboro, ethnicity and class).

as likely to feature as partners in work as were the children's own parents, and Porto Alegre, where the partners were evenly distributed across fathers, mothers, child-care providers, and other children.

When breaking the results down by class and ethnicity (see Figure 7.18), we can see that in the Black communities in Greensboro other children and grandparents (specifically, grandmothers) were more common partners, proportionally speaking, than was the case in the White communities, where the mother and father represented approximately 50% of the children's partners in work.

The same situation was found in northeastern Europe, where the mother and father were the children's partners in work in 40% to 60% of all cases. Mothers, as is clearly shown in Figure 7.19, were the children's primary partners in all cases although working-class fathers in both Tartu and Oulu constituted approximately 20% of the children's partners in work.

The situation in the remaining cities was a good deal more variable. As was true for the play in which children were involved, Suwon mothers were by far the most likely partner in the work in which their children were engaged, in approximately 60% of all cases (see Figure 7.20). In Kisumu, by contrast, other children were heavily involved in work with "our" children (in around 40% of the cases), although the children's mother was also a common partner, particularly in the working-class community. In Porto Alegre, as also was true for children's play, mothers and fathers played a more equal role as partners in the work that the children did, especially in the middle-class community.

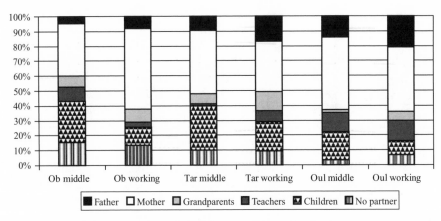

Figure 7.19. Main partners in work (northeastern Europe, by class).

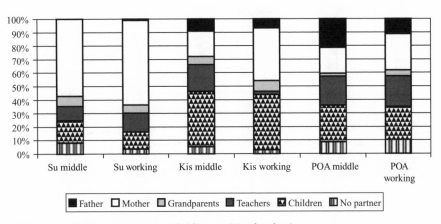

Figure 7.20. Main partners in work (diverse cities, by class).

Partners in Lessons

The remaining two categories of activities, lessons and conversation, almost by definition do not go on without partners. As we can see in Figure 7.21, as was true for both play and work, when children were involved in lessons, their mothers were also likely to be involved with them. Other children were also likely to be involved, particularly in Kisumu, and child-care teachers also took a larger role in all cities except Tartu, where few of the children spent any time in child care, whether formal or informal.

Looking at the data separately by ethnicity and class, when Greensboro children were involved in lessons, 20% to 30% of their partners were

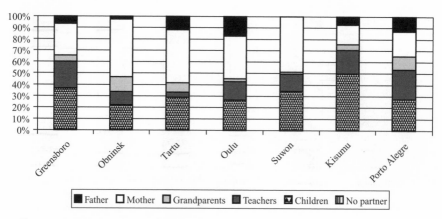

Figure 7.21. Main partners in lessons.

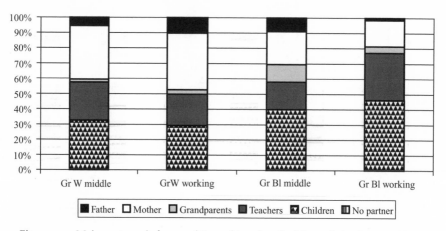

Figure 7.22. Main partners in lessons (Greensboro, by ethnicity and class).

teachers, although consistently a larger proportion consisted of other children (see Figure 7.22). This is primarily because when children were in a child-care setting they were far more likely to have a lesson in the company of a teacher and several other children. In the Black community, particularly among middle-class families, we also can see the greater role of grandparents (specifically grandmothers).

In the northeastern European cities, by contrast, we can see that mothers comprised the major partner in the lessons in which their children were involved in all cases except in the Oulu middle-class families, where other children played a larger role. It is also clear from Figure 7.23 that in both Tartu and Oulu fathers were more involved than they were in Obninsk. For

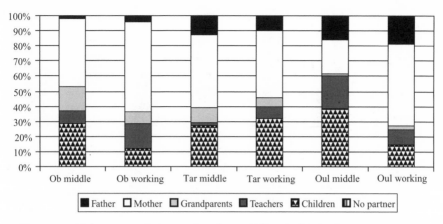

Figure 7.23. Main partners in lessons (northeastern Europe, by class).

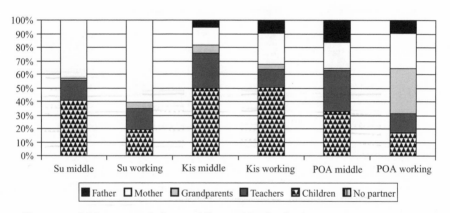

Figure 7.24. Main partners in lessons (diverse cities, by class).

middle-class Finnish children from Oulu, in fact, fathers were almost as likely to partner their children in lessons as were mothers and teachers.

In the remaining cities (see Figure 7.24), perhaps the most notable finding is that Kisumu adults served as their children's partners in half of their lessons, a far greater proportion than in either play or work. It is also interesting to see that when working-class children in Porto Alegre were involved in a lesson, they were most likely to be in the company of a grandparent and that when their middle-class counterparts were involved in a lesson, they were almost as likely to be involved with their fathers as their mothers. In Suwon, as we've seen in the other activities, the children's mothers were the most common partner in lessons.

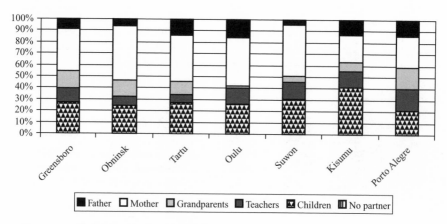

Figure 7.25. Main partners in conversation.

Partners in Conversation

When the children were involved in conversation, that is, talking about things that were not part of the ongoing situation, a similar pattern of partners was found as was true of lessons (see Figure 7.25). In most of the cities (the exception being Kisumu), mothers were the main person with whom the children engaged in conversation. In the Kenyan city, by contrast, other children constituted approximately 40% of the conversational partners. In Porto Alegre, partners were fairly evenly distributed across the major groups of partners.

Working-class fathers in Greensboro were more likely to be involved in their children's conversations than were their middle-class counterparts (see Figure 7.26). In the Black families, fathers constituted more than 20% of their children's partners in conversation, more so than mothers in the working-class Black community. As we have seen in the observations of play and work, grandparents also played a larger role as conversational partners than we found in the other cities.

In the northeastern European cities (see Figure 7.27), also as we saw in the cases of play and work, fathers were more likely to be involved in their children's conversations in Tartu and Oulu than they were in Obninsk, but, in all cases, mothers were far more likely to feature as partners than were fathers. In both Obninsk and Tartu, however, grandparents were more likely to feature as partners in conversation than they were in Oulu.

The remaining cities, as we saw with regard to the other major categories of activities, are dissimilar from one another in terms of the main partners in

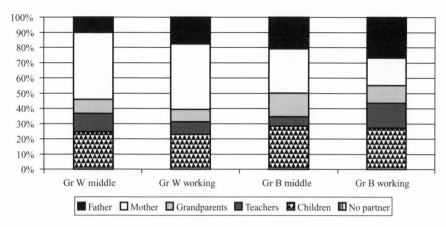

Figure 7.26. Main partners in conversation (Greensboro, by ethnicity and class).

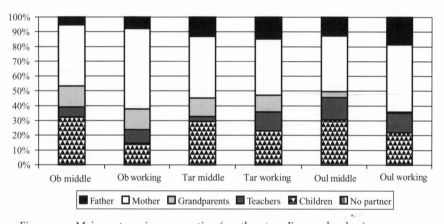

Figure 7.27. Main partners in conversation (northeastern Europe, by class).

conversation (see Figure 7.28). In Suwon, the Korean mothers again featured as the primary partner, but fathers also had some role, although still much less than in the other cities. In Kisumu, in the middle-class community, teachers were the second most common partners in the children's conversations (after other children), and, in the working-class community, the children's fathers constituted almost 20% of the children's partners in conversation. In the working-class Porto Alegre families, grandparents were their children's predominant partners in conversations, filling a similar role in that Brazilian city as they had with regard to their children's lessons.

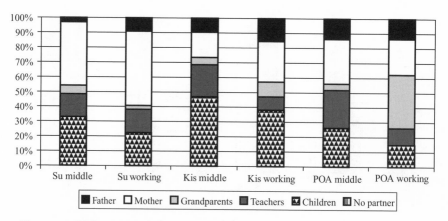

Figure 7.28. Main partners in conversation (diverse cities, by class).

Summary

As we saw in Chapter 6, the majority of these children's time was spent in play, with work, lessons, and conversation occupying a far smaller proportion of their daily activities. It's worth stressing this, because when we want to get a sense of who are the children's most common partners in activities, it's clear that other children take that position, given that play is their predominant activity. Of the various adults who are involved with the children, in all groups, it is the mother who is most likely to be involved. That's even the case in Kisumu, where adults are less involved in children's activities than we found in the other cities. Although the Luo mothers were only occasionally involved with their children in play, they were the most common adult partner in work and, although only in the case of the working-class children, in lessons and conversation. In all of the remaining cities except for Porto Alegre, mothers were the children's most common partner in work, lessons, and conversations, most obviously in Suwon. In Porto Alegre, by contrast, teachers were typically at least as likely as mothers to be involved in these activities as were mothers. This should not be such a surprise, given that children in Porto Alegre were more likely than children in the other cities to spend time in a child-care center.

Children in each of the groups were far less likely to be involved in activities with their fathers than they were with their mothers, although fathers played a more active role, proportionally, in their children's work, lessons, and conversations than they did in their children's play. As for grandmothers, they were most commonly found as the children's partners in the Black communities in Greensboro, in Obninsk and Tartu, and among the working-class group in Porto Alegre. Why do we find this different distribution of partners in children's everyday activities? In part, the answer can be found in beliefs about who should be involved with children. But another, somewhat related, explanation has to do with the availability of partners.

THE AVAILABILITY OF PARTNERS

The graphs presented in the previous few pages show nicely the proportions of people with whom our children interacted in the course of their main types of activities. In the case of Kisumu, I pointed out that the relative dearth of adult partners, compared with child partners, in this Kenyan city stemmed in part from a belief that adults are not appropriate play partners for their children. Other variations, however, stemmed from the types of settings in which children were situated and the company they had available to them in those settings. For example, children who spent a greater proportion of their time in a child-care center obviously had greater access to teachers (and typically to other children) than children who did not. By the same token, they clearly would have had less possibility for engagement with either parent. The fact that the children in Porto Alegre were observed, on average, 30% of the time in child care, whereas their counterparts in Tartu were only observed in a child-care setting in 5% of our observations and children in Suwon even less, obviously has implications for the availability of partners. Similarly, children who spent more of their time in and around the home were more likely to spend time with the people who were at home with them.

In groups in which fathers are either more likely than mothers to work outside the home or, when both parents work outside the home, are more likely to work longer hours, mothers are likely to be more available to their children. In groups in which the mother is more likely than the father to have custody of the child following divorce, children of divorced parents are likely to spend more time with the mother than the father. In groups in which fathers and mothers need neither marry nor live together following the birth of their child and in which the child lives with the mother, fathers will be less available to their children than will mothers.

Thus, in Suwon, where mothers tend to stay home with their young children and fathers work long hours outside the home, it is not surprising that mothers constitute the primary partners of the children there. Similarly, when the family was a mother-headed household, as was the case with some of the Black families in Greensboro, some of the Obninsk families, and some of the working-class families in Porto Alegre, the mother obviously featured more than the father as a partner in the child's activities. In groups in which

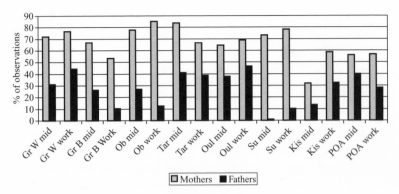

Figure 7.29. Availability of mothers and fathers.

children are cared for by their grandmothers when the mother is working outside the home, grandmothers will be more available; where children are more likely to be placed into some type of formal child-care center, teachers and other children will be more available to them than would be the case otherwise. In this section, therefore, I discuss involvement as a function of availability.

In recent years, scholars (Lamb, 1987, 1997, 2000; Lewis, 1997; Lewis & Dessen, 1999; Parke, 2000; Pleck, 1997; Tamis-LeMonda & Cabrera, 2002) have started to pay a good deal more attention both to the availability and involvement of fathers in the rearing of young children. (Lamb [1997, 2000] and Parke [2000] also noted the importance of examining the extent to which fathers take on responsibility for their children, but this is not something on which we focused in our research.) For this reason, we always noted, while doing the observations, whether the mother or father was in the same vicinity as the child – that is, within reasonable earshot or eyeshot, so that he or she could be called to participate in some activity or to help the child if he or she were in trouble.

As one might expect, given the previous discussion of the mother as a main partner in her children's activities, mothers were with their children a lot of the time, across all of our groups in about two thirds of our observations (see Figure 7.29). Fathers were in the same vicinity as their children less than half as often, in less than 30% of the observations, across all communities. However, there was also a great deal of variation across all groups; the middle-class Luo mothers were available to their children in only 30% of our observations, whereas White mothers in Greensboro and mothers in Obninsk, Tartu, and Suwon were available to their children in more than 70% of the observations. Fathers also varied greatly in the extent to which they were available to their children, from a low of 1% in the case of the middle-class families in Suwon, to around 40% in the White working-class families in Greensboro, families in Tartu and Oulu, and middle-class families in Porto Alegre.

Some of these variations, as I mentioned, may be explained by beliefs about who should spend time with children. Others, however, require different explanations. In the White working-class group in Greensboro, one father was divorced and did not see his daughter during the week of the observations. In the African American communities, the fathers from one middle-class and two working-class families were no longer living with the family, and the children (a girl and two boys) had no contact with him. In Obninsk, three children, a middle-class girl and two working-class boys, were living only with their mother, because of divorce (in the girl's case), because the mother had never lived with the boy's father, or because the father was away looking for work. In Porto Alegre, four working-class children (three boys) were living in mother-only families. In none of these cases were father figures involved; had they been, they would have been counted as fathers. The situation was somewhat different in Kisumu, where two of the families were polygamous. In these cases, the father was necessarily spread somewhat thinner than might otherwise have been the case.

Overall, it's clear that children spend more of their time with their mothers than they do with their fathers. However, the question still remains about the extent to which mothers and fathers actually engage with their children in these various activities when they are around. Lamb (1997, 2000) and Parke (2000) have suggested that fathers may be as involved as are mothers, at least when taking into account fathers' typically less frequent availability, although the prevailing view is that the nature of those activities is different. "Mothers actually play with their children much more than fathers, but as a proportion of the total amount of child–parent interaction, play is a much more prominent component of father–child interaction" (Lamb, 2000, p. 34). As the Boston fathers studied by Harkness and Super (1992) pointed out, their time may have been limited with their children but, they argued, it was balanced by the quality of the interactions. Whether these conceptions of the father's role are justified can be examined in our data. In the following section, therefore, I take into account the availability of both the mother and father and address the question of whether fathers are involved in the various activities as much as mothers, given the extent to which they are present.

In terms of the lessons in which the children were involved, as we have seen, mothers were more involved than were fathers. Even when taking into account the fathers' lesser availability, mothers played a greater role than

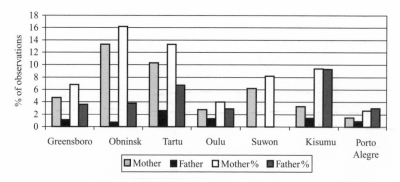

Figure 7.30. Mothers and fathers as partner in lessons (raw and proportional).

did fathers, in all cases except Kisumu and Porto Alegre (see Figure 7.30). It is interesting to note that in those cities in which neither mothers nor fathers were frequently observed as partners in their children's lessons (Oulu, Kisumu, and Porto Alegre), fathers and mothers were most similar in the extent to which they partnered their children in lessons, when expressed as a percentage of availability.

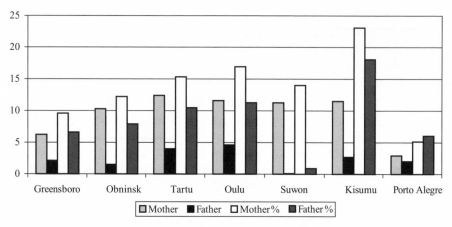

Figure 7.31. Mothers and fathers as partners in work (raw and proportional).

In terms of work, mothers were again more likely to be the children's partners than were fathers, and this was true both in absolute terms and when expressed as a percentage of availability (see Figure 7.31). In all cities except Suwon, however, fathers were almost as likely to engage in work with their children as were mothers (given their availability), and in Porto Alegre fathers were actually more likely to be involved in work with their children than were mothers.

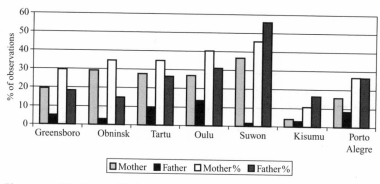

Figure 7.32. Mothers and fathers as partners in play (raw and proportional).

In terms of play, our expectation was that fathers might have played more with their children than did mothers, at least when expressed as a percentage of their availability. We found this expectation to be supported only in the cases of Suwon and Kisumu (see Figure 7.32). As I mentioned with regard to lessons, it is interesting to note that these two cities featured families in which the fathers rarely played with their children. These data indicate, however, that when they were involved with their children, particularly in Suwon, they were (proportionally speaking) a good deal more likely to play with their children than were the mothers. In Porto Alegre, as we have seen consistently throughout this discussion of children's partners in activities, although mothers were more likely than fathers to play with their children in absolute terms, when fathers were around their children, they were just as likely to play with them as were their mothers. In the remaining cities, however, mothers were more likely to play with their children both in absolute and proportional terms.

Finally, mothers were more likely to converse with their children than were fathers, in absolute terms, but in most of the cities, fathers were almost as likely as mothers to be involved in conversation with their children when expressed as a proportion of availability (see Figure 7.33). The exceptions were Oulu, where fathers conversed less than mothers with their children even when they were present, and Suwon, where they conversed more. When the Suwon fathers were around their children (a rather infrequent situation in the families we observed), they were highly likely to be involved with them either in play or in conversation.

It thus seems fairly clear that, in each of these cities, with data gathered in precisely the same way, we see that children are much more likely to be engaged in activities that feature the mother than the father. Nonetheless, once we break down the data into the different socioeconomic and, in

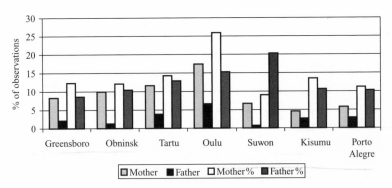

Figure 7.33. Mothers and fathers as partners in conversation (raw and proportional).

Greensboro, racial/ethnic groups, some groups of fathers were actually more involved with their children than were mothers after we take into account differences in the extent of availability to their children.

In Greensboro, Black middle-class fathers were somewhat more likely to be involved in their children's lessons (6.4% of their time with the child, compared with 5.6% of the time the children's mothers were with them). Similarly, working-class Black fathers spent a slightly greater proportion of their time with their children conversing with them than did the children's mothers (9.8% vs. 8.8%). Among families in the northeastern European cities, working-class fathers in Obninsk (17.3% vs. 12.3%) were more likely and middle-class fathers in Tartu were as likely (16.3% in each case) to spend their time with their children conversing as were the children's mothers. In the "diverse" cities, middle-class fathers in Porto Alegre typically spent a greater proportion of their time with their children engaging in lessons (4.4% vs. 3.6%), work (6.8% vs. 4.2%), and play (30.6% vs. 24.1%), and working-class fathers there spent a greater proportion of their time conversing with their children than did mothers (10.7% vs. 7.7%).

In Kisumu, too, middle-class fathers spent a greater proportion of their time with their children engaging in lessons (9.7% vs. 6.3%) and playing with their children (36.5% vs. 14.5%), and working-class fathers in Kisumu spent a greater proportion of their time engaging in lessons with their children (9.7% vs. 6.3%) and conversing with them than did the children's mothers (12.7% vs. 12%). However, it was in Suwon that the greatest discrepancies were seen. Middle-class fathers spent a much greater proportion of their time playing with their children than did the children's mothers (88.7% vs. 50%) and conversing with them (37% of their time vs. 13%); working-class fathers there also spent a greater proportion of their time with the children conversing with them (7% vs. 5.1%).

We should be cautious about putting too much weight simply on these proportional figures, however. It's true that our Korean fathers in Suwon were much more likely to play and talk with their children when they were together, but the fact still remains that they were together a tiny portion of time. As in the old *Doonesbury* cartoon in which a father proudly boasted of the 10 minutes of "quality" time that he spent with his child, the fact still remains that the mothers in our study were far more involved with their young children than were their fathers, simply because they spent, on the whole, much more of their time with their children. The only evidence to support the views of Lamb (1997, 2000), Parke (2000), and Harkness and Super (1992) that once fathers' availability is taken into account, they are as involved as are mothers in the play of their children was found in Suwon and Kisumu (where fathers were least likely to be available or involved) and in Porto Alegre. These Brazilian fathers best exemplify what Lamb, Parke, and others have argued. However, the situation in Greensboro, Obninsk, Tartu, and Oulu does not provide good evidence for their position.

Nonetheless, we still need to bear in mind the individual variations that are disguised by these group averages. Just as children engage in different activities in part because of their different inclinations, their temperaments, and their motivations, so, too, do parents have their unique qualities. In just over 10% of our cases (15 of the 141 families that participated in this study), fathers were actually more involved in their children's activities – not in proportional but actual terms. These fathers were from the White working-class community in Greensboro (this father had a son), two from the working-class Black community from Greensboro (both fathers had daughters), a working-class father of a boy in Obninsk, two fathers of boys from Oulu (one from each social-class group), four middle-class fathers, two of boys and two of girls, in Kisumu, and five fathers from Porto Alegre (three from middle-class backgrounds, each of whom had sons), and two working-class fathers (one with a son and one with a daughter).

CONCLUSION

In this chapter, I have focused primarily on aspects of the context. As many scholars (e.g., Weisner, 1989; Whiting, 1980) have pointed out, culture's importance is in part as a provider of settings. The types of settings in which children are situated have clear implications for the activities in which they are likely to engage and the people with whom they are likely to interact. In the data presented here, we can see this most obviously in the case of Kisumu, where those Luo children who attended child care had very different experiences from those they had outside child care and from the experiences of children who did not attend child care at all. However, we also saw the impact of setting on Black working-class children from Greensboro. These children had approximately half the lessons and one third of the conversations compared with their White middle-class counterparts; however, the one place where they were likely to get such interaction with adults was in child-care centers, where they were involved, proportionally speaking, in twice as many such interactions as in other settings. As I pointed out earlier, setting is particularly important in these cases as child-care centers may be viewed by some families and teachers in Kisumu and Greensboro as places in which children should be helped to prepare for school.

However, it's equally clear that there are other groups for whom child care has no such meaning. For the working-class White children who attended child care, the activities in which they engaged were strikingly similar to those they had outside of child care; the same was true for children in Oulu and Porto Alegre. For these children, the prevailing sense was likely to have been that child care was an opportunity for play and entertainment.

Toward the end of Chapter 6, I discussed the differences between the time-use data, gathered by interviewing parents about how their young children spend their time, and the data that we gathered. I noted there that our finding that the Greensboro children, on average, spent approximately 16% of their time in some type of formal child-care setting closely matched what the national time-use data found, but that the parents, not surprisingly, could not report on *how* their children spent their time while in child care (or, for that matter, in any setting in which the parents were not with them). Only by following the children can one get a sense of how their time is spent when their parents are not with them.

We found, when following children in Greensboro who spent a significant amount of time in child care, that their activities inside and outside child care revealed some striking similarities and differences. On average, they spent about as much time in play within child care (56.7% of the time) as in other places (55.8%), slightly more time involved in academic lessons (1.8% within child care; 1.2% elsewhere), were less likely to engage in conversation (3.8% vs. 10%) and in work (5.1% vs. 9.1%), and were less likely to watch television (4.4% vs. 11.8%) in child care than elsewhere.

In addition, of course, by following the children, it is possible to go beyond the generic data reported in the time-use studies; our data allow us to provide far more detail about the types of play in which the children were involved, who initiated their various activities, who their partners were (and what the children were doing when they were alone), and so on. To be sure, it is possible to get at more of the details of exactly what the children are doing by asking the mothers more specific questions. As we reported elsewhere (Tudge et al., in press), when mothers of preschool-aged children were asked to report on the extent to which their children engaged in things mathematical (but with no specific prompting), they indicated that the children did so once or twice a day; when prompted for various types of mathematical activities, they responded that the children engaged in most of them several times a week! We reported in the same paper that the method of collecting data (asking parents to report, listening to audiotaped mother–child interactions, doing live observations in the home and child-care center, or videotaping children's play) was heavily implicated in the extent to which children appear to be involved in mathematics.

Settings are important not only for the types of activities they encourage or discourage; they also have implications for the types of people with whom children can interact on a regular basis. In the industrialized world, at least as represented by the United States and England (where much of the more ethnographic work on young children's experiences in the industrialized world has been done), the prevailing view is that young children's main partners in activity are their mothers. I believe that this view is partly a function of when these interviews and observations were carried out (a period when many more mothers did not work outside the home), but mostly a function of the approach taken. When parents are telephoned or interviewed at home and asked to report on their children's activities, or when observations are restricted to the homes (choosing times when mothers are at home with their children), it's not altogether surprising that mothers are viewed as their children's primary partner. By contrast, when cultural anthropologists try to find out who spends time with young children in various parts of the majority world, they rely on observations in any of the places young children are likely to be found.

When adopting this more anthropological approach to data collection, what my colleagues and I found is far more varied than has typically been reported. Even in those groups in which the mother was available to (that is, in the immediate environment of) her child in more than 70% of our observations (in Greensboro, Obninsk, Tartu, and Suwon), she was only the child's partner in approximately 20% to 30% of our observations of the child playing. Children played either alone or had other children as partners in a much larger percentage of the observations. Mothers were their partners in the play of the children far less in Kisumu, as might have been expected given the prevailing literature, but also in Porto Alegre. To be sure, she occupied a larger role, proportionally speaking, in terms of the other activities (30%–60% of the work in which the children were involved, 20%–50% of the lessons, and 20%–50% of the conversations) in which the children were involved. However, given that the children in all of these cities were far more involved in play than in any other activity, it is difficult to argue on the basis of our data that the mother is the child's primary partner.

It's also worth stressing that even in Kisumu, where the mothers were only available in 30% of the observations of the middle-class children and in 60% of the observations of the working-class children, they still partnered their children in about 30% of the work in which their children were involved and about 20% of their children's lessons and conversations. This does not accord well with the view that Kenyan mothers are not important social partners for their children, although I need to stress that they were, as many authors have pointed out, much less involved in play with their children than was the case in the other cities.

The fathers in this study, on the whole, were not heavily involved in their young children's everyday activities, although there were some notable exceptions. In part this was simply because they were far less available to their children. However, even taking their lesser availability into account, fathers were not as involved as were mothers. In Obninsk and the Black communities of Greensboro, grandmothers were more involved than were fathers in all the children's activities, including play, and in each of the cities in which a significant number of the children attended a formal child-care setting teachers (all of whom were women) were as involved as were fathers. Although the exceptions should not be forgotten, it is generally the case that the adult world with which these young children engaged was a female world.

To this point, then, we have examined the children's main activities, the settings in which they experience these activities, and the social partners with whom they interact in the course of these activities. In the next chapter, I focus more on the individual children themselves, to give a sense of how they actually spent their everyday lives.

8   Everyday Lives

One is constantly wondering what sort of lives other people lead, and how they take things.

George Eliot, *Middlemarch*, 1872/1988, p. 268

To this point, I have concentrated on the various types of activities in which the children were involved, how the children became involved in those activities, where they were situated, and the extent to which their differing settings changed the extent to which they were involved in various activities, and their main partners in their activities. However, this approach has not allowed us to see the ebb and flow of children's lives, to view children's everyday lives in a more holistic way. In this chapter, therefore, I focus on the children themselves, drawing on the field notes that the observers wrote as they did the live observations. I've chosen four periods during the day: in the morning; early afternoon; late afternoon/early evening; and the time leading up to the children going to sleep.

It's important to specify that I haven't chosen children to illustrate any particular points. There were only two criteria for choosing specific children. The first was that I should draw equally on children from each city (the only exception being in Greensboro, where we collected data from two ethnic/racial groups), with equal numbers of children from middle-class and working-class families. The second was that, having decided to illustrate these four times of the day, the observations had to cover a minimum of two hours. In the case of some children, for example, the observations stopped on one day in the middle of the period I wanted to describe and started at the same time on another day, and I was therefore unable to use these notes. My selection of the children followed no other rules.

MORNING

Andy, in Greensboro

Andy, a middle-class White boy, has been awake for a little more than an hour by 8:15 on a Friday morning in February. His father had made him, his younger sister, and their mother their breakfast while Andy was being washed and dressed, and at 8:15 he's watching the news on TV with his father. The news is showing images of the first United States–Iraq Gulf War. "It's about the war; it's about the army," he says several times. His mother, shortly after, is helping him brush his teeth and talking to him about what he's seen on TV, and how he's learning about what's happening in the world. When they're done, they go into his bedroom where he starts playing with one of his "Ninja Turtles," and he explains to his mother about how the turtles use swords to hurt "the bad guys." His mother sets the timer to give him five minutes more play before they have to leave for preschool, and soon thereafter his mother drives him there.

It's almost 9 when they get there, and while Andy takes off his coat his mother talks to the teacher, and Andy wanders around the room, apparently looking for something to do or someone to play with, and joins several children who are looking at a fireman's helmet. The teacher tells the children that they'll have to take turns. Andy joins another boy playing at being firemen driving a fire engine, but shortly thereafter the teacher tells the group that it's "circle" time. Another boy sits next to Andy in the circle and tells him that he loves him. The teacher talks to the children about the number three, and the children have to find shirts that have three things on them. The children then go to various areas of the room, with some pasting the number three and three apples onto some paper. Andy joins them, and when he's finished with this task, about 10 minutes later, he gets himself a "block pass" (something that allows him to play in the blocks), puts it on, and goes over to the block area to a structure a girl has built. He tells her he is going to "cut" it and begins to start removing blocks. She tells him "No," then he changes and says he's going to fix it and make it "more better." He works on it and says, "there, isn't that better?" and the girl says "yes" and he keeps working on it. By 10, the girl has left the area and Andy and two other boys have built a larger structure and are now pretending that they are "army guys" and defending it against "attackers" ("Here they come!"). When the structure falls down, they move on to the Tinker Toys and start to make "sprayers" with them. One teacher comes over and says that she hopes that they're not using them as guns, which isn't allowed, and another teacher tells them that they need to put something round on the ends.

Naomi, in Greensboro

A Friday morning in May has begun rather differently for Naomi, a Black middle-class girl. She had gone to bed after 10 the night before and was rather resistant to getting out of bed soon after 6. By 8, she's already been at her child-care center for an hour and has just finished eating a snack. Naomi goes over to the block area and joins two boys and a girl who are building things with Legos. She complains to a teacher that the girl has taken her car, and when she gets it back, she and the boys play cars together, making the sounds of police sirens. Naomi has brought a doll and a book to school for "share" day and shows both to her teacher who is busy taking the clothes off dolls and washing them in a small tub. The teacher tries to persuade Naomi to help her, but soon after it's time for "group time" and the children all sit down, some with the books that they've brought from home. The teacher chooses one and reads it to the group, calling on the children to repeat names of the characters, while Naomi listens and plays with some Legos.

At about 8:30 a second teacher brings in some food, and the teacher says that it's time to clean up, and for the children to put their books and toys back into their cubbies, where they keep their personal belongings. She hands out Wet Wipes for the children to clean their tables, and tells Naomi to take it to the trash when Naomi tries to hand back to her the dirty wipe. Before passing out the food, the teacher leads the children in prayer and then asks who wants some oatmeal. Naomi says that she doesn't and accepts some crackers and milk instead. "You're being too loud," says a teacher. "We're inside; we don't need to use our outside voices." Naomi is at a table with four other children, but she turns her chair around so that she can see what children at another table are doing. She calls for the teacher, but the teacher responds, "Quit calling me!" and goes back to handing out cloths to the children so that they can wipe their faces. The other teacher is also cleaning up the children and the room, until the lights are turned out and the children are asked to sit down and be quiet. It's then time for the girls to line up to use the toilet, and a teacher goes with them and helps Naomi take off her trousers.

Back inside the classroom, the other teacher is still sweeping the floor, and some of the children are singing and dancing to an exercise song that is playing. Naomi joins in when she comes back from the toilet. The teacher, when she's finished sweeping, tells the children to listen to what the song is telling them to do, and reaches up into the air with the children. After a while the other teacher calls Naomi to her – she's doing some type of physical examination of her – and writes something down before letting her return to the group, where the first teacher asks the children to get their books once again and sit and wait for their story to be read. The children get to listen to a "Winnie the Pooh" story, and then one about a zoo. Naomi is listening attentively, and when the teacher asks the children to name various animals Naomi calls out: "That's an elephant!" "That's right," says the teacher. "I went to the circus," explains Naomi. As the story-reading comes to an end it's almost 10, and Naomi tries to help one of the teachers line up chairs for a game of musical chairs. The teacher tells her not to, but Naomi pays no attention and keeps on lining up chairs. "OK, you want this chair? Then why don't you sit in this one," says the teacher. As music comes on, Naomi runs to find a seat, but it doesn't take long before she's "out" and she's told to go and sit in another chair. As the observation period comes to an end, she's standing in the doorway threatening to hit a boy if he doesn't stop crying.

Boris, in Obninsk

The day for Boris, a middle-class Russian boy, starts at almost 8 A.M., when he wakes on a Tuesday in May, exercises his arms and legs while still lying in bed, and talks to his grandmother about the visit to a friend's house the day before. His mother is busy preparing breakfast, and while his grandmother puts away the fold-away bed, she talks to Boris about what he's going to eat. After a visit to the toilet with the baby, the two adults talk to him about the roach extermination that's going on in the corridor, warning Boris not to pick up anything from the floor because of the poison that's been sprayed. Boris's mother brings in the hot kasha (a type of porridge made from cereals), and they wait for it to cool, talking about the trip to the countryside that they're going to take. Boris says that he'll bring a tractor and a ball with him, and that he'll go and put his things in a bag. "Yes, I'll buy a bookpack for you and you'll carry it yourself!" says his grandmother.

As breakfast finishes, everyone agrees how tasty it was. His grandmother tries to get Boris to thank his mother for the food, but Boris replies that he's embarrassed. "You're always embarrassed when it comes to saying 'thank you'." Boris remembers the name of a poem about an absentminded mother, and both the mother and grandmother supply quotes. Boris gargles with his tea, and his grandmother tells him not to, on the grounds that he's an elder brother now and has to set a good example for the younger one. By now, it's a little after 9, his grandmother has gone to the shops, his mother is cleaning up, and Boris has taken out his coloring book and is drawing and painting. His younger brother is doing the same thing. The radio is on, Boris talks to his mother about the program, and then pretends to be holding a pig, so that he can do a "pig dance" while his mother and brother watch him. He's looking for something to do, and so his mother fetches a book, and reads to the two children, talking about the various characters. She calls a tiger a cat at one point, and when Boris argues that it's a tiger, not a cat, she explains: "Tigers are elder brothers of cats; they are one family." Boris gets another book and worries, after his brother wets himself and the floor, whether the book also got wet. It's OK, and Boris tries to get his mother to read to him, but she is now busy preparing some food, and instead gets him to look in the book for two flowers that are exactly alike, and helps him in the process. By 10:30 she is once again reading with the two children.

Peeter, in Tartu

The day for Peeter, a middle-class Estonian boy, begins at 8 on a Thursday in May, when his mother is helping him to dress, and notices that he has holes in his socks. She tells him: "You must wear slippers, so you don't get holes in your socks." They talk about various presents that he got the previous Christmas, and then about the fact that others are still sleeping, but that he (Peeter) and his brother are early risers. By 8:30 Peeter is playing with a large beach ball, and his mother cautions him that if the ball goes into the ocean, it's not safe to go after it. Peeter wants to know why not, even if using a paddleboat, and his mother explains to him; the water is too deep, and the people who rent paddleboats don't allow it. "Then it's possible to go with a ship" Peeter says, and his mother replies: "Yes, ships can sail in deeper water, because they've been built to allow that."

Shortly after, Peeter is playing with some jars in the kitchen cabinets, but his mother warns him that they may fall on his head, and so (as she puts his younger brother back to bed) he starts playing with water and cups in a bowl. He wants more water in the bowl, but his mother tells him that he'll need to move to the bathroom if he wants more water, where "you won't make the floor and carpet wet." He wants to know, "How can I get water from the bowl; there's so little" and his mother replies: "Make your brain work!" "I did, but I still can't." They continue talking: "How do you get soup from your plate?" "With a spoon." "That's right, but if the soup is at its end?" "I say 'thank you'." "But the last drops?" "I tip the bowl" And that's just what he does!

By 9, his mother is washing the dishes, and talking to Peeter about giving his little brother some jam when he wakes up, something that Peeter agrees would be greatly appreciated; they both like to empty the pot. Instead, the two boys play together, while their mother eats and reads.

Jukka, in Oulu

At 8:15 one Friday in May, Jukka, a middle-class Finnish boy, is already at his child-care center and playing there with another boy and an infant. Jukka is careful to stop the baby putting something into its mouth. He then goes over to a teacher, and gets a board and some play-dough, and goes over to a table where two other boys are sitting. He sings to himself, and plays with his play-dough for over 20 minutes, occasionally looking around at what others are doing. The two teachers are going around the room looking at what the children are doing, and one of them asks Jukka about the things that he has been making. At that point Jukka goes over to watch a girl who is being helped by the teacher. She is doing some printing, using a stamp, and Jukka wants to do the same, and he makes prints of flowers, talking to the girl about what they're doing. He shows his work to the teacher, and continues to make prints before going over to join three children who are playing with Legos at the next table. Although this little group is doing the same activity, they each work on their own individual model.

By now, it's 9:15, and Jukka has made a gun out of Legos and is "shooting" one of his teachers. "Please don't shoot at me," she says. "I don't feel good about that." When she starts tidying up the room, Jukka shoots one of his friends, who at first doesn't pay any attention. Jukka tells his friend that the two of them should play together, and they do so, while in the other room the children start to get ready for "outdoor time." Jukka and his friend decide not to shoot each other but instead pretend that there's a ghost in the room, and each try to shoot it. They then decide that the observer is the ghost, and shoot her, but then start playing with a train set, while the other children are getting dressed for going outside. Jukka continues playing with the train for a while, but then joins his friend who has a plane, and they pretend that they are flying. Other children are on their way outside, however, and a teacher takes Jukka to the toilet and gets him ready to go outside. She tells him how much better he's able to dress himself these days, and he goes outside and joins another boy on a little bicycle. They talk to each other about what they should do and which other children should be allowed to play with them. Part of the play involves pretending to drive cars around, but they also spend some time eating the snow that's still on the ground in the middle of May.

Jonghee, in Suwon

It's already 10 a.m. on Wednesday, and Jonghee, a middle-class Korean girl, is still sleeping while her mother is using the bathroom, and it's probably this noise that makes her wake up. While her mother cleans up in the bathroom, Jonghee goes into the kitchen, gets herself some snacks, and eats. Her mother comes into the main room and puts a record on, while Jonghee talks to her about a friend. Her mother heats up some milk for her, while Jonghee watches her use the microwave. While her milk cools, Jonghee turns on the TV, but it's her mother who watches while she plays with some puzzles that are designed to help her learn numbers (Arabic, rather than Korean). Her mother watches TV, looks at the newspaper, and watches her daughter playing.

While Jonghee is drinking her milk, her mother chooses an educational video, turns it on, and starts to watch it with her daughter. She then makes a phone call, and Jonghee watches the video by herself, singing along in places. This goes on until almost 11, when Jonghee gets herself some picture books and starts drawing. After about 10 minutes, she decides to get another videotape to watch, and tries to put it into the VCR, and so her mother comes to help. They watch together for a while, and then, while her mother does some cooking, Jonghee watches alone, sometimes joining in with the songs, sometimes clapping her hands, sometimes accompanying the music on her toy horn. She also does some more drawing, while continuing to keep one eye on the TV. By 11:30 she has mostly stopped watching TV and instead is playing with various toys – including one of her dolls, a toy rabbit, and riding a toy car – while her mother cooks nearby. She tells her mother that she'd like a snack, and her mother brings something to her, and the two of them sit and watch TV, putting a different tape in, while her mother brushes Jonghee's hair. By 11:50 her mother has got out a children's book designed to help children with pre-kindergarten skills, and between then and noon she helps Jonghee learn colors, the concepts of "big" and "small," how to write those words, and finally teaches her Arabic numerals.

Fredah, in Kisumu

Fredah, a middle-class Kenyan girl, is in her preschool class one Friday morning at 8:40 when the observations begin. The teacher finishes writing some letters on the board and gets the children to say their names. The alphabet gradually appears, and the children have to repeat it. Fredah does so, while playing with her fingers for a while, and then is busy watching two other children playing with each other's hands, all the while going over the alphabet. The teacher continues with the lesson for almost an hour, occasionally admonishing the children for not sitting straight. The children continue to repeat letters, but also play with things that are available – one child plays with his own shirt, Fredah waves her hands in the air, looks out of the window from time to time, and toward the end of the hour tells one of her classmates to take his feet from her chair.

After an hour, the teacher tells the children to put their books away, and while they're doing that she washes the floor. Fredah watches her while she does that, and then she and the other children sit down. Their teacher tells them the meaning of the word "to kick a ball" and then says that it's time for them to go outside and play. She, Fredah, and the other children do some exercises, which involve jumping up and down, and then Fredah and some other children get a ball and start playing with it. Fredah plays for a while, watches other children play ball, and watches the teacher as she dresses another child. Finally she goes over to an area for sand, and starts scooping it with a group of other children, both boys and girls, until the teacher tells them that it's time to go in for a snack. Fredah goes inside, washes her hands and, before they can eat, the teacher leads the children in prayer.

Gabriela, in Porto Alegre

Gabriela, a middle-class Brazilian girl, is already awake at 8 A.M. on a Thursday in September, wandering around the house in her pajamas, which her mother wants her to take off. She starts to play with some marbles, with her mother helping, but then goes back to bed. Her mother tells her to get up, and they go into the kitchen to get something to eat (she eats a yogurt), while Gabriela talks with her mother about the time that she burned her finger, and about whether she needs to take a bath. She asks for another yogurt, and proceeds to feed her mother! She then plays with the baby's face, and her mother explains that that's not something one should do with babies, and so they start making some sandwiches together, and talk about who's going to wash the dishes afterwards. While Gabriela's mother continues making sandwiches and also cooks some eggs, they talk about the preschool that Gabriela attends and about the other children who go there.

By now it's 9 A.M., and it's time to get dressed. Together Gabriela and her mother decide what she's going to wear and talk about "Fada Sininho" (Tinkerbelle, from Peter Pan*) and about Gabriela's grandfather. Gabriela puts on some perfume, and plays with some dolls, before helping her mother prepare her bag for preschool. She uses the toilet, and her mother helps her to wash her hands and brushes her teeth for her. When Gabriela is clean and dressed, she and her mother get out some photos, and Gabriela tells the observer that she's going to her grandmother's house at Christmas. She and her mother talk about Christmas, and about one of Gabriela's friends. By now it's 9:45, and they're about to leave for preschool. Her mother brings her some sweets to take to school, and they get in the car. On the way to preschool, Gabriela sings some songs by herself, and then sings along with a CD as her mother drives.*

Summary

All of these children are from middle-class homes, and at first sight their experiences, although different from one another, appear interchangeable, in the sense that whether the children spend their morning at home or in a child-care center they could have had similar experiences in any of the other cities. However, closer inspection reveals the impact of culture. This is most easily seen in the various experiences within child care. In Fredah's case, half of the two-hour observation is taken up with a formal lesson on the alphabet. As I pointed out in Chapters 5 and 7, preschool in Kenya is currently viewed primarily as a way to help children enter a more prestigious school, and given the fact that entrance exams are used, some parents place a premium on their children getting a rigorous academic start.

It's not that things academic don't occur in the child-care centers in the other cities, but they are much less the focus of attention. Andy, for example, also participates in a formal lesson, dealing with the number three, but it only lasts about 15 minutes and involves both listening to the teacher and then participating in a couple of related activities (finding objects on people's shirts and pasting onto some paper the number and three apples). In the case of the other children whom we see in child care, Naomi (Greensboro) spends more of her time listening to stories, naming animals, and eating while Jukka (Oulu) plays. These vignettes support the impression gained from the data I presented in Chapter 7, namely, that the goals for child-care centers are different in different cultures.

What of the children who were not observed in child care during the morning? In Gabriela's (Porto Alegre) case, she's on her way to her preschool at 10, unlike Naomi who's been there already since 7 in the morning and who spends all day there. Jonghee (Suwon), on the other hand, only wakes at 10 and stays at home with her mother, as do both Boris (Obninsk) and Peeter (Tartu). All of these children, however, seem to be involved in at least as many lessons as do the children who are in child care, with the exception of Fredah. Their lessons are more varied, however, including interpersonal lessons (Boris's grandmother trying to get him to thank his mother and about how he has to set a good example for his younger brother and not gargle with his tea; Gabriela's mother telling her about inappropriate ways of handling her baby sister), lessons about the world (Andy's mother, prior to him going to child care, talking about what he's seen on television about war; Peeter's mother talking about not going into the ocean and helping him with the skill of tipping a bowl to get the remaining water out; Boris's mother warning about the roach poison that's been put down and pointing out the relationship between cats and tigers), and academic lessons on the part of Jonghee's mother.

Jonghee illustrates nicely what we already saw in more general terms – the fact that middle-class Korean children seem to be involved in a good deal of play with academic objects. Although both Andy and Naomi watch television or videos, the former watching the news about the ongoing war and the latter preparing to watch a film at her child-care center, Jonghee plays with puzzles that are designed to help her with her numbers while her mother watches television, and then when Jonghee starts to watch, her mother picks out a video with an academic focus, with songs about numbers and information about colors. At the end of the observational period, her mother is helping her learn mathematical concepts.

Culture is thus clearly implicated in the types of activities in which children become involved, partly because of the particular settings in which they are placed and partly because of cultural variations in beliefs about what should go on in those settings. However, we can just as clearly see the ways in which the children, too, change both the activities and the interactions in which they are involved. Andy, for example, finds an effective way to join a girl who's already playing with the blocks, telling her that what he's doing is going to make her structure "more better." Naomi uses her teacher's "name this animal" task to link the activity with her own experiences: "I went to the circus," she says, although her teacher doesn't build on Naomi's comment. Jukka creatively turns the injunction not to shoot at people into a ghost-shooting experience, and both Gabriela and her mother seem equally comfortable starting new conversational topics.

It's also worth noting the relative absence of men in these vignettes. Andy's father is watching television with him and had been involved prior to the observational period, but other fathers are conspicuous by their absence. Interestingly, although all of the fathers in this study either worked outside the home or were not a part of their children's lives, they play more of a role in the next set of vignettes, featuring children from working-class families, during the afternoons.

AFTERNOON

Mike, in Greensboro

It's a Tuesday afternoon in February, close to 2:30, and Mike, a boy from a working-class White American family, is in a family child care. The children we follow wear a wireless mike, and this afternoon Mike doesn't want to wear his at first. He's persuaded to, and then runs around the yard and climbs a tree, singing, "He's a hero; he's a bad guy" (presumably to himself, as the observer is Sarah). He gets a stick and digs for a while, and then calls out "Hey Sarah!" and "aims" his stick at her. Four more children arrive, and an adult sends them over to a table for a snack. Two children, one older and one the same age, come over to Mike who is breaking up some dirt in a sandbox with his stick, and he explains that his stick is a gun. The stick then becomes a bow and arrow, and he "shoots" the older boy with it, and the boy falls over. He tries to get the boy to play more with him, but the boy ignores him. Mike then climbs a tree with another boy and a girl, but when he gets down, he's upset because one of his peers has broken his weapon. "Me bad guy; he's a hero; he's a bad guy." He goes into the front yard, where some older children are riding bikes, and he starts to put rocks into a toy car. One of the adults tells him not to do that, and a peer chimes in: "Don't put rocks!" "No, we don't put rocks in there" the adult repeats, but then has to physically prevent Mike from doing exactly that. She then asks him if he'd like to help her push her baby in its stroller, and the two of them do that for a while. An older boy playing basketball gets Mike's attention, and he takes the ball, runs with it, and then throws it toward the hoop, then climbs on Sarah's (the observer) car. The adult tells him to get off, which he does, and then pushes a toy lawn mower into the neighbor's yard, and the adult calls him back and tells him to put it away. She brings him a toy tractor instead, but says that he'll have to put his stick down if he wants to ride it. He chooses to keep the stick and goes into the house.

It's now almost 3:30, and one of the caregivers asks if the children want to play with shaving cream. Mike says "No" but does so anyway. The adult turns the TV on to a children's program, for some to watch while others are playing with the cream. Some of the children smear shaving cream on the table, and Mike makes tracks in it using a toy car, continuing to do so for 10 minutes or more, until it's time for him to wash his hands and let others play with it. An older boy helps him to clean himself, and he watches a children's program on TV for a while, before going into the playroom, where he starts playing with a toy set of cooking utensils while one of his peers, at the same table, uses play-dough. Mike starts using it as well but yells at the other child when the latter takes his car. "Be nice!" says an adult, and soon thereafter Mike is playing with two other children and the play-dough. Then he starts to watch TV, first Donald Duck and then the Disney version of Peter and the Wolf.

Sandra, in Greensboro

One Wednesday in May Sandra, a working-class Black American girl, is at her child-care center at 2:30 P.M., as the regularly scheduled nap time comes to an end. The center's director is talking to two adults, and a teacher has turned on a toy that makes music as she goes round to wake up the remaining sleeping children – including Sandra, who then needs to use the bathroom. When she comes back from the bathroom, she sits at a table and watches one of the teachers feeding an infant. The director tells Sandra to get ready for a snack, and she walks over to a table, where she sits, resting her head on her arms and looking at the two same-age children and one older boy who are talking to each other. One of the teachers hands out cups of milk, and an older child passes out napkins, while Sandra talks to one of her friends at the table behind her. Sandra says grace, by herself, and then eats the cookies she's been given. One of the teachers says that they can go outside when everyone's finished, but first they have to be quiet. She starts counting so that all the children will sit down, and tells them that they're all being very rude. Sandra asks the teacher for a grape, and pretends to give it to another child. A child tells the group that everyone needs to be good and quiet, and the director asks everyone to put their heads down on the table. "Ya'll see we have a guest [Fabienne, the observer] and you're showing out like this." An older girl reinforces the message: "OK, everybody heads down" and that's what Sandra does, while the director and teachers put away the cots the children have been sleeping in.

By now, it's 3:30, and Sandra is singing a song about days of the week, as one of the teachers lines up the children to go outside. "Are you going to be everybody's friend, or are you gonna sit in the office? We are not gonna have anybody talking like that." The teacher tells everyone to put their hands over their mouths ("We will not go outside until everyone is quiet, and when we get outside we are going to make a big circle"), and as Sandra holds hands with two young boys, the teacher continues: "I'm going to count to 10 and everyone who is not in the circle will sit and watch us play" and some of the children count along with her. Sandra, finally outside, plays on the swings and sings to herself. After about five minutes, however, she goes back inside, where some children are watching a Disney movie, but a teacher then gets the children to get into a circle and do the "hokeypokey," and Sandra joins in. After a teacher tells the children that they can have about five more minutes outside ("you can run as hard as you can before it starts raining"), Sandra asks another girl if she can join her on the swing, and they swing together for a while, until Sandra jumps down and joins another girl who is picking flowers. She then runs around the yard, calling to an older girl: "I'm going to put you in jail." Her friend joins in the game and says that Sandra is going to have to feed her. "I'll get you something to eat" and throws grass at her. Finally Sandra gets drawn into various games started by an older girl: "Red light, green light," "Ring around the roses," and "London Bridge." Finally, two hours after Sandra woke up, she returns to the swings, where she has an argument with two girls who are in the swings that she wants.

Kolya, in Obninsk

Kolya, a boy from a working-class Russian family, is at home with his grand-mother and grandfather at 2 in the afternoon one Saturday in June. His grand-mother gives him an apple, explains to him about sharing it with her, and asks him what he'd like to eat for lunch. While she prepares something for him, he plays by himself, talking to himself as he does it. She calls him when the food is ready, and he eats it quickly, by himself, rocking himself on his chair, while his grandmother washes the dishes. Kolya goes into the family's main room, and his grandmother brings him a cup of tea, and persuades him to drink it. She goes back into the kitchen, and he plays alone, until Kolya's father comes home. While the two adults talk, Kolya listens to them. His grandmother mentions that it's about time for Kolya to have his nap, but instead the boy chases the cat, becoming quite excited in the process, rolling around on the sofa and turning somersaults as his grandmother tries to stop him. No doubt hoping to calm him down, she gets down a photo album, and talks to him about the various people in the photos.

It's almost 3 by now, and Kolya's grandmother tries to get him to sleep, stroking him and telling him that his eyes are tired, his hands are tired, and so on, but Kolya runs into the main room, and plays there loading blocks onto his toy truck and taking them into the other room. After a quick break to use the bathroom, he goes back to his toy play, and his grandmother watches him and talks to him about his toys and his play. She tries to persuade him to pick up his toys before having a nap, and the two of them talk about how he's getting sleepy. He asks for a fairy tale and lies on the sofa as his grandmother reads to him for about 15 minutes. As she reads, he gets up from time to time, looking at the pictures in the book, asking questions and commenting on the story. He's getting tired, and his grandmother covers him with a blanket, kisses him, and leaves for the kitchen. Kolya whispers to himself the story that he's just heard. At about this time, Kolya's grandfather wakes up, and his wife sets the table and serves him his lunch, and while they eat Kolya sleeps.

Heino, in Tartu

One Wednesday in June, at 2 p.m., Heino, a boy from a working-class Estonian family, is at home with his grandmother and a caregiver (Tiia) who comes to the house when Heino's parents are working. While Heino goes into the kitchen to use his potty and his grandmother is washing dishes, Tiia starts to wrap a present and tells Heino when he comes back that he's going to a birthday party soon. He wants to go now, but Tiia tells him that it's too early and that he should play now. Heino, instead of playing, gets milk in a bottle and lies on the floor drinking it, listening to the radio and then uses a tin whistle to accompany the music. Tiia sends Heino to his grandmother to ask what time the party starts; she reads from the invitation and tells him at 4. "What time is it now?" she asks the child. "It's half past seven four" he replies. His grandmother tells him that he has to wait one more hour. Heino gives this information to Tiia and then starts playing with stickers, then again with his whistle, and then draws. In the meantime, Tiia has been going from room to room while his grandmother is wrapping the present. The latter comes in to see Heino, and realizes that he's been drawing on his own body. Tiia is asked to take him outside and wash him thoroughly.

When Heino comes back in, it's almost 3, and he starts playing with the family's cell phone, and then with a screwdriver with which he's "repairing" his car. The two adults are getting the clothes ready for ironing. When his grandmother comes into the room to see what he's doing, he's lying on the bed and sucking on the nipple of the now-empty bottle. She notices that he's broken a number of things and comments: "Are you a baby that you break things? All the time only breaking!" She takes out a flyswatter and starts killing flies, and Heino takes over from her once she gets out some clothes for him to wear. When he's being dressed and using the potty again, Tiia starts swatting flies, and then they leave for the party just before 4.

Jonas, in Oulu

At 2 on a Wednesday afternoon in June, Jonas, a working-class Finnish boy, is in the garden at home, wearing his Peter Pan outfit. His mother and father are there as well, talking about gardening. Jonas's five-year-old brother, Asko, says that the two boys should go upstairs to play, but they come down quickly, and Jonas crawls on the floor with his younger sister. His father comes in and tickles him for a while but then tells him that he needs to go upstairs to play. Asko is drawing, and their mother is in the kitchen, and Jonas asks for some paper. "You don't need paper; you can't draw" his father says, but then starts looking for some, although he can't find any. Asko gives Jonas some, and the children begin to draw. Asko asks which letter some words start with, and the children talk about their drawing. Asko asks his father to draw for him, but the latter says, "Leave me alone!" and the mother calls from the kitchen to say that children should draw by themselves or otherwise they won't be given paper again. "I'll take your pencil away." Instead the children use some type of stencils for their drawing, and Asko tries to guess what it is that Jonas has drawn. Their mother has been preparing some food in the kitchen, and Asko goes in to get some, followed by Jonas, but their parents tell them to leave the kitchen. "When are we going to make balloons?" Jonas asks his father, but the latter is reading and doesn't answer. Asko asks if they can go outside, and both parents say that they can't. The children eat, and talk about going to the play park. Their mother says that Dad might make a train track later on but spends most of the time telling the children what they should or should not do while eating and that they have to eat everything that they've been given. Jonas, having finished, cleans his face with his shirt and is told not to do that as his mother cleans his face for him.

It's now about 3:30, and Asko asks over and over again for the train track to be set up. Jonas watches his father put the pieces together, but the latter gets annoyed when his daughter comes over to the box. "Go away! Don't disturb this now," he says. Asko is allowed to help, and Jonas watches intently, as their mother takes their sister off for a nap. Once the track is ready, Asko first plays with it alone, with Jonas watching, and then the two play together, putting decorations around the track, building a "hill" with books, and so on. The train keeps coming off the rails, and their father explains how they can repair it. Jonas sits in his little rocking chair and watches his brother, and at the end of the two hours is saying that he needs to go to the toilet.

Mikyung, in Suwon

It's a little after 2 on a Monday in October, and Mikyung, a working-class Korean girl, is playing with one of her friends, a little boy, in his house. As the observations start, the children are playing with a robot, but within a few minutes Mikyung goes down to her house, crying, telling her mother that the boy was bothering her. Her mother gives her something to eat, and Mikyung goes out again, first calling at another friend's house, and then going to a children's playground, where she continues eating, playing with a net for catching insects, and watching other children playing on the swings. She makes her way round various parts of the playground, first on the swings, then on the jungle gym, and on a seesaw. She sees some trash on the ground, and puts it into a trash can, before going back to the swings, where there are a couple of other children, another girl and an older boy. She talks to the girl about preschool, and the two of them keep swinging together, sometimes joined by one or two other children, but not talking.

By now it's 3:30, and Mikyung goes to say "hello" to another child, and goes to watch other children swinging on a different swing set, before settling down in the sand lot. After a while she gets some kitchen utensils and uses them with the sand, but she's been playing by herself for the past 15 or 20 minutes, and starts looking around for something more interesting. She sees a friend playing with some ants and goes to join her, playing with the ants. As the observation time comes to an end, Mikyung, with another little girl and a boy, is pretending to cook dinner with the sand.

Brendah, in Kisumu

Brendah, a working-class Kenyan girl, is with a group of other children on the street close to her house at 2 one Wednesday afternoon in October. Another child tells her that she's too young and can't play with them. So she goes back home and watches various activities going on in and around the house: her six-year-old sister sweeping; another child playing with some bottle tops, strung together; a child of about the same age carrying an infant and another one playing with a teddy bear; her sister washing the dishes. Brendah then plays first with a stick and then with an iron rod, before watching her brothers bringing water for her sister. They carry it into her house, and Brendah helps her sister to wash the dishes for a short while.

At 3 one of Brendah's brothers and her sister are discussing the weather, before Brendah plays with the water that her brothers have brought and her sister dusts the house. One of her brothers starts to clean the bathroom, and Brendah goes to help him, and then watches her sister tidying the living room, with the radio playing. While her sister continues to work, Brendah plays with some paper and seems to be listening to the radio. She finds a mango and plays with it for a while, but her sister tells her, "You should not play with your food," and so she climbs onto a chair and starts pushing the window back and forth. Finally her sister sends her to first bring a broom, and then to bring the mango to her so that she can wash it.

Mariana, in Porto Alegre

Mariana, a working-class Brazilian girl, is at child care one Friday afternoon in September at 2, and one of her teachers is reading a story about a bad wolf (lobo mau) and the children have to illustrate it as she's reading. And that's what Mariana does for the next 10 minutes, until she goes to get a drink of water, and listens to two teachers talk about another child. When her teacher leaves the room to get some music, so that the children can dance, Mariana hugs one of the other children, and for the next 20 minutes, the children dance to the music, before lining up to go outside. Once she's there, she plays on the slide with some other children, in a doll's house, on a spinning wheel with two other children, with a little stove, and in the sand, where she and another little girl pretend to be cooking.

The pretend cooking goes on for 10 minutes or more, before she goes back to the spinning wheel and to the doll's house and to the slide. She runs inside to use the toilet and then watches other children at play, and one of the teachers and a child sweeping the patio area where they've been playing. Mariana plays with a toy telephone, pretending to call people, and then with some keys, and then starts to make bubbles with soapy water. She continues playing with these various things until she goes into the bathroom to wash her hands. While inside she sees a teacher give some medicine to a child, and she makes some strange noises, as though she were taking the medicine herself. Two other children are talking there, and she goes over to them and joins in their conversation, while one of the teachers starts giving cups of water to the children.

Summary

Mike and Sandra, from Greensboro, like Andy and Naomi, were also in child care, although Mike's child care is not a formal center, but one that's been set up in someone's home (a family child care). However, for both of these working-class children, the experiences seem quite different from those of their middle-class counterparts. It may be in part because these observations are from the afternoon, rather than morning, but the time for both children features having snacks, a lot of playing, and having to follow the rules. This is particularly clear in the case of Sandra, who (along with the other children) is told off for being rude for not following the rules and who has to put her head onto the table to be quiet, is threatened with being sent to the office rather than going outside to play or with having to sit and watch others play unless they're being "good and quiet." By contrast, Mariana's (Porto Alegre) experiences in her child-care center feature a story and lots of play both by herself and with other children.

The remaining children are at home during the observational period, but Jonas (Oulu), like Mike and Sandra, also seems to be getting a lot of experience with rules that need to be followed (he and his older brother won't be allowed to have paper to draw on if they bother their father, and their mother repeatedly tells them what they should or should not do while eating). Their father is particularly brusque with the children but finally agrees to set up the train track for the two boys and explains how they can fix the problem of the train coming off the tracks. Kolya (Obninsk) also spends some time in the company of men – his father comes home from work and his grandfather, who was at home sleeping, wakes up during the observational period. Kolya listens to the two men talking but only interacts with his grandmother, who for the first hour is mostly preparing food and for the second hour is getting Kolya ready for his nap. Much of Heino's (Tartu) time is also spent waiting for something to happen – his grandmother and a caregiver are taking him to a birthday party, and he amuses himself in various ways (not always appropriate) while waiting to go.

Mikyung (Suwon) and Brendah (Kisumu) spend almost no time with adults during their entire vignettes – the former goes upstairs from the play area outside her apartment complex to complain about another child, but the two girls spend almost all of their time in the company of other children, in the case of Mikyung, and siblings in Brendah's case. However, whereas Mikyung's time is almost all spent in play at a playground designed precisely for this purpose, Brendah spends a good deal of her time either watching other children at play or work or helping in the work that her siblings are doing, whether it's washing dishes, cleaning the bathroom, or bringing things that her sister needs. None of the play that she observes or that she's involved in features the sorts of toys that are commonly found in the other cities; instead she plays with a stick, a rod, some paper, a mango, and the curtains.

In comparison with the middle-class children who featured earlier, we see far fewer examples of academic lessons or using school-related materials, even in child care, although Mariana does listen to a story, Heino has a lesson about time, and Jonas hears his brother ask about the names of some letters. However, far more of the lessons that these working-class children have are about appropriate behavior and following the rules, and numbers (in Sandra's case) are used only for warning purposes. The child-care experiences of Mike and Sandra on the one hand and Mariana on the other reinforce the view that the goals that people have for child care are quite different in different societies. But so, too, are the expectations that adults have for children, and Brendah's experiences helping her siblings clean house while their parents are at work are quite different from those of the children in the other cities.

We also now can see the influence of siblings. Whereas the middle-class children whose siblings were present during the particular vignettes were younger, both Jonas and Brendah have older siblings. Having a younger brother or sister can lead to lessons about appropriate behavior (Boris on not setting a bad example by gargling and Gabriela learning how to touch the baby's face), having an older brother helped involve Jonas in drawing, as well as learning the names of some letters and how to prevent a train from going off the tracks. Brendah, as we've seen, is easily drawn into the world of work by her six-year-old sister and older brothers.

EARLY EVENING

Cassandra, in Greensboro

Cassandra, a middle-class White American girl, is out walking with her mother and a neighbor a little after 5 one Friday in March. Or rather, Cassandra is in a stroller, being pushed by her mother. The two adults are talking to one another, and Cassandra is listening to them and watching the things that she passes. The walk lasts for about 40 minutes, and then they're home again. The neighbor goes into her house, where Cassandra's brother is watching TV and her sister and a friend are in the sister's room. Cassandra goes into her sister's room saying, "I want to jump rope," but her mother and her friend's sister are busy talking about the friend spending the night. Her father and brother come to the bedroom door, hear that they're talking, and leave. Cassandra's grandparents arrive, and everyone starts to get ready to leave for a party, with Cassandra's grandmother and mother talking about plans for the party, with Cassandra listening to them.

By 6 o'clock, Cassandra, her immediate family, and her sister's friend are in the car, with Cassandra and her father talking about the party, the grandparents following in their car. Her mother, father, and brother then talk to each other, about a basketball league and about a possible trip to New York. Cassandra is also talking – a pretend conversation. The mother and father tease Cassandra's brother about how he used to shop for cemeteries for his father when he was the same age that Cassandra is now. They arrive at the party by 6:20. It's a party for a cousin who is turning four, held in a large child-care center owned by the cousin's grandmother. At first Cassandra stands, watching people, listening to people chatting, and then goes into the cafeteria area, which is laid out with basketball goals and court markings. Cassandra rides on a "flying turtle" toy (a sort of scooter, with wheels) with a cousin and a friend, and then joins two other children jumping from chairs onto a tumbling mat (set up for them to do precisely that). She divides her time between these two activities for a while, goes to get a basketball and plays with her cousin, and then moves on to tossing a balloon back and forth with him, while eating the food that's being passed around.

Kevin, in Greensboro

At 5 on a Wednesday in May, Kevin, a middle-class Black American boy, has just turned on his computer and is with his mother, who's asking him what sort of game he'd like to play. Kevin's older sister, Gloria, is also there. Kevin has to spell his name, and his mother helps him: "You've got the K, what's next? OK." The computer game is related to The Jungle Book *and is telling Kevin the story.*

*His mother and sister leave, and he continues watching and playing by himself.
He has to click with the mouse to go to the next page, bangs on the screen at a
wolf saying, "bad, bad," and gets frustrated with the fact that the game requires
him to connect some dots. He's done so but says, "I can't click!" But then it
works again, and allows him to color the wolf's face. He continues playing until
almost 5:30, when his mother comes back and asks what he's doing. She opens
another game and leaves. He doesn't appear particularly interested, but when
the computer asks him to do something, he looks up and starts trying. Then the
doorbell rings, and Kevin runs to answer it and then goes into the kitchen to see
if dinner is ready. His mother tells him to turn off the computer, but he returns
to his room and starts playing again. His mother comes in and asks him how to
turn it off: "Do we go to this screen? Then what?" Kevin tells her: "Then we go
to the shortcut."*

*Kevin walks into the kitchen, plays with some magnets on the fridge, and
then walks into his sister's room to see what she's doing, but his mother tells him
to wait until she's finished and then they can eat. "Or do you want to go outside
first?" He does, but first goes into the kitchen, looks at the things that are being
prepared, gets a cup, and opens the fridge. "What are you doing?" his mother
asks, and when he tells her that he's getting something to drink, she says, "Hold
on" and comes to help – but he's already helped himself and is drinking. He
grabs a shirt and starts playfully slapping his mother with it. She laughs, takes
it from him, slaps him with it, puts him on the ground, and tickles him. He's
laughing, then coughing, and finally throws up! His mother takes him into the
bathroom to clean him up. Gloria appears with her paper and shows it to her
mother. "Doesn't that look better? Doesn't that look like an 'A' now?" asks her
mother.*

*Before going outside, Kevin is asked to brush his hair, and his mother explains
to him how to do it properly. In the playground that's close to the house, Kevin
and Gloria run over to the swings, and their mother joins in, and then challenges
them to race to another set of swings. She tells Kevin to put his shoes back on.
He doesn't want to, and she says "We don't go barefoot in the park because
there could be glass or rocks." They all run over to the horses, and Kevin and his
mother each get one. Gloria hits Kevin, because she wants to be on one, and her
mother slaps Gloria's hand, saying, "No!" When it's time to go back home, they
all run home, chasing Kevin, and the two children get ready for dinner. While
they eat, their mother reads. Kevin says that Gloria is eating with her spoon;
their mother says that she can eat with whatever she wants, but she might want
to save her spoon for dessert. After they've finished, their mother runs a bath
for Kevin, telling him after the bath he can watch a movie. He goes to the toilet
and then gets into the bath, playing with a boat. He then asks his mother for*

another toy. She wants to wash him, but he says that he can do it himself. He's only partially successful but sings to himself, plays with his toys and other things in the bath, and then it's time to get out, just after 7.

Liuba, in Obninsk

At 5 on a Thursday in May, Liuba, a middle-class Russian girl, is fast asleep, as is her older brother. Her father has gone to the shops, her mother is cooking, and her grandmother is cleaning. It's around 5:30 when Liuba wakes, and her mother brings her an apple to eat. She does so, and then goes to the toilet, while her mother clears away the bed sheets and covers. Her mother encourages Liuba to dress herself, encouraging her to do it for herself, making it easier by getting down the clothes that she'll need from the closet. As her mother brushes her hair, Liuba counts her fingers. Both children come into the kitchen, their mother cuts sandwiches for them, and they eat. They have tea to drink, and Liuba gargles hers, something her mother tries to stop her from doing. She says that the children can go outside, and they go to get dressed, with his father helping Misha, Liuba's brother, and her mother helping Liuba. Their grandmother is doing the laundry. They spot some letters and tell each other what they are.

It's now a little after 6, and Liuba is waiting outside the apartment for her mother to get dressed. A neighbor's little girl comes out of her door, and the two children stare at each other. When Liuba's mother is dressed, they go downstairs to the playground. It's the middle of May, and Liuba's mother tells her, "Don't sit down on the sand; it's cold and your tummy will hurt." She also tells her that she should breathe through her nose and not through her mouth because it's better for her. At the playground, Liuba plays with sand and a shovel. Another girl is there, playing with her own things for a while, as well as four older boys, playing by themselves. Her mother explains that for a "cake" to be good, the sand must be damp. Liuba says that she's made an "airoplane" out of sand. Two other children arrive, and the mother of one of them asks if Liuba's mother can look after her daughter while she "runs to the shops." "Get up from your knees," Liuba's mother tells her, "Your tummy will hurt" (she's already mentioned that Liuba has some bladder problems). Liuba is playing in the company of four older children, and as the observation comes to an end, an older girl has arrived and starts to organize a game: "Let's be a family. You'll be a mother, you a father."

Epp, in Tartu

When the observations begin, close to 5:30 on a Monday in June, Epp, a girl from a middle-class Estonian family, is at home, and her aunt and two cousins have come to visit. The two other girls are skipping together, and Epp goes into the kitchen to complain to the adults that they won't play with her and she's bored. Her aunt tells her that she shouldn't come into the kitchen as she (the aunt) is smoking in there, and adds: "Go tell them that they should play with you, or they could read to you." Epp goes back to the other room, switches on the TV, but then goes back to the aunt and says that the girls won't read to her, and her aunt tells her that she'll come to read and does so. Epp's mother, meanwhile, is preparing things to eat in the kitchen, and Epp's younger brother is waking up from his nap. At the end of the story, Epp asks her aunt to read some more, and she reads to Epp and to one of her own daughters, while the other one reads by herself. When that book has been read, Epp asks for another one, but that this one has to be with pictures. Epp's uncle then arrives, together with his son, and Epp wants to put on her new tights to show her cousins. "You should take those off, Epp, they'll tear," and when Epp doesn't want to, her mother continues: "It's not a holiday." Epp replies, "But I'm a woman, and women want to be beautiful." "Let me help you get them off, dear woman," says her aunt. Epp tries to get her uncle to play with her, but he switches on his laptop and works on it for a while, and Epp drinks a little and gets out Plasticine to play with.

It's now almost 6:30, and Epp's mother is still preparing food in the kitchen. Epp goes in and says, "I want to cut, too," but her mother tells her, "This is peeling, and you're too young for that." She picks up her own knife, a blunt one that she uses to eat with, and pretends to cut her sock, and then goes into the bedroom and lies on her parents' bed as if sleeping. Her brother pretends to wake her up, while her cousins play with a balloon. Epp gets her toy broom and pretends to sweep the room, and then starts playing with a vase. One of her cousins questions whether she's allowed to play with it, and Epp assures her that she is. However, she leaves it alone and starts arranging the towels, saying to herself as she does, "Why have you touched those? I put the washing away neatly." She then watches a little TV, plays with some toys, and goes back to her Plasticine. She asks her mother when her father is coming home and is told that he'll be back soon. She gets out a calculator to play with while her mother reads. At 7:30, Epp's brother wakes up, and Epp gets him to push the buttons of the calculator.

Teija, in Oulu

A little after 5 P.M. on a Thursday in December, Teija, a middle-class Finnish girl, is at home with her father and older sister, Jaana. Their father has prepared a meal of pancakes for them, and they're eating. Jaana and their father talk about what she ate earlier today, and he asks Teija if she likes the pancakes and offers to get her some jam for them. Once she's had enough, she starts playing with her food, and her father asks her not to. The doorbell rings, and a woman arrives with some flowers. While the two adults talk in the living room, Teija gets a spoon from the drawer and plays with her food, talking to herself while doing so, and then she joins the others in the living room, where Jaana is reading. Teija talks a little with the woman, but then gets her own book, reads for a while, and then talks to Jaana about her sister's book. When the woman leaves, the girls' father finishes his food and cleans the kitchen table. Teija wants to read the book her sister has and sits on her sister's lap. Their father asks them if they went on any trips today (they'd spent the earlier part of the day in child care), and Jaana talks about going to a church. Teija sits on the sofa and looks at the pictures on the front cover, then talks to her sister about the book. Jaana shows her some of the pictures inside, while Teija crawls over her. Teija asks her sister if she can sit on the sofa (Jaana has been stretched out on it, taking all the space), and then says, "I'll make the bed" while organizing the pillows.

A little after 6, their father helps the girls to get dressed and to put their coats on because "We want to fetch mother." Getting dressed takes some time, as the girls sit in their room, singing, playing with various objects, including their father's ATM cardholder. He says, "Oh, you want to have this; are you going to play with it?" and Teija says that she isn't going to. About 15 minutes later, they're all ready, and are driving to meet the girls' mother. Teija is talking quietly to herself and seems about ready to fall asleep in her car seat. Her father phones his wife and parks, and she comes to the car and talks to the children. Teija wants to have a hamburger, but instead they all drive to the supermarket, where their mother pushes the cart and their father brings things. Their mother asks the girls about the various things that they should buy and then stands talking to a friend whom she meets in the store. At the cashier, Teija tries to persuade her mother to buy some sweets for her, but instead they leave, and on the way home, her mother asks her about her day in child care.

Juwon, in Suwon

At 5 on a Thursday afternoon in September, Juwon's mother, from a middle-class Korean family, has just picked him up from child care and is on the way home after a quick visit to a grocery store with Juwon and a friend of his. His friend's mother is driving them, and Juwon is eating some ice cream and his friend a banana. Juwon tries to get a toy out of the bag of groceries and talks about wanting some sweets. When the neighbor drops them off by their home, Juwon refuses to go in, and instead plays on the slide and rides his bike. Some of the neighbors are there with their children, and Juwon goes up to one of their babies and kisses him. By about 5:45, his mother has persuaded him to come into the house, and his father arrives. Juwon asks his mother to read to him, and he brings her various picture books. They read together, interrupted only when Juwon and his father talk briefly about what happened at child care. Then Juwon goes outside and plays with his toy top for a while, before going into a friend's house. The two boys play with the friend's train and with a gun, while his mother prepares dinner. The mother tells Juwon not to hit his friend and for the children not to shout. She gives them both ice cream, and they run around the house, playing with various toys.

By 6:30, Juwon goes back to his own house to find that his father has gone out, but his sister's friend arrives. Juwon's mother asks her whether she's told her grandmother that she's here, and she must have done so, because she can stay. She plays the piano, and Juwon joins her and plays as well for a while, until the two girls get dolls out and get some colored paper for Juwon to play with, while their mother prepares dinner. He then watches a videotape, a cartoon, while eating cookies.

Brandon, in Kisumu

Brandon, a middle-class Kenyan boy, is playing outside his home, one Tuesday in December at 5:30, with Samuel, one of his friends, a boy of roughly the same age. Samuel finds an old tire, from a car, and starts to play with it, while Brandon watches him from the gate. There's a pile of rubbish nearby, and Brandon picks up an old container of Vaseline. He throws it up and down for a while, before throwing it away, and, getting a spoon for serving ice cream, plays with it in the sand, scooping and pouring it. Samuel, meanwhile, has been attracted to some plants nearby, and he begins pulling them up and Brandon joins him in this activity. Tiring of that, Brandon runs over to an electricity pole, and Samuel joins him swinging around and around it, then running to a pole supporting the fence, and the two boys swing on that.

By now, it's about 6:30 in the evening, and the children are still playing on the fence, when Brandon's mother walks by. He asks her where she's going, and she says that she's going for a walk. Samuel calls him back to the tire; Brandon sits on it, and Samuel tries to push the tire, as Brandon pretends to drive it. His parents' car is more attractive, however, and he goes over to it, and plays with the mirror, until a man (not his father) comes out of the house and tells him to leave the car alone. The cleaner or "home-help" that the family employs takes the trash can into the house as Brandon watches her, pretending to be a driving. She comes back out and starts picking up rubbish from the compound as Brandon watches her work, climbing on his parents' car as the observation comes to an end.

Francisco, in Porto Alegre

Francisco, a middle-class Brazilian boy, is still in child care at 5 one Thursday in July, and the teacher has just given the children some food. She's talking to the children, including Francisco, about the names of their mothers, the jobs their fathers have, and so on. Some of the children are talking about brushing their teeth, as the teacher serves more salad. She goes to get more, and Francisco and some other children start singing. When the teacher comes back, she organizes the children to go and brush their teeth, and Francisco goes to the bathroom to do this, with an adult helper's assistance. He then shows the teacher, who asks him to wash his hands. He does that but also wets himself, and he has to change his trousers and wash himself, also with the assistance of the helper. When he comes back into the room, some of the other children are being picked up. He plays with a friend, and they gather up bits of food from the floor and eat them, until the teacher tells them and the rest of the children to sit in one corner of the room so that a cleaner can sweep the floor. Francisco talks to a friend about where one of their friends has gone and about the toys that they've each brought to the child-care center.

At about 5:45, the teacher tries to get the children ready to leave. Francisco runs and spins around until the teacher suggests that while they're waiting, the children sing a song about a little witch, and several do so, although Francisco playfully hits one of his friends, and other children join in, hugging and pushing each other. The teacher puts on a CD, and she dances and sings with some of the children. Two teachers organize the children to sit at a table, and one of them hands out paper, suggesting that the children draw pictures to take home with them. Some of the children are picked up by their parents, and others, including Francisco, draw. He asks the teacher for more paper but then uses one of the crayons to put "lipstick" on one of his friends; a teacher takes the crayon away from him, saying that children don't use lipstick. The teacher puts on a CD of stories, first of "Peter Pan" and then "Puss in Boots," and shows the children who are still there pictures from a book that has the same stories. This continues for about 20 minutes, until it's almost 6:40, by which time Francisco is playing on the floor and jumping. Some of the children are restless; they're running around, hitting one another, and one little boy has hurt himself. The teacher has put ice on his forehead.

At about 6:45, Francisco's parents arrive to collect him, and a couple of minutes later they're in the car on the way home, which is not very far away.

When they get there, Francisco wants to look at his parents' motorbike, while his parents talk about their respective days at work. His mother turns on the TV, and the adults go into the kitchen where his mother prepares a sandwich. She offers it to Francisco, but he's not hungry and still interested in the motorbike and the crash helmet that's next to it. As the observation comes to an end, his parents are still in the kitchen, and Francisco is sticking something onto the wall.

Summary

Late afternoon to early evening, and only one of the children (Francisco) is still in child care, although their experiences in child care feature as subjects for discussion for both Teija (Oulu) and Juwon (Suwon). Francisco's time seems almost exclusively devoted to activities designed to fill the time until he, and the other few remaining children, are collected. Given the time of day, it's not so surprising that fathers are now more likely to be in the picture. This is the case for Cassandra (Greensboro), Liuba (Obninsk), Epp (Tartu), Francisco (Porto Alegre), and even Juwon, although the fathers of the children in Suwon were almost never present during our observations. Unlike the other children, however, only Teija's father is exclusively present and takes Teija and her sister to collect their mother from work.

What is noticeable in many of these vignettes, particularly after reading about the focus on following the rules that was so evident in several of the working-class children's experiences, is the fairly consistent attempt on the part of many of the parents to follow the child's lead where possible, but, when that wasn't possible, to explain why a course of action should not be followed. Kevin's mother (Greensboro), when she wants him to turn off his computer, asks him to explain to her how to do it. He's given lots of choices, and toward the end of the vignette, when she wants to wash him, he tells her that he can do it by himself. Even when Kevin points out the apparent infraction of a rule, telling his mother that Gloria, his older sister, is eating her meal with her spoon, his mother simply replies that they can use what they like, although she might prefer to save her spoon for dessert! Liuba, too, is encouraged to dress herself, and when she's told not to sit in the damp sand, her mother states this not as a rule that has to be followed but as something for which a reasonable explanation can be offered. Both Epp and Juwon find it easy to get someone else to read to them – her aunt in Epp's case, his mother in Juwon's. It's not that there are no rules to be followed – Kevin's mother tells him that he has to put his shoes on, Juwon's mother tells him not to shout in the house or hit his friend, and Epp clearly should not be wearing her "special" tights, although she's encouraged to remove them with humor rather than by the simple evocation of a rule.

As was seen in the case of the working-class children whose vignettes were described earlier, it's possible to see the benefits of being around older children and, in all cases except Brandon (Kisumu), adults. Cassandra listens in on several adult conversations, and both Juwon and Teija have conversations with their parents (both father and mother, at different times, in Teija's case) about what happened that day in child care. Kevin's mother explains to him that he needs to have his shoes on in the park because of the danger of hidden glass and rocks. Having an older brother means that Liuba has experiences with letters that she otherwise might not have had, and Teija sits on her older sister's lap to listen to the book that Janna is reading and is able to get her sister to show her the pictures.

It's interesting to note that whereas Brendah, the working-class girl from Kisumu, was well integrated into the world of real work, Epp has a toy broom with which she pretends to clean the bedroom. In effect, she is encouraged to learn appropriate adult roles in the course of imaginative play, unlike Brendah and her siblings, for whom work is serious business. All of the children but Brandon have access to various toys and other things designed for children, from Kevin's computer, Cassandra's "flying turtle," the playgrounds where Liuba and Juwon play, the various books that Epp, Teija, and Juwon read, and the CD of stories that Francisco listens to. Brandon, by contrast, plays with an old tire, a discarded jar of Vaseline, a spoon for serving ice cream, an electricity pole, and with (and on) his neighbor's and parents' car. Unlike the other children, Brandon has almost no interaction with adults except with a man who tells him not to play with the car; his time is almost exclusively spent in the company of a peer, It's not that the other children don't play with things from the adult world – Epp plays with a vase, with folded clothes (having clearly internalized a lesson that she must have heard a few times in the past!), and with a calculator, and Teija plays with her father's card holder, but this play is not in the absence of toys of their own. As I showed in the earlier chapters, in many ways, the experiences of the children from Kisumu were quite different from those of the children in the other cities.

PREPARING FOR SLEEP

Patty, in Greensboro

Patty, from a working-class White American family, is at home on a Sunday evening in March at 7. Her father, who works the night shift, has left for work an hour earlier, and her grandparents and a cousin have arrived. Patty's playing a bowling game with her cousin Roger, a boy who is somewhat older than she is, and play fighting with her grandmother. Patty kicks her grandmother who grabs her leg and won't let go, saying that she'll take Patty home with her and will "straighten her up." She continues, "She'll come home with a red behind." When Patty screams, her grandmother calls her "mouth of the south." Her mother says how nice Patty looked when they were in church earlier on. Roger wants to look at a book with her, but Patty threatens to hit him with it and is told not to by her mother. Patty asks for a model gun, and her mother gets it for her, and Patty pretends to shoot everyone in the room. The TV is on, and the adults are watching, when Patty sees a dog while her grandfather is switching channels. She demands to see the "doggie" again, but it was on a commercial, and they can't find it. She starts to cry. Her grandfather turns the channel to wrestling, and everyone watches, while Patty's mother and grandmother talk about going to see wrestling. "I wouldn't go. It's all fake," says the grandmother, but her mother says, "I used to go. You could hear them smack each other. They're really hitting each other." Grandmother responds, "I don't like it when people are hitting each other. I want to do the hitting!" By now some dogs have reappeared, and Patty is watching.

Patty's grandparents and cousin are leaving, a little before 7:30, and Patty is crying. Her mother offers her some cereal, and she eats it while watching TV and her mother is tidying the room. Her mother asks her if she'd like a bath, and she says that she would and gets a toy to play with in the tub. After Patty is in the bath, her mother goes to lock the front door, then comes back to play with her. Patty is using a puzzle that sticks to the wall when wet and is taking mouthfuls of water and spitting it out. Her mother says, "Keep it in the water!" and squirts "mermaid" soap onto various parts of her body, before washing her hair. Patty puts something around her waist (it's part of a puzzle) that looks like a short dress and dances, telling her mum to clap and say "that's great!" over and over (the last thing that Patty watched on TV was ice-skating). They continue to do this, although her mother changes to "that's terrific" and "that's wonderful" as time goes on. She drinks bath water from one of her toys as her mother tells her, "These girls are in here ice-skating. Do you want to watch?" and helps her to get out of the bath. In her room, Patty wants to wear her new dress, and her mother allows her to, but puts a T-shirt on her under the dress. When she starts combing her hair, Patty screams and knocks the hair drier onto the floor. While continuing to dry her hair, her mother asks her: "Did you write on your table?" "Yeah," Patty replies. "Why'd you do that?" "It's hot." "It's not hot!"

By 8:30, Patty is lying in her bed, and her mother puts a videotape on the TV in her room, but Patty asks for another tape, one of Winnie the Pooh. *"Are you sure that's what you want to watch, 'cause I'm not changing it again," says her mother. The tape has to be rewound, and while that happens, Patty's mother reads to her. Patty wants more reading and gets some more books. They read for 15 minutes until the phone rings. Her mother answers, puts on the video, and gives Patty some sweets to eat. Patty finishes the sweets, jumps on the bed, and kicks the wall while her mother is elsewhere in the house, but then settles down to watch the tape and is asleep within 5 minutes.*

Noel, in Greensboro

At 8 P.M., Noel, a working-class Black American boy, has just arrived in church with his mother, grandmother, and older sister on a Wednesday in September. Someone compliments him on his new clothes, and his grandmother tells him to take his hat off in church. Noel spots another boy and wants to play with him, and someone warns the other boy to be careful when playing because he's holding a pen in his hand. Noel's mother asks him to sit down, because people have started to pray, and while his mother looks at the bible, Noel is looking around at the others who are there, including the other boy who is pretending to write on some paper. The congregation starts to sing, and the child claps along. His mother lifts him into her arms, and while Noel claps, his mother rocks him in time to the singing. He seems to be looking around at everyone and everything and starts to clap as soon as others do. The other little boy has been stopped from doing something and has started to cry. Noel laughs and then climbs on the pew and pretends to be hiding from the boy, and then waves to him, but the boy just ignores him. So Noel watches the people sing, his mother in Bible study, and the other activities going on. He looks under the pew and plays with the carpet, then starts hitting the pew. His mother says that he'll have to stop and that they'll have to leave if he doesn't sit down. She gives him some paper and a pen, and Noel draws something and shows his mother as she continues with her Bible study, interrupting it only to stop him from writing on the pew itself. He continues doing this for 10 minutes and then starts singing to himself ("Old MacDonald Had a Farm"). His mother tries to stop him and gives him a new piece of paper. She glances at what he's doing, turns the paper over for him when it's covered, and then goes back to the Bible. Noel tries to see who's talking at the front of the church, and continues writing and singing.

By now it's 9:15, and everyone's getting ready to leave church. His mother takes the pen and paper away from him, and Noel starts to put on his hat, but his mother says that he shouldn't yet because they're still inside. She puts his jacket on for him and takes him to the bathroom. On the way to the car, he tries to walk backward, but his mother stops him because a car is coming. Instead he runs with his sister to the car, and his mother straps him into his car seat. Nicole, his sister, is dancing and singing, and then she and Noel start playing with each other, first tickling and then hitting. Noel tells Nicole to stop after a while, and then kicks her. His mother and grandmother have been talking about a bill that needs to be paid, but now his grandmother tells Noel to stop kicking. He continues, but it turns back into a game with his sister. Noel asks where they're going, and his mother tells him they're on their way home and that he's going to get a bath and go to bed. He starts playing with his lips and making blowing noises as his mother sings while driving, and then they get home. His mother tells Noel to take off his jacket; he does so and then gets some crackers to eat, while his mother is running water in the tub. Noel turns on the TV in his sister's room and plays briefly with some of her toys, before his mother calls him into the bathroom and starts undressing him. He gets into the bath and plays with the bubbles, splashing water onto both himself and his mother. While soaping him down, his mother asks Noel if he's going to sing her a song later on, but he says that he won't. He "swims" in the water to get the soap off him, and then his mother asks him to get out of the tub so that she can dry him. While she does so, he talks to her about all of the water that's going down the drain. She asks him what color his pajamas are, and rather than saying, Noel points to the same color on the wallpaper. His mother tells him to get into bed so that she can turn on the tape for him to watch, but he gets his truck and starts to play with it. She has him take it into bed with him, and he starts to watch the video (of a family trip) as his mother tidies up the room. She takes the truck from him because it's time for him to sleep. He has to climb over the rack that's at the side of the bed to go over to the dresser and takes a belt from it and swings it around, and then gets a book. It's now 10, and he gets back into bed as his mother gives him some medicine, and before long he's asleep.

Volodya, in Obninsk

Around 8:15 on a Monday evening in June, Volodya, from a working-class Russian family, is outside in the play area that is in the middle of a cluster of large apartment blocks, one of which is where he lives. He is with his mother and three other children, playing on a large "pirate ship" that has been built there. They've been playing for about 15 minutes already. Volodya runs over to his mother to tell her something, and she shows him the dark clouds that have gathered and tells him that this is a sign that a thunderstorm may be coming, and they decide to go back home. Before they enter their apartment building, Volodya asks his mother to lift him up so that he can see the mailbox better, and she explains to him the meaning of the postcode that's written there. Volodya then decides to "wash" his boots in a puddle, and then thunder is heard. His mother explains what it is, and then they go inside. In the kitchen, Volodya's mother plugs in the telephone, and Volodya runs into another room so that he can listen in to the conversation on the other phone. He then picks up a book and takes it to his mother so that she can read to him, and she does so, with Volodya listening attentively. There's a picture of a bee in the book, and he asks his mother how it bites, and she explains about its sting, while wiping Volodya's nose.

It's now a little after 9, and his mother tells Volodya to look at the pictures while she prepares some macaroni and meat for him. She explains that she has to beat the meat to make it more tender, and Volodya gets out the hammer and says that he wants to do the beating. So she cuts the meat into small pieces and gives him a wooden board on which to do that. She then fries the meat. Volodya wants to do that, but she explains that the pan is very hot and it might "spit" at him but lets him coat the pieces of meat in breadcrumbs. "We'll put some mayonnaise on the meat" says his mother, and Volodya gets the jar out of the fridge and asks his mother to help him open it, which she does. Before she rinses the macaroni, she pulls up a small stool to the sink so that he can watch what she's doing. Volodya unplugs the fridge, and his mother asks him to put the plug in again, quickly. He does so, and then tries to fold up her umbrella. His mother calls him to the table and gives him his dinner, telling him to chew well. It's hot, and his mother cuts the meat into small pieces for him. "Bon appétit," she says, and asks him what he has to say in response. "Thank you," he replies. As the two eat, his mother talks about the cats that they had seen a few days earlier at the cottage in the countryside. Volodya finishes his meal and drinks his juice, and his mother tells him that it's just about time for bed. He tells her that he doesn't want to go to bed and gets some toys out to play with, but when she asks him to undress and get into bed he does so, and she reads him a story, very quietly, as Volodya drops off to sleep.

Eva, in Tartu

It's a Tuesday evening in July, at 8, and Eva, a working-class Estonian girl, is at home with her mother, her brother, and her sister. She's watching TV, a typical evening program in Estonia. Her brother and sister watch for a while but then start chasing each other around the room, as Eva continues to watch. Her mother is doing a crossword puzzle. She goes to use the potty, which is in the toilet, and then comes back to the TV program, but after a while, she starts playing, first with the family cat, then with her feet, then with a toy, and finally with her mother's arm. Her mother continues doing the puzzle but watches Eva from time to time. Eva goes back to her potty and empties it into the toilet (without being asked to do this). She then goes back to her mother, who is by now watching TV, and plays with her arm as she watches. Her brother and sister are play fighting, dragging each other across the floor. Eva watches them as her mother tells them not to do that because they're going to get hurt. She goes back to her newspaper, reading it and then working some more on the crossword, as Eva's siblings play and Eva plays with some toys by herself.

It's a little after 9 by now, and Eva's mother is still reading the newspaper, but tickling Eva's leg while doing so. Her sister comes into the room with some toys, and her mother asks her not to mess up the room before bedtime. Eva watches TV for the next 20 minutes with her mother and talks to her mother occasionally. By 9:30 or so, Eva appears sleepy, and her mother says, "Don't fall asleep in here [i.e., in front of the TV]. Should I prepare your bed for you?" but Eva doesn't want her to, and keeps on saying "Don't go, don't go," but her mother does indeed go to make up the bed, Eva gets into it, and is asleep before 10.

Piia, in Oulu

Piia, a working-class Finnish girl, is playing outside on a playground near her house with her mother, father, and the baby at 8 on a Thursday evening in June. Piia is on the swings, and her mother tells her to put her shoes back on and continues talking with another child's mother. Piia goes over to the slide, and she and some other children count to decide the order in which they go down. When she's had her turn, her mother takes her home, where she has a snack and then cleans the table. Her father has been reading a magazine, and Piia says that she wants to do a crossword puzzle. Her mother, after heating some food for the baby, asks her if she'd like a bath and starts running it. Piia is working on the puzzle while the bath is filling. At 8:30 she's in the bath, playing with her toys, while her mother tells her husband what she did during the day and feeds the baby. Piia calls her mother into the bathroom to ask what's in some packages and talks to her mother while the baby is getting its bath. Piia then calls her father in to let him see the strange sight of the baby being bathed in the sink, and her mother asks him to wash Piia's hair, which he doesn't do. Piia continues playing in the bath, with plastic bottles and a duck, which she washes and talks to, and she's still in the bath at 9.

Her mother again tries to get her husband to wash Piia's hair, and Piia herself calls him to do it; finally he comes in to do so. Piia gets upset with him, and her father tries to explain to her that her mother is better at washing hair. Piia asks him for a towel, which he gives her, but it's her mother who dries her, cuts her toenails, and cleans her ears. They seem to be having fun while doing that, and Piia's father washes the dishes in the kitchen. Piia gets ready for a story and tells her mother which one she wants. Her mother reads the story to her, and Piia plays with the baby (who's on her mother's lap) while listening. Piia tries to get her father to read, but he says that he's still busy in the kitchen, and so her mother reads another book to her, before suggesting that she go to bed.

By 9.30, Piia's in bed, the baby's in his bed, and her mother is talking with her, when she remembers that Piia has not yet brushed her teeth, and there's a quick trip to the bathroom. Afterward they talk for a while about what Piia had done earlier than day in child care, and then her mother says a prayer and leaves the room. Piia quickly falls asleep, but the baby cries, and Piia's mother comes in to feed her, and Piia wakes. She gets her father to bring her a doll, and her parents leave the room again. Piia goes back to sleep.

Dongki, in Suwon

Dongki, a working-class Korean boy, is watching television on a Saturday night in September, a little before 9. As his mother and younger sister come into the room, he doesn't seem particularly interested in the program and lies down for a while. His mother has brought some laundry into the room and is busy folding it, and Dongki starts playing with his sister, Eunhye, running around the room, until they decide to play a video game together. Their mother tells Eunhye not to fight with her older brother; she continues to fold laundry as her own mother, the children's grandmother, arrives home from work. As his mother goes into the kitchen to prepare a meal for the grandmother, Dongki eats some cookies and goes into his grandmother's room with his spinning top. As he plays, his grandmother comes into the other room and watches TV until she's told that it's time for dinner. Dongki decides to play in the closet and is trying to find something there, until his mother tells him to come out and asks him to take his vitamins. After he's taken them, with his mother's help, he gets a pen out and draws a picture on the wall. "Don't draw on the wall!" says his mother, "Use a piece of paper." By now it's almost 10, and their mother has persuaded the two children to eat some dinner, which they do (with her help) while watching television.

After dinner is over, Dongki gets out a toy car and starts to play with it. He wants his mother to mend it, but she's busy, first with the dinner things and then on the phone, and so Dongki plays alone with his car and a gun, and then puts batteries in the car as his mother watches him. He tries to tear off a sticker from the car, but his mother tells him not to. He continues to play but watches television at the same time, interrupting those activities once to get himself some more vitamins. He tries once again to play with his spinning top, and his mother shows him how to do it. She then starts to repair some torn books, and Dongki plays with something to make bubbles, until his mother reads a book to him for a few minutes. Dongki then asks for some juice, and continues playing until it's almost 11 P.M. and time for the observer to leave!

Derrick, in Kisumu

At about 6:45 on a Tuesday in October in a working-class Kenyan home, Derrick's sister Dolphine is busy sweeping the room and his brother Brandon is changing a lightbulb while Derrick eats a mango that Dolphine has just washed for him. Dolphine starts doing some knitting, and Derrick watches her for a while and plays with some cards. He goes into the kitchen and tells Dolphine that he's hungry, and she gives him some tea to drink and starts cooking. He asks her if he can play with some of her wool, and she gives him some. He pretends to weave a basket with it, until Dolphine asks him to put plates on the table, and his mother asks him to get a cloth to wipe the table. Derrick does that but then starts playing with a stick and his mother tells him not to put it into his mouth because it's dirty.

Derrick keeps playing with it until his mother calls him to the table, and the whole family prays together before eating. Derrick's father talks about the maize harvest, and Derrick listens to the conversation and also to the radio, which is playing in the background. "Look at your food while you're eating," says his father. The conversation continues about the harvest, and their father talks to Brandon about the work that he's doing. Derrick goes to wash his hands. When he comes back to the table, he's picked up some thread and is playing with it while listening to the conversation. Derrick goes into the bedroom, still playing with the thread, and lies on the bed for a while, before folding back the sheets. Rather than get into bed, however, he goes into the room where his mother is. She's weaving a basket, and he climbs into her lap as she continues to weave and has fallen asleep in her lap as the observation comes to an end at 8:45.

Daniel, in Porto Alegre

Daniel is at home with his mother and grandmother a little before 8 on a Friday evening in September in a working-class home in Porto Alegre. He's been looking at a notebook, turning the pages, but when his grandmother starts talking to him, Daniel begins to play with her. He tears out one of the pages, and says, "How pretty!" He then turns a chair upside down, and his mother asks him put it back; when he doesn't, she makes him do it, and then sits him on her lap for a while. When he gets down, he plays first with the TV remote control and then tries to climb onto the bookcase. His mother tells him to get down, which he does. She makes a paper airplane for him, and he plays with that for a while, while asking where his father is. But then he goes into the bedroom and crushes the plane. His mother puts him at the table, whereupon he tries to take off the cloth covering it, and when his grandmother goes out of the room she tells him that she's going to call a witch! Daniel stops wiggling around; he's waiting for his grandmother to come back with the witch, but when she comes back, the two adults start chatting while putting food on the table, and Daniel watches TV, eats, and tells his mother that he hurt his knee at child care that day. They also talk about the TV programs. When his grandmother comes to the table to eat, Daniel asks her why she's eating with a spoon. "That's the way to eat soup," she explains. She then changes the channel, switching from a children's program to a soap opera (one of Brazil's famous novellas), and Daniel starts playing with his food. His grandmother is annoyed with him and complains to him about his behavior. He eats a little more but then starts banging his plate with his spoon, until his mother tells him to stop and takes the food away. Daniel asks her to take off his bib, which she does, and he gets down from the table and starts playing with a toy tricycle, talking to his mother from time to time, while she continues chatting with her mother, who is still watching the soap opera on TV. But when Daniel needs to go to the toilet, it's his grandmother who takes him.

By now it's nearly 9 P.M., and Daniel and his mother are playing in his room, getting things out of his box of toys and building things out of blocks. This continues for the next 20 minutes or so, interrupted only by the arrival of Daniel's aunt, who kisses him. It's then time for him to start getting ready for bed, but he takes out some action figures and asks for some cake. He goes into the kitchen to get some and talks a little to his aunt while playing with the cake. When he goes back into the other room, his aunt calls him to ask whether he wants to take a bath, and his mother says that she's going to put his toys back into their box. Daniel gives her a hug, and she hugs him back, saying "My big buddy!" (amigão, amigão), and then he runs back and forth between the bedroom and the kitchen, with his mother, aunt, and grandmother watching him. His mother gets him his pacifier, but he shows no signs of being ready for bed, and talks to the adults. The TV is still on, with his grandmother still watching the same soap opera. Finally, his mother takes Daniel to brush his teeth and get ready for bed.

Summary

It's clear that it's not just middle-class parents who follow the lead of their young children. Patty's (Greensboro) mother does this to a great extent: giving her the toy gun that her daughter wants; changing the TV channel to search for the "doggie" that Patty had seen briefly; asking her whether she wants to take a bath; allowing her to put on her new dress; changing the videotape that Patty watches before sleeping. Volodya's mother, too, helps him see what's on the letter box and explains the meaning of the postcode; reads to him when he asks her to; explains to him how a bee stings in response to his question; allows him to help her cooking even while explaining why he can't help with the actual frying. Piia's (Oulu) mother asks her daughter whether she'd like a bath.

But these examples are not common in the vignettes of the other children. Noel (Greensboro), for example, spends most of his time during the observational period fitting in with his mother's wants, including spending more than an hour in church with little to occupy him. His attempts to make contact with another boy who's in church are not successful, and he entertains himself mostly by drawing on some paper his mother finds for him and singing to himself. Derrick, for the most part, seems to be finding ways of amusing himself, and although he gets someone to prepare him some tea, it's his older sister who does this rather than either of his parents. The other children spend a lot of their time watching TV, but this means Daniel (Porto Alegre) watching the soap opera that his grandmother wants to see, Patty watching the wrestling that her grandfather turns on, Eva (Tartu) watching the typical evening programs in Estonia, or Dongki (Suwon) watching what his grandmother is watching.

None of the fathers, even when physically present, spend a great deal of time interacting with their children. Piia and her mother try quite hard to get Piia's father to help with his daughter's bath time, but it's only with some urging that he tries to wash her hair and explains, when he doesn't do a good job of it, that her mother is much better at this task than he is. But he is also asked to dry her and to read to her, and does neither. Derrick's father does speak to him, during the evening meal, but it's only to admonish him. The other fathers are not present at all during the observations, although only one of the families is headed by a single mother (Volodya's mother had never been married to his father, who had never had a role in Volodya's life).

It's interesting to see the different bedtime routines that we find in the various cities. Patty and Noel, from Greensboro, both go to sleep to the sounds of videos – *Winnie the Pooh* in her case, a family trip in his. Volodya's mother reads quietly to him until he falls asleep and Piia's mother talks to her, leaving her after a prayer. Eva just gets into bed and falls asleep, and Derrick falls asleep in his mother's lap, while she continues to work – weaving baskets. Dongki and Daniel both stay awake longer than anticipated, and the observers unfortunately have to leave before they sleep.

CONCLUSION

I hope that these vignettes have given a sense of the types of activities and social interactions in which the children in the various cities are involved. They give every appearance, I think, of everyday life as it happens, despite the fact that during two of the episodes the observer is brought into the picture – once as a target to be shot at (Mike in Greensboro) and once (Sandra, also in Greensboro) as an apparent reason for the children not to show bad behavior. As I said at the start of the chapter, the vignettes were not chosen to illustrate any particular points but simply to describe what was happening in these children's lives during four periods of the day. These descriptions allow us to put some "flesh" onto the drier "bones" of the data that have been presented in the previous two chapters.

In part, they illustrate the similarities across all the children featured in the vignettes – all of whom spend a good part of the time in play, whether in child care or not. It's also possible to see from these vignettes what is generally apparent in the data, namely, that mothers are far more likely than fathers to feature in these children's daily experiences, and even when both mothers and fathers are present, it's far more likely for the mother to be involved than the father. Teija's father in Oulu seems to be the exception that proves the rule!

However, cultural differences, at the level of the city, are also quite clear. For example, although the children spend most of their time in play, the objects with which they play are different in Kisumu, as Brendah and Brandon most clearly show, and Fredah's time in preschool also provides her with few opportunities for play. The children's experiences in Kisumu also appear to be different from those in the other cities in at least one other way: none of the four Kenyan children who feature in these vignettes spends much if any time in interaction with adults, something that isn't true of the children in any of the groups. It's also possible to see, in the experiences of Boris and Liuba from Obninsk and Peeter and Epp from Tartu, the reasons so many lessons about the world occurred in the lives of children from these two cities.

However, the vignettes just as clearly illustrate the fact that it is the intersection of society and social class that is at least as interesting as are these citywide differences. For example, Fredah's time in preschool is devoted, in large part, to the provision of academic lessons, something that we saw was true for all of the middle-class children who attended child care. By contrast, both Derrick and Brendah, from working-class homes in Kisumu, are far more integrated into the world of work than are any other children. The experiences of Jonghee (but not Juwon), from Suwon, illustrate the important role that middle-class Korean mothers give to the provision of academic lessons. In Greensboro, in both the White and Black families, middle-class parents (and teachers in child care) were far more likely to try to fit in with the wishes of their children (as in the cases of Andy and Kevin) and less likely to have the children follow the rules, seen clearly with Mike and Sandra.

Regardless of the extent to which adults try to follow their children's lead or encourage their children to follow rules that they, the parents, have established, the children themselves are highly active. They try to draw adults into activities and interactions with them: Jonas and his brother Asko, in Oulu, try hard to get their father to put a train track together, and finally he does so; Kolya, in Obninsk, gets his grandmother to read to him, Epp persuades her aunt to do the same, and Juwon's mother is asked to read to him, and does so, and Piia tries to involve her father in reading a story to her, and although she fails in that attempt, her mother reads with her; Patty (Greensboro) pretends to be an ice-skater, and her mother is asked to act the part of the highly appreciative audience; Volodya (Obninsk) draws his mother into a conversation about bees and how they sting. Children also actively start activities that are not so appreciated by others: Dongki draws a picture on the wall; Daniel (Porto Alegre) tries to climb into the bookcase; Heino, in Tartu, plays with the family's cell phone, takes a screwdriver to "repair" his car, and ends up breaking various things; Mike ignores both a peer's and a teacher's admonishments not to put rocks into a toy car. The cultural world, important though it is, is far from a determinant of what occurs in children's lives; children themselves play a major role in influencing the nature of the activities and interactions in which they're involved.

Why is it important to focus on these activities and interactions, assuming that they are reasonably typical of these children's experiences? To answer this question, we have to return to theory, and that's what I'll do in the next, and final, chapter.

9   The Cultural Ecology of Young Children

"Our deeds are fetters that we forge ourselves." . . . "Ay, truly: but I think it is the world that brings the iron."

George Eliot, *Middlemarch*, 1872/1988, p. 29

In the previous three chapters, I've focused on the everyday activities in which young children from different cultural communities are engaged, how they get involved in those activities, the various settings in which they spend their time, and the different people with whom they interact. In this chapter, I return to the earlier discussion of why it's so important to examine these typically occurring activities and interactions, namely, that it is one way in which to understand how culture and human development are related. First, I'll discuss the issues in more abstract ways and then will tie these abstractions to cultural–ecological theory and to the data that have been presented in this book.

CULTURE AND HUMAN DEVELOPMENT

How can we understand the relations between culture and human development? As I described in Chapter 3, the answer to this question depends in large part on one's paradigm, or worldview, and paradigms, as I pointed out in that earlier chapter, vary in terms of ontology, epistemology, and methodology. Ontological questions have to do with the nature of reality. Those who position themselves within the mechanistic paradigm are comfortable with a view that culture (or any aspect of the environment in which people live or are placed, as in the case of experimental research) has a reality separate from that of the individuals within. The relevant epistemological and methodological questions deal with how that reality can be known and the methods used for coming to know reality. Mechanists therefore have no problem designing studies in which variables can be treated as independent (when they are hypothesized to have some causal effect, whether direct or indirect) or dependent (when they are hypothesized to be the result of those independent causes). Culture, in this approach, can thus be viewed as a *cause* of human development. Smedley and Smedley, for example, wrote that "the evidence from history and the study of thousands of diverse cultures around the world are testament to the overwhelming and coercive power of culture to mold who we are and what we believe" (2005, p. 17). Van der Vijver and Poortinga reacted to the opposing position that culture cannot simply be reduced to an independent variable as follows:

> The issue is not whether or not cultures can be "reduced" to independent variables, but whether or not a reduction of cultural elements to independent variables can advance our knowledge of behavior. As an experiential category, culture is clearly molar. From an analytic point of view, however, it is counterproductive to restrict ourselves to a molar conception. . . . It is only by abstracting from daily contexts and reducing culture to a set of core variables relevant for the construct under study that we can carry out culture-comparative studies. (2002, p. 253)

Mechanists thus clearly accept a dualistic position on the nature of reality; individual and context, or mind and body, either are or can be treated as though they are separate phenomena.

From the contextualist point of view, however, dualism is untenable, and three approaches have been taken to build a nondualist psychology. One, which is not contextualist, is simply to deny the reality of the social group altogether and to argue that groups (including cultural groups) are nothing other than collections of individuals (i.e., the social world has no reality apart from the individuals within it). This position of "methodological individualism" (Sawyer, 2002a, 2002b) is that the individual is thus the appropriate unit of analysis.

Contextualists typically take one of the remaining two approaches. One is to take a holistic view, arguing that the whole (the social group, or culture) is more than the sum of its parts and therefore has a reality that cannot be reduced to the individuals within. The other is to take a dialectical position, in which both the social world and the individuals within have separate realities but that these two realities are in constant dynamic interaction.

The holistic view, in essence, denies that there is any meaningful boundary between individual and context. This is the position taken by Barbara Rogoff and some of her colleagues and former students. Rogoff (1995), for example, argued that her sociocultural approach is one "in which the boundary [between individual and context] itself is questioned, since a person who is participating in an activity is a part of that activity, not separate from it" (p. 153). This means that individual development is "inseparable from interpersonal and community processes" (Rogoff, Baker-Sennett, Lacasa, & Goldsmith, 1995, p. 45) and should be studied holistically, "as dynamically integrated constellations of cultural practice" (Rogoff & Angelillo, 2002, p. 213). Matusov (1998), similarly, contrasted an "internalization" model as being one in which there is a separation of the social and the individual with a "participation" model in which "social and psychological planes mutually constitute one another and are inseparable" (p. 329).

Those taking a dialectical position argue that individuals and their social worlds are separate entities but attempt to deal with the dualistic problem by treating the two as dynamically interrelated. To contrast a dualistic separation with one that is dialectic, Valsiner (e.g., 1991, 1998a) coined the terms "exclusive separation" and "inclusive separation." The former involves separation of the type favored by mechanists, namely, that various aspects of the context can be treated as independent of the individuals within those contexts and there is not a "whole" of which the separate variables are linked parts. By contrast, inclusive separation recognizes that two (or more) aspects are included within a whole, and therefore interrelated, but which nevertheless can be distinguished analytically.

I think that the holistic argument, built around the inseparability of individual and social world, has a number of difficulties. What exactly is meant by the "whole" when talking about society, culture or, more generally, the social world? Societies are heterogeneous, as are the cultural groups that exist within societies. It becomes difficult to talk about something that is holistic when the entity being discussed is typified by unequal relations of power and wealth in which conflicts of interests are at least as likely to be found as shared interests and harmonious relations (Corsaro et al., 2002; Erickson, 2002; Gjerde, 2004; Lewis & Watson-Gegeo, 2005; Packer & Goicoechea, 2000; Schousboe, 2005; Turiel & Perkins, 2004). It may be in the interests of those with access to power to stress the notion of society or culture being an integrated and seamless whole and to downplay existing socioeconomic, race or ethnic, gender, or age differences, but that does not mean that those differences do not exist.

It is possible to tackle this issue of within-society heterogeneity in various ways. One way is simply to accept that cultures are heterogeneous and to take a "polycontextual" approach (Cole, 2005a). It certainly is the case that none of us are members of a single culture but members of multiple cultures; which of these cultural groups we identify with at any particular time depends in part on which groups we are comparing ourselves with – an American when talking with a group of Japanese, a Southerner when thinking about

Northerners, middle class when thinking about the poor, and so on. Cole's view also fits well within the contextualist ontology – that there is no single reality but multiple realities, as I mentioned in Chapter 3. This polycontextual position seems difficult to reconcile with holism, however.

Another attempt to tackle this issue is to argue, as Rogoff has (see, for example, Rogoff, 2003; Rogoff & Angelillo, 2002), that because culture is not a "category" in the way that ethnicity or social class is it would be better to talk not about culture at all but instead to focus on people participating in different "communities of practice." This notion of communities is designed to limit the unit of analysis to more manageable groups of people who share approaches to participation, while at the same time not always agreeing. Communities, Rogoff wrote, consist of "groups of people who have some common and continuing organization, values, understanding, history, and practices" and culture consists of "the *common ways* that participants share (even if they contest them)" (2003, pp. 80–81).

Smaller groups, or communities of practice, can of course be studied in their own terms, and in this case I think that the holistic argument makes more sense. However, one cannot ignore the impact of the broader social structural forces that influence the relations of particular communities with other communities, as well as larger groups, within the society (or culture) at large. Every society has its shared history, no matter the extent of within-society heterogeneity.

The position of Blacks within the United States can be seen as just one example of what I mean, even if this requires oversimplifying dramatically by not considering the class, ethnic, and regional variations that exist within the Black community. As I discussed in Chapter 3, this cultural group has been viewed from a position of weakness (the discredited "culture of deprivation" view) or from a position of the strengths that derive from the specific cultural heritage of African Americans (Boykin & Allen, 2004; García Coll et al., 1996). However, the Black community within the United States can never be understood outside of the context of the society as a whole, with its history of slavery, current relations between Blacks, Whites, and immigrant groups, issues relating to unequal power, and past and continuing differential access to resources among these groups. Equally, of course, it is (or should be) impossible to discuss the White community (or any other ethnic group) within the United States outside of the same context, although far too often this happens (Perry, 2001).

At the same time, any racial/ethnic group within any society is far from homogeneous itself. It is therefore important to take seriously the hetero-geneity that exists within all societies and particularly the intersections of the main sources of heterogeneity, for example, social class, ethnicity, and race in the United States (see, for example, Hill & Sprague, 1999; Lareau, 2002; Lee, 2002; McLoyd, 2004; Smedley & Smedley, 2005). These multifaceted relations within and between groups make it difficult to take seriously a holistic view of social groups.

Another major difficulty with the holistic position is that focusing on the whole may occur at the expense of examining what the individual brings to bear. One doesn't have to go to the extreme of methodological individualism (that the social group has no reality apart from the individuals within) to recognize that individuals are heavily implicated in the creation and recreation, with each new generation, of culture. It's certainly difficult to find any theory of human development, whether mechanist, organicist, or contextualist, that doesn't include the notion of the active individual, whether we consider radical behaviorism, social cognitive theory, or the theories of Piaget, Erikson, Vygotsky, and Bronfenbrenner.

It is partly for this reason, I think, that scholars such as Barbara Rogoff or Jean Lave talk about communities of practice, whether the communities are school classrooms (Rogoff, Turkanis, & Bartlett, 2001) or groups of workers (Lave & Wenger, 1991), because it's relatively easy to see the ways in which the communities, the individuals within those communities, the forms of interaction among those individuals, and the practices themselves change in the course of individuals participating in those practices. It is no doubt for this reason that Rogoff (1995; Rogoff & Angelillo, 2002) accepted that for the purposes of analysis, one can treat what is inseparable as separable, by using separate "lenses" to focus first on one plane (the individual, for example) and then on one of two other planes (the interpersonal and the community).

As Lawrence, Dodds, and Valsiner (2004) noted, it is all too easy to reify cultural practices and treat them as immutable or unchanging – something that culture hands down to its members – whereas in fact they are always coconstructed by those who participate in them, more competent and less (or non-) competent alike. This is as true for children drawing other children into current classroom practices as for adults trying to pass down to children aspects of the current cultural repertoire (Corsaro et al., 2002; Gjerde, 2004). Practices considered normal or appropriate, that is, those within the cultural repertoire, are important, but so, too, are those that arise as a way of dealing with unexpected situations, new technologies, or new ideas, as well as those that emerge in opposition to traditional cultural norms. Even in situations in which the power relations and directions of influence seem clear, such as the school classroom, children also have power, both forcing their teachers to act in ways they might not otherwise have acted (Packer, 2002), as well as "interpretively reproducing" the power relations of which they are aware with other children in the classroom or on the playground (Corsaro, 1997; Corsaro et al., 2002).

A dialectical approach to the relations between culture and human development therefore makes sense to me because it can consider at one and the same time the joint realities of the social world and the individuals who make up that world by treating them in dynamic interaction. This, of course, is the essence of cultural–ecological theory, as I've laid it out in the earlier chapters. This theory, in common with other contextualist theories, focuses attention on the types of activities and interactions that occur frequently in the lives of developing individuals, while showing how those activities and interactions are altered both by the characteristics of the individuals who are participating in them and by the context in which they are occurring.

Context, as I have made clear, includes not only the particular setting (home, child care, workplace, etc.) in which the activities and interactions are occurring but the interactions among the various settings in which the developing individuals typically spend their time and the various broader contexts (spatial, social, and temporal) that provide meaning to the rest. Development proceeds via the interplay of these various mutually influencing factors, with none of them, alone, determining the course of that development.

ILLUSTRATING A DIALECTICAL APPROACH TO CULTURE
AND HUMAN DEVELOPMENT

It's easy to write the previous sentence; it's more difficult to describe development as a phenomenon that emerges from the dramatic interplay of forces without some degree of artificial separation. You'll have noted that it was in Chapter 5 that I focused primarily on historical features that, I argued, were helpful in explaining the particular set of activities and engagement with others that featured in one or another cultural group. I noted there that knowing about the historical changes was essential to our understanding the differences between the data we gathered in Kisumu and those reported by others. Similarly, it is impossible to imagine writing about children developing in Russia and Estonia without linking their activities and interactions to the changes that have occurred since the collapse of the Soviet Union. The impact of history on young children's everyday activities and interactions in Greensboro, Oulu, Suwon, and Porto Alegre may be less obvious than the examples from Kisumu, Obninsk, and Tartu but is equally important.

In the following two chapters, I paid little attention to historical changes. Instead, in Chapter 6, I focused on variations in activities both at the group level (citywide, social class, and, in Greensboro, race differences) and because of individual differences, particularly in initiating activities and interactions. In Chapter 6, I showed how these variations could in part be explained by the immediate context (in particular, by the child's presence in some type of child-care setting) and by interactions with the children's main social partners. However, this type of separation of factors (of history, of the social group, of activities, of the role of the individual, of the impact of the immediate setting, and of the partners in activities) has to be seen as being purely for ease of display and should not in any sense be taken as implying that the various factors have independent roles.

In the sections that follow, I again describe each of the interacting factors in turn. However, it will also become clear why it's so important to put engagement in activities and interactions at the center of any theory that deals with the relations between culture and human development. In essence, this allows us to see both the ways in which culture influences engagement in activities and the ways in which, through such engagement, cultures themselves change.

Cultural and Social-Class Influences on Development

Although there are likely to be some exceptions, I take it as given that parents want their children to grow up to be successful — by which I mean able to fit well into their cultural group and be able to prosper economically and emotionally, although the ways in which this can be achieved will vary greatly. For some cultures, this means raising children to be self-sufficient; for others, the goal is to achieve economic *inter*dependence. These differences in values, like all others that distinguish one culture from another, should be reflected in the cultures' varying practices. If this is the case, at least some of the activities encouraged by parents, and by other people charged with looking after children, should be those that are viewed, within that culture, as likely to lead to success. Because culture influences the types of activities that occur and the manner of interactions, we cannot think that engagement in more of any type of activity (or greater interaction of a certain type) by members of one cultural group than another indicates that the members of the first group are in any way better or worse than members of the second. Rather, we need to think about the reasons for the variation between the groups.

We can see some of these reasons by contrasting experiences that seem to be designed to help children do well in school. The Korean children in this study spent a good deal of their time in the company of their mothers. Further, as I showed in Chapter 6, mothers in Suwon provided a good deal of school-related material for their children, whether books, toys that included things mathematical, or videotapes that were designed to teach their children things that might help them in school. The Suwon mothers seemed to view these activities as helpful to their children and actively encouraged their children to engage in them. Some of the parents in Kisumu, too, appeared interested in providing their children with experiences that might help them in school, but their approach was different. As we saw in Chapter 7, neither these Luo children's mothers nor their fathers engaged them in many academic lessons, and the children did not play with objects designed to help them learn school-related things in and around the home. On the other hand, those Kisumu children who were placed into a formal child-care setting were far more likely to spend their time with things academic than was true for any of the groups of children. Clearly, here are two different approaches with the same goal – to prepare children to do well in school. The children are involved in different types of activities, with different people, but it would be ridiculous for someone to argue that one set of activities or partners is somehow better for development than the other without taking into account the cultural norms in these two societies.

A different insight into what parents view as important when their children are in child care was provided by the parents in Porto Alegre. It seems apparent, judging by the types of activities that occurred in the centers where we observed the children, that parents' primary goal in having their children in child care was not to have them be explicitly prepared for school. The centers, by contrast, seemed to offer a place in which children could safely play with others (as well as allowing both parents to have paid employment).

The same argument can be made for examining cultural differences within societies, whether a function of race/ethnicity or social class. Building on Kohn's ideas discussed in Chapter 3, if social class is an important cultural factor, it is because the experiences of life (both educationally and in their work) for professional, middle-class parents are different from those of parents who did not have higher education and whose jobs require them to follow other people's rules.

In all of the cities except Obninsk, children from middle-class families were more likely than those from working-class families to play with objects designed with school in mind and to engage more in academic lessons. It's difficult to avoid the view that these middle-class families were more likely than working-class families to provide their children with more opportunities to engage in these activities because they viewed them as more important. The implication again seems to be clear, that parents from each group are preparing their children for success in different domains by giving them different experiences. In turn, these types of differences support the position that social class is akin to culture – defined as a group whose values, beliefs, and practices distinguish them from other groups and which tries to pass on those values, beliefs, and practices to the next generation.

Is there evidence that the Black–White differences in Greensboro also qualify for the status of cultural differences, given this definition? The Black children were twice as likely to be observed playing with no objects (singing, dancing, running and chasing, playing rough and tumble) than were their White peers and were less likely to receive interpersonal lessons and to engage in conversation with adults. The settings in which they were situated were also somewhat different – Black children were more likely than their White counterparts to spend their time in the company of grandparents or some other type of child-minder, and this is reflected in the greater role played by grandparents in the children's various activities. The White children's fathers were more available to them than were the Black children's fathers, but it's also worth noting that the Black children's mothers were also less available to them.

However, it is the intersection of social class and race that is the most interesting; it was the White middle-class children who were involved in far more conversation than any of the other communities in Greensboro, the White working-class children who were involved in the fewest academic lessons, and middle-class children, both White and Black, were involved in more play with academic objects than were their working-class counterparts. Also interesting is the fact that of the three cases in Greensboro in which fathers were more involved in their children's activities than were mothers, all were in working-class families, two of which were Black. Skin color in Greensboro translates into some striking differences in experiences, at least part of which have to do with values, beliefs, and practices of the two groups, but those differences are clearly moderated by social class.

Of course, as I mentioned earlier, when dealing with cultural variations within a single society the situation is more complex than when considering cultures from different societies. In Greensboro, class and race are interwoven; the experiences of professional Blacks and those from a working-class background are in some ways similar (both will experience prejudice and discrimination in ways that Whites will not) but in some ways very different, just as the life experiences of middle-class and working-class Whites are very different. It's necessary to remember that culture is not simply about values, beliefs, and practices, important though these things are. Culture also relates to access to resources, something that is just as relevant (if not more so) when considering cultural differences within any given society, where differential resources will be far more visible than is the case of societies that are far from one another. In a city such as Greensboro, for example, access to child care (and particularly child care that is considered to be of high quality) is heavily dependent on resources; the choice of placing one's child with an unlicensed child-minder may have less to do with what a parent values or believes will help the child's development and far more to do with a lack of money. Similarly, although more obviously during an earlier period of history, racism denied Blacks in the United States access to resources, schooling, and positions of influence in society. In other words, children's experiences in the United States, as in any society, are related not simply to their parents' values and beliefs but to structural and resource constraints as well.

Despite these class and racial differences, however, each of these four groups in Greensboro shares the experiences of living in the United States at the start of the 21st century. All those aspects of life that currently make Americans different in important ways from Russians, Estonians, Finns, Koreans, Kenyans, and Brazilians are experienced by members of these four American groups. Images of success, of status, of what counts as "appropriate" family life are shared across the society, while at the same time, given the variations in experiences at the group level, are different. For example, it may be the case that, in comparison to Koreans, Americans are individualistic; however, thanks to the history of Blacks in the United States, Blacks tend to have a more group-oriented approach to family than is the case for many Whites.

Individual Influences on Development

It's thus possible to see the ways in which cultural influences are experienced and expressed in the course of the typically occurring everyday activities and interactions in which people in different cultural communities engage. However, cultures do not simply influence the individuals within them; they are equally influenced by those individuals. Cultural–ecological theory is not a theory about cultural influences on individual behavior and development; rather it is about the interweaving of cultural and individual aspects of development in the course of engaging in activities, particularly those that occur commonly. Thus, although a good claim can be made that cultures vary in terms of the types of settings they provide and the encouragement that they give to some activities rather than to others, culture never is a *determinant* of activities.

Although cultures change, in part, because of contact from outside the culture, most changes cannot be understood only by reference to forces from outside. Change occurs largely because each new generation never simply copies what previous generations had done but appropriates the old and transforms it in the process of appropriation. The extent of change, from one generation to the next, obviously varies greatly. During some periods of historical time, the rate of change seems rapid, but at others much slower. Even within the same historical period, one society can experience rapid change and another society change that may not seem perceptible. During periods of rapid technological change, members of an older generation may have little or no use for a technology invented by members of a younger generation, but a still younger generation will not only grow up with that new technology but appropriate it in ways not foreseen by the inventing generation.

Even in times of relatively slow change, however, the same forces are at work. Members of the youngest generation have to learn the ways of the older generations to fit into the cultural group into which they have been born. Yet it's impossible for a novice to understand an activity, practice, event, or symbol in the same way an expert does; the latter, by definition, brings entirely different experiences to bear. How, then, does the novice become an expert, in turn ready to pass on to the following generation those things that the culture considers important? By engaging in those activities, practices, events, symbols, and the like not only with those who are already more competent but also with those who are merely as competent (peers) and with those who are even less competent. Because humans are so variable, individually, we will necessarily engage in these activities in slightly different ways, and so appropriate them differently.

The extent of the difference is a function not only of these individual variations, but also of the pace of the society's change – where the change is slow, traditional ways of doing things will be more highly valued than in societies in which the rate of change is relatively fast, when novelty and creativity are more likely to be valued. Some of us seem more disposed to rebel, others less so, and some societies are more tolerant than others of the rebellions of the young against the ways of those who are older. But generally speaking, it is by engaging in the typically occurring practices of a group, with others of that group, in ways the group approves that ensures the continuity of what we think of as culture. This is equally true when considering culture as a single community of practice, as a minority group (whether of high or low status), or as a society as a whole. Engagement in everyday activities and interactions, then, is the key to understanding development.

In part, children engage in activities because they are available to them and viewed as appropriate. However, they also do so because the activities in which they choose to engage are those that they enjoy. Enjoyment may outweigh the appropriateness of an activity (both children and adults engage in activities that are not sanctioned by the culture), and so may necessity or the perception of necessity. Children also engage in activities and interactions because of a developing sense of identity as someone who engages in those sorts of things in the ways in which they do. This is, of course, a coconstruction with the others with whom they engage. For example, depending on the practices in which they participate and their interactions with others in the course of those activities, they form a view of themselves as relatively skilled in some arenas, incompetent in others. As Packer and Goicoechea (2000) argued, we become who we are and how we think about ourselves in the course of the practices in which we engage.

As soon as we introduce issues such as enjoyment or perception, we are necessarily introducing individual temperament, characteristics, desires, and so on. Whether children read, watch television, play with a friend, or clean their room obviously depends on what objects and people are available, and perhaps on what they are asked or encouraged to do, but it also depends on what they want to do. What one wants to do is not purely an individual characteristic, of course; it is likely to be related either to things that one has been encouraged to do in the past (and perhaps rewarded for) or to the opposite (deliberately choosing something that one's parents do not want one to do), but in either case, the role of the surrounding social world cannot be easily separated from individual desires. This having been said, it still is the case that most parents who have more than one child are quite clear on the fact that the two (or more) of them were unlike right from the start and that those differences helped to change the nature of the interactions between parents and child. This type of statement, of course, need not be accepted completely at face value; having a second child is a different experience in all sorts of ways from having the first one, not least of all because the process has been experienced before. Changes in patterns of interaction cannot be so simply viewed as the responsibility of the different nature of the second child.

In the study reported in this book, it's clear that the cultural groups we identified were far from homogeneous. Although I concentrated in Chapter 6 on activities and interactions at the group level, presenting the averages for each group, I also discussed the individual variation within each group. If cultures *determine* engagement in activities, there clearly would be no room for this type of variation. Further, some of the variation in the activities in which the children in this study engaged clearly came about because some of the children were more likely to do something to start the activity than were others. As I already mentioned, middle-class children in most of the cities were more likely to be involved in lessons than were their working-class peers. It was not simply the case, as I implied earlier, that middle-class parents provided more opportunities for such lessons to occur; middle-class children were also far more likely to initiate lessons (by asking questions) than were children from working-class families. This was most clearly the case in the White communities in Greensboro, in Obninsk, Tartu, Suwon, and Kisumu. (Although children from middle-class Black families and middle-class families in Porto Alegre were involved in more lessons than their working-class counterparts, this was not because they initiated more of them.)

Across the entire study, children who initiated more lessons were also more likely to start both conversations and work by themselves, which might be evidence that these children had a temperamental propensity to play a more active role in starting the activities in which they were involved. However, without collecting data on their temperament from their birth and beyond, it's impossible to say whether they were simply reacting to their middle-class parents encouraging them to exercise more self-direction, something that we know is commonly done in many middle-class households in many societies (Kohn, 1977, 1995; Kohn & Slomczynski, 1990). The main point that I want to stress is the fact that individual characteristics and aspects of the cultural surround cannot be easily separated, one from the other. Members of a culture that values the exercise of initiative might be more likely to view their young children as showing initiative than do members of a culture that values tradition and following the lead that elders set.

It's worth recalling the vignette in which Kevin, a Black child from a middle-class family, is playing with his computer. The game is one in which Kevin is in effect being told the story of *The Jungle Book* but is able to go at his pace as he determines when to move to the next page. When his mother wants him to turn off the computer, he doesn't do it until she comes in and asks him *how* to do it, allowing him to show her while at the same time doing what she wants. When he's thirsty, Kevin gets himself a drink from the fridge. Later that evening, his mother says that she wants to wash him in the bath, which leads him to say that he can do it by himself. In this way, she accomplishes a task that she wants done, while allowing him to exercise self-direction. The culture is one in which computers are available (along with software explicitly designed for young children to use by themselves), the mother clearly wants her child to exercise some freedom of choice, and the child wants to be able to do things by himself. It's easy to see the interweaving of culture, parent–child interaction, and child desires, and impossible to single out any one of them as being uniquely responsible.

Similarly, we can think about Volodya, in Obninsk, asking to see things, wondering about how bees "bite," wanting to help cook, in conjunction with a mother who obviously is more than ready to accommodate to her child's wishes. The cultural component cannot be ignored, however, because we are talking about a culture in which it is considered appropriate for a mother to engage with her child in these ways. By contrast, middle-class Luo children in Kisumu such as Brandon were able to exercise a lot of self-direction, at least when they weren't in child care, playing with other children and amusing themselves with all sorts of found objects, but not in conjunction with their parents. Culture is clearly implicated in both sets of relations, but in different ways.

The Influence of Time on and in Development

Because in this study, we collected data from different cultural groups, it's easy to see cultural variations in activities, adult–child interactions, and so on. It's less easy to see the impact of time, given that all of the data were gathered at approximately the same time, covering the final decade of the 20th century and the first years of the 21st century. And yet, as I described in Chapter 5 and mentioned briefly earlier in this chapter, historical time is as interwoven as is culture. Just as studies conducted in a single culture (particularly the researcher's own culture) typically do not consider the role played by culture, so, too, studies conducted at any one point of historical time tend to ignore its impact. Time, as well as space, is the final frontier that researchers need to conquer to understand development.

The influence of time on the ways in which these children are developing is seen relatively easily in Kisumu, where schooling has taken on a much more important role than was true 50 years ago when the Whitings and their colleagues started their *Six Cultures* work. Yet it's just as easily seen when comparing the social experiences of the Greensboro children (including those from middle-class families) with those observed by the Fischers in Orchard Town in the 1950s or with the English families from a variety of class backgrounds who were interviewed by the Newsons a decade later (see Chapter 2). In the 1950s, compared with the present day, it was common for women (particularly from middle-class backgrounds) not to work outside the home and therefore be available virtually all the time to be their children's social partners. In our work in Greensboro, although mothers were still far more available to their children than were fathers, they were available only a little over 50% of the time to the working-class Black children and around

70% of the time to the other groups in Greensboro. The desire or necessity for both parents (or the mother, in the case of our single-parent families) to work outside the home and the availability of child care, not to mention changes in prevailing views about working mothers, has changed children's social landscapes dramatically. Along with the changes in social partners have come other changes, with children in formal child-care settings engaging in different types of activities than those who do not go.

In Kisumu, too, we can see the same impact on the social landscape following the increased likelihood of children, particularly from middle-class families, to spend their time in a formal child-care setting. As we know, Luo mothers were not likely to feature as partners to their children in any of their activities, but whereas working-class mothers were available to their children (in the same locale) in about 60% of our observations, they were available only half that often in the middle-class community, primarily because half of the middle-class children spent a significant amount of their time in a child-care center.

Another way in which the influence of time is relatively easily visible is in both Obninsk and Tartu. As I pointed out in Chapter 5, these families had lived through the dramatic changes that accompanied the collapse of the former Soviet Union, and the parents were currently experiencing life in societies very different from those in which they had been raised. I provided in that chapter some of the comments that Russian and Estonian parents made about the changes that had occurred and how their families had been affected by those changes, both for the better and for the worse. Although I can only speculate, not having any relevant data from the period prior to independence for Estonia and the separation of Russia from the other former republics, it's possible that the reason why children in these two cities were involved in far more lessons than were children from any other city (three times more than children in Oulu, for example) stems from the parents' desire to help provide their children with the skills they might need to succeed in these uncertain times (Elliott & Tudge, 2007).

It's one thing to talk about the influence of historical time on development, but another to talk about development itself. Development, after all, involves change over time. This book does not describe such changes, however, and does not allow us to see development. What I've provided is a view of a slice of life in different cultural communities in different countries, with perhaps some possibility of imputing how things have developed because of current expectations. When we see Gabriela, in Porto Alegre, having breakfast with her mother, talking about the things that are going to happen later on that day in preschool and about the time she burned her finger, it seems clear that the pair of them have developed the sort of relationship in which they can engage in these sorts of conversations. When Epp, in Tartu, says to herself as she arranges some towels, "Why have you touched those? I put the washing away neatly," surely we are seeing a developed appropriation of her mother's voice.

What I have shown, in these previous chapters, is a little like our own development – we can reflect on our own past development, are most clearly aware of what's happening now, and can anticipate (with more or less degrees of certainty) what might happen in the future. But what is happening *now* is what we're experiencing, "the event alive in its present . . . doing, and enduring, and enjoying . . . [activities that are] like incidents in the plot of a novel or drama. They are literally the incidents of life" (Pepper, 1942, pp. 232–233). Or, as Tom Stoppard expressed it: "Life's bounty is in its flow" (2002, p. 100).

CONCLUSION

I hope that by now it is clear why I think that examining typically occurring activities and interactions is a good foundation on which to build an understanding of how culture and human development are related. It's not sufficient, of course. Aspects of what I described in Chapter 1 as the psychological, sociological, and anthropological modes of studying humans need to be incorporated into our research. Thus, as psychologists would argue, we cannot lose sight of what the individual brings to the activities and interactions of which he or she is a part. Similarly, as sociologists would stress, it's necessary to account for the influences of societal (and extrasocietal) structural forces as they developed over historical time and which help shape human lives. Finally, in keeping with the goals and methods of cultural anthropologists, our focus should be on the cultural nature of activities and interactions. Regardless of whether our studies include participants from different cultural groups, we need to be aware of the cultural nature of the everyday and taken-for-granted things that people do.

Cultural–ecological theory can help us by making explicit these different, yet interwoven strands – the individual, social–structural, and cultural–anthropological facets that are played out in the course of the everyday activities and interactions in which humans are involved in the course of their development. This is not the only theory that is relevant – as I pointed out in Chapter 3, there are other contextualist theories that, by virtue of their contextualist nature, make explicit the dialectical relations between individuals and the contexts in which they are situated and which have, in the foreground, the typically occurring activities that constitute the "historical events" of Pepper's (1942) contextualist metaphor.

What I've tried to accomplish in this book is to make explicit the metatheoretical foundations for the theory, to show how the methods for gathering data were explicitly based on the theory, and to illustrate how the methods can be put into practice in research on children engaged in everyday activities and interactions in a variety of different cultural contexts. It should now be clear why it's so important to mesh the methods with the theory. If the theory requires a focus on what typically occurs, in such a way as to find out what activities are generally available to young children, how they get involved in these activities, and who their usual social partners are, it makes little sense to try to control aspects of the setting or the presence or absence of any specific individuals.

Can methods such as those my colleagues and I used to collect our data really "capture" everyday life, the typical things that go on between children and their social partners, the normal ways in which activities start and end, and so on? As I wrote in Chapter 4, our aim was to change activities, behaviors, and interactions, in as few ways as possible – to be, in effect, the proverbial "fly on the wall." I won't repeat the various limitations to this approach, but it's clear that we were not always successful. Looking back at the vignettes, we can see Mike "shooting" at Sarah, the observer – perhaps in reaction to the fact that he didn't want to wear the wireless microphone that day. Yet for the most part, the vignettes seem, at least, to have the smell of reality about them. The reason that we wanted to observe for as long as we did was not simply to be able to cover the equivalent of a complete day but also to be with each child long enough for the children and, we hoped, the others who were around them to behave as they would without us being there.

Observation is not sufficient, however, to get a good sense of how children spend their time; it depends on where the observations take place. If we observe just in the home, particularly at times when a parent (typically the mother) is at home, we will be likely to observe a good deal more mother–child interaction than when we observe in all the settings in which children can be found. It's thus not surprising that virtually all of the "naturalistic" observations conducted in the United States and England, discussed in Chapter 2, clearly overemphasize (by comparison to our findings) the extent to which mothers are involved in their young children's activities. The goal of cultural anthropologists, using ethnographic methods, of describing what occurs naturally, rather than naturalistically, in parts of the majority world provides a far more reasonable sense of how children spend their time, and with whom. However, the problem of much of this anthropological work, as I pointed out in Chapter 2, is that it has not done such a good job of taking into account the changes that have occurred, particularly with the growth of schooling, or of moving beyond studies in rural areas to observe city life. Perhaps for these reasons, prior research has tended to underemphasize the extent to which Kenyan parents are involved with their children, and to overemphasize dramatically the extent to which young Kenyan children are involved in work; as our data clearly show, middle-class children in Kisumu did not work any more than children from the other cities.

I think it should be clear, then, that differences in the types of methods used to collect data from children and families from the industrialized world on the one hand and from the majority world on the other, the emphasis on comparing cultures that are in many ways highly dissimilar, and the relative lack of attention to the heterogeneity that exists within any cultural group has left an important void – a void that this book seeks to start filling. For this reason, the families that I chose to study were from different societies, drawing both from the industrialized and majority worlds. Because all of the children were living in cities and because from each city we chose equal numbers of middle-class and working-class families, I was able to compare like with like as a way of examining cultural variations in children's activities and interactions both across and within societies.

I have argued throughout this book that everyday activities and interactions are key to development, and that they cannot be understood without reference to the individuals who are involved in them and the various contexts in which those activities are situated. It is clear, then, that cultural–ecological theory does not accept the position that individuals and contexts can be conceived of as separate, independent entities. The ontological position that I take, in other words, is that both social worlds and the individuals within those worlds have a reality that cannot be subsumed under the other, and I think that Valsiner's notion of inclusive separation fits well with this theory.

First, the social world does have reality that cannot be explained simply by the individuals within, as can be seen by the patterning of activities in different social contexts. In our data, these different patterns are visible at the level of society (at least as indexed by the single city from each society in which we observed children); in several important ways, the everyday activities and interactions of our children in Korea, in the United States, in Kenya, in Brazil, and in the three northeastern European cities were different from one another. Admittedly, these differences were not great, certainly by comparison with the differences that can be found when contrasting middle-class White children from an industrialized society with those from a rural area of the majority world. This should not be such a surprise, however, given that we deliberately chose to observe children who were not "maximally dissimilar" (Hallpike, 2004) but came from families that looked similar in terms of parental education and occupation, all of whom lived in medium- to large-sized cities. The differences that we did find can be explained, in part (but only in part) by reference to views about what activities are appropriate, which should be encouraged, and which discouraged, within the society from which the families were drawn.

Evidence of the reality of social context can also be drawn from social class, with clear differences in the patterns of activities and interactions provided by children who came from working-class families and those whose parents were classified as middle class in terms of their education and occupation. These differences were fairly clear in each of the cities but were strikingly so in the case of Kisumu. One might be tempted to explain Kisumu's clear class distinction by virtue of Kenya being a part of the majority world; however, the fact that social-class differences were far less clear in Brazil than in Kenya should give one pause. On the basis of these class differences, it is immediately apparent that cultures are not homogeneous; even within a single city from each society, growing up in a middle-class family meant experiencing activities and interactions to a different extent than in a working-class family.

The reality of social context can also be seen, at least in the case of Greensboro, in terms of race – or rather the social arrangements that are related to the color of people's skin. The experiences of the Black and White children that we observed were not identical, but nor was it the case that either race only, or social class only, could be invoked to explain the patterns that we found. Instead, it was the intersection of race and social class that turned out to be critical. We did not examine ethnic variations in other cities (this would have been relatively easy in Tartu or Kisumu but more difficult in the other cities), nor did we try to study other differences such as rural–urban differences, regional differences, or recency of immigration, although one would surely expect to find equally clear differences in the experiences of children from different ethnic, regional, or immigrant groups.

The reality of social context could also be seen at a more microlevel (at least in some of the societies), by examining the experiences of children who attended some type of formal child-care setting and those who did not. Here again, it was clear that context had a reality that could not simply be explained by the specific individuals who were observed inside that setting; when looking at the same children when they were in child care and when they were not, it was apparent that their experiences were different inside and outside of that setting. Most interestingly, the extent to which those experiences differed and the manner of the differences could be traced to broader levels of context, whether racial (in the case of Greensboro), socioeconomic, or society.

In none of these situations can the different patterns we observed be attributed to individual differences – social contexts have a reality that cannot be explained by adopting an approach of methodological individualism. The reality of social contexts is also seen beyond the level of communities of practice, at much broader levels. On the other hand, it is equally clear that context, at whatever level, does not, by itself, explain anything.

As was obvious from the data presented in Chapter 6, within each group of children, even when considered at the most micro of levels, there was a good deal of individual variation, with some children engaging in the activities of interest to a far greater extent than others. As I showed, in part this could be explained by the fact that some children were far more likely to initiate these activities than were others. Moreover, as is clear from the various vignettes provided in several chapters, particularly Chapter 8, even when children don't start particular activities, those in which they become engaged often are those in which they seem to be interested. At other times, of course, they are involved in activities that others chose for them, such as when they have to take a bath or go to buy something from a local shop. It would be impossible, however, to make the argument that aspects of the setting or context were solely responsible for the activities in which the children engaged; their own individual characteristics, as well as those of the other people with whom they are interacting, are as important as are the characteristics of the settings. In other words, individuals have a reality that is separate from that of the social contexts they inhabit.

As Cole (1985) wrote about the zone of proximal development, everyday activities and interactions are the crucible in which culture and the individual are jointly created. They are thus the most meaningful unit of analysis from a contextual perspective, given that it is impossible to consider an activity or an interaction separate from the personal characteristics of the individual or individuals involved or from the contexts in which that activity or interaction is occurring. I wrote "contexts" deliberately, because not only is there the local context in which the activity is occurring – for example, a child preparing to sleep in a specific place – but also the broader contexts that give additional meaning to the activity. Whether it's a child, like Patty, going to sleep to the sounds and images of a videotape playing in her room, or a child such as Derrick, laying himself down in his mother's lap as she continues to work, or one such as Volodya, being read to as he falls asleep, one has to invoke systems of values, beliefs, access to resources, and availability of culturally powerful artifacts, to understand what is occurring.

When thinking about any interaction between a child and her parents, the manner in which the parents treat the child is an amalgam of the parents' own individual ideas about how to deal with the child at that time, their collective ways of dealing with each other and with the child, the child's own individual characteristics at that time, her ways of dealing with her parents, and notions about dealing with children that are common in the groups of which the parents and child are a part. Each of the individual influences, which are of course not independent of one another, serve at one and the same time to change the family system of which the individuals are a part and have the potential to change the wider groups of which the family is a part.

For example, it may be the norm for members of one group to allow their young children to go to sleep when they are tired and not to try to enforce a set bedtime. If one of those children appears to be doing poorly once she has gone to school in part because it's difficult to wake her up in the morning and she seems sleepy when at school, her parents might take the advice of her teacher to put her to bed earlier, look at the bedtime practices of other children from a different cultural group from the same society, or look at the school behavior of other children from the same group who like to go to bed earlier. As a result of these interactions with people outside the family, this family's practices may alter. Subsequently, this family's members might talk about the beneficial effect of the changed practices with other families from the same cultural group and thus bring about wider changes.

Finally, let's return to the children who featured in the brief vignettes provided at the start of Chapter 1. As I mentioned there, it's difficult to tell, from a sentence or two, which cultural group these children came from, although describing a full day in each child's life would be far more likely to provide a picture of cultural groups that are in many ways different. However, it's also possible to use those brief descriptions to illustrate some of the important similarities and differences among cultural groups that I have described in the course of this book.

I wrote about Felicia, playing with other children at the Brownie meeting. As was true of all of the children who feature in this book, by far the most common activity in which they are involved is some sort of play. It's important not to forget that in many ways all three-year-olds are similar, despite my focus in this book on aspects of their daily lives that distinguishes children in one group from those in other groups. The type of play, and the materials with which children play, vary across cultures, and in the case of Felicia and her friends, from White families in Greensboro, we can perhaps see the impact of television on the nature of their play, with Felicia being captured and put in jail, followed by discussion of who is to play the good guys and who the bad ones.

Jonghee was at home with her mother in Suwon and, as was true of many of the Korean children from middle-class homes that we observed, her mother obviously had decided to provide her with some learning opportunities at home and was busy teaching her both colors and mathematical concepts from a workbook designed to help her once she went to school. By contrast, both Daniel, from Porto Alegre, and Andrea, from the Black community in Greensboro were in a child-care setting. Both children are from working-class homes, but Daniel was in a formal child-care center, safely protected from the outside world by metal bars, on which he was playing, that surrounded the center. As I showed in Chapters 6 and 7, children are not much involved in school-related lessons in Porto Alegre, and child care seems to be primarily a place in which children can play in a safe place while their parents work. Andrea, by contrast, was in a family child-care setting, and it's interesting to note that the television was on, given that working-class children in Greensboro spent more time than all others watching television.

Volodya and Olev were also playing in those first examples provided in Chapter 1. Volodya, from Obninsk, was watching TV but also playing with his toys, which he didn't want to put away. However, it's also worth pointing out that during this brief episode Volodya's mother was repairing a broken toy. In the current conditions of life in Obninsk, as was true during Soviet times, repairing things to make them last longer, rather than buying something new, is common. She also used the television as an opportunity to give her son a lesson about where baby ostriches come from, nicely illustrating what we found generally – namely, that middle-class children were far more likely than their working-class counterparts to be involved in various types of lessons. It's thus not surprising to find that children in Obninsk were twice or three times more likely to be involved in "world" lessons (which included lessons about how to fix things and about the workings of the natural world) than were children in all other cities except Tartu, where the situation was similar, for the same reasons.

Olev, from Tartu, was playing with other children, but unlike in the case of several of the children, who were in a setting designed for young children, he was playing with his older siblings at home. His mother was also at home, but in this example, she only interacted with the children to tell them to stop jumping on the bed. The children did what they were told, unlike Volodya, and engaged in some imaginative pretend play, going off to the seaside in their car. In much of the literature on young children, mothers are treated as the primary social partners. However, despite the fact that mothers were in the same setting as their three-year-olds in 50% to 85% of our observations in all the communities except in Kisumu (see Chapter 7), they consistently featured as partners in children's play far less than did other children. In fact, children were more likely to play alone than they were to play with their mother.

In the first few descriptions, the children's fathers were conspicuous by their absence, and in the study as a whole we found that fathers were in the same settings as their children about half as often as were mothers and actually engaged with their children even less than their limited presence would suggest. However, in the brief snapshot from Kisumu, Gisela's father asked her and her older sister to go on an errand to a local shop. It's not surprising, given what I wrote in Chapter 6, to find that Gisela is from a working-class family and that involving children as young as three in work was not uncommon in that Kenyan community. The importance of academic lessons for both working- and middle-class children in Kisumu was seen in this description, too, although the person providing the lesson was an older sibling rather than a teacher.

The final description that I provided was of Simo, from Oulu, who was being collected from child care by his father and brother. As I mentioned in Chapter 6, the staple images of White middle-class children who are heavily involved in conversation and the "silent Finn" were belied in our study. Although it's certainly true that the White middle-class children from Greensboro were more involved in far more conversations than were children from the other groups from that city (and more than children in most of the other cities), the Finnish children that we observed were actually involved in more conversations than those from any other group.

As I mentioned early in Chapter 1, these brief descriptions, or verbal snapshots, of everyday events in the lives of children from different parts of the world can only give a sense of the similarities and differences in their lives. The book, as a whole, has provided more of a verbal equivalent of a film, one in which it's possible to see how different cultures arrange settings, activities, and types of interactions for the children growing up in them. At the same time, it's possible to see how the children themselves both reproduce, although in transformed fashion, aspects of the world in which they live and how they help transform that world.

Are Greensboro, Obninsk, Tartu, Oulu, Suwon, Kisumu, and Porto Alegre adequately representative of their respective societies, and are these seven societies adequately representative of the rest of the world? Clearly not – but I would hope that rather than this be treated as a failure (remember, the goal was never to generalize to other cultural contexts), it should serve as the impetus for others to collect data in similar ways from different groups. For it is only by doing this that we will really gain a good understanding of the interrelations of children's development and the cultural contexts in which that development occurs.

Rather than leave you with the typical "more research is needed" statement that ends many a thesis, dissertation, or scholarly article, I'll conclude with the opening lines of *Middlemarch*'s final chapter. "Every limit is a beginning as well as an ending. Who can quit young lives after being long in company with them, and not desire to know what befell then in their after-years? For the fragment of a life, however typical, is not the sample of an even web" (George Eliot, 1872/1988, p. 677). As I wrote toward the end of Chapter 4, we have continued to follow many of these children through their early years of school, and my next book will focus more on their "after years."

References

Abell, E., Clawson, M., Washington, W. N., Bost, K. K., & Vaughn, B. E. (1996). Parenting values, attitudes, behaviors, and goals of African American mothers from a low-income population in relation to social and societal contexts. *Journal of Family Issues, 17*, 593–613.

Adamopoulos, J., & Lonner, W. J. (2001). Culture and psychology at a crossroad: Historical perspective and theoretical analysis. In D. Matsumoto (Ed.), *The handbook of culture and psychology* (pp. 11–34). Oxford: Oxford University Press.

Anderson, D., Field, D., Collins, P., Lorch, E., & Nathan, J. (1985). Estimates of young children's time with television: A methodological comparison of parent reports with time-lapse video home observation. *Child Development, 56(5)*, 1345–1357.

Aristotle. (1985). *Nichmachean ethics* (T. Irwin, Trans.). Indianapolis, IN: Hackett. (Original work written in the fourth century B.C.)

Asante, M. K. (1987). *The Afrocentric idea.* Philadelphia: Temple University Press.

Atkinson, P., Coffey, A., Delamont, S., Lofland, J., & Lofland, L. (Eds.). (2001). *Handbook of ethnography.* London: Sage.

Bardi, A., & Schwartz, S. H. (1996). Relations among sociopolitical values in Eastern Europe: Effects of the communist experience? *Political Psychology, 17(3)*, 525–549.

Barker, R. G., & Wright, H. F. (1951). *One boy's day.* New York: Harper.

Barker, R. G., & Wright, H. F. (1954). *Midwest and its children.* Evanston, IL: Row, Peterson.

Bateson, P. P. G., & Hinde, R. A. (1976). (Eds.). *Growing points in ethology.* Cambridge: Cambridge University Press.

Baumrind, D. (1989). Rearing competent children. In W. Damon (Ed.), *Child development today and tomorrow* (pp. 349–378). San Francisco: Jossey-Bass.

Baumrind, D. (1996). The discipline controversy revisited. *Family Relations, 45(4)*, 405–414.

Bearison, D. J. (1991). *"They never want to tell you": Children talk about cancer.* New York: Cambridge University Press.

Benedict, R. (1959). *Patterns of culture.* Boston: Houghton-Mifflin.

Berger, P. L., & Luckmann, T. (1966). *The social construction of reality.* New York: Doubleday.

Bernstein, B. (1971). *Class, codes and control.* London: Routledge & Kegan Paul.

Billingsley, A. (1988). *Black families in white America* (2nd ed.). New York: Simon & Schuster.

Bloch, M. N. (1989). Young boy's and girl's play at home and in the community: A cultural-ecological framework. In M. N. Bloch & A. D. Pellegrini (Eds.), *The ecological context of children's play* (pp. 120–154). Norwood, NJ: Ablex.

Blurton-Jones, N. (1972). (Ed.). *Ethological studies of child behaviour.* Cambridge: Cambridge University Press.

Bodrova, E., & Leong, D. J. (1996). *Tools of the mind: The Vygotskian approach to early childhood education.* Englewood Cliffs, NJ: Prentice-Hall.

Bolger, N., Davis, A., & Rafaeli, E. (2003). Diary methods: Capturing life as it is lived. *Annual Review of Psychology, 54,* 579–616.

Bornstein, M. H. (2002). Parenting infants. In M. H. Bornstein (Ed.), *Handbook of parenting* (2nd ed.), *Vol. 1: Children and parenting* (pp. 3–43). Mahwah, NJ: Erlbaum.

Bornstein, M. H., & Cote, L. R. (2001). Mother-infant interaction and acculturation: 1. Behavioural comparisons in Japanese American and South American families. *International Journal of Behavioral Development, 25*(6), 549–563.

Bornstein, M. H., & Cote, L. R. (2004). Mother's parenting cognitions in cultures of origin, acculturating cultures, and cultures of destination. *Child Development, 75*(1), 221–235.

Bornstein, M. H., Haynes, O. M., Azuma, H., Galperin, C., Maital, S., Ogino, M., et al. (1998). A cross-national study of self-evaluations and attributions in parenting: Argentina, Belgium, France, Israel, Italy, Japan, and the United States. *Developmental Psychology, 34*(4), 662–676.

Bornstein, M. H., Tal, J., & Tamis-LeMonda, C. S. (1991). Parenting in cross-cultural perspective: The United States, France, and Japan. In M. H. Bornstein (Ed.), *Cultural approaches to parenting* (pp. 69–90). Hillsdale, NJ: Erlbaum.

Bornstein, M. H., Tamis-LeMonda, C. S., Pascual, L., Haynes, O. M., Painter, K. M., Gelperín, C. Z., & Pêcheux, M.-G. (1996). Ideas about parenting in Argentina, France and the United States. *International Journal of Behavioral Development, 19*(2), 347–367.

Boykin, A. W. (1994). Afro-cultural expression and its implications for schooling. In E. Hollins, J. King, & W. Hayman (Eds.), *Teaching diverse populations: Formulating a knowledge base* (pp. 243–273). Albany: State University of New York Press.

Boykin, A. W., & Allen, B. A. (2004). Cultural integrity and schooling outcomes of African American children from low-income backgrounds. In P. B. Pufall & R. P. Unsworth (Eds.), *Rethinking childhood* (pp. 104–120). New Brunswick, NJ: Rutgers University Press.

Bradley, R. H., Corwyn, R. F., McAdoo, H. P., & Coll, C. G. (2001). The home environments of children in the United States: Part I. Variations by age, ethnicity, and poverty status. *Child Development, 72*(6), 1844–1867.

Brewer, J. D. (2000). *Ethnography.* Buckingham, UK: Open University Press.

Bronfenbrenner, U. (1958). Socialization and social class through time and space. In E. E. Maccoby, T. M. Newcomb, & E. L. Hartley (Eds.), *Readings in social psychology* (3rd ed., pp. 400–424). New York: Holt, Rinehart and Winston.

Bronfenbrenner, U. (1979). *The ecology of human development: Experiments by nature and design.* Cambridge, MA: Harvard University Press.

Bronfenbrenner, U. (1988). Interacting systems in human development. Research paradigms: Present and future. In N. Bolger, A. Caspi, G. Downey, & M. Moorehouse (Eds.), *Persons in context: Developmental processes* (pp. 25–49). Cambridge: Cambridge University Press.

Bronfenbrenner, U. (1993). The ecology of cognitive development: Research models and fugitive findings. In R. Wozniak & K. Fischer (Eds.), *Development in context: Acting and thinking in specific environments* (pp. 3–44). Hillsdale, NJ: Erlbaum.

Bronfenbrenner, U. (1995). Developmental ecology through space and time: A future perspective. In P. Moen, G. H. Elder, Jr., & K. Lüscher (Eds.), *Examining lives in context: Perspectives on the ecology of human development* (pp. 619–647). Washington, DC: American Psychological Association.

Bronfenbrenner, U. (1999). Environments in developmental perspective: Theoretical and operational models. In S. L. Friedman & T. D. Wachs (Eds.), *Measuring environment across the life span: Emerging methods and concepts* (pp. 3–28). Washington, DC: American Psychological Association.

Bronfenbrenner, U. (2005). The bioecological theory of human development. In U. Bronfenbrenner (Ed.), *Making human beings human: Bioecological perspectives on human development* (pp. 3–15). Thousand Oaks, CA: Sage. (Original work published 2001.)

Bronfenbrenner, U., & Ceci, S. (1994). Nature-nurture reconceptualized in developmental perspective: A bioecological model. *Psychological Review, 101*(4), 568–586.

Bronfenbrenner, U., & Crouter, A. C. (1983). The evolution of environmental models in developmental research. In P. H. Mussen (Series Ed.) & W. Kessen (Vol. Ed.), *Handbook of child psychology, Vol. 1: History, theory, methods* (4th ed., pp. 357–414). New York: Wiley.

Bronfenbrenner, U., & Evans, G. W. (2000). Developmental science in the 21st century: Emerging questions, theoretical models, research designs, and empirical findings. *Social Development, 9*(1), 115–125.

Bronfenbrenner, U., & Morris, P. A. (1998). The ecology of developmental processes. In W. Damon (Series Ed.) & R. M. Lerner (Vol. Ed.), *Handbook of child psychology: Vol. 1. Theoretical models of human development* (5th ed., pp. 993–1028). New York: Wiley.

Buchmann, C. (2000). Family structure, parental perceptions, and child labor in Kenya: What factors determine who is enrolled in school? *Social Forces, 78*(4), 1349–1379.

Busse, T. V., & Busse, P. (1972). Negro parental behavior and social class variables. *Journal of Genetic Psychology, 120*(2), 287–194.

Carew, J. V. (1980). Experience and the development of intelligence in young children at home and in day care. *Monographs of the Society for Research in Child Development, 45* (6–7, Serial No. 187), 1–89.

Carew, J. V., Chan, I., & Halfar, C. (1976). *Observing intelligence in young children: Eight case studies.* Englewood Cliffs, NJ: Prentice-Hall.

Cassidy, D. J., Hestenes, L. L., Hegde, A., Hestenes, S., & Mims, S. (2005). Measurement of quality in preschool child care classrooms: An exploratory and confirmatory factor analysis of the early childhood environment rating scale-revised. *Early Childhood Research Quarterly, 20*(3), 345–360.

Chao, R. K. (2000). Cultural expectations for the role of parenting in the school success of Asian-American children. In R. D. Taylor, & M. C. Wang (Eds.), *Resilience across contexts: Family, work, culture, and community* (pp. 333–363). Mahwah, NJ: Erlbaum.

Chase-Lansdale, P. L., Gordon, R. A., Coley, R. L., Wakschlag, L. S., & Brooks-Gunn, J. (1999). Young African American multigenerational families in poverty: The context, exchanges, and processes of their lives. In E. M. Hetherington (Ed.), *Coping with divorce, single parenting, and remarriage: A risk and resiliency perspective* (pp. 165–191). Mahwah, NJ: Erlbaum.

Chernykh, N. S. (2000). *Obninsk na perevale epokh* [Obninsk at the turn of the century]. Obninsk, Russia: Printer Publishers.

Christensen, P., & Prout, A. (2005). Anthropological and sociological perspectives on the study of children. In S. Greene & D. M. Hogan (Eds.), *Researching children's experience: Approaches and methods* (pp. 42–60). London: Sage.

City of Greensboro Data Book. (2003). Retrieved on October 25, 2006, from http://www.greensboro-nc.gov/NR/rdonlyres/62B4BD2D-48A7–49EF-8D14-EF9EC18F9260/0/ CompleteFinalConPlanDocument.pdf

Clarke-Stewart, K. A. (1973). Interactions between mothers and their young children: Characteristics and consequences. *Monographs of the Society for Research in Child Development, 38* (6–7, Serial No. 153), 1–109.

Cole, M. (1985). The zone of proximal development: Where culture and cognition create each other. In J. V. Wertsch (Eds.), *Culture, communication and cognition: Vygotskian perspectives* (pp. 146–161). Cambridge: Cambridge University Press.

Cole, M. (1996). *Cultural psychology: A once and future discipline.* Cambridge, MA: Harvard University Press.

Cole, M. (1998). Can cultural psychology help us think about diversity? *Mind, Culture, and Activity, 5*(4), 291–304.

Cole, M. (2005a). Cross-cultural and historical perspectives on the developmental consequences of education. *Human Development, 48*(4), 195–216.

Cole, M. (2005b). Cultural-historical activity theory in the family of socio-cultural approaches. *International Society for the Study of Behavioural Development Newsletter, 47*(1), 1–4.

Cole, M., Cole, S. R., & Lightfoot, C. (2005). *The development of children.* New York: Worth.

Corsaro, W. A. (1985). *Friendship and peer culture in the early years.* Norwood, NJ: Ablex.

Corsaro, W. A. (1992). Interpretive reproduction in children's peer cultures. *Social Psychology Quarterly, 55*(2), 160–177.

Corsaro, W. A. (1997). *The sociology of childhood.* Thousand Oaks, CA: Pine Forge Press.

Corsaro, W. A., & Molinari, L. (2000). Entering and observing in children's worlds: A reflection on a longitudinal ethnography of early education in Italy. In P. Christensen & A. James (Eds.), *Research with children: Perspectives and practices* (pp. 179–200). London: Falmer Press.

Corsaro, W. A., Molinari, L., & Rosier, K. B. (2002). Zena and Carlotta: Transition narratives and early education in the United States and Italy. *Human Development, 45*(5), 323–348.

Corsaro, W. A., & Rosier, K. B. (1992). Documenting productive-reproductive processes in children's lives: Transition narratives of a Black family living in poverty. In

W. A. Corsaro & P. Miller (Eds.), *Interpretive approaches to children's socialization* (pp. 67–91). San Francisco: Jossey-Bass.

D'Andrade, R., & Strauss, C. (Eds.). (1992). *Human motives and cultural models.* New York: Cambridge University Press.

Dansky, J. L. (1980). Make-believe: A mediator of the relationship between play and associative fluency. *Child Development, 51*(2), 576–579.

Deyhle, D., & Swisher, K. (1997). Research in American Indian and Alaska Native education: From assimilation to self-determination. In. M. W. Apple (Ed.), *Review of research in education* (Vol. 22, pp. 113–194). Washington, DC: American Educational Research Association.

Dickinson, D. K., St. Pierre, R. G., & Pettengill, J. (2004). High-quality classrooms: A key ingredient to family literacy programs' support for children's literacy. In B. Wasik (Ed.), *Handbook of family literacy* (pp. 137–154). Mahwah, NJ: Erlbaum.

Dickinson, D. K., & Tabors, P. O. (Eds.). (2001). *Beginning literacy with language: Young children learning at home and in school.* Baltimore: Brookes.

Dixon, S. D., LeVine, R. A., Richman, A., & Brazelton, T. B. (1984). Mother–child interaction around a teaching task: An African-American comparison. *Child Development, 55*(4), 1252–1264.

Donald, M. (2000). The central role of culture in cognitive evolution: A reflection on the myth of the "isolated mind." In L. P. Nucci, G. B. Saxe, & E. Turiel (Eds.), *Culture, thought, and development* (pp. 19–38). Mahwah, NJ: Erlbaum.

Doucet, F. (2000). *The transition to school in middle-class and working-class African American families: A study of beliefs, values, and practices.* Unpublished doctoral dissertation, University of North Carolina at Greensboro.

Doucet, F., & Tudge, J. R. H. (2007). Co-constructing the transition to school: Reframing the "novice" versus "expert" roles of children, parents, and teachers from a cultural perspective. In R. Pianta, M. Cox, & K. Snow (Eds.), *School readiness and the transition to kindergarten in the era of accountability* (pp. 307–328). Baltimore: Brookes.

Dunn, J. (1988). *The beginnings of social understanding.* Cambridge, MA: Harvard University Press.

Dunn, J. (2005). Naturalistic observations of children and their families In S. M. Greene & D. M. Hogan (Eds.), *Researching children's experience: Approaches and methods* (pp. 87–101). London: Sage.

Dunn, J., & Brown, J. (1991). Becoming American or English? Talking about the social world in England and the United States. In M. H. Bornstein (Ed.), *Cultural approaches to parenting* (pp. 155–172). Hillsdale, NJ: Erlbaum.

Eckensberger, L. H. (1979). A metamethodological examination of psychological theories from a cross-cultural perspective. In L. H. Eckensberger, W. J. Lonner, & Y. H. Poortinga (Eds.), *Cross-cultural contributions to psychology* (pp. 255–275). Amsterdam: Swets and Zeitlinger.

Eckensberger, L. H. (2002). Paradigms revisited: From incommensurability to respected complementarity. In H. Keller, Y. H. Poortinga, & A. Schölmerich (Eds.), *Between culture and biology: Perspectives on ontogenetic development* (pp. 341–383). Cambridge: Cambridge University Press.

Edwards, C. P., & Whiting, B. B. (1993). "Mother, older sibling, and me": The overlapping roles of caregivers and companions in the social world of two- to three-year-olds in

Ngeca, Kenya. In K. MacDonald (Ed.), *Parent–child play: Descriptions and implications* (pp. 305–329). New York: SUNY Press.

Edwards, C. P., & Whiting, B. B. (2004). *Ngecha: A Kenyan village in a time of rapid social change*. Lincoln: University of Nebraska Press.

Elder, G. H., Jr. (1974). *Children of the great depression*. Chicago: University of Chicago Press.

Elder, G. H., Jr. (1996). Human lives in changing societies: Life course and developmental insights. In R. B. Cairns, G. H. Elder, Jr., & E. J. Costello (Eds.), *Developmental science* (pp. 31–62). New York: Cambridge University Press.

Eliot, G. (1981). *Adam Bede*. Harmondsworth: Penguin Books. (Original work published in 1859.)

Eliot, G. (1985). *Silas Marner*. Harmondsworth: Penguin Books. (Original work published in 1861.)

Eliot, G. (1988). *Middlemarch*. Oxford: Oxford University Press. (Original work published in 1872.)

Elliott, J. G., Hufton, N. R., Willis, L., & Illushin, L. (2005). *Motivation, engagement and educational performance*. London: Palgrave Press.

Elliott, J. G, & Tudge, J. R. H. (2007). Change and resistance to change from the West in post-Soviet Russian education. *Comparative Education, 43*(1), 93–112.

Ember, C. R. (1981). A cross-cultural perspective on sex differences. In R. H. Munroe, R. G. Munroe, & B. B. Whiting (Eds.), *Handbook of cross-cultural human development* (pp. 531–580). New York: Garland Press.

Ensminger, M. E., & Fothergill, K. E. (2003). A decade of measuring SES: What it tells us and where to go from here. In M. H. Bornstein & R. H. Bradley (Eds.), *Socioeconomic status, parenting, and child development* (pp. 13–27). Mahwah, NJ: Erlbaum.

Erickson, F. (2002). Culture and human development. *Human Development, 45*(5), 299–306.

Farver, J. M. (1999). Activity setting analysis: A model for examining the role of culture in development. In A. Göncü (Ed.), *Children's engagement in the world: Sociocultural perspectives* (pp. 99–127). New York: Cambridge University Press.

Farver, J. M., Kim, Y. K., & Lee, Y. (1995). Cultural differences in Korean- and Anglo-American preschoolers' social interaction and play behaviors. *Child Development, 66*(4), 1088–1099.

Farver, J. M., & Shin, Y. L. (1997). Social pretend play in Korean- and Anglo-American preschoolers. *Child Development, 68*(3), 544–556.

Fischer, J. L., & Fischer, A. (1963). *The New Englanders of Orchard Town U.S.A.* In B. B. Whiting (Ed.), *Six cultures: Studies of child rearing* (pp. 869–1010). New York: Wiley.

Fischer, J. L., & Fischer, A. (1966). *The New Englanders of Orchard Town U.S.A.* New York: Wiley.

Freitas, L. B. de L., & Shelton, T. L. (2005). Atenção à primeira infância nos EUA e no Brasil [Young children's care and education in the USA and Brazil]. *Psicologia: Teoria e Pesquisa* [Psychology: Theory and Research], *21*(2), 197–205.

Freitas, L. B. de L., Shelton, T. L., & Tudge, J. R. H. (in press). Conceptions of U.S. and Brazilian early childhood care and education: A historical and comparative analysis. *International Journal of Behavioral Development*.

García Coll, C. T., Lambert, G., Jenkins, R., McAdoo, H. P., Crnic, K., Wasik, B. H., & Garcia, H. V. (1996). An integrative model for the study of developmental competencies in minority children. *Child Development, 67*(5), 1891–1914.

Gaskins, S. (1999). Children's daily lives in a Mayan village: A case study of cultur-ally constructed roles and activities. In A. Göncü (Ed.), *Children's engagement in the world: Sociocultural perspectives* (pp. 25–61). New York: Cambridge University Press.

Gauvain, M. (1999). Everyday opportunities for the development of planning skills: Sociocultural and family influences. In A. Göncü (Ed.), *Children's engagement in the world: Sociocultural perspectives* (pp. 173–201). New York: Cambridge University Press.

Gauvain, M. (2001). *The social context of cognitive development.* New York: Guilford Press.

Geertz, C. (1973). *The interpretation of cultures.* New York: Basic Books.

Geertz, C. (1977). From the native's point of view: On the nature of anthropolog-ical understanding. In J. Dolgin, D. Kemnitzer, & D. Schneider (Eds.), *Symbolic anthropology: A reader in the study of symbols and meanings* (pp. 480–492). New York: Columbia University Press.

Gjerde, P. F. (2004). Culture, power, and experience: Toward a person-centered cultural psychology. *Human Development, 47*(3), 137–157.

Goldhaber, D. E. (2000). *Theories of human development: Integrative perspectives.* Mountain View, CA: Mayfield.

Göncü, A., Mistry, J., & Mosier, C. (2000). Cultural variations in the play of toddlers. *International Journal of Behavioral Development, 24*(3), 321–329.

Göncü, A., Tuermer, U., Jain, J., & Johnson, D. (1999). Children's play as cultural activ-ity. In A. Göncü (Ed.), *Children's engagement in the world: Sociocultural perspectives* (pp. 148–170). New York: Cambridge University Press.

Goodnow, J., & Collins, W. A. (1990). *Development according to parents: The nature, sources, and consequences of parents' ideas.* Hillsdale, NJ: Erlbaum.

Gottlieb, G. (1996). Developmental psychobiological theory. In B. Cairns, G. H. Elder, Jr., & E. J. Costello (Eds.), *Developmental science* (pp. 63–77). New York: Cambridge University Press.

Gottlieb, G. (2000). Understanding genetic activity within a holistic framework. In L. R. Bergman, R. B. Cairns, L.-G. Nilsson, & L. Nystedt (Eds.), *Developmental science and the holistic approach* (pp. 179–201). Mahwah, NJ: Erlbaum.

Graham, S. (1992). "Most of the subjects were white and middle class": Trends in pub-lished research on African Americans in selected APA journals, 1970–1989. *American Psychologist, 47*(5), 629–639.

Graue, M. E., & Walsh, D. J. (1998). *Studying children in context: Theories, methods, and ethics.* Thousand Oaks, CA: Sage.

Greene, S. (1997). Child development: Old themes and new directions. In R. Fuller, P. Noonan Walsh, & P. McGinley (Eds.), *A century of psychology* (pp. 36–53). New York: Routledge.

Greenfield, P. M. (1997). Culture as process: Empirical methods for cultural psychol-ogy. In J. W. Berry, Y. H. Poortinga, & J. Pandey (Eds.), *Handbook of cross-cultural psychology, Vol. 1: Theory and method* (pp. 301–406). Boston: Allyn and Bacon.

Guba, E. G., & Lincoln, Y. S. (1994). Competing paradigms in qualitative research. In N. K. Denzin & Y. S. Lincoln (Eds.), *Handbook of qualitative research* (pp. 105–117). Thousand Oaks, CA: Sage.

Hagen, J. W., & Conley, A. C. (1994, Spring). Ethnicity and race of children studied in *Child Development*, 1980–1993. *SRCD Newsletter*, 6–7.

Haight, W. L. (1999). The pragmatics of caregiver-child pretending at home: Understanding culturally specific socialization practices. In A. Göncü (Ed.), *Children's engagement in the world: Sociocultural perspectives* (pp. 128–147). New York: Cambridge University Press.

Haight, W. L., & Miller, P. J. (1993). *Pretending at home: Early development in a sociocultural context.* Albany: State University of New York Press.

Hale, J. E. (1986). *Black children: Their roots, culture, and learning styles.* Baltimore: Johns Hopkins University Press.

Hallpike, C. R. (2004). *The evolution of moral understanding.* London: Prometheus Research Group.

Harkness, S., & Super, C. M. (1985). The cultural context of gender segregation in children's peer groups. *Child Development, 56*(1), 219–224.

Harkness, S., & Super, C. M. (1992). The cultural foundations of fathers' roles: Evidence from Kenya and the United States. In B. S. Hewlett (Ed.), *Father–child relations: Cultural and biosocial contexts* (pp. 191–211). New York: Aldine de Gruyter.

Harkness, S., & Super, C. M. (1999). From parents' cultural belief systems to behavior: Implications for the development of early intervention programs. In L. Eldering & P. Leseman (Eds.), *Effective early education: Cross-cultural perspectives* (pp. 67–90). New York: Falmer Press.

Harkness, S., & Super, C. M. (2002). Culture and parenting. In M. H. Bornstein (Ed.), *Handbook of parenting, Vol. 2: Biology and ecology of parenting* (2nd ed., pp. 253–280). Mahwah, NJ: Erlbaum.

Harkness, S., Super, C. M., Axia, V., Eliasz, A., Palacios, J., & Welles-Nyström, B. (2001). Cultural pathways to successful parenting. *International Society for the Study of Behavioral Development Newsletter, No. 1* (serial no. 38), 9–13.

Harkness, S., Super, C. M., Pai, S. G., Rios, M., Axia, G., Ughetta, M., & Blom M. (1999, April). *Building children's competence through everyday activities: A cross-cultural study in four communities.* Presented in D. M. Hogan & J. R. H. Tudge (Chairs), Creating and acquiring cultural competence through everyday activities: A focus on children's use of time. Symposium presented at the Society for Research in Child Development biennial meetings, Albuquerque, NM.

Hart, B., & Risley, T. R. (1995). *Meaningful differences in the everyday experiences of young American children.* Baltimore: Brookes.

Hart, B., & Risley, T. R. (1999). *The social world of children learning to talk.* Baltimore: Brookes.

Hauser, R. M. (1994). Measuring socioeconomic status in studies of child development. *Child Development, 65*(6), 1541–1545.

Heath, S. B. (1983). *Ways with words: Language, life, and work in communities and classrooms.* New York: Cambridge University Press.

Heath, S. B. (1986). Separating "things of the imagination" from life: Learning to read and write. In W. H. Teale & E. Sulzby (Eds.), *Emergent literacy: Writing and reading* (pp. 156–172). Norwood, NJ: Ablex.

Herrnstein, R. J., & Murray, C. (1994). *The bell curve: Intelligence and the class structure in American life.* New York: Free Press.

Hill, S. A. (1999). *African American children: Socialization and development in families.* Thousand Oaks, CA: Sage.

Hill, S. A. (2001). Class, race, and gender dimensions of child rearing in African American families. *Journal of Black Studies, 31*(4), 494–508.

Hill, S. A., & Sprague, J. (1999). Parenting in black and white families: The interaction of gender with race and class. *Gender and Society, 13*(4), 480–502.

Hoff, E. (2002). Causes and consequences of SES-related differences in parent-to-child speech. In M. H. Bornstein & R. H. Bradley (Eds.), *Socioeconomic status, parenting, and child development* (pp. 147–160). Mahwah, NJ: Erlbaum.

Hoff, E., Laursen, B., & Tardif, (2002). Socioeconomic status and parenting. In M. H. Bornstein (Ed.), *Handbook of parenting, Vol. 2: Biology and ecology of parenting* (2nd ed., pp. 231–252). Mahwah, NJ: Erlbaum.

Hofferth, S. L., & Sandberg, J. F. (2001). How American children spend their time. *Journal of Marriage and Family, 63*(2), 295–308.

Hofstede, G. (1980). *Culture's consequences: International differences in work-related values.* Beverly Hills, CA: Sage.

Hofstede, G. (1991). *Cultures and organizations: Software of the mind.* London: McGraw-Hill.

Hogan, D. M. (2005). Researching "the child" in developmental psychology. In S. Greene & D. M. Hogan (Eds.), *Researching children's experience: Approaches and methods* (pp. 22–41). London: Sage.

Hogan, D. M., Etz, K., & Tudge, J. R. H. (1999). Reconsidering the role of children in family research: Conceptual and methodological issues. In F. M. Berardo (Series Ed.) & C. Shehan (Vol. Ed.), *Contemporary perspectives on family research, Vol. 1: Through the eyes of the child: Re-visioning children as active agents of family life* (pp. 93–105). Stamford, CT: JAI Press.

Hogan, D. M., & Tudge, J. R. H. (1999). Implications of Vygotsky's theory for peer learning. In A. M. O'Donnell & A. King (Eds.), *Cognitive perspectives on peer learning* (pp. 39–65). Mahwah, NJ: Erlbaum.

Holden, G. W. (1995). Parental attitudes toward childrearing. In M. H. Bornstein (Ed.), *Handbook of parenting, Vol. 3: Status and social conditions of parenting* (pp. 359–392). Mahwah, NJ: Erlbaum.

Holland D., & Quinn, N. (Eds.). (1987). *Cultural models in language and thought.* New York: Cambridge University Press.

Jahoda, G. (1993). *Crossroads between culture and mind: Continuities and change in theories of human nature.* London: Harvester Wheatsheaf.

James, A. (2004). Understanding childhood from an interdisciplinary perspective: Problems and potentials. In P. B. Pufall & R. P. Unsworth (Eds.), *Rethinking childhood* (pp. 25–37). New Brunswick, NJ: Rutgers University Press.

James, A., Jenks, C., & Prout, A. (1998). *Theorizing childhood.* New York: Teachers College Press.

James, A., & Prout, A. (Eds.) (1997). *Constructing and reconstructing childhood: Contemporary issues in the sociological study of childhood.* London: Falmer Press.

Johnston, T. D., & Edwards, L. (2002). Genes, interactions, and the development of behavior. *Psychological Review, 109*(1), 26–34.

Juster, F. T., & Stafford, F. P. (1985). *Time, goods, and well-being.* Ann Arbor: Survey Research Center, University of Michigan.

Kağitçibaşi, C. (1996). *Family and human development across cultures: A view from the other side.* Mahwah, NJ: Erlbaum.

Kamii, C. K., & Radin, N. (1967). Class differences in the socialization practices of Negro mothers. _Journal of Marriage and Family, 29_(2), 302–310.

Keller, H. (2003). Socialization for competence: Cultural models of infancy. _Human Development, 46_(5), 288–311.

Keller, H., Hentschel, E., Yovsi, R. D., Lamm, B., Abels, M., & Haas, V. (2004). The psycho-linguistic embodiment of parental ethnotheories: A new avenue to understanding cultural processes in parental reasoning. _Culture & Psychology, 10_(3), 293–330.

Keller, H., Lamm, B., Abels, M., Yovsi, R. D., Borke, J., Jensen, H., et al. (2006). Cultural models, socialization goals, and parenting ethnotheories: A multicultural analysis. _Journal of Cross-Cultural Psychology, 37_(2), 155–172.

Kelley, M. L., Power, T. G., & Wimbush, D. D. (1992). Determinants of disciplinary practices in low-income black mothers. _Child Development, 63_(3), 573–582.

Kim, U., Triandis, H. C., Kağitçibaşi, C., Choi, S.-C., & Yoon, G. (Eds.). (1994). _Individualism and collectivism: Theory, method, and applications._ Thousand Oaks, CA: Sage.

Kohn, M. L. (1977). _Class and conformity: A study in values_ (2nd ed.). Chicago: University of Chicago Press.

Kohn, M. L. (1979). The effects of social class on parental values and practices. In D. Reiss & H. Hoffman (Eds.), _The American family: Dying or developing?_ (pp. 45–68). New York: Plenum Press.

Kohn, M. L. (1995). Social structure and personality through time and space. In P. Moen, G. H. Elder, Jr., & K. Lüscher (Eds.), _Examining lives in context: Perspectives on the ecology of human development_ (pp. 141–168). Washington, DC: American Psychological Association.

Kohn, M. L., & Slomczynski, K. M. (1990). _Social structure and self-direction: A comparative analysis of the United States and Poland._ Oxford: Basil Blackwell.

Kuczynski, L., & Daly, K., (2003). Qualitative methods as inductive (theory-generating) research: Psychological and sociological approaches. In L. Kuczynski (Ed.), _Handbook of dynamics in parent–child relations._ Thousand Oaks, CA: Sage.

Kuhn, T. S. (1962). _The structure of scientific revolutions._ Chicago: University of Illinois Press.

Lamb, M. (2000). The history of research on father involvement: An overview. _Marriage and Family Review, 29_(2–3), 23–42.

Lamb, M. E. (Ed.). (1987). _The father's role: Cross-cultural perspectives._ Hillsdale, NJ: Erlbaum.

Lamb, M. E. (Ed.). (1997). _The role of the father in child development_ (3rd ed.). New York: Wiley.

Lancy, D. F. (1996). _Playing on the mother ground: Cultural routines for children's development._ New York: Guilford Press.

Lareau, A. (2002). Invisible inequality: Social class and childrearing in black families and white families. _American Sociological Review, 67_(5), 747–776.

Larson, R. W., Moneta, G., Richards, M. H., & Wilson, S. (2002). Continuity, stability, and change in daily emotional experience across adolescence. _Child Development, 73_(4), 1151–1165.

Larson, R. W., & Verma, S. (1999). How children and adolescents spend time across the world: Work, play, and developmental opportunities. *Psychological Bulletin, 125*(6), 701–736.

Lave, J., & Wenger, E. (1991). *Situated learning: Legitimate peripheral participation*. New York: Cambridge University Press.

Lawrence, J. A., Dobbs, A. E., & Valsiner, J. (2004). The many faces of everyday life: Some challenges to the psychology of cultural practice. *Culture & Psychology, 10*(4), 455–476.

Lee, C. D. (2002). Interrogating race and ethnicity as constructs in the examination of cultural processes in developmental research. *Human Development, 45*(4), 282–290.

LeVine, R. A. (1989). Cultural environments in child development. In W. Damon (Ed.), *Child development today and tomorrow* (pp. 52–68). San Francisco: Jossey-Bass.

LeVine, R. A., Dixon, S., LeVine, S., Richman, A., Leiderman, P. H., Keefer, C. H., & Brazelton, T. B. (1994). *Child care and culture: Lessons from Africa*. New York: Cambridge University Press.

LeVine, R. A., & LeVine, B. B. (1963). Nyansongo: A Gusii community in Kenya. In B. B. Whiting (Ed.), *Six cultures: Studies of child rearing* (pp. 14–202). New York: Wiley.

Lewis, C. (1997). Fathers and preschoolers. In M. Lamb (Ed.), *The role of the father in child development* (3rd ed., pp. 121–142). New York: Wiley.

Lewis, C., & Dessen, M. A. (1999). O pai no contexto familiar [Fathers in family life]. *Psicologia: Teoria e Pesquisa* [Psychology: Theory and Research], *15*(1), 9–16.

Lewis, J. L., & Watson-Gegeo, K. A. (2005). Fictions of childhood: Toward a sociohistorical approach to human development. *Ethos, 32*(1), 3–33.

Lonner, W. J., & Berry, J. W. (1986). *Field methods in cross-cultural research*. Newbury Park, CA: Sage.

Lubeck, S. (1985). *Sandbox society: Early education in Black and White America*. London: Falmer Press.

Lubeck, S., Jessup, P., deVries, M., & Post, J. (2001). The role of culture in program improvement. *Early Childhood Research Quarterly, 16*(4), 499–523.

Lugaila, T. A. (2003). *A child's day: 2000 (Selected indicators of child well-being)*. Current Population Reports, P70–89. Washington, DC: U.S. Census Bureau.

Luster, T., & McAdoo, H. P. (1994). Factors related to the achievement and adjustment of young African American children. *Child Development, 65*(4), 1080–1094.

Luster, T., & Rhoades, K. (1989). The relation between child-rearing beliefs and the home environment in a sample of adolescent mothers. *Family Relations, 38*(3), 317–322.

Luster, T., Rhoades, K., & Haas, B. (1989). The relation between parental values and parenting behavior: A test of the Kohn hypothesis. *Journal of Marriage and Family, 51*(1), 139–147.

Lynd, R. S., & Lynd, H. M. (1929). *Middletown: A study of modern American culture*. New York: Harcourt, Brace.

Lynd, R. S., & Lynd, H. M. (1937). *Middletown in transition: A study in cultural conflicts*. New York: Harcourt, Brace.

Malinowski, B. (1966). *The father in primitive psychology*. New York: Norton.

Marx, K. (1978). The 18th Brumaire of Louis Napoleon. In R. C. Tucker (Ed.), *The Marx-Engels reader* (2nd ed.). New York: Norton. (Original work published 1852.)

Matsumoto, D. (2006). Culture and cultural worldviews: Do verbal descriptions about culture reflect anything other than verbal descriptions about culture? *Culture & Psychology, 12*(1), 33–62.

Matusov, E. (1998). When solo activity is not privileged: Participation and internalization models of development. *Human Development, 41*(5/6), 326–349.

McLoyd, V. C. (1990). The impact of economic hardship on Black families and children: Psychological distress, parenting, and socioemotional development. *Child Development, 61*(2), 311–346.

McLoyd, V. C. (2004). Linking race and ethnicity to culture: Steps along the road from inference to hypothesis testing. *Human Development, 47*(3), 185–191.

McLoyd, V. C., Cauce, A. M., Takeuchi, D., & Wilson, L. (2000). Marital processes and parental socialization in families of color: A decade review of research. *Journal of Marriage and Family, 62*(4), 1070–1093.

Mead, M. (1961). *Coming of age in Samoa.* New York: New American Library. (Original work published 1928.)

Miller, J. G. (1997). Theoretical issues in cultural psychology. In J. W. Berry, Y. H. Poortinga, & J. Pandey (Eds.), *Handbook of cross-cultural psychology, Vol. I: Theory and method* (2nd ed., pp. 85–128). Boston: Allyn & Bacon.

Miller, P. J., & Garvey, C. (1984). Mother–baby role play: Its origins in social support. In I. Bretherton (Ed.), *Symbolic play: The development of social understanding* (pp. 101–130). Orlando, FL: Academic Press.

Minturn, L., & Lambert, W. W. (1964). *Mothers of six cultures: Antecedents of child rearing.* New York: Wiley.

Morelli, G. A., Rogoff, B., & Angelillo, C. (1992, December). *Cultural variation in young children's opportunities for involvement in adult activities.* Paper presented at the American Anthropology Association Meeting, San Francisco.

Morelli, G. A., Rogoff, B., & Angelillo, C. (2003). Cultural variation in young children's access to work or involvement in specialized child-focused activities. *International Journal of Behavioral Development, 27*(3), 264–274.

Morelli, G. A., Rogoff, B., Oppenheim, D., & Goldsmith, D. (1992). Cultural variation in infants sleeping arrangements: Questions of independence. *Developmental Psychology, 28*(4), 604–613.

Moynihan, D. P. (1965). *The negro family. A case for national action.* Washington, DC: Department of Labor.

Munroe, R. L., & Munroe, R. H. (1992). Fathers in children's environments: A four culture study. In B. S. Hewlett (Ed.), *Father–child relations: Cultural and biosocial contexts* (pp. 213–229). New York: Aldine de Gruyter.

Narusk, A., & Hansson, L. (1999). *Estonian families in the 1990s: Winners and losers.* Tallinn: Estonian Academy Publishers.

National Institute of Child Health and Human Development Early Child Care Research Network. (2003). Modeling the effects of child care quality on children's preschool cognitive development. *Child Development, 74*(5), 1454–1475.

Newson, J., & Newson, E. (1963). *Infant care in an urban community.* New York: International Universities Press.

Newson, J., & Newson, E. (1968). *Four years old in an urban community.* Chicago: Aldine de Gruyter.

Newson, J., & Newson, E. (1976). *Seven years old in the home environment.* New York: Wiley.

Nobles, W. W. (1974). Africanity: Its role in black families. *Black Scholar, 5,* 10–17.

Ochs, E. (1988). *Culture and language development: Language acquisition and language socialization in a Samoan village.* New York: Cambridge University Press.

Odero, D. A. (1998). *Everyday activities and social partners of Luo children in an urban Kenyan setting: The roles of culture, class, and gender.* Unpublished doctoral dissertation, University of North Carolina at Greensboro.

Odero, D. R. (2004). Families of Kenya. *National Council on Family Relations Report, 49*(4), F13–F14.

Ogbu, J. U. (1981). Origins of human competence: A cultural-ecological perspective. *Child Development, 52*(2), 413–429.

Overton, W. F. (1984). World-views and their influence on psychological theory and research: Kuhn–Lakatos–Laudan. In H. W. Reese (Ed.), *Advances in child development and behavior* (Vol. 18, pp. 191–226). New York: Academic Press.

Overton, W. F., & Reese, H. W. (1973). Models of development: Methodological implications. In J. R. Nesselroade & H. W. Reese (Eds.), *Lifespan developmental psychology: Methodological issues* (pp. 65–86). New York: Academic Press.

Packer, M. (2002). Accounting for change: Priming, power, and plot. *Human Development, 45*(5), 349–354.

Packer, M. J., & Goicoechea, J. (2000). Sociocultural and constructivist theories of learning: Ontology, not just epistemology. *Educational Psychologist, 35*(4), 227–241.

Parke, R. D. (2000). Father involvement: A developmental psychological perspective. *Marriage and Family Review, 29*(2–3), 43–58.

Pepper, S. C. (1942). *World hypotheses: A study in evidence.* Berkeley: University of California Press.

Perry, P. (2001). White means never having to say you're ethnic: White youth and the construction of "cultureless" identities. *Journal of Contemporary Ethnography, 30*(1), 56–91.

Piaget, J. (1962). *Play, dreams and imitation in childhood.* New York: Norton. (Original work published 1951.)

Piccinini, C. A., Tudge, J. R. H., Lopes, R. S., & Sperb, T. M. (1998). O impacto de fatores iniciais do desenvolvimento nas interações pais-crianças e no comportamento social de crianças: Estudo longitudinal da gestação ao 7th ano de vida das crianças [The impact of initial factors of development on parent-child interactions and on the social behavior of children: A longitudinal study from gestation to the 7th year of life]. Unpublished research proposal, Porto Alegre, Brazil.

Pleck, J. H. (1997). Paternal involvement: Levels, sources, and consequences. In M. E. Lamb (Ed.), *The role of the father in child development* (3rd ed., pp. 66–103). New York: Wiley.

Plewis, I., Mooney, A., & Creeser, R. (1990). Time on educational activities at home and educational progress in infant school. *British Journal of Educational Psychology, 60*(3), 330–337.

Prout, A., & James, A. (1997). A new paradigm for the sociology of childhood? Provenance, promise and problems. In A. James & A. Prout (Eds.), *Constructing and reconstructing childhood: Contemporary issues in the sociological study of childhood* (pp. 7–33). London: Falmer Press.

Putnam, S. E. (1995). *Everyday activities of North American preschoolers: Social class as cultural community.* Unpublished doctoral dissertation, University of North Carolina at Greensboro.

Realo, A. (1998). Collectivism in an individualist culture: The case of Estonia. *Trames,* 2(1), 19–39.

Realo, A. (2003). Comparison of public and academic discourses: Estonian individualism and collectivism revisited. *Culture & Psychology,* 9(1), 47–77.

Realo, A., & Allik, J. (1999). A cross-cultural study of collectivism: A comparison of American, Estonian, and Russian students. *Journal of Social Psychology,* 139(2), 133–142.

Rebhun, L.-A. (2005). Families in Brazil. In J. L. Roopnarine & U. P. Gielen (Eds.), *Families in global perspective* (pp. 330–343). Boston: Allyn and Bacon.

Richards, M. P. M. (1977). An ecological study of infant development in an urban setting in Britain. In P. H. Leiderman, S. R. Tulkin, & A. Rosenfeld (Eds.), *Culture and infancy: Variations in the human experience* (pp. 469–493). New York: Academic Press.

Richards, M. P. M., & Bernal, J. F. (1972). An observational study of mother–infant interaction. In N. Blurton-Jones (Ed.), *Ethological studies of child behaviour* (pp. 175–197). Cambridge: Cambridge University Press.

Richters, J. E. (1997). The Hubble hypothesis and the developmentalist's dilemma. *Development and Psychopathology,* 9(2), 193–229.

Robinson, J. P. (1977). *How Americans use time: A social psychological analysis of everyday behavior.* New York: Praeger.

Robinson, J. P. (1985). The validity and reliability of diaries versus alternative time use measures. In T. F. Juster & F. P. Stafford (Eds.), *Time, goods, and well-being.* Ann Arbor: Institute for Social Research, University of Michigan.

Robinson, J. P., Andreyenkov, V. G., & Patrushev, V. D. (1989). *The rhythm of everyday life: How Soviet and American citizens use time.* Boulder, CO: Westview Press.

Robinson, J. P., & Godbey, G. (1997). *Time for life: The surprising ways Americans use their time.* University Park: Pennsylvania State University Press.

Rogoff, B. (1990). *Apprenticeship in thinking: Cognitive development in social context.* New York: Oxford University Press.

Rogoff, B. (1993). Children's guided participation and participatory appropriation in sociocultural activity. In R. H. Wozniak & K. W. Fischer (Eds.), *Development in context: Acting and thinking in specific environments* (pp. 121–153). Hillsdale, NJ: Erlbaum.

Rogoff, B. (1995). Observing sociocultural activity on three planes: Participatory appropriation, guided participation, apprenticeship. In A. Alvarez, P. del Rio, & J. V. Wertsch (Eds.), *Perspectives on sociocultural research* (pp. 139–164). Cambridge: Cambridge University Press.

Rogoff, B. (2003). *The cultural nature of human development.* New York: Oxford University Press.

Rogoff, B., & Angelillo, C. (2002). Investigating the coordinated functioning of multifaceted cultural practices in human development. *Human Development,* 45(4), 211–225.

Rogoff, B., Baker-Sennett, J., Lacasa, P., & Goldsmith, D. (1995). Development through participation in sociocultural activity. In J. Goodnow, P. Miller, & F. Kessel (Eds.), *Cultural practices as contexts for development* (pp. 45–65). *New Directions for Child Development* (67). San Francisco: Jossey-Bass.

Rogoff, B., Mistry, J., Göncü, A., & Mosier, C. (1991). Cultural variation in the role relations of toddlers and their families. In M. H. Bornstein (Ed.), *Cultural approaches to parenting* (pp. 173–183). Hillsdale, NJ: Erlbaum.

Rogoff, B., Turkanis, C. G., & Bartlett, L. (2001). *Learning together: Children and adults in a school community*. New York: Oxford University Press.

Savin-Williams, R. C. (1982). A field study of adolescent social interactions: Developmental and contextual influences. *Journal of Social Psychology, 117*(2), 203–209.

Sawyer, R. K. (2002a). Emergence in psychology: Lessons from the history of nonreductionist science. *Human Development, 45*(1), 2–28.

Sawyer, R. K. (2002b). Unresolved tensions in sociocultural theory: Analogies with contemporary sociological debates. *Culture & Psychology, 8*(3), 283–305.

Scarr, S., & Weinberg, R. (1986). The early childhood enterprise: Care and education of the young. *American Psychologist, 41*(10), 1140–1146.

Schieffelin, B. B. (1990). *The give and take of everyday life: Language socialization of Kaluli children*. Cambridge: Cambridge University Press.

Schousboe, I. (2005). Local and global perspectives on the everyday lives of children. *Culture & Psychology, 11*(2), 207–225.

Schwartz, S. H. (1994). Beyond individualism/collectivism: New cultural dimensions of values. In U. Kim, H. C. Triandis, C. Kağitçibaşi, S.-C. Choi, & G. Yoon (Eds.), *Individualism and collectivism: Theory, methods, and applications* (pp. 85–119). Newbury Park, CA: Sage.

Schwartz, S. H., & Bardi, A. (1997). Influences of adaptation to communist rule on value priorities in Eastern Europe. *Political Psychology, 18*(2), 385–410.

Scott-Jones, D. (2005). Toward varied and complementary methodologies in the study of ethnic identity in childhood. In T. Weisner (Ed.), *Discovering successful pathways in children's development: Mixed methods in the study of childhood and family life* (pp. 165–169). Chicago: University of Chicago Press.

Scribner, S. (1985). Vygotsky's uses of history. In J. V. Wertsch (Ed.), *Culture, communication, and cognition: Vygotskian perspectives* (pp. 119–145). Cambridge: Cambridge University Press.

Scrimsher, S., & Tudge, J. R. H. (2003). The teaching/learning relationship in the first years of school: Some revolutionary implications of Vygotsky's theory. *Early Education and Development, 14*(3), 293–312.

Serpell, R. (1993). *The significance of schooling*. New York: Cambridge University Press.

Seymour, S. C. (1999). *Women, family, and child care in India*. New York: Cambridge University Press.

Shiraev, E., & Gradskova, J. (2005). The Russian family. In J. L. Roopnarine & U. P. Gielen (Eds.), *Families in global perspective* (pp. 277–290). Boston: Pearson Education.

Shweder, R. A. (1990). Cultural psychology – what is it? In J. W. Stigler, R. A. Shweder, & G. Herdt (Eds.), *Cultural psychology: Essays on comparative human development* (pp. 1–43). New York: Cambridge University Press

Shweder, R. A., Jensen, L. A., & Goldstein, W. M. (1995). Who sleeps by whom revisited: A method for extracting the moral goods implicit in practice. In J. J. Goodnow,

P. J., Miller, & F. Kessel (Eds.), *Cultural practices as contexts for development* (pp. 21–39). *New Directions for Child Development* (67). San Francisco: Jossey Bass.

Sigel, I. E., McGillicuddy-DeLisi, A. V., & Goodnow, J. (Eds.). (1992). *Parental belief systems: The psychological consequences for children* (2nd ed.). Hillsdale, NJ: Erlbaum.

Sigman, M., Neumann, C., Carter, D. J., D'Souza, S., & Bwibo, N. (1988). Home interactions and the development of Embu toddlers in Kenya. *Child Development, 59*(5), 1251–1261.

Silvia, P. J. (2007). *How to write a lot: A practical guide to productive academic writing.* Washington, DC: American Psychological Association.

Singer, J. L. (1973). *The child's world of make-believe: Experimental studies of imaginative play.* New York: Academic Press.

Smedley, A., & Smedley, B. D. (2005). Race as biology is fiction, racism as a social problem is real: Anthropological and historical perspectives on the social construction of race. *American Psychologist, 60*(1), 16–26.

Smilansky, S. (1968). *The effects of sociodramatic play on disadvantaged preschool children.* New York: Wiley.

Smith J. C., & Horton, C. P. (Eds.). (1997). *Statistical record of Black America.* Detroit: Gale Research.

Smith, P. K., & Connolly, K. (1972). Patterns of play and social interaction in pre-school children. In N. Blurton-Jones (Ed.), *Ethological studies of child behaviour* (pp. 65–95). Cambridge: Cambridge University Press.

Steinberg, L., Darling, N. E., & Fletcher, A. C. (1995). Authoritative parenting and adolescent adjustment: An ecological journey. In P. Moen, G. H. Elder, & K. Lüscher (Eds.), *Examining lives in context: Perspectives on the ecology of human development* (pp. 423–466). Washington, DC: American Psychological Association.

Stone, P. J. (1972). Child care in twelve countries. In A. Szalai (Ed.), *The use of time: Daily activities of urban and suburban populations in twelve countries* (pp. 249–264). The Hague, The Netherlands: Mouton.

Stoppard, T. (2002). *Shipwreck.* New York: Grove Press.

Strauss, C. (2000). The culture concept and the individualism–collectivism debate: Dominant and alternative attributions for class in the United States. In L. P. Nucci, G. B. Saxe, & E. Turiel (Eds.), *Culture, thought, and development* (pp. 85–114). Mahwah, NJ: Erlbaum.

Suina, J. H., & Smolkin, L. B. (1994). From natal culture to school culture to dominant society culture: Supporting transitions for Pueblo Indian students. In P. M. Greenfield & R. R. Cocking (Eds.), *Cross-cultural roots of minority child development* (pp. 115–130). Hillsdale, NJ: Erlbaum.

Super, C. M., & Harkness, S. (1982). The infant's niche in rural Kenya and metropolitan America. In L. Adler (Ed.), *Cross-cultural research at issue* (pp. 47–55). New York: Academic Press.

Super, C. M., & Harkness, S. (1997). The cultural structuring of child development. In J. W. Berry, P. R. Dasen, & T. S. Sarasthwati (Eds.), *Handbook of cross-cultural psychology, Vol. 2: Basic processes and human development* (pp. 1–35). Boston: Allyn and Bacon.

Super, C. M., & Harkness, S. (2002). Culture structures the environment for development. *Human Development, 45*(4), 270–274.

Super, C. M., & Harkness, S. (2003). The metaphors of development. *Human Development, 46*(1), 3–23.

Szalai, A. (Ed.). (1972). *The use of time: Daily activities of urban and suburban populations in twelve countries.* The Hague, The Netherlands: Mouton.

Tamis-LeMonda, C. S., & Cabrera, N. (2002). *Handbook of father involvement: Multidisciplinary perspectives.* Mahwah, NJ: Erlbaum.

Taylor, R. J., Chatters, L. M., Tucker, M. B., & Lewis, E. (1990). Developments in research on Black families: A decade review. *Journal of Marriage and Family, 52*(4), 993–1014.

Tharp, R. (1994). Intergroup differences among Native Americans in socialization and child cognition: An ethnogenetic analysis. In P. M. Greenfield & R. R. Cocking (Eds.), *Cross-cultural roots of minority child development* (pp. 87–105). Hillsdale, NJ: Erlbaum.

Tharp, R. G. (1989). Psychocultural variables and constants: Effects on teaching and learning in schools. *American Psychologist, 44*(2), 349–359.

Timmer, S. G., Eccles, J., & O'Brien, K. (1985). How children use time. In F. T. Juster & F. P. Stafford (Eds.), *Time, goods, and well-being* (pp. 353–382). Ann Arbor: Survey Research Center, University of Michigan.

Tizard, B., & Hughes, M. (1984). *Young children learning: Talking and thinking at home and at school.* London: Fontana.

Tobin, J. T., Wu, D. Y. H., & Davidson, D. H. (1989). *Preschool in three cultures.* New Haven, CT: Yale University Press.

Triandis, H. C. (1995). *Individualism and collectivism.* Boulder, CO: Westview Press.

Tudge, J. R. H. (2000). Theory, method, and analysis in research on the relations between peer collaboration and cognitive development. *Journal of Experimental Education, 69*(1), 98–112.

Tudge, J. R. H., Doucet, F., & Hayes, S. (2001). Teoria, método e análise: As interconexões no estudo das crianças e das famílias. [Theory, method, and analysis: Necessary interconnections in the study of children and families.] *Contrapontos: Revista de Educação* [Counterpoints: The Journal of Education], *1*(3), 11–22.

Tudge, J. R. H., Doucet, F., Odero, D., Sperb, T., Piccinini, C., & Lopes, R. (2006). A window into different cultural worlds: Young children's everyday activities in the United States, Kenya, and Brazil. *Child Development, 77*(5), 1446–1469.

Tudge, J. R. H., Gray, J., & Hogan, D. (1997). Ecological perspectives in human development: A comparison of Gibson and Bronfenbrenner. In J. Tudge, M. Shanahan, & J. Valsiner (Eds.), *Comparisons in human development: Understanding time and context* (pp. 72–105). New York: Cambridge University Press.

Tudge, J. R. H. & Hogan, D. (2005). Naturalistic observations of children's activities: An ecological approach. In S. M. Greene & D. M. Hogan (Eds.), *Researching children's experiences: Approaches and methods* (pp. 102–122). London: Sage.

Tudge, J. R. H., Li, L., & Stanley, T. K. (in press). The impact of method on assessing young children's everyday mathematical experiences. In O. N. Saracho & B. Spodek (Series Eds.) & O. N. Saracho & B. Spodek (Vol. Eds.) *Contemporary perspectives in early childhood education: Mathematics in early childhood education.* Greenwich, CT: Information Age.

Tudge, J. R. H., Odero, D., Hogan, D., & Etz, K. (2003). Relations between the everyday activities of preschoolers and their teachers' perceptions of their competence in the first years of school. *Early Childhood Research Quarterly, 18*(1), 42–64.

Tudge, J. R. H., Putnam, S. A., & Valsiner, J. (1996). Culture and cognition in developmental perspective. In B. Cairns, G. H. Elder, Jr., & E. J. Costello (Eds.), *Developmental science* (pp. 190–222). New York: Cambridge University Press.

Tudge, J. R. H., & Scrimsher, S. (2003). Lev S. Vygotsky on education: A cultural-historical, interpersonal, and individual approach to development. In B. J. Zimmerman & D. H. Schunk (Eds.), *Educational psychology: A century of contributions* (pp. 207–228). Mahwah, NJ: Erlbaum.

Tudge, J. R. H., Sidden, J., & Putnam, S. A. (1990). *The cultural ecology of young children: Coding manual.* Unpublished manuscript, Greensboro, NC.

Tudge, J. R. H., Tammeveski, P., Meltsas, M., Kulakova, N., & Snezhkova, I. (2001, April). *The effects of young children's everyday activities: A longitudinal study in the United States, Russia, and Estonia.* Presented at the biennial meetings of the Society for Research in Child Development, Minneapolis, MN.

Tulviste, T., Mizera, L., De Geer, B., & Tryggvason, M.-T. (2003). A silent Finn, a silent Finno-Ugric, or a silent Nordic? A comparative study of Estonian, Finnish and Swedish mother-adolescent interactions. *Applied Psycholinguistics, 24*(2), 249–265.

Turiel, E., & Perkins, S. A. (2004). Flexibilities of mind: Conflict and culture. *Human Development, 47*(3), 158–178.

Valsiner, J. (1991). Building theoretical bridges over a lagoon of everyday events. *Human Development, 34*(5), 307–315.

Valsiner, J. (1998a). Dualisms displaced: From crusades to analytic distinctions. *Human Development, 41*(5/6), 350–354.

Valsiner, J. (1998b). *The guided mind: A sociogenetic approach to personality.* Cambridge, MA: Harvard University Press.

Valsiner, J., & Litvinovich, G. (1996). Processes of generalization in parental reasoning. In C. M. Super & S. Harkness (Eds.), *Parents' cultural belief systems* (pp. 56–82). New York: Guilford Press.

Van der Veer, R., & Valsiner, J. (1991). *Understanding Vygotsky: A quest for synthesis.* Oxford: Basil Blackwell.

Van der Vijver, F. J. R., & Poortinga, Y. H. (2002). On the study of culture in developmental science. *Human Development, 45*(4), 246–256.

Vygotsky, L. S. (1978). *Mind in society: The development of higher psychological processes* (M. Cole, V. John-Steiner, S. Scribner, & E. Souberman, Eds.). Cambridge, MA: Harvard University Press. (Original work published 1930–1935.)

Vygotsky, L. S. (1993). *The collected works of L. S. Vygotsky, Vol. 2: The fundamentals of defectology* (R. W. Rieber & A. S. Carton, Eds.; J. E. Knox & Carol B. Stevens, Trans.). New York: Plenum. (Original work published or written 1924–1935.)

Vygotsky, L. S. (1994). The problem of the environment. In R. Van der Veer & J. Valsiner (Eds.), *The Vygotsky reader* (pp. 338–354). Oxford: Basil Blackwell. (Original work published 1929.)

Vygotsky, L. S. (1997a). *The collected works of L. S. Vygotsky, Vol. 3: Problems of the theory and history of psychology* (R. W. Rieber & J. Wollock, Eds.; R. van der Veer, Trans.). New York: Plenum. (Original work published or written 1924–1934.)

Vygotsky, L. S. (1997b). *The collected works of L. S. Vygotsky, Vol. 4: The history of the development of higher mental functions* (R. W. Rieber, Ed.; M. J. Hall, Trans.). New York: Plenum. (Originally written in 1931; chapters 1–5 first published in 1960, chapters 6–15 first published in 1997.)

Weisner, T. S. (1979). Urban–rural differences in sociable and disruptive behavior of Kenya children. *Ethnology, 18*(2), 153–172.

Weisner, T. S. (1989). Cultural and universal aspects of social support for children: Evidence from the Abaluyia of Kenya. In D. Belle (Ed.), *Children's social networks and social supports* (pp. 70–90). New York: Wiley

Weisner, T. S. (1996). Why ethnography should be the most important method in the study of human development. In R. Jessor, A. Colby, & R. A. Shweder (Eds.), *Ethnography and human development: Context and meaning in social enquiry* (pp. 305–324). Chicago: University of Chicago Press.

Weisner, T. S. (1997). Why ethnography and its findings matter. *Ethos, 25*(2), 177–190.

Weisner, T. S. (2002). Ecocultural understanding of children's developmental pathways. *Human Development, 45*(4), 275–281.

Weisner, T. S., & Gallimore, R. (1977). My brother's keeper: Child and sibling caretaking. *Current Anthropology, 18*(2), 169–190.

Weisner, T. S., Gallimore, R., & Jordan, C. (1993). Unpackaging cultural effects on classroom learning: Hawaiian peer assistance and child-generated activity. In R. Roberts (Ed.), *Coming home to preschool: The sociocultural context of early education* (pp. 59–87). Greenwich, CT: Ablex.

Wells, C. G. (1981). *Learning through interaction: The study of language development.* Cambridge: Cambridge University Press.

Wells, C. G. (1985). *Language development in the pre-school years.* Cambridge: Cambridge University Press.

Wenger, M. (1989). Work, play, and social relationships among children in a Giriama community. In D. Belle (Ed.), *Children's social networks and social supports* (pp. 91–115). New York: Wiley.

Westcott, H. L., & Littleton, K. S. (2005). Exploring meaning in interviews with children. In S. Greene & D. Hogan (Eds.), *Researching children's experiences: Approaches and methods* (pp. 141–157). London: Sage.

Wertsch, J. V., & Tulviste, P. (1992). L. S. Vygotsky and contemporary developmental psychology. *Developmental Psychology, 28*(4), 548–557.

Whiting, B. B. (Ed.). (1963). *Six cultures: Studies of child rearing.* Cambridge, MA: Harvard University Press.

Whiting, B. B. (1980). Culture and social behavior: A model for the development of social behavior. *Ethos, 8*(2), 95–116.

Whiting, B. B. (1996). The effect of social change on concepts of the good child and good mothering: A study of families in Kenya. *Ethos, 24*, 3–35.

Whiting, B. B., & Edwards C. P. (1988). *Children of different worlds: The formation of social behavior.* Cambridge, MA: Harvard University Press.

Whiting, B. B., & Whiting, J. W. M. (1975). *Children of six cultures: A psycho-cultural analysis.* Cambridge, MA: Harvard University Press.

Willie, C. V., & Reddick, R. J. (2003). *A new look at Black families* (5th ed.). Walnut Creek, CA: Altamira Press.

Willis, M. G. (1989). Learning styles of African American children: A review of the literature and interventions. *Journal of Black Psychology, 16*(1), 47–65.

Winegar, L. T. (1997). Developmental research and comparative perspectives: Applications to developmental science. In J. R. H. Tudge, M. Shanahan, & J. Valsiner (Eds.),

Comparisons in human development: Understanding time and context (pp. 13–33). New York: Cambridge University Press.

Wood, D. J., Bruner, J. S., & Ross, G. (1976). The role of tutoring in problem solving. *Journal of Child Psychology and Psychiatry, 17*(2), 89–100.

Woodhead, M., & Faulkner, D. (2000). Subjects, objects or participants? Dilemmas of psychological research with children. In P. Christensen & A. James (Eds.), *Research with children: Perspectives and practices* (pp. 9–35). London: Falmer Press.

Yeung, W. J., Sandberg, J. F., Davis-Kean, P. E., & Hofferth, S. L. (2001). Children's time with fathers in intact families. *Journal of Marriage and Family, 63*(1), 136–154.

Index